Barry Barack Hussein Soetoro Obama: Identity and Racial Hypocrisy in America

Double Standards, Double Speak, and Double Binds

Barry
Barack
Hussein   Identity and Racial
Soetoro   Hypocrisy
Obama: in America

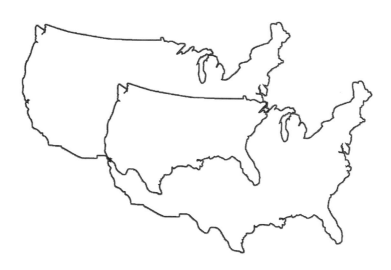

Double Standards, Double Speak, and Double Binds

Peter J. McCusker

iUniverse, Inc.
Bloomington

Barry Barack Hussein Soetoro Obama: Identity and Racial Hypocrisy in America
Double Standards, Double Speak, and Double Binds

Cover Art by Peter J. McCusker ™

iUniverse books may be ordered through booksellers or by contacting:

iUniverse
1663 Liberty Drive
Bloomington, IN 47403
www.iuniverse.com
1-800-Authors (1-800-288-4677)

ISBN: 978-1-4620-3260-0 (sc)
ISBN: 978-1-4620-3262-4 (hc)
ISBN: 978-1-4620-3261-7 (ebk)

Printed in the United States of America

iUniverse rev. date: 09/08/2011

Table of Contents

DEDICATION vii

PREFACE   Racial Identity Sham and Scam ix

CHAPTER 1   Our First Black President? 1

CHAPTER 2   The Development of a Race-Preoccupied
Future President 13

CHAPTER 3   He's Got Personality 27

CHAPTER 4   Barack Hussein Obama:
Disingenuous, Elusive, and Protean 59

CHAPTER 5   What Made "President" Obama Possible? 69

CHAPTER 6   From the Slavery of Servitude
to the Slavery of Attitude 87

CHAPTER 7   Racial Atrocities:
Equal Opportunity Abominations 109

CHAPTER 8   Roots: Origins of Black Male Identity 132

CHAPTER 9   The Incontrovertible Reality of Race Need Not Be a
Really Big Thing 143

CHAPTER 10   People-of-Color 167

CHAPTER 11   Forces That Maintain the Racial Divide 178

CHAPTER 12   Popular Media: American Pravda 206

CHAPTER 13   Tell Michelle 212

CHAPTER 14   Barack Obama: Epitome of Racial Hypocrisy
and the Doubles 249

CHAPTER 15   General Racial Reconciliation Impediments
and General Solutions 257

CHAPTER 16   Shedding a Little Light
on Individual Mentality Regarding Race 268

CHAPTER 17   Obama, Identity, Race, and America 286

CHAPTER 18   Con Vick 310

CHAPTER 19   Forgive? Forget? 321

CHAPTER 20   Rorschach Barack, the Dreamy-Eyed Electorate,
and the Future 327

EPILOGUE 337

REFERENCES 343

DEDICATION

To Eric Himpton Holder junior, who encourages Americans to be racially courageous, a book that asks him to differentiate racial courage from racial discretion. Also, a suggestion: identify racial double standards, double speak, and double binds, and campaign against them. We must not only change what we talk about, but also how we talk about it—inter-racial communication premises and processes. More than anything else, doing so will foster authentic and constructive black-white dialogue and progressive reconciliation.

PREFACE
Racial Identity Sham and Scam

At the start of the 2008 presidential primary, like most Americans, I knew very little about Barack Obama but seriously considered voting for him. He seemed intelligent, energetic, and committed. He said most things that seemed reasonable. However, the more I learned about him, the more I knew that I could not vote for Obama. Because I believed that America needed a change, I simply could not vote for another middle-aged, white male.

But wait, you say, Obama is black. That's the way he has been "marketed" politically. That's how he has been portrayed by the worldwide media, especially the U.S. media. Everyone from Reverend Jeremiah Wright to George Stephanopoulos has referred to Obama as our first "black" president. (This is nothing less than shared delusional disorder on a grand scale.) So I ask myself: What makes Obama a one hundred percent bona fide every day black man? And I conclude: Not his genes, not his mother nor her lineage, not his sibling, not his upbringing, not the neighborhoods in which he has bought homes, not his lifetime modal environments, not his education, and not his social circle.

When I was a boy in Philadelphia, some black guys with whom I played sports occasionally would verbally joust by "playing the dozens," a series of alternating, outrageously derogatory, but facetious, slurs against each other's mother. The insults would go something like this: "Yo momma so ugly, she scare stripes off a zebra." "Yeah, well yo momma so ugly, she scare dirt out a rug." The dozens usually began light-heartedly, with uproarious laughter, but, as the "game" progressed, things often heated-up, sometimes ending with flying fists.

Barack Obama and his supporters do not play the dozens with America, but they play their own self-serving verbal game: identity manipulation and racial doubles—double standards, double speak, and double binds. While everyone knows what double standards are, for some, double speak and double binds may be new. I am using the terms in very specific ways. Double speak is manipulative talk that is duplicitous, disingenuous, deceptive, and destructive. Double bind—more than damned if you do and damned if you don't—is best described by example. For instance, when white people express racial opinions, they frequently are called racists. When white people resist talking about their racial opinions, the Attorney General of the United States calls them racial cowards. And now the bind: white people are not permitted to question the unfair racial language and unfair racial rules of the game. If whites challenge the language or rules, they are shouted down, told that they "don't know what it means to be black," meaning that white people not only have no credibility from which to express an opinion, but also have no opportunity to argue for a level playing field. Whites, then, are left with unresolved dysphoric feelings, such as frustration, resignation, or anger that militate against racial harmony and reconciliation.

The doubles constitute the heart and soul of what I have to say here. Each element—double standards, double speak, and double binds—exerts profound social and linguistic affects on the American people. Each element can do so implicitly or explicitly, consciously or unconsciously. And each element can present singly or in combination with either or both of the other two elements. The doubles, clearly, are most powerful when all three elements synergistically reinforce each other, as they do in racial matters, generally, and in the Obama story, specifically.

Ex-President Bill Clinton insightfully, albeit unwittingly, addressed the doubles when, commenting about Barack Obama, he said, "Give me a break. This whole thing is the biggest fairy tale I've ever seen." For the sake of America, I pray that the Obama saga does not turn out to be an old world, un-sanitized fairy tale with its archetypal gruesome ending.

Barak Obama has packaged himself for political gain as though he were a typical black man when he clearly is not. Rather he is an incarnate metaphor of racial hypocrisy in America. In carefully selected venues, for personal advantage or expediency, Obama recites a script acknowledging and even underscoring that he had a black African father and white American mother. However, his spontaneous words and actions routinely discredit himself, his mother, and her heritage by impassioned oral and written references to being a "black man" only—nothing more or less. I have never heard or seen from him a self reference in which he acknowledges being a "white man," or, more correctly, being a "biracial man." In fact, his autobiographical memoire, *Dreams from my Father*, literally does not even contain the term "biracial," although Barack does use the derogatory term, "mulatto."

Before white, but not black, crowds Obama occasionally, opportunistically has touted his black and white family. But he was born into that condition; he did not choose it. The composition of Barack's friends and partners shows that he often has chosen angry, Afrocentric, America disparagers who give voice to his pseudo-black biases in ways from which he can distance himself when that serves his self interest.

Barack Obama, always black, briefly black and white when convenient, and never white, has been advertised as destined to bring the races together despite his inability to embrace, or even to fully accept, his own biracial identity. What is even more startling is that while all literate people know in their hearts that Obama is biracial, most watch him parade by masquerading as a homogenous black man and say nothing. Taking a page from Bill Clinton's fairy tale analogy, I feel like a 21st century adult version of the proverbial child who asserts that the emperor has no clothes while an adoring throng stands mesmerized and enthralled by his sartorial splendor.

You no doubt are thinking, "Who is the person writing this book?"

The answer, of course, is central to what I have to say, and to whatever credibility with which I can say it. But before addressing who I am, I am compelled to tell you who I am not. Unlike the majority of white and black authors who try to address Obama and race, I am not an Ivy League graduate. I never owned a Lexus, BMW, Mercedes, or a Porsche. I've never vacationed in the Hamptons. I don't belong to a country club. In fact, I don't even play golf or tennis.

I did grow up in a working-class neighborhood in Philadelphia. From about 13 to 17, I "hung out" at an approximately 60% African American housing project where I and other white and black kids played sports together. One of the high schools that I attended was about 95% white and the other, about 50% white and 50% black. Like many from my neighborhood, I quit high school. In the Marines, en route to South Viet Nam, I turned eighteen. While in the service, I lived amicably with black and white "leathernecks," and I had enough sense to study for and earn a GED-type diploma. Four years in the Marine Corps impressed me with the stark reality that I had acquired no marketable skills, so, after discharge, I went to college through the GI Bill. Half-way through undergraduate school I married my wife of over 40 years. Just before I received my bachelor's, we had our first child. We repeated that basic formula for my master's and doctoral degrees, resulting in our claim to fame—three wonderful daughters. Having earned my degrees in psychology, I have been, for 35 years, a colleague to black and white professionals and a doctor for many hundreds of black and white patients—with a mostly even split between black and white—practicing in virtually every clinical psychological setting imaginable. Two particularly relevant experiences were my over two-decade long service to pre-adjudicated and adjudicated "delinquents," about 70% of whom were black, and my occasional evaluations of prison inmates with a similar racial imbalance.

Through the years, I have learned at a gut level what in contemporary America sometimes not always is appreciated: that racial differences are superficial and virtually meaningless in the grand scheme of things. I know that the black people with whom I have associated and worked are much more like I am than I am like the typical white or black writers of race-oriented books. More relevant, I know that everyday black people have infinitely more in common with me than they do with Barack Hussein Obama who spent the majority of his childhood in elite private schools, and the majority of his adulthood cavorting with multi-millionaires and billionaires.

Please note that I do not agree with those who say that Obama flat out hates white people. Neither do I accept the ludicrously ironic statement, often made during the 2008 presidential campaign, that Obama is "comfortable in his own skin." Rather, I assert the opposite: Barack

Obama is pathologically alienated from his own skin. He harbors a deep, pervasive, and profound racial identity conflict. I believe that Obama has spent most of his life unsuccessfully struggling against his own personal race-based demons—always suspicious of whites, always operating with the default assumption of white racism, always believing that he, and he alone, knows the pernicious, occult animosities lurking behind positive white overtures toward blacks.

Since childhood, Barack Obama has been racially obsessed. As a result, he has developed a compensatory cognitive style by which his perceptions and thoughts are secreted into a racial funnel and filtered through a race-based semi-permeable membrane. Anything remotely racial is caught in the membrane, the exudate is tagged with an emotional valence, and Barack responds by celebrating anything that is black positive, and by blaming whites for anything that can be construed as black negative. Because Obama cannot reconcile the black and white within himself, because he must choose black versus white within himself, he naturally generalizes this either-or tendency onto the social field, perceiving white people and black people as dichotomous alternatives.

Just after the 2008 presidential election, MSNBC announced "Barack Obama elected 44th president: 'Change has come to America,' first African American leader tells country." But what change? One change, for sure, is the change in national consciousness and reality testing by which an educated electorate permits itself to be duped into acting as though they believe what they want to believe: that Barack Obama is black rather than biracial. He surely has proven to be a lifelong masterful racial manipulator. After receiving all the benefits of middle class white childrearing and childhood development, he managed to accrue to himself all the social and political benefits of calling himself a black man. Barack Obama is a racial ringer who instinctively and deftly tacks from white to black or black to white whenever it suits his purposes. When the wind is right, he might even briefly acknowledge some minimal elements of biraciality, then quickly and resolutely swing black after achieving his short-term end: the only concession that Obama makes to his biracial inheritance—a biraciality that he recognizes and acknowledges only when convenient and expedient for his purposes. On a race basis, he maligns his mother as racially naïve, his grandmother as harboring racial stereotypes, and his white grandfather as "too troubled" to provide direction for him; Obama also implies that his black grandfather hated white people.

Barack tried to frame his election as "not about race," but, in fact, it was mostly about race. Many blacks saw the election as a way to get "one of our own" into power as shown by their 96% vote for Barack Obama. Many whites saw it as a way to be "on the right side of history" and/or to prove how righteous and progressive they were. For a subset of the latter, the fact that Obama "wasn't Bush" just sweetened the pot.

Barack Obama has had an historic, probably unique, opportunity to provide a foundation on which America can begin to build a bridge spanning the black-white racial divide. Why has he failed to seize the opportunity? Is it because that there is no self-serving political advantage to underscoring his biracial identity? Does he fear that he would lose the votes of blacks who want to regard him as an authentic, un-amalgamated extension of themselves? Does he fear that he would lose the votes of a substantial number of white subgroups who regard him as a candidate the support of whom shows them to be eminently virtuous in advocating a "black man" for president?

What does Obama's denial of the reality of his dual racial heritage say to the millions of biracial people who look up to him? Is his message that a biracial person should deny half of him- or her-self? Cut off the white nose to spite the black face, or vice versa? To be at war with oneself? To be ashamed? To be a human chimera who opportunistically casts off an out-of-favor aspect of the self whenever discussing his or her racial identity?

As applied to Americans generally, the implicit malignant message of Barack Obama clearly is that one, in fact, must choose sides in contemporary society's inane, destructive double standards, double speak, and double binds concerning identity, race, racial harmony, and racial equality. Americans are assailed with a constant barrage of Obamafuscation—implicit and explicit race-based lies. The practice has troubled me such that I am compelled to challenge it and the social matrix from which it arises.

Using Barack Obama as common ground and point of departure, *Barry Barack Hussein Soetoro Obama, Identity, and Racial Hypocrisy in America: Double Standards, Double Speak, and Double Binds* addresses the twin psychopathologies of disturbed racial identities and disturbed racial attitudes in the contemporary United States. I choose to write in order to grapple with nagging questions. The most primary of these are: First, why would an intelligent, accomplished grown man play hide and seek with the incontrovertible reality of his biracial essence? What fuels the formation and maintenance of this disingenuous identity? Second, why would the American people and popular media not only permit him to promulgate the lie but also collude in the deception? And, finally, what do both of the aforementioned questions imply about the broader issues of identity, race, and race relations in the United States?

The book is both a dissertation of my beliefs about race in America and a social experiment that asks whether society will tolerate a white man honestly addressing some tough racial issues that keep the racial cauldron bubbling. The visceral nature of racial polarity also determines the language that I employ—often vernacular and occasionally sarcastic and crude. After all, isn't authentic race-talk just what Eric Himpton Holder junior is advocating? Caustic and cynical language is "honest," given the balkanized, often covert, racial attitudes prevalent in 21ˢᵗ century America. This is the talk that real people use in real situations to address real racially-charged issues. The rational, pretty words of social science do not helped us combat racism because racism is not rational and racism is not pretty. Moreover, vernacular, sarcastic and, even, crude talk is the talk that traditional race "advocates" regularly employ to make their positions crystal clear.

Initially I had planned a standard, cerebral, rigidly academic approach, with arguments carefully sequenced and meticulously referenced. But, ultimately, I concluded that the effort would be both unappreciated and unproductive. While superficial issues regarding race can be debated rationally, the underlying substantive gut-level ones have yet to yield to dispassionate, logical discourse. For that reason, I do not attempt methodically to argue all the relevant data, reference each and every fact or opinion that I have discovered, or to neatly tie together all the loose ends. Rather, I merely initiate and encourage a black-white dialogue that highlights and begins to work through some of the most salient, fundamental, and neglected issues that trouble Americans—black and white.

Respectful, yet honest, race-oriented talk presents a formidable challenge. In the United States, a country that prides itself, above all, on openness and the free flow of ideas, frank discussion of race is the single most tabooed, distorted topic. Race discourse historically has been incredibly divisive and intractable, despite the best efforts of a host of well-intentioned black and white citizens. Blacks who dare deviate from the conventional race script that ascribes all black problems to white America routinely are derided as "Uncle Toms." White Americans who speak honestly about race invariably are labeled as "racists." It is inevitable that my attempts to communicate honestly will cause some to try to label me similarly.

What bedrock assumptions undergird *Barry Barack Hussein Soetoro Obama, Identity, and Racial Hypocrisy in America: Double Standards, Double Speak, and Double Binds?* First and foremost, I assert the obvious and indisputable fact that blatant racism and slavery had been the most virulent, most destructive factor affecting black Americans. Second, institutionalized racism was its own hypocrisy that white America had permitted to exist alongside airy statements regarding the dignity and equality of all people. Third, black America has harbored its own racist, anti-white attitudes that neither they nor white America have been willing to confront. Fourth, for many Americans, important divergent black-white attitudes and biases usually remain hidden during superficial or highly scripted interracial interaction, obscuring real differences lying just beneath the surface. It is mostly when emotions or stakes are high that true black-white differences and biases reveal themselves. Fifth, the expectation of complete racial equality is a delusion, if by racial equality we mean that all Americans will treat each other solely and completely in terms of the "quality of their character." (Are we to assume that intra-racial people *always* treat each other purely in terms of the quality of their character?) Some attitudes and behaviors labeled "racism" are not racism at all, but instead are preferences for that which looks and seems similar to one self over those that do not. By acknowledging the possibility of differences in racial preferences that are non-racist, we provide space that permits racial pride and racial affinity to coexist with good-enough racial equanimity. Sixth, and most critically, both races have been colluding in a grotesque Orwellian-like conspiracy that prevents the honest dialogue necessary to sincerely address underlying racial tensions. Nothing is as important or as challenging to racial reconciliation as is breaking through the stone wall of dialogue deception. George Orwell, himself, has advised that "Freedom is the freedom to say two plus two makes four. If that is granted, all else follows." Superlatively simple, superlatively succinct and superlatively clear—physicists would say, "elegant"—in 18 words Orwell implicitly advises us that freedom provides us both the contents, and, more important, the processes that lead inexorably to truth.

Dialogue deception occurs in part because the language of race is stacked against any white person who attempts to speak honestly, such as by asserting that most problems masquerading as inter-racial have little, if anything, to do with race per se. Emotionally balanced white people do not mindlessly stereotype blacks or see them as one ill-defined mass of protoplasm. Common parlance, however, coerces us into describing blacks by the color of their skin; it does not provide words that can be used to differentiate blacks according to the contents of their characters. For instance, if a white person speaks critically of a black person, the default assumption is that the white person is racist and the verbal assault against him begins. In this book, I start to build a lexicon that fills the void by defining some personality types and associated activities that promote racial tension. Toward that end, I employ four new terms: "Racializers" detect race-oriented, especially anti-black, bias wherever they cast their eyes. "Raceketeers" derive power, prestige and profit from imagined or grossly exaggerated race-oriented, especially anti-black or pro-black, sentiment. "Race cadets" aspire to raceketeer status. And "bimps" (black inner-city male persona) adopt a marauding, destructive black inner-city male personality caricature epitomized by "gangsta rap" bearing and behavior. By employing the new lexicon, we have language suitable for exploring the intended and unintended consequences that follow for black and white communities when racializers, raceketeers, race cadets, and bimps play their destructive games.

So where am I going with this book?

In Chapters One and Two, I do what psychologists are trained to do: I construct a relatively general profile of Barry Barack Hussein Soetoro Obama in the context of his family that integrates his history, his verbalizations, and his overt acts—each data base informing the other. I must underscore that I am not merely investigating the personality of a man who became a president. Rather, I am showing how a man with a particular personality and like-minded cohorts use race to manipulate a country and, to a lesser extent, the world.

Obama's two autobiographies help structure my investigation in that much of what I say frequently references what Barack has written or said about himself. The material from his books are evaluated to determine how it articulates with all that we have learned about Barack Obama since publication of *Dreams from My Father* (that I regard as *Delusions from My Father*) and *The Audacity of Hope* (that I consider as *The Mendacity of Hype*). You will see in his communications varying degrees and combinations of five critical elements: truth, hyperbole, structured myth, obfuscation, and deliberate self-serving omissions and distortions intended to sell a book and a political career. Since Obama, his publisher, and an army of promoters and admirers will continue to trumpet the truths, I present information regarding the other five elements.

The particulars of Barack Obama's personality are targeted in Chapter Three. Because I have never met Barack, and do not expect to, this chapter is, at best, my second hand account of his personality. We see here that the Obama character can be explained in large part by applying a modification of the "dark-triad" personality construct, an amalgam of narcissism, Machiavellianism, and psychopathy. The narcissism of Obama is so patently obvious that it needs little explanation at this point in the manuscript. His Machiavellianism, documented in many books and articles, concerns Barack's penchant for political manipulation. The psychopathy of our President is less obvious but clearly present in the way that he manages his identity, relationships, and emotions. For instance, Obama regularly employs the psychopathic defenses of "isolation" and "splitting," rigidly dichotomizing people into good versus evil in order to coldly and self-servingly exploit them. Psychopathy also is apparent in how Obama has used his associations with criminal types to get what he wanted—for instance, with Bill Ayers of the Weather Underground

Terrorist group who, in reflecting on his seditious past recently, said, "I don't regret setting bombs . . . I feel we didn't do enough," and with Tony Rezko, convicted in 2008 on sixteen counts of fraud and money laundering.

The fourth chapter investigates how Barack Obama and his handlers masterfully manipulate the American psyche in order to promote him. Primarily this involves their deftly plucking all the right strings to transform the dissonance between black and white America into beautiful music for Barack. The Obama people play to their self-serving manipulative advantage all the notes of white yearning to put black-white division behind them, and all the rhythms of black longing for self-esteem through identity validation.

Separatist propaganda and pressure by raceketeers are the bases for Chapter Five. I suggest that what began as an essential need for guidance and leadership for blacks by blacks has been corrupted, now enslaving black identity consciousness while lining the pockets of raceketeer leaders. To a considerable extent, black demagogues have been able to dictate their narrow views of what "proper" black identity is. That restricted range of legitimacy not only keeps everyday black people in identity servitude, but also elicits white backlash that further deepens racial divisions.

Chapter Six elaborates some specifics of raceketeers' efforts to manipulate black people and the overt and covert white reactions to those ostensibly "pro-black" racialized standards and practices. I assert that many of the manipulations cause, rather than cure, the problems of inner-city black families.

In Chapter Seven I take a reluctant look at the grim reality of racial violence. It is acknowledged that, since antiquity, all races have committed gross cross-group atrocities. However, in contemporary America, white on black crimes are reported far, wide, and interminably, while black on white crimes are glossed over and precipitate a flood of excuses, "soul"-searching, and recommendations that more social programs are needed to correct the institutionalized white racism that caused the "conditions" that led the poor African American perpetrators astray.

The epidemic of black crime and incarceration is attributable to a relatively small number of repeat offenders who, Chapter Eight shows, have fashioned an identity built around an anti-social lifestyle. The "bimp" identity has at its core a hyper-masculine, dark-triad personality structure that disdains law and order. Rather, their unspoken creed expresses a desire for immediate and unconditional self-gratification, with no consideration for the needs of others—white or black. In fact, since these hard-core, dark-triad psychopaths live in black neighborhoods, purely on a numbers basis, African Americans are victimized the most.

There never has been an America free from racial dissention, but I once heard a most quotable comment, "Things that never were happen every day." Chapter Nine asserts that we can overcome black-white differences, or at least make them less onerous, by taking personal responsibility for our own inter-racial attitudes, rather than allowing raceketeers to dictate them. To do so, we must develop an internal locus of control with particular attention to the language that we use to frame the race-oriented comments that we deliberately and inadvertently utter to ourselves and to others.

Chapter Ten also begins language-oriented, considering the meanings and implications of the term, "people-of-color" (POC). I suggest that, regardless of the professed intention for using it, POC pits the entire human race on one side of a racial Berlin Wall and white people on the other. POC is merely one more way to make race, rather than individual character, the litmus test of who sides with whom. The supreme hypocrisy of the POC concept is that when one checks local newspapers, as I do, he finds that many black bimps just delight in exploiting and terrorizing people-of-color when it serves their dark-triad personality needs.

Language is important for race relations but so are actions, some of which begin with good intentions but end with unforeseen negative consequences. Chapter Eleven discusses how the civil rights movement and what initially were salutary pro-black attitudes have been corrupted to work against racial reconciliation and against the best interests of the black community itself. Profiteering raceketeers, an "our turn" mentality, an anti-law bias and a popular media that forgives black self-destructive behavior are four of these. But the most debilitating consequence of the pro-black mindset has been to create an environment that enables bimps to control the streets of inner-city black America.

In Chapter Twelve, I show that our print and broadcast institutions are a kind of America Pravda who make it their business to promote personal views of what our country is or is not, rather than to objectively present the facts. Like their beloved Barack, many so-called journalists and their bosses truly believe that they know what is best for the huddled masses, and they are intent to shove their notions of truth and propriety down our collective throat.

Addressing Michelle Obama's "for the first time in my adult life I am proud of my country" disrespect for America is the raison d'être of Chapter Thirteen. Contending that Michelle really was complaining not about America but about white America, I report both about white grievances and about whites who have performed outstanding, selfless service to blacks. I challenge Obama to go one-on-one with me about the ratio of white to black cross-race compassion and assistance.

Chapter Fourteen, rather than thirteen, might be considered unlucky for Barry Barack Hussein Soetoro Obama, since it summarizes the racial hypocrisy, double standards, double speak, and double binds that he perpetrates. The major purpose of this chapter is to assert that the American people cannot wait for a racial savior, even if he has been preceded by John the Baptist-like prophets who have promoted him and have attempted to prepare hapless souls for his coming. The lesson is obvious: Being half black and half white does not ensure that the person in question will adequately understand or empathize with either race.

While Barack Obama, raceketeers—professional and amateur—media, and others contribute mightily to America's racial discord, only individual black and white citizens can affect constructive change in black-white sensibilities. Chapter Fifteen details some general social impediments and general solutions to collaborative cross-racial dialogue. These impediments are natural human tendencies that make Americans so vulnerable to manipulation by raceketeers and other racializers.

Chapter Sixteen complements the previous chapter's general social focus by shedding light on specific individual mental processes that underlie the racial confusion and frustration that many of us feel. Here we consider over a dozen cognitive-emotional mechanisms that cause us to attend to the negatives of race and that paralyze us from acting to correct what obviously is wrong with the way we perceive and treat each other racially. Knowing the mechanisms, of course, is only a start. The hard work comes in implementing the language and behavior change necessary to help Americans focus on all people as individuals and not as groups of colors.

American culture barrages us daily with messages about how important black identity is. Barack Obama even devoted his first book to a tedious, self-aggrandizing, Machiavellian treatment of his heroic almost-black self. Now, as a psychologist, I accept that identity is critically important but, for emotionally healthy people, identity is much more than racial identity. Chapter Seventeen explores how raceketeers and others manipulate black identity to their own self-serving advantage, and, in the process, contribute to creating and sustaining many of the problems experienced by 21st century African Americans.

In Chapter Eighteen, Michael Vick, pro football superstar, provides a counterpoint to Barack Obama in the succeeding chapter. The story of Vick is a story of a hardcore dark-triad bimp personality that, nevertheless, is inner city, authentically black: in contrast to Barack Obama, a synthetic, knob hill, Ivy League, pseudo-black. The rise and fall of Michael Vick illustrates that some bimp characteristics are the very qualities that enable some "street kids" to become outstanding athletes and rappers, and the very qualities that ultimately lead to their undoing.

Religious, social science, and government leaders preach to us about the power of forgiveness in all areas except race relations. There, they are intent on inculcating whites with guilt and blacks with feelings of entitlement. In Chapter Nineteen, I offer a format for thinking about racial reconciliation. As is true throughout this book, I focus on what individuals can do on their own, given the absence of support by most of our "leaders" and the divisive interference by some others.

In 1967, Martin Luther King junior published his last book, *Where Do We Go from Here: Chaos or Community?* The question remains. Chapter Twenty indirectly addresses King's question by summarizing some essentials from earlier chapters and using them to point us toward a better future. I restate why I believe that Barack Obama is the embodiment of racial identity hypocrisy, both a beneficiary and a perpetrator of the racial doubles—double standards, double speak, and double binds—and how Americans unwittingly have colluded with him, due to our intense longing to prove our racial virtue and to "do the right thing." I suggest that there is hope, however, since Obama continues to have a unique opportunity to help bridge the racial divide and to support our country's growing biracial and multi-racial citizens. I caution him that someday there will be a "purely black" president who will identify Barack as the biracial that he is, and I implore Barack Obama to evidence the "racial courage" that Eric Himpton Holder junior feels is so essential to the social and inter-racial health of the United States of America.

CHAPTER 1

Our First Black President?

Delusions from My Father

Virtually every autobiography is a self-serving historical fiction fashioned to bring coherence, consistency, and approbation to its creator. Real, distorted, or blatantly erroneous ideas are culled from an ongoing life script toward those ends. No one should be faulted for a fallible memory. Anyone writing an autobiography can and will make some mistakes. It is the pattern of the mistakes that is revealing, especially when the pattern points to a utilitarian purpose. Regardless of the truths or lies contained within the autobiography, the personality of the autobiographer determines what he chooses to say and what he chooses not to say. Each reveals as much about him as does the other.

The fact that Obama contrives some aspects of his first book, then, is of no special consequence. There are some things that make the Barack Obama's autobiographies atypical, however. For one, by age forty-five he already had written two autobiographical works. What might this suggest? Was it indicative of narcissistic elitism? Was it an attempt to manipulate social opinion to promote political avarice? Was it a way to work through a profoundly conflicted racial identity? Was it coldly calculating, psychopathological, or both?

As the old saying goes, timing is everything. One might argue that the author-politician Barack Obama has been just plain lucky, but I believe that it has been much more than luck. *Roots*, its own plagiarized historical fiction, aired on television to rave reviews in 1977 when Obama was sixteen years old. Perhaps it was the anticipated 20th anniversary of the

1

series that helped motivate Times Corporation on July 18, 1995 to publish the 34-year-old Obama in hopes of another Africa-inspired blockbuster. Moreover, the fact that Barack had been elected the first "African American" president of the *Harvard Law Review* in 1990 virtually guaranteed that anything that he wrote about race would garner free widespread media attention and advanced publicity; he simply was a publisher's dream.

It certainly strains credulity to think that the book's release was only coincidentally related to Obama's almost contemporaneous push to launch his political career. Sharon Churcher of London's *Daily Mail*, in fact, speculated that *Dreams from My Father* constituted Obama's "preemptive strike" against those who might challenge his political candidacy. The most obvious example of this strategy was the fact that in the book he dubbed himself as "a black man with a funny name," the very self appellation that he repeatedly would use during future campaign speeches. Speaking in the *Dreams* book, Obama claimed that because he did not trust his childhood recollections, he sat at his father's grave "trying to rewrite" the stories of his life. He suggested that the dialogue in his book presents "an approximation" of what he learned in Africa, that some characters are "composites," and the chronology is unreliable.

The *Dreams* introduction says much about Barack Obama and his strategy. Here, as often, he is looking to control the dialogue and preempt relevant inquiry. He mentions hiding from himself, the skepticism of others about him, and the mythology of his youth—just what one would expect from a presidential candidate and president who vigorously had resisted or totally refused to let the light of day shine on his birth certificate, school transcripts, and Lord knows what else. Obama tries to evoke pathos for the struggling young man by claiming to have been virtually prostrate at his father's grave. He acknowledges his revisionist efforts at identity reconstruction. But the single most revealing aspect of the aforementioned memoir introduction is that it lays bare the manipulative, disingenuous nature of Barack Obama in that he tells us that we can never be sure which parts of his memoir are real and which are contrived. In so doing, Obama can take credit for whatever others ultimately laud and minimize or otherwise disassociate himself from whatever others criticize. That strategy presages the Machiavellian tactics that Barack Obama employs concerning his identity in general and his racial identity in particular.

By introducing himself to America in cleverly edited autobiographical print, Obama is able to make light of, rationalize, and minimize his weaknesses while exploiting and over-stating his strengths on his own terms at the times of his own choosing. Check for yourself that every one of the scores of books written about Barack Obama, including this one, uses his *Dreams* book as a primary source. One cannot overestimate the advantage of this "first out" strategy that has enabled Barack to frame the political discourse. Paul Watkins in the August 6, 1995 Sunday *New York Times* seems to be on the same page as I, so to speak, when in reviewing *Dreams from My Father* he comments: "Although Mr. Obama is no more black than he is white, his quest for acceptance is aimed at the African Americans with whom he shares his organizational duties, and his story bogs down in discussions of racial exploitation without really shedding any new light on the subject."

The Mendacity of Hype

Acceptance by the black electorate had to be central in Obama's political calculus. As any Chicago Democrat politician, he needed the African American vote, if he were to have any chance of reaching first base. But black acceptance, even adulation, meant much more to Obama than mere politics. Black acceptance was the reassuring identity elixir that he needed to overcome his profound racial self doubt and conflict.

Two desperate antidotes for self doubt are hubris and narcissism. These traits permit a person to be his own lover, his own mother, his own father, and his own best friend. Hubris and narcissism enable him to maintain the illusion of personal superiority and to justify saying one thing and doing another with nary a hint of compunction. Could anyone be so crass as to accuse Barack Obama of such things? Does this sound like right-wing propaganda or white racist venom?

If you believe so, then ask why Hillary Clinton called Barack Obama "elitist and divisive." Why in commenting about Obama did Jesse Jackson say that he wanted to "Cut his nuts off because Barack . . . he's talking down to black people . . . telling niggers how to behave." Why did Sir Nigel Sheinwald, British ambassador in Washington, refer to Barack Obama as "aloof'?" Even the journalist Peter Nicholas of the Los Angeles Times, who spent one and one-half years covering the 2007-2008 presidential campaign, regarded Barack Obama as robotic and self-absorbed.

What made Barack Obama first agree to accept federal campaign funds and the limits pertaining thereto in order to improve the American political system and then to renege on the promise when he saw personal advantage in doing so? What kept him from ever being able to admit that the surge helped radically reduce the levels of violence in Iraq? I will cite a slew of examples to show the presidential candidate Obama claiming that he would not proceed with "politics as usual" and then doing exactly that during the campaign and after being elected.

The Lighter Side of Barry Obama

A Girl Named Stanley

On November 29, 1942, Madelyn Dunham delivered onto the maternity ward of Fort Leavenworth a baby girl who would be her one and only child. This presumably delighted Madelyn, but not her soldier husband. Rather, Stanley expressed unabashed, profound disappointment at being denied a son. To compensate himself for the narcissistic wound, he decreed that the child should be named after him and, amazingly, his wife consented.

Self interest of father pitted against that of daughter: a dynamic that only would intensify over time. Just as whiskey-swigging, chain-smoking Stanley could not accept his daughter for the person she was, Stanley Ann increasingly grew to reject him and all that he represented. The child needed to distance herself from her egotistical namesake in order to survive emotionally.

According to Barack, Stanley Ann developed into an "introverted" child: "shy and awkward," inclined to "bury her head in a book or to wander off on solitary walks." He stated that his grandmother worried about the youngster's "eccentricities." He added that his mother made few friends at school. He directly referred to how she was "teased mercilessly for her name." Christopher Andersen claimed that during childhood and adolescence, as her son later would, Barack's mother adopted a preemptive identity strike strategy by introducing herself as, "Hi. I'm Stanley. My dad wanted a boy." Her friend noted that Stanley Ann discharged tension by "constantly cracking her knuckles." As a young woman, she allegedly "never dated crew-cut white boys;" nor did she babysit, as most of her girlfriends did. One classmate recalled showing Stanley Ann her newborn brother and the latter replying, "When are you sending him back?"

By adolescence, Stanley Ann was profoundly alienated from her explosive and depreciating father. Their relationship had devolved into an endless series of tumultuous, sometimes violent, interactions. Stanley frequently belittled his daughter. If he perceived any sign of defiance, he slapped her. At times, the intrusive, attention-seeking Stanley tried to insinuated himself into Stanley Ann's discussions with her friends. Mortified and irritated, she frequently responded with passive-aggressive contempt, stepping back from him and surreptitiously rolling her eyes.

Having completed high school in Washington state and desperate to escape her father's imperious control, Stanley Ann applied for a scholarship to the University of Chicago. Acceptance letter in hand, she prepared to launch herself over the barbed-wire enclosure of home life. But this was not to be. Stanley senior informed her that she would not be accepting the offer; rather, she was commanded to relocate with her parents to Hawaii. Profoundly disgruntled, she reluctantly acceded to her father's demands.

What did Stanley Ann do to assert her independence? The year was 1960. Racial tensions had begun roiling. There were scores of prohibitions concerning race relations, the greatest being a taboo concerning black-white sexual relations. White, as well as black, fathers of little girls lived in mortal fear that their daughters somehow could become involved in cross racial intimacy.

Within a few weeks of relocation, eighteen-year-old Stanley Ann started dating a black African six years older than she. In his memoire, Barack junior stated that his grandparents probably regarded the liaison ". . . as a trial that would pass." If so, they were guilty of parental malfeasance. According to him, despite the lovers being polar opposites—his father, "black as pitch;" his mother, "milky white"—they were irresistibly attracted to each other. Peter Firstbrook noted that, "By November 1960, within weeks of meeting Obama senior, Ann was pregnant . . ." Historylink.org commented: ". . . it is something of a mystery whether the pregnancy or true love brought on the marriage." President Obama wrote that ". . . how and when the marriage occurred remains a bit murky, a bill of particulars that I've never quite had the courage to explore. There's no record of a real wedding, a cake, a ring, a giving away of the bride. No families were in attendance; it's not even clear that people back in Kansas were fully informed. Just a small civil ceremony, a justice of the peace."

Stanley Ann's high school friends reportedly were shocked by news of her pregnancy, since, allegedly, she never had a steady boyfriend and was disinterested in children. So, a young woman who once joked that a baby boy should be returned to wherever it came from, a young woman who had a most troubled relationship with the only consistent male in her life, her tyrannical father, had a sexual liaison with an essentially unknown, "forbidden" man. Thus, while Stanley Ann may or may not have had a "murky" marriage ceremony, she definitely did have a precipitous "romantic" liaison that, for better or worse, produced a baby boy of her own.

If there was a marriage, it certainly was not a marriage made in heaven, but a most effective way for an eighteen-year-old daughter metaphorically to stick her finger in the eye of a domineering father. Stanley Ann proved that she was liberated and fully independent. Given his African tribal, post-colonial roots, Barack senior proved that he was as good as any white man and had the trophy white woman to prove it. As we shall see, perhaps predictably, Stanley Ann managed to swap a despotic, alcoholic father for a despotic, alcoholic first husband who would abscond within two years, ultimately proving himself to be little more than a sperm donor for his son, "Barry." The story of Barry's birth, then, seemed to be one in which his mother and father had a brief, impulsive relationship during which they acted out private, forbidden fantasies and conflicts, shared gametes, and quickly bade each other adieu.

In January 1964, about the time little Barry was two and a half, his mother divorced Barack senior. By August, 1967 Stanley Ann already had courted and married Lolo Soetoro, another alcoholic, sullen non-American who soon left her after being conscripted into the Indonesian Army. One year later, she and six-year-old Barry rejoined Lolo in Indonesia. Two years afterwards, in August of 1970, Stanley Ann gave birth to Barry's half-sister, Maya. Approximately one year after her birth, Barry, age ten, was shuttled back to Hawaii to live with the maternal grandparents, but not before he had noticed that his mother had been "weeping on a daily basis." Within the next year, 1972, Stanley Ann's second marriage bit the dust: she left Lolo, taking Maya with her and rejoining her son and parents in Hawaii. This time she stayed for a grand total of three years before hustling back to Indonesia with Maya, but leaving her son behind.

Reportedly never reestablishing a wife-husband relationship with Lolo (who eventually died of liver disease that probably was alcohol-induced), Stanley Ann finally divorced him in1980. Apparently, interpersonal relationships never were her strong suit. Associates described Stanley Ann as distant from American expats, perceiving them as haughty, and distant from Indonesians, regarding them as untruthful. According to Barack, his mother occasionally became so flustered and frustrated during conversations that she literally burst into tears. The tendency toward being interpersonally overwhelmed apparently was matched by other sectors of low self confidence, presumably accounting for the fact that Stanley Ann never learned to drive an automobile.

On the other hand, Stanley Ann Dunham did have academic competencies, earning a Ph. D. in anthropology from the University of Hawaii, thus supporting Barack's belief in her "bookish" nature. As one might expect from an interpersonally distant person who saw Indonesians as untruthful, she spent much of her time in small rural villages among indigents who presumably expected little from her emotionally.

Having suffered through so many troubled relationships with people, in general, and with men, in particular, Stanley Ann's attachment to the maturing Barry became increasingly perfunctory and episodic. Unlike the situation with her son, however, she never allowed Maya to leave her during the daughter's childhood. Apparently, Barry reciprocated the loose attachment to his mother with an out of sight, out of mind mentality, as when in his high school year book he thanked his maternal grandparents for their support, but not Stanley Ann.

How did the "milky white" mother try to win the affection of her profoundly identity-conflicted biracial son, so preoccupied with being a "real" black? According to him, despite what he disparaged as her child-like understanding of race-relations, she proselytized ceaselessly to instill in him a sense of black pride. Stanley Ann spoke glowingly of the brilliance of Barack senior, talked up civil rights heroes, and even suggested that "Harry Belafonte is the best looking man on the planet."

We gain insight into the depth of Barack's gratefulness for his mother's black pride-inculcating efforts from an anecdote reported by him in *Dreams from My Father* ("father," of course) wherein Obama notes that during his college years he and his mother argued vociferously about the civil rights struggles. He mentions perceiving her as "racially naïve" when she complained that blacks were painting all whites as racist. In the course of one of these race-based altercations, Barack unwittingly placed his mother in a personal identity double bind reminiscent of the struggles she experienced as a little girl. Just as Stanley Ann was expected to compromise her gender self-esteem to placate a tyrannical father, she felt compelled to apologize to a racially overbearing son for her racial self-esteem, pleading "I never felt white. That's not my identity."

If he could not subdue her through argument, Barack sometimes shunned his mother when she hurt his black pride. For example, he reports being so embarrassed by her child-like infatuation with "Black Orpheus," a movie that they had attended together and that had insulted his black sensibilities, that "for the next several days," he literally avoided situations that might "force" him to talk to Stanley Ann. In so doing, Barack ignored his mother, much as her peers did during childhood. The tactic also reveals the personality of Obama since he notes that while they were viewing the Black Orpheus film together he not only felt embarrassed by his mother but ". . . irritated with the people around me." Here the coping formula seems to be: When one's racial identity is threatened, project blame onto anyone and everyone within sight; it will make you feel better—a paranoid defense mechanism of the first order.

Given the distant mother-child relationship, it is not surprising that the son would write a book centered on a quasi-mythical, philandering, boorish, self-absorbed father, virtually ignoring his devoted mother. Stanley Ann complained weak-heartedly at first about the inequity of the book's focus; then, true to form, she gave "little Barry" a pass for it, excusing his need to find himself racially.

Just as Barack senior abandoned Stanley Ann to pursue his career and other interests, Barack junior was on the road pursuing his own personal political and economic agendas as his mother lay dying. That is, he chose to accompany the black raceketeers Jeremiah Wright, Marion Barry, and Louis Farrakhan on their Million Man March to promote his political career over allegiance to white flesh and blood, and to promote his *Dreams from My Father* rather than to fly to his mother's side as his grandmother, sister, and wife had implored him to do. How could he pass-up an opportunity to market his hoped-for best seller? How could he risk not winning an election? Never mind that every year approximately a half-million United States candidates lose a political election, only to have an opportunity to run again in the future. Never mind that not a single election winner or loser ever has a second chance to comfort his mother in the last hours of her life.

The circumstances of Stanley Ann's death in November 1995 reveal more about Barack than almost any other single event in his history. Think about it. As his white mother is dying, he is promoting a book based on his black father; marching in a procession celebrating the importance of black fathers; and marching side-by-side with the white-hating Louis Farrakhan, organizer of the march, and the crack-smoking-convicted, drug-addicted black hero Marion Barry, one of its major stars. Moreover, to do this, he had to inure himself against repeated entreaties of his grandmother, sister, and wife who virtually begged him to see his mother one last time before she died. (One would have thought that the unanticipated death of Michelle's father four years earlier, in 1991, as a result of kidney surgery complications would have sensitized Barack to the importance of being at the side of his terminally ill mother.) More than anything else, black racial identity obsession, fame and fortune avarice, and a megalomaniacal need for black acceptance have made Barack, Barack.

The Darker Side of Barack Hussein Obama

Barack Obama senior: Luo Prince

Even before the hard finality of his father's desertion fully ossified, Barry had begun creating elaborate identity-assuaging fantasies to compensate for disappointing father-son realities. In *Dreams from My Father*, he writes of an incident in grade school in which he lied to his classmates, telling them that his grandfather was an African chief and his father, a prince.

So who was Barack senior? No prince; not even a prince of a fellow.

Senior's own father, Hussein Onyango Obama both profited from and despised Englishmen. His hatred of whites, however was not limited to the British; rather, it was so pervasive, enduring, and complete that, according to Barack junior, when told that Barack senior intended to marry a white person, Hussein wrote Stanley Ann's father ". . . this long nasty letter saying that he didn't approve of the marriage. He didn't want the Obama blood sullied by a white woman, he said." Ultimately, however, Barack senior did his father proud when it came to white women. Not only did he expeditiously abandon Stanley Ann, he also reportedly married, abused, and abandoned another white lady, Ruth Nidesand, after procreating two sons with her. (When it came to misogynistic abuse, Barack senior apparently identified with his own father who Peter Firstbrook in *The Obamas* claimed "attempted to murder" his wife, our President's African grandmother.) On November 18, 2009, CNN reported an interview that they had conducted with one of the sons, Mark, regarding a memoir that he had published. Mark said this about his father, Barack senior:

> "What I wanted to do is write about my father," he said. "My father beat me. He beat my mother." Mark Obama went on to say that oftentimes, he heard thuds coming from the living room and would "hear my mother's screams and my father shouting. I wanted to protect her . . . but I couldn't do anything."

Author Janny Scott reported a violent streak in Senior as well. She noted that, "One evening . . . Ann had cooked dinner for Obama. She put the food on a plate and put the plate in front of him at the table. 'You expect me to eat this?' he barked. Then he grabbed the plate and hurled it against the wall."

Considering the family antipathy toward Caucasians, Barack senior also exploited them career-wise. The white British establishment provided his early education, and the white American establishment, his higher education.

In a valiant but unsuccessful attempt to squeeze out yet another drop of benefit from the Barack senior educational legacy, during the presidential primaries, Barack was outed when he tried to push an I-am-heir—to-JFK mythology by erroneously claiming that the senior Obama came to America in a program funded by the Kennedys. On the other hand, Barack conveniently failed to name Elizabeth Mooney Kirk, the white woman who, in fact, did provide Senior with financial support, perhaps because no personal gain would have accrued to him by acknowledging her contribution.

Barack admits that his mother was ". . . quick to explain or defend the less flattering aspects of my father's character." And he, himself, notes that his father was a "myth," one jointly created by him and by the white side of his family, presumably to fashion a compensatory positive black role model for little Barry.

Senior never established a constructive fatherly identity where Barry was concerned. When Barack senior was interviewed by the *Honolulu Star Bulletin* on June 20, 1962, he did not mention having a son, nor a wife for that matter. In fact, not only did senior abscond to graduate school at Harvard just before his son's first birthday, his rejection was so extreme that he did not bother to see Barry again until the child was 10 years old. During that approximately month-long Christmas reunion at Stanley Ann's parents' house in Hawaii, the time was rife with tension and dissention. In *Dreams from My Father*, Barack spoke of the immense relief that he felt when his father finally left, never to see him again.

As noted earlier, Barack's mother was an apologist for the father's aberrant personality characteristics while Grandmother Toots thought he was "straaaange." Barack junior referred to his father as a "womanizer."

Others who knew Barack senior were not so circumspect, proffering characterizations that disclosed grim realities: loud, opinionated, preachy, egotistical, self-involved, impulsive, and bitter, to name a few. The aforementioned physically abused Ruth Nidesand, Barack senior's third wife, in fact, called him "quite crazy" and said that he was even worse on those frequent occasions when he was drunk. In *Barack and Michelle*, Christopher Andersen quoted Africans who said that even Senior's friends reached a point at which "they couldn't stand to be around him" and that he was "always very intoxicated" and "unable to do his job." He deteriorated to the point of driving drunk daily. Barack senior became so reckless that, allegedly, he once committed vehicular homicide, later injured one leg in a car accident, still later destroyed both legs to the point of double amputation, and, finally, when driving a car specially adapted for a double amputee, died in a final, presumably drunken, wreck.

CHAPTER 2

The Development of a Race-Preoccupied Future President

Racial Identity under Construction: Barry Soetoro Obama

Abandoned by his "black as pitch" father in one fell swoop during infancy and by his "milky white" mother multiple times during childhood, Barry learned to distrust parents. Who was left? There was a white grandmother whose racial comments made him "cringe." Thus Toots proved irrevocably flawed precisely in the personality sector at the core of her grandson's being—race. Then there was the white grandfather who the future president readily dismissed as "troubled." Distrustful and rejecting of parents, grandparents, and, by extension, of authority while obsessively, compulsively attentive to all things racial, this was the young Barry Obama. He turned his back on the reality of the white privileged world in which he lived and fancied about the pantheon of black heroes propagandized by his "dreamer" mother in what likely was an unconsciously motivated attempt to live up to Stanley Ann's standards while simultaneously addressing his infantile desire to unite with the mostly mythical, absconded black father whom he never knew.

Surrounded by a flawed white family and embedded in a broader flawed white social environment, Barry decided that whites could not be trusted, that he needed to break away from them in order to be black. If we are to accept *Dreams from My Father*, his alienation from himself began early. In addressing his troubled identity, Barack, the adult, says: ". . . I ceased to

advertise my mother's race at the age of twelve or thirteen, when I began
to suspect that by doing so I was ingratiating myself to whites . . ."

To advertise is to calculatingly and self-servingly put forth an idea that one
wants others to buy. Is that what identity is? Do we want to advertise our
race to others, so that others will see us as being a race? I, like Martin Luther
King, think that a person should strive to be seen for the individual that
he or she is: not a race, not a gender, nor any other single defining feature.
Isn't each individual an amalgam of an infinite array of characteristics?
Isn't that, in fact, the very definition of an "individual?" If one perceives
race as something to be advertised or defended, only then will he become
obsessed with ingratiating himself to one racial caste or another. But if he
is comfortable in his own skin, he will just be himself.

Now you might say, "Wait a minute. Barry was only twelve or thirteen
years old at the time quoted." To which I rejoin, "Really? I don't think so."
It was not the twelve or thirteen–year-old Barry who wrote *Dreams from
My Father*, but the 33-year-old Barack who wrote it, a 33-year-old who
admitted to having written *Dreams* in large part to launch his political
career, just as Obama believed JFK had done with *Profiles in Courage*.
Like much of the content in *Dreams*, the "advertising race" comment
was advanced as its own adult advertisement, an advertisement designed
to promote Obama as a black racial hero who has regarded whites as
adversaries to be studied so that their weaknesses can be exploited.

Obama discloses the depth of his racial paranoia in describing an incident
during high school. At the suggestion of Ray, a black friend, Barry brought
two white so-called buddies, Jeff and Scott, to an otherwise all black party.
Arriving together, the three cruised around the room and the white boys
even danced with black girls. Within an hour, however, his white friends
had become so "self-conscious" that they asked Barry, who had driven, to
take them home. According to Obama,

> In the car, Jeff put an arm on my shoulder, looking at once contrite
> and relieved "You know, man," he said, "that really taught me
> something. I mean, I can see how it must be tough for you and
> Ray sometimes, at school parties . . . being the only black guys

and all." I snorted. "Yeah Right." A part of me wanted to punch him right there.

Did Barry appreciate Jeff's sentiments? No. Instead he responded with an urge to "punch him right there." Am I missing something? Seems to me that Jeff was being understanding and empathic, but paranoids, by definition, see nefarious hidden meanings wherever they cast their eyes. When Obama reflected on the incident and on one from the previous day, he could only conclude that ". . . any distinction between good and bad whites held negligible meaning." The experience allegedly launched him into an obsessive search "Over the next few months . . . to corroborate this nightmare vision." In other words, to feed his racialized biases.

And Barry knew just where to look, reading every angry black raceketeer that he could find. Malcolm X impressed him the most. Quick to pardon and downplay Malcolm's "blue-eyed devils" harangues, Obama asserted that one of the Black Muslim's comments especially resonated with him: It was X's wish to expunge any lingering trace of white blood from his body. While the comment was essentially a relatively abstract social statement for Malcolm X, however, it was painfully and palpably real to Barry, referencing the primary identity conflict at the heart of his psychodynamics, interpersonal relationships, and, inconveniently, half-white self.

The future U.S. president's anti-white-folks education was not limited to his own sterile, solitary literary musings; he received a practicum in race-baiting by his black militant and communist mentor, Frank Marshall Davis. When Barry told Frank that he intended to go to a "white" college, the inimitable, the honorable Mr. Davis replied that Obama would be "trained" rather than educated, trained to accept white lies about equal opportunity. He injected Barry with poisonous, hateful ideas such as, "They'll yank on your chain and let you know that you may be a well-trained, well-paid nigger, but you're a nigger just the same."

Speaking of training, Frank Marshall Davis did his best to "train" Barry to accept black hatred of whites as being both natural and expected. On one occasion the young Obama confided a story to Davis about his grandmother who had told Barry that a panhandling vagrant had accosted Toots, insisting that she give him money. She characterized the panhandler

15

as being increasingly demanding and aggressive, wanting more money despite her already having given him some. She anxiously added that she was extricated from the terrorizing situation only when her bus arrived. Continuing his story to Davis, Barry added a punch line by noting that his grandfather said that the panhandler was "black," and that Gramps had believed that to be the "real" reason for his wife's terror. In *Dreams*, the melodramatic Barry says that his grandfather's revelation was ". . . like a fist in my stomach, and I wobbled to regain my composure."

One thread of honest self-disclosure by his grandmother, then, provided Barry a pretense to rent the entire fabric of his bond to both grandparents as he concluded: "Never had they given me reason to doubt their love; I doubted if they ever would. And yet I knew that men who might easily have been my brothers could still inspire their rawest fears."

Rather than embracing his alleged love for his grandparents and accepting his grandmother's fear for what it was, the teen-aged Barry rushed to Frank, the black militant, to share a shot of whiskey and talk things over. The sagacious Mr. Davis provided both, including just the following uplifting message that the young man needed, saying that his grandmother should be frightened of blacks, since blacks "have a reason to hate," and advising Barry to "get used to it."

The race-melodramatic Barry alleged that after he left Frank that night: "The earth shook under my feet, ready to crack open at any moment. I stopped, trying to steady myself, and knew for the first time that I was utterly alone." What torment, what anguish, what a heroic figure bent upon an epic quest to find his racial identity. He could have been Kunta Kinte, searching for his "roots." But Barry was not Kunta Kinte. He had never suffered at the hands of the evil white man. According to Ray, the close black friend who had encouraged Obama to invite Jeff and Scott to the aforementioned all-black party, Barry's angst centered on the troubled relationships he had with his family and his feelings of parental abandonment more than any other single factor. After all, as quoted earlier, Barry had said that ". . . I've never quite had the courage to explore . . ." the roots of the mother-father union that led to his conception.

Conflicted parental relationships and racial paranoia need not be distinct and separate, of course. And, in fact, both were inextricably intertwined in the case of Barry Obama. He could not be comfortable with his parents not only because of the rage that he felt attendant to their abandoning him, but also because he knew that he was like neither of them—not white and not black. Barry's grandmother, Toots, was not spared, either; he dismissed her as being "a typical white person" in the way that she harbored racial stereotypes of black people. The ambiguity of being biracial was too much for this need to know-it-all, got-to-figure-it-all-out future president. Biracial was too messy; too many loose ends; too many unanswered questions. Biracial was not chic. Twentieth-century America mostly failed even to acknowledge the presence of biracials. No one boasted of being biracial. What glory, what advantage could Barry derive from being biracial? None and none.

No. Biracial was not for Barry; it provided neither an outlet nor an elixir for his ego. He needed to be black, all black, and nothing but black. By pretending to be all black, Barry could follow a well-defined course toward actualizing the heroic persona that he had read about, fantasized about: the one celebrated by his family and by cultural media of all types. Ally with other like-minded heroes to rebel against decadent, racist white America, champion the indigent, organize the ghettos, redistribute the wealth: This was the can't-miss formula for a black messiah want-to-be, a boy determined to remake America in his own image and likeness. Well, maybe only his fancied image and likeness; certainly not in his true biracial image or likeness.

By the time he reached Occidental College in 1979, the eighteen-year-old Barry Obama had derived maximal advantage from being Barry, the boy raised exclusively by the white people who had contributed one-half of his genome. It was time to convince whoever would listen that he was black through and through, and to derive the benefits appertaining. What better way to do so than to embrace his African name? So, aside from his family, who never relinquished "Barry," the wider world soon became acquainted with "Barack." Accordingly, from this point forward, I will use the name Barack to refer to Barack junior and specify Barack senior to refer to Junior's father.

In Barack's mind, every word communicated by a white person needed to be scrutinized to find its explicit or implicit racial threat. Literature, of course, was no exception. If written by a white man, even fiction, no matter how dated or fantastic, underscored for him not just the depravity of its Caucasian communicator, but of the entire white race. Barack said as much at Occidental. When a black friend chastised him for reading *Heart of Darkness*, Obama replied that he was reading it to learn about white people, as if he did not know them. He expressed particular interest in knowing how whites learn to hate, as if white people invented hatred, and he melodramatically thought to himself that his very life depended on such knowledge.

In addition to fueling his perverse racial ideas, how else did the Occidental years contribute to the identity formation of Barry Barack Soetoro Hussein Obama? Cocaine, marijuana, and alcohol, in which he regularly and eagerly partook. Further, he learned to disrespect indigent, so-called, "people-of-color," as revealed by an anecdote related by his soul brother, Reggie, who reminisced gleefully and drunkenly to Obama about a previous weekend dorm party that they had attended together. Recalling that the party goers trashed the dorm, Reg laughingly commented that, "those little old Mexican ladies" responsible for the clean-up "started to cry" when they saw the mess awaiting them.

After two years at Occidental, Barack transferred to Columbia University from which he graduated without honors in 1983. Here, too, he reportedly indulged his penchant for drugs and alcohol until, if you can believe him, he had an epiphany that helped sober him up. On the other hand, he did not hesitate in his relentless march toward becoming racial paranoid in chief. He notes "I had grown accustomed, everywhere, to suspicion between the races." Given the circles in which he traveled, including the Black Students Organization, I am sure racial animosity and contempt did rule the day. Speaking about Columbia University's restrooms, Obama claimed that "the walls remained scratched with blunt correspondence between niggers and kikes."

In researching this book I found few details regarding Barack's time at Columbia. Ross Goldberg comments similarly, and, in a September 2, 2008 special to the *New York Sun*, he says that Obama's political handlers had declined being interviewed about Goldberg's article or even to explain Barack's refusal to allow his Columbia transcript to be published. Mr. Goldberg quotes the political historian Geoffrey Kabaservice who claimed that Barack had acknowledged benefiting from affirmative action in the past, but he did not elaborate. Given that Obama did not achieve honors while at Columbia, affirmative action very well might explain how he managed to gain acceptance to Harvard Law School. The mystery around Obama's Columbia years proves once more that, if nothing else, Barry Barack Hussein Soetoro Obama has been and continues to be a transcendent, even nonpareil, manipulator of his personal history and identity.

One social fact that *Dreams from My Father* did reveal about the Columbia years was that Barack roomed for a time with a Pakistani illegal alien. While at Columbia, Obama mastered the fine art of remaining mum about illegals, preparing him as president, emotionally and strategically, to deny knowing that his African aunt, a convicted illegal immigrant, was hiding out in the USA, and to deftly ignore the "undocumented" (illegal) Mexican problems on our southern border.

Barack also disclosed that while in New York he and his friend mocked whites for sport. Thus, he wrote that the two of them would sit on the fire escape and watch "white people" walk their dogs who would "shit on our curbs," then Barack and his buddy would scream at the whites to clean up the messes, and laugh uproariously when they did.

Obama, obviously, lived in a very special part of town. This was a place where only white people had dogs, only white people walked dogs, or only white people walked dogs capable of shitting. At the time of Barack's malign-the-white-folks campaign, our hero was twenty-one years old—no kid—but rather a young adult in training to become a president prepared to bridge America's racial divide. I suppose Obama and his illegal resident buddy believed that white people conspired to walk their dogs with the sole purpose of shitting in black neighborhoods, but that non-whites never did similar things. The lesson: if one white person does something offensive, it must be characteristic of whites in general.

It is not only blacks who employ racial demagoguery in a misguided attempt to lift up their own "people." One would not be surprise to learn that George Wallace, the racist governor of Alabama, once said: "Desperate times call for desperate measures, and for many whites, times have become chronically desperate. If the white power movement can create a strong and effective insularity, deliver on its promise of self-respect, then the hurt it might cause well-meaning blacks, or the inner turmoil it would cause people like me, would be of little consequence."

George Wallace certainly could have said the aforementioned. However, substitute white for black and black for white and you have a quip from Barack Obama's *Dreams from My Father* in which our president quotes himself. Moreover, three paragraphs earlier he opined: "Yes the nationalist would say, whites are responsible for your sorry state, not any inherent flaws in you. In fact, whites are so heartless and devious that we can no longer expect anything from them. The self-loathing you feel, what keeps you drinking or thieving, is planted by them."

Obama went on to say that while these racial scapegoating tactics ran counter to the guidance imparted to him by his white mother, they "might" need to be tolerated temporarily for the greater good of the black population.

Maybe someone should tell Obama that sanctioning black on white scapegoating is a Black Liberation-like strategy that inevitably leads to black on white violence, explaining, perhaps, the United States Department of Justice finding that, on average, blacks murder whites at a rate 277 percent higher than whites murder blacks.

Given that Barack and his family remained in the Black Liberation church of Jeremiah Wright for nearly 20 years, contributed at least $22,500 in 2006 alone, and listened to all the anti-white America scapegoating propaganda endemic to that setting, I must conclude that Obama succeeded heartily in coming to peace with his earlier alleged disquiet over race baiting. In fact, even after he had reluctantly distanced himself from Wright for political expediency, on March 14, 2008 Barack Obama wrote admiringly of Wright in the *Huffington Post,* noting that the Reverend had been a United States Marine, a scholar, and a "pillar" of Chicago who always preached love of God and neighbor. Of course, the kudos to Jeremiah were delivered during the height of the presidential campaign season when blacks were being especially attentive to Barack's racial allegiances in general and to his comments about Wright in particular.

Age Twenty-One and Beyond: The "Racially Mature" Barack Hussein Obama

Despite his academic mediocrity at Columbia, Barack had no trouble being admitted to Harvard Law. Affirmative action? We will never know for sure. That is not to detract from Obama's intellectual capabilities. He is smart enough in the textbook sense of the term. No, intelligence is not the issue; it is personality, that is the key to Barry Barack Hussein Soetoro Obama, and while race is central, it is only one major facet of what makes Barack Barack.

Obama had no substantive, concrete achievements on which to campaign politically. His only real non-political jobs were brief: those of a financial consultant and of a community organizer. And, as an organizer, his accomplishments were miniscule, his only confirmed success being an asbestos clean-up program at Chicago's Altgeld Gardens public housing project in the mid-1980s, and, even here, he was no more than a co-leader. Community organizing was really Obama's black resume padding for the future. When he left his community organizer job, Altgeld Gardens was little different from when Barack had started; it was not a matter of change that the community could believe in.

No, Obama cannot boast that he saved Altgeld from itself. You probably remember the horrific televised scene of September 2009 when Derrion Albert, a 16-year-old black boy, was being beaten to death in a black bimp melee. Well, two of the four adults charged in Albert's murder were Altgeld Gardens public housing residents. One month later, Layton Ehmke, Justine Jablonska and John Lund, graduate journalism students at Northwestern University's Medill school, wrote in Medill Reports:

> Altgeld Gardens looks like a war zone. From burned-out CHA
> [Chicago Housing Authority] structures to potholes deep enough
> to make streets unpassable, it looks and feels more like war-torn
> Baghdad than Chicago.

If you live in the housing project, off 130th Street on Chicago's Far South Side, a few things are within convenient walking distance: A wastewater treatment plant, a rolling mountain range of Chicago's garbage, a polluted river.

A decent grocery store, however, is three separate bus rides away.

This is where President Barack Obama did his community organizing. Obama worked under Hazel Johnson, his mentor. Obama now lives in the White House, but those who remain in Altgeld—including Hazel's daughter Cheryl—continue to fight as the community boils over from too many years of alternately being pushed around or neglected.

Obama did not campaign for elective office on his record of real-world accomplishments, but on his identity, verbiage, and uncommon ruthless desire to do whatever it took to win.

Barack likes to talk about his persistence, his determination, and he certainly has those. But what truly sets him apart is his icy psychopathic insensitivity to the effects that his persistence, determination, and actions have on those who come between him and his political ambitions.

Obama's first victim of record was Alice Palmer, an African American Illinois state senator from Chicago's 13th Legislative District who announced in June, 1995 that she would not seek reelection to the state senate, but instead would run for the 2nd Congressional District seat of United States Representative Mel Reynolds who had been indicted on fraud and sexual misconduct charges. Palmer enthusiastically endorsed and supported Barack Obama for the state senate seat that she would be vacating. However, when she lost the special primary election for the U.S. Congress in December, 1995, Palmer held a press conference, saying that she had changed her mind and would run to retain her state senate position. She later asked Obama to withdraw from the race, but he promptly refused. Rather than risk having the people of Chicago's 13th decide who they wanted to represent them, Obama challenged Palmer's nominating petitions and won, knocking her out of the election before a single vote was cast. Giddy with the success, he enacted similar challenges to all three of his other Democrat primary opponents, dispatching them and running unopposed on the Illinois ballot. So much for choice we can believe in!

In 1999, three years after winning Palmer's seat, it was Barack's turn to attempt to "move-up" to the U. S. House of Representatives. In trying to doing so, however, Obama had allowed his mega-ambition to get the best of him, resulting in a staggering defeat. His incumbent opponent, Bobby L. Rush, a founding member of the Illinois Black Panther Party, asserted that Obama was neither black enough nor genuine enough to lead the African American community, and the electorate apparently accepted the assertions. The word on the street was that Barack was an "Uncle Tom," sent and owned by "the Jews." For his part, Rush did not mince words, saying "Barack Obama went to Harvard and became an educated fool. Barack is a person who read about the civil-rights protests and thinks he knows all about it." He crushed Obama by a two to one margin. Even more important, he exposed the black racial Achilles heel of the Barack Obama identity; Rush sure knew how to hurt a guy.

What to do about his troublesome black identity and the barrier that it posed to attaining political nirvana? Obama knew that he could handle white voters. Whoever heard a white say, "He's not black enough or white enough?" Who did not know that white Democrat liberals fed their flagging egos by sanctimoniously carping about how they plan to vote for "the black guy," even if the black guy is half-white? Barack had no doubt that he could double- and triple-speak his way through the white community. But black folks, black folks can be tough. Book knowledge of how to be black would not suffice. Obama needed street "cred," a way to blacken himself up in words and actions, such that any African American could be duped into accepting him as the "real deal"—a change that the "hood" could believe in.

Enter Michelle Obama, you know, the one who exclusively sees the world through dark-colored glasses, the one who famously boasted:"You don't get any blacker than me." She pulled no punches in her initial critique of her husband's bearing. Michelle felt that he looked and sounded like a boring, white college professor when speaking to the masses. He needed to

23

loosen up and talk in the stereotypic way that she believes a stereotypically black man speaks. Now who could he model himself on?

Michelle concluded that the Honorable Reverend Jeremiah Wright—the god damn America preacher—was just the guy to serve as a template for Barack's black male presence and oratory. Christopher Anderson claimed that Michelle and Barack Obama attended Reverend Wright's Trinity United Church of Christ virtually every Sunday and enthusiastically participated in Wright's "call and response" conduct of the church. Anderson suggested that Barack literally and painstakingly "studied" all the particulars of Jeremiah's approach including tone, gesture, and rhythm. Moreover, according to him, Barack Obama refined his new found method in many of the same churches where he previously had flopped, and that he typically invoked Wright's name in order to "connect" with the parishioners there.

Barack even appropriated Reverend Wright's "audacity of hope" phraseology in titling one of his books. Copying the catchy verbal expressions of others became his political stock-in-trade to sound profound, particularly profoundly black. Barack, for instance, evidenced a special fondness for quoting variants of "the arc of the moral universe is long, but it bends toward justice," an erudite-sounding comment that most believed Martin Luther King junior had coined. In 2010, President Obama even commissioned and received a rug for the White House Oval Office that included the inscription along its edge. Unfortunately, we now know that the "arc" quote really began with Theodore Parker, a white man. Just one more example of how damn hard it is to be racially pure!

As mentioned earlier, despite attempting to be as black as could be, Barack Hussein Obama knew that anyone who runs nation-wide must appeal to white voters, no less than black. What quotable quip could see him through? At the time, Democratic presidential co-contender John Edwards railed about how there were two Americas, with references to segregation, discrimination, and African Americans. But Obama felt compelled to counter that idea. If voters were permitted to think of America as divided white and black, white people might be inclined to vote for an all-white candidate. Barack came up with a sure fire antidote: just take Edwards' slogan and spin it one hundred eighty degrees: "There is not a black America and a white America . . . There is only the United States of America." What an incredible display of cognitive-moral perspicacity! Who would have thought? The answer, of course, is: Nearly anyone with a second grade education. What about those who criticized the fact that Obama had no accomplishments, only words to offer America? Simple: Just imply that actions are superfluous; words are what really count. By applying this logic we get:

> Don't tell me words don't matter! 'I have a dream.' Just words. 'We hold these truths to be self-evident, that all men are created equal.' Just words! 'We have nothing to fear but fear itself.' Just words—just speeches!

These Obama lines admittedly are stirring, almost in the "Give me liberty or give me death" tradition. But, once again, the pretty words did not originate in the mind of Barack Obama. Rather, Howard Wolfson, Hillary Clinton's communications director, exposed the plagiarism of Obama's aforementioned quote by juxtaposing it with a speech that Deval Patrick delivered two years earlier, in October, 2006, when running against Lieutenant Governor Kerry Healy for governor of Massachusetts:

> But her dismissive point, and I hear it a lot from her staff, is that all I have to offer is words—just words. 'We hold these truths to be self-evident, that all men are created equal.' Just words—just words! 'We have nothing to fear but fear itself.' Just words! 'Ask not what your country can do for you, ask what you can do for your country.' Just words! 'I have a dream.' Just words!

"Just words" often has taken center stage where Barack Obama is concerned. The man who never could admit that the John McCain-inspired Iraq surge succeeded is the same man who double spoke his way through an NBC interview by Chuck Todd on November 18, 2009. Just after Attorney general Eric Holder defied popular American opinion, declaring that Khalid Sheikh Mohammed would be tried in civilian rather than military court, Todd wondered aloud whether the nation would be offended, since a civilian trial would afford Mohammed all the rights appertaining to United States citizens. Obama quickly replied, "I don't think it will be offensive at all **when he's convicted and when the**

death penalty is applied to him [emphasis added].'' Todd, apparently surprised that a former "constitutional lawyer" glibly risked prejudicing the case against KSM, then replied, "One of the purposes of doing the justice system—criminal justice—going with justice, the legal and not the military, court is to show off to the world our fairness, the fairness of our court system, but you've also now just said that he's going to be convicted and given the death sentence." Barack, master of double speak, adamantly rejoined, "**What I said** [emphasis added] was, people will not be offended **if** [emphasis added] that's the outcome. **I'm not pre-judging** [emphasis added], I'm not going to be in that courtroom, that's the job of prosecutors, the judge and the jury What I'm absolutely clear about is that I have complete confidence in the American people and our legal traditions and the prosecutors, the tough prosecutors from New York who specialize in terrorism."

The Barack Obama who so glibly lies about what he had said seconds earlier is a man adept at the double speak tradition that enables him to talk and write about a racial reconciliation imperative, despite checking only the black rather than black and white slots on his 2010 census form. Someday perhaps, the president will develop the courage and integrity to communicate honestly about inconvenient, uncomfortable racial realities.

How is it that an otherwise intelligent man so shamelessly and disingenuously misrepresents himself, his identity in general, and his racial identity in particular? To say that Barack Hussein Obama is racially obsessed merely is to state the obvious. Any psychoanalyst worth a leather couch would give his goatee to have a shot at treating our 44th president. Barack is a case study of the explanatory power of the repetition compulsion, the tendency for an individual continually to seek out situations associatively linked to original emotional traumas in order to master them. The sad reality is that by reliving the situations, most often the traumatized person merely reinforces his conflicts, making them more intractable with each repetition. Over time the traumatic events and the efforts to contain them become essential parts of his identity and primary motivating forces driving his feelings, thoughts, and actions. Once circumscribed and resolvable conflicts then become pervasive and intractable, entombed within his personality, or, in the case of Obama, as will be explained shortly, within the "dark-triad" of his personality.

CHAPTER 3

He's Got Personality

    More than just a pretty face, that's what the world-wide media said. MSNBC's Chris Matthews gushed that Barack possessed such animal magnetism that he sent a "thrill" up the commentator's leg. (A therapist might ask: "Which leg? Please tell me more about that.") Matthews then concluded the issue with: "And that is an objective assessment." On October 27, 2008, *Time* magazine ran a cover story entitled "Does Temperament Matter?" cooing about the cool, cool, supercool Obama, contrasting him with the hot, hot, super hot-head John McCain. Beginning with their ill-defined, vague notion of temperament, the article pseudo-scientifically advocated for Obama as being the guy with the presidential goods.

This is not the time or place for a treatise about temperament or personality as psychological constructs, but I must say that most psychologists regard temperament as akin to the more biological, more innate physiological action and reaction patterns already visible in the first months and years of life, such as one's activity level, sensory thresholds, and distractibility, to name a few. Personality, on the other hand, includes not only temperament but also action and reaction patterns that evolve throughout life, contingent on an individual's environment and experiences. The "Big Five Personality Factors," for example, is a personality construct that goes beyond temperament by identifying essential personality features that include openness, conscientiousness, extraversion, acceptance, and nervousness.

Temperament and the Big Five notwithstanding, to my way of thinking, the essence of Barack Obama, the man, is best distilled by three aberrant personality traits—narcissism, Machiavellianism, and

27

psychopathy—subsumed under the term, "the dark-triad." As President Barack Obama is wont to say, "Make no mistake; let me be clear about this," the dark-triad is a type of personality disorder, not an emotional disorder. I am not saying that Obama is insane in the colloquial sense of that word. The hallmark of personality disorders, as opposed to purely emotional disorders, is that unlike neurotic people who are troubled by symptoms, such as by anxiety or depression, those with personality disorders are not troubled by their symptoms; their symptoms trouble others, as when dark-triad persons act out their grandiosity, emotional coldness, manipulation and aggressiveness toward their own self-centered ends.

The three dark-triad traits have in common a gluttonous preoccupation with the self and everything self-associated. All three also are love focused. The narcissist loves himself and tolerates anyone who attends to and who dotes on him; the Machiavellian loves power and prestige; and the psychopath loves his emotionless unflappability that he wields as an ultimate weapon against others whom he regards as weak or vulnerable. As you no doubt have surmised, only highly permeable membranes separate the tripartite dark-triad personality. What distinguishes each triad leg is more quantitative than qualitative—all crave attention, love, power, and prestige, and all prey upon the weak and vulnerable.

Narcissism is the dark-triad's keystone, an inflated, self-absorbed preoccupation with feeding one's self-esteem and receiving acclaim. Machiavellianism describes a proclivity for manipulating and exploiting others, especially to attain power, prestige, and profit. And psychopathy, a term somewhat eclipsed in the psychological literature by "antisocial personality," defines a personality trait in which one self-servingly acts out impulses in a virtually immediate and unrestrained manner without empathy or regard to the consequences of the actions upon those around him.

Delroy L. Paulhus and Kevin Williams of the University of British Columbia have pioneered the dark-triad concept and state that it entails ". . . a dark, socially destructive character with behavior tendencies such as grandiosity, emotional coldness, manipulation and aggressiveness." I want to underscore that despite the prerogative sound of the term, an individual with a dark-triad personality need not be insane or criminal, and he almost never evidences all the symptoms that define the condition. The dark-triad circumscribes an aberrant personality that ranges from mild to severe; one person can be incapacitated by his dark-triad personality while another can so skillfully manage it that he becomes president of the United States.

Although Not Completely Black, Barack Definitely Is Dark

If anyone can be "diagnosed" as having a dark-triad personality, it is Barry Barack Hussein Soetoro Obama. The core of Barack's constituent dark-triad characteristics is race. More than anything else, his narcissism-Machiavellianism-psychopathy evolved as a natural consequence of a troubled little boy's futile attempts to come to grips with his not-quite-black identity. In his insecurity, Obama forever has rummaged through every nook and cranny of his being, vainly and obsessively searching for something purely and authentically black on which to cling. For instance, in referring to Hussein Onyango Obama, his grandfather, Obama says that his original mental image of Hussein had been of a person both cruel and autocratic, but one with a fierce sense of independence and opposition to white control. He explains that he equated his grandfather's Muslim religion with the Nation of Islam, implying militancy. For that reason, Barack states that his African Granny's unflattering description of Hussein Onyango caused him disquiet, to wonder whether his grandfather might have been an "Uncle Tom. Collaborator. House nigger."

So, let's think about this a moment: Barack can forgive cruel and autocratic behavior, and anti-white racism is laudably equated with black patriotism and black racial purity. Moreover, thoughts such as these are associatively linked in Obama's mind with extremist pro-black advocacy, such as practiced by Nation of Islam adherents who see whites as devils. All this sits well with the narcissistic need of Barack Obama to be descended along an authentic black nationalist bloodline. If he can't be a real African American hero, he, at least, can be the grandson of a hero from the African continent. Not quite a Luo prince, but close enough. Then, when his delusion is shattered with the injection of information that challenges his mythology, he entertains thoughts of the other extreme—that his grandfather might have been an Uncle Tom, House Nigger, and Collaborator.

The Narcissist

Narcissism comprises one leg of the dark-triad. We all know one or more narcissists. Among other things, they exhibit pervasive grandiosity, lust for attention and admiration, and lack empathy. Narcissists presume that they are extraordinarily intelligent, powerful, and desirable. They sincerely think that they, and only they, not only know what is best for themselves, but also for virtually everyone else. Wounded identity is the linchpin of the narcissistic personality. Having suffered an early and profound blow to their sense of self, narcissists develop into identity addicts, constantly searching for an esteem-assuaging fix. They have an abiding need to prove themselves superior through downward comparison with those they encounter. Once anchored in their superiority, they see no contradiction in setting moral and ethical self-standards at variance with standards that they apply to others. For instance, while quick to regard the people around them as haughty, arrogant, or condescending, narcissists view themselves as nothing less than self-assured, assertive, and straight-talking.

Barry presents as a strong candidate for the dubious distinction of having suffered an early and profound blow to his sense of self, in general, and to his racial identity, in particular, a blow that has fueled in him a relentless quest for power and prestige. The vicissitudes of his name hint at some possibilities. "Barry" served him well during childhood and adolescence; it also was good enough for black baseball star Barry Bonds and the celebrated black soul singer Barry White. But Barack jettisoned Barry at Occidental College, hoping that his Nation of Islam-like African name would bring him notoriety among his militantly black buddies. Fast forward about thirty years and consider the "Hussein" in Obama. You doubtless recall that "Hussein" was verboten during the election campaign. You may not remember that on June 16, 2008 at a Detroit pro-Obama campaign rally, in a virtuoso Machiavellian performance, Obama identity obfuscators refused to allow Muslim-garbed women to sit behind the podium where our hero was speaking, fearing that their presence would "Muslimize" him. But, in typical have it both ways style, Barack later sent the ladies an "I'm sorry" message. Who knows? Maybe they also got an "If I get elected, IOU one night in the Lincoln bedroom" message.

In any case, while Barack and his band of not-so-merry men and women bristled and protested vociferously whenever anyone included "Hussein" when mentioning Obama's name, our illustrious president asserted his Hussein credential "loud and proud" during the presidential oath.

Elements of the mother-son relationship seem to have been especially central in Barack's tortured internal racial struggle regarding not only his name, but also his essence. Even as an adult, he often has spoken of his mother not only as white but as "milky white" and his father not only as black but "pitch black," underscoring that the elusive mother and absconding father were antitheses. Obama also has "joked" about how, often during his youth, acquaintances teasingly had substituted "Yo Mama" for "Obama." When Barry was growing up, "Yo Mama" had been the ultimate, stereotypically black street talk insult. For the racially preoccupied Barry, this had to reinforce negatively, again and again, the mental image that he had of himself as the "black" son of a whiter-than-white momma and a blacker-than-black poppa. In short, conflicted racial identity has been, and continues to be, the liet motif of Barry Barack Hussein Soetoro Obama's life, sometimes a soft melody playing in the background and sometimes a deafening cacophony drowning out everything else.

Saying that Barack Obama has identity conflicts and narcissism is like saying that Bill Gates has a few bucks. Obama, himself, admitted to his identity struggle, albeit in his characteristically self-serving way, by penning a book about black identity angst that that he claimed cured his who-am-I affliction (If identity transformation were that easy, the treatment of emotional and personality disturbances, substance addiction, and criminality would be achieved in writing class.), but he never fessed up to his associated narcissism.

An examination of Barack the narcissist must begin with his tic-like tendency literally to lift his nose in the air during pontifications. Let's not forget the swaggering gait, acclaimed regularly by raceketeers, black and white. To cite one example, on April 25, 2009 CNN's black commentator T.J. Holmes "crowed" about Obama's "swagga," claiming that this showed the president surely to be "a brotha." White anchor Kyra Phillips, in turn, chortled to Holmes in pubertal-like ecstasy: "So, bottom line, every white president has had absolutely no "swagga!" Is that what you're saying?"

Holmes replied that ". . . you can go from Billy Dee Williams to Shaft to whoever you want to talk about. There's just a bit, like I said, swagger sometimes [laugh]—Ha. The song comes on [The theme from the film Shaft is playing in the background]—people associate with black men." Just for the record, I must add that wordnetweb.princeton.edu. defines "swagger" as: "to walk with a lofty proud gait, often in an attempt to impress others. He struts around like a rooster in a hen house." (For those of you who without swagga, "shaft" is street lingo for "penis." Shaft was one of cinema's first bimp prototypes, a so-called "black exploitation" character created by Gordon Parks, a black movie director.)

In addition to swagga, there's the familiar Barack vocal style. The hallelujah aspect is Jeremiah, the whole Jeremiah, and nothing but the Jeremiah Wright, so help me God: a style deliberately stolen and practiced. On the other hand, the wait-with-baited-breath-for-me-to-finish-my-comment-I'm-about-to-say-something-profound aspect of Obama's vocal pattern only could have been independently crafted by the narcissistic master himself. Never missing an opportunity to elicit adulation, Barack reportedly is fond of smugly inquiring "Whose idea was that?" to his cabinet and other advisors whenever he believes that he has advocated an opinion that he thinks has proven correct. According to Jonathan Alter, in the summer of 2007, when speaking to David Axelrod, the great and powerful Barack boasts about his presidential qualifications: "The weird thing is, I know I can do this job. I like dealing with complicated issues. I'm happy to make decisions. I'm looking forward to it. I think it's going to be an easier adjustment for me than the campaign. Much easier." The boasting certainly is personality-consistent for the narcissist Obama who has done whatever he can to promote a view of himself as being the equivalent of political superstars such as Abraham Lincoln, John F. Kennedy junior, and Franklin Delano Roosevelt, to name only three.

Already in November 2010, Colin Powell, a man who earlier had abandoned his then-friend of 25 years, John McCain, to support Barack Obama during the election, complained publically that Obama had lost his sense of direction and had tried to do too much too fast.

By early 2011, even the popular press's "slobbering love affair" (Goldberg, 2009) with Barack had lost some of its drool. The February 21 edition of

Newsweek cover-featured "Egypt: How Obama Blew It" by Niall Ferguson, lamenting the president's stumbling, fumbling, bumbling leadership style. The piece quoted the Prussian statesman Otto von Bismarck as having said, "The statesman can only wait and listen until he hears the footsteps of God resounding through events; then he must jump up and grasp the hem of His coat, that is all." Ferguson complained that the previous week Obama, for the second time, had failed to act decisively when given the chance to promote democracy in the Middle East. He underscored the president's international double speak statements of alternating assertion and passivity. To Ferguson, Obama's policy had been a "debacle" that "alienated everybody," including the Egyptian government and its opposition, and that "disgusted" Saudi Arabia and Israel. Niall Ferguson also indicted the identity politics of Barack by asserting that "I'm not George Bush" is an inadequate strategy by which to conduct foreign affairs.

Within 24 hours of the on-line release of Niall Ferguson's aforementioned *Newsweek* article, MSNBC's pandering political pundits had set their trap for the heretical professor. On *Morning Joe*, March 14, 2011, Joe Scarborough and Mika Brzezinski were taking no chances, having recruited Jonathan Capehart, Mark Halperin, and Willie Geist as reinforcements in their search and destroy mission. When was the last time you saw a television station align four hit-men and one hit-woman against a "guest"? MSNBC apparently regarded the get-Ferguson campaign as a high-stakes partisan political battle.

Brzezinski began the assault against the infidel Ferguson and his blasphemy. Feisty Mika asserted, "Yeah I want to hear more about how you think he [Obama] blew it with Egypt, because looking at all the different reports coming in, and the pictures, and the peacefulness on the streets of Cairo, so far so good. It actually seems like it went pretty damn well."

"Yeah" and "damn?" Sounded a bit testy, and not especially well-received, by Niall who countered that Obama's previous attention to Egypt has been limited to little more than a "touchy feely" June 2009 speech. In his opinion, the uprising had taken the administration totally unawares.

The MSNBCers struck again and again, from Brzezinski to Capehart, to Halperin, to Scarborough, to Geist, and back to Scarborough, even trying to use the old "what about George Bush" red herring to obfuscate the extant issue. But Niall Ferguson would not be deterred, ending by saying that while George Bush had a "great deal" of Middle East influence, Obama's was "almost completely absent."

How could MSNBC "read" Niall Ferguson so terribly wrong? This man has more ivy than Princeton: currently Professor of History and Business Administration at Harvard University, senior Research Fellow at Oxford and Stanford. Incredible that, despite all his book learning, Niall Ferguson fails so miserably in his ability to recollect and comply with the Barack Obama Audacity of Hype media script.

Please note that Niall Ferguson recognized the alternating paralytic-spasmodic quality to Barack Obama's identity-based action tendencies. A president preoccupied with his own identity and with the ways that others construe it is a hesitant, non-spontaneous, obsessive, ineffectual presidential procrastinator.

Although Ferguson focused almost exclusively on Obama's inept leadership, Bret Stephens of the Wall Street Journal cited Barack's general arrogance and stupidity. He noted that the President has boasted of being a better speech writer than his speech writers, a better policy director than his policy directors, and of being the "LeBron" (James) of the democrat party. Stephens went on to say that Obama forever advertises how much he knows about everything and regards himself "immune from error." The journalist summed-up the presidential dark-triad personality by concluding that Barack Obama:

> makes predictions that prove false. He makes promises he cannot honor. He raises expectations he cannot meet. He reneges on commitments made in private. He surrenders positions staked in public. He is absent from issues in which he has a duty to be involved. He is overbearing when he ought to be absent.

Everyday non-Ivy League Americans are in accord with Bret Stephen's views on Obama. A viral email that I received on February 26, 2011 has something germane to say about our great leader's presidential acumen:

> Yes indeed, we got change. Two years ago, Barack Obama was inaugurated as president of the United States. Are you better off today than you were two years ago?

Numbers don't lie, and here are the data on the impact he has had on the lives of Americans.

	January 2009	TODAY	% chg	Source
Avg. retail price/gallon gas in U.S.	$1.83	$3.104	69.6%	1
Crude oil, European Brent (barrel)	$43.48	$99.02	127.7%	2
Crude oil, West TX Inter. (barrel)	$38.74	$91.38	135.9%	2
Gold: London (per troy oz.)	$853.25	$1,369.50	60.5%	2
Corn, No.2 yellow, Central IL	$3.56	$6.33	78.1%	2
Soybeans, No. 1 yellow, IL	$9.66	$13.75	42.3%	2
Sugar, cane, raw, world, lb. fob	$13.37	$35.39	164.7%	2
Unemployment rate, non-farm, overall	7.6%	9.4%	23.7%	3
Unemployment rate, blacks	12.6%	15.8%	25.4%	3
Number of unemployed	11,616,000	14,485,000	24.7%	3
Number of fed. employees, ex. military (curr = 12/10 prelim)	2,779,000	2,840,000	2.2%	3
Real median household income (2008 v 2009)	$50,112	$49,777	-0.7%	4
Number of food stamp recipients (curr = 10/10)	31,983,716	43,200,878	35.1%	5
Number of unemployment benefit recipients (curr = 12/10)	7,526,598	9,193,838	22.2%	6
Number of long-term unemployed	2,600,000	6,400,000	146.2%	3
Poverty rate, individuals (2008 v 2009)	13.2%	14.3%	8.3%	4
People in poverty in U.S. (2008 v 2009)	39,800,000	43,600,000	9.5%	4
U.S. rank in Economic Freedom World Rankings	5	9	n/a	10
Present Situation Index (curr = 12/10)	29.9	23.5	-21.4%	11
Failed banks (curr = 2010 + 2011 to date)	140	164	17.1%	12
U.S. dollar versus Japanese yen exchange rate	89.76	82.03	-8.6%	2
U.S. money supply, M1, in billions (curr = 12/10 prelim)	1,575.1	1,865.7	18.4%	13
U.S. money supply, M2, in billions (curr = 12/10 prelim)	8,310.9	8,852.3	6.5%	13
National debt, in trillions	$10.627	$14.052	32.2%	14

Just take this last item: In the last two years we have accumulated national debt at a rate *more than 27 times as fast* as during the rest of our entire nation's history. Over 27 times as fast!

Metaphorically, speaking, if you are driving in the right lane doing 65 MPH and a car rockets past you in the left lane 27 times faster, it would be doing 1,755 MPH! This is a disaster!

Sources: (1) U.S. Energy Information Administration; (2) Wall Street Journal; (3) Bureau of Labor Statistics; (4) Census Bureau; (5) USDA; (6) U.S. Dept. of Labor; (7) FHFA; (8) Standard & Poor's/Case-Shiller; (9) Realty Trac; (10) Heritage Foundation and WSJ; (11) The Conference Board; (12) FDIC; (13) Federal Reserve; (14) U.S. Treasury

In fact, soon after Obama began to produce a track record of action and inaction versus mere rhetoric, people around the world began to see that the big time talker is a two-bit actor. On September 17, 2009, Jonathan Freedland reported that Dan Gillerman, former Israel ambassador to the United Nations, characterized Barack as making dangerously naïve assumptions and statements regarding international relations. He specifically cited how Barack Obama foolishly suggested that he could talk the Iranians out of their nuclear ambitions, praise Russian President Medvedev while criticizing Putin, and solve the Israeli-Palestinian conflict to produce an ipso-facto cooling of the simmering Middle East cauldron. May 18, 2011, on Fox News, Gillerman had not changed his opinion, saying that Obama had been "talking the talk" on the Middle East, but still had not "walked the walk."

Sounds as though Powell, Ferguson, Stephens, the email originator, and Gillerman were not so sure that the job of president is easier, ***much easier*** [emphasis added] than that of a presidential candidate. Seems to me that the latter job concerns words, mostly words, whereas the former involves actions, mostly actions. The supreme irony of the whole "easier" saga is that the *New York Times*' Mark Landler and Helene Cooper reported on March 10, 2011 that when speaking about the then-extant political unrest occurring in the Middle East, Barack Obama had "told people that it would be so ***much easier*** [emphasis added] to be president of China," since the Chinese president is not "scrutinized" the way the United States president is. That is, the American president's actions and positions, not just statements, are what counts.

While Obama's body language and vocal style reveal much about him, his narcissistically self-centered, hypocritical actions speak far louder than his words. In two memoirs written by age 45, he celebrates his father and his father's heritage while mostly ignoring his mother and hers; enhances his black identity at her expense; derides his grandmother about race to provide cover for himself regarding his own race cadet past; celebrates the race-mongering Wright until his public statements threaten Obama's ambitions at which time he then throws the good reverend under the bus; and lectures America about fatherhood after choosing a job that ensures he will be physically and/or emotionally absent from his two daughters during four to eight of their formative years, thus replicating the parenting style bequeathed to him by his own parents. Obama makes this choice even after being virtually assured that he would be vice president to Hillary Clinton, a position permitting him to be infinitely more physically and emotionally present to his children while also affording him the training and opportunity to stage his own presidential bid later when Malia and Sasha were more mature.

As a special person, the narcissistic Obama never has had any compunction against saying one thing and doing another. Until America noticed, Barack, the environmentalist, drove a gas-guzzler. According to Jeff Zeleny of the New York Times, in mid-March, 2009 Barack, savior of the financial meltdown, chided American business to be fiscally responsible and criticized their lavish lifestyles. Two weeks later, Dale McFeatters wrote for Scripps Howard News Service a piece about Obama at London's G-20 Summit Meeting entitled, "An entourage more royal than the Queen's." That entourage was described as having included: 500 staff; among them 6 doctors, 200 Secret Service agents; Barack Obama's personal water and food, and the White House kitchen staff and cook to provide it; 12 teleprompters; 4 speech writers; and 35 vehicles. (Frugal, eh?) Barack, the advocate for animal welfare, first boasted that he would choose his family dog from a shelter, and then selected a Portuguese water dog, a dog worth about $1500 to $3000, one who had spent several weeks being trained in Virginia by Ted Kennedy's dog handler—a dog just like any other that the average American would pick up at their local shelter. As a sterling role model for health and self restraint, Obama cautioned children against alcohol and drugs but used both. He rebuked children who would consider smoking and he signed anti-smoking regulations into law. At the same time, like a wayward child himself, Barack sneaked smokes on the White House lawn while furtively scanning the scene to be sure that no cameras were present to record the event to expose his "do as I say" charade.

If fear of being shown to be a hypocrite finally has motivated Obama to refrain from smoking indoors, then hail to the chief. For the sake of his family, one only can wish that the conversion had come sooner. As is widely known, Malia Obama has suffered from life-long asthma, a condition aggravated by cigarette smoke. In *Barack and Michelle: Portrait of an American Marriage*, Christopher Anderson writes that Michelle repeatedly cautioned her husband about the effects of second hand smoke on their daughter, but Barack proceeded so recklessly and self-centeredly that spent cigarettes littered the house and cigarette smoke discolored portions of the wall, as well as the future president's fingers and teeth.

Seems that Barack failed to follow his wife's advice about smoking to the same extent that he failed to heed her when she begged him to visit his mother as she lay dying from double cancer.

Could it be that Barack Obama simply did not care enough for his daughter and his mother? Possible, but highly unlikely. It is not that he loved them less, but that he loves himself more. With his father and mother as examples, Obama learned early that when one REALLY wants something, relationships take a back seat. Most of us are accustomed to hearing the term "blind ambition" to refer to political or business avarice, and that definition certainly fits Obama. But blind ambition also is properly applied to Barack's proclivity for intellectualizing and rationalizing himself to himself in order to justify doing whatever he wants to do, regardless of the consequences, even to people he loves. This is the duplicity of separating emotion from intellect. Barack Obama does not "know" at a gut level that intellect devoid of emotion is an illusion.

Of all the duplicity that derives from his haughty condescension, however, nothing matches Barack's relentlessly preaching that all citizens, regardless of race or station, must be treated with respect and then in an unguarded moment on the Jay Leno program, Obama inadvertently comments that his 129 bowling score is "like the Special Olympics or something." The lesson: Everyday white people should censor each and every word that passes their lips; God forbid that they refer to a black as articulate. But an extraordinary black president, who actually is biracial, can harbor disparaging stereotypes and malign people in any way that he chooses.

The superiority complex of Obama has not escaped Ken Hutcherson, African American and former NFL linebacker, who, on July 1, 2009, was quoted by onenewsnow.com's Jim Brown as observing, "I think this president has a disdain for anyone who disagrees with anything about him—don't just limit it to Christians and conservatives. Brother, this man doesn't like anyone who doesn't think he's the smartest man in the world."

Barack's supporters, "friends," and Democratic colleagues also, occasionally, have seen through him. Americans never will forget Jesse Jackson's contemptuously saying that he would like to cut Barack's "nuts" off because he "talks down to black people." Lynn Forester de Rothschild, member of the Democratic National Committee's Platform Committee, called Obama "an elitist." Hillary and Bill Clinton regularly referred to Obama not only as "elitist" but also as "condescending." In September, 2007, on Meet the Press, when referring to Obama's vote against funding the troops in Afghanistan and Iraq, Joe Biden implied that Barack Obama put blind ambition above concern for our nation and servicemen. To quote, "If you tell me I've got to take away this protection for these kids in order to win the election, some things aren't worth it." A renegade member of the generally Obama-sycophantic media, Maureen Dowd, in a New York Times op-ed piece observed that Barack behaved in an aloof, irritable manner with reporters, apparently presuming that they should be uncritically, eternally supportive of him. She felt that he was "elitist . . . thin-skinned and controlling." Dowd even contrasted Obama's attitude of coarse disdain with George W. Bush's graciousness.

Dowd's observations jibe with those of Peter Nicholas, a Los Angeles Times staff writer who spent months shadowing Obama during the presidential campaign. Nicholas regarded Barack as an up-tight, emotionally distant boor with no spontaneity, a "robo-candidate," intent only on achieving his self-serving ends. When Nicholas' unsatisfying Obama tour of duty mercifully ended, the reporter concluded that "After all this time with him, I still can't say with certainty who he is."

I cannot help wondering whether Barack would have been more welcoming if Nicholas had been a black newsman from the black media, such as from Ebony, the Chicago Defender, The Baltimore Afro-American, or The Philadelphia Tribune.

The Machiavellian

Barack Obama's abilities to change names as readily as races and to hustle Muslim-garbed women from the stage presaged his later penchant for Machiavellian manipulation of the entire nation. For instance, Obama, the president, stalwart of racial reconciliation and proponent of rationality, was at his Machiavellian best in pandering to Mexican Americans during the Arizona immigration debacle when this crass demagogue tried to obamafuscate discussion of the law by saying, "Now suddenly if you don't have your papers and you took your kid out to get ice cream, you can be harassed; that's something that could potentially happen." (And a wayward asteroid *potentially* could impale itself on the Washington monument this Tuesday, too.)

Barack Obama simply cannot resist the self-enhancing allure of the divide and conquer strategy, returning to it again and again in the 2010 mid-term elections. The man intent on bringing America together advises, "If Latinos sit out the election instead of saying we're going to punish our enemies and we're gonna reward our friends . . ." and then proceeds to equate illegal immigration with the black civil rights struggle. The Mexican and liberal vote clearly provide more political power and prestige to the president than does doing the right thing by the nation as a whole, just another example of how comingled race and self-interest regularly determine Obama's decisions and actions.

Parading before the world all that he considers wrong with America is a tried and true Barack Obama strategy intended to raise his stature with America's detractors, overseas and within the United States, while at the same time enlisting support that he hopes will empower him to bully our nation into accepting whatever he knows is best for us. Expertise in lifting himself up by putting America down is a natural consequence of Obama's education at the foot of such raceketeers as Frank Marshall Davis, the pornographic novel writer and white hater of Barry's youth, the Reverend Jeremiah Wright of Obama's adulthood, a mentor whose orientation is obvious to all, and Barack's wife Michelle who is expert in both defiling and exploiting America.

A variation on the "find something wrong with America and exploit it" theme is obvious in Obama's Machiavellian penchant for exploiting family, friends, and colleagues. We already have noted that Barack: snubbed his loving white mother to write a book about his absconded black father and later failed to be by his mother's side as she lay dying of double terminal cancer, despite family urging to rush to her; racially maligned the white grandmother who sacrificed relentlessly for him; first trumpeted Jeremiah Wright as an avuncular mentor and then avoided him like the AIDS virus. In each case, Obama's traitorous abandonment was all about his tortured racial identity conflict. We also have mentioned the Machiavellian tactics that launched Obama's political career, such as how Barack stepped all over Alice Palmer to step up to national office. There, too, was manipulation of the Kennedy clan. Everyone remembers that Ted Kennedy outspokenly supported our first biracial president during the 2008 elections. Few realize that half the Kennedys supported Hillary Clinton, not Barack Obama. And, because of the pandering popular media, almost no one learned that Robert F. Kennedy's son, Chris, successfully led the fight to block emeritus status for University of Illinois professor and former terrorist Bill Ayers, Barack's friend and advocate, who once had said, "I don't regret setting bombs . . . I feel we didn't do enough" when he was a member of the Weather Underground. So, you see, Obama has used and abused the Kennedys as if they were a part of his family.

Only political stalwarts dare stand up to the play-pretend black president who manipulates everyone in sight with impunity, and only an especially intrepid political colleague forcefully does so. Enter Frank Caprio, 2010

Democrat candidate for Rhode Island governor, whom Barack Obama refused to endorse. Said Caprio, "He can take his endorsement and shove it" and, then, he opined that Obama was practicing "Washington insider politics at its worst." John Edwards, no saint himself, also had the temerity to confront the Machiavellian Barack Obama, albeit in a self-serving way, during a January 2008 Democratic presidential primary debate, challenging Obama's having voted "present" more than 100 times instead of taking principled positions on "hard issues."

Gay rights, for instance, has been an especially hard issue for Barack. He always has wanted gay votes—a badge of righteousness—but not enough to alienate the powerful black and white constituencies that strongly oppose gay marriage.

August 17, 2008, Obama and McCain square off at Rick Warren's Saddleback Presidential Forum. When the moderator asks, "define marriage," Barack Obama does not hesitate: "I believe that marriage is the union between a man and a woman. Now, for me as a Christian—for me—for me as a Christian, it is also a sacred union. God's in the mix." June 18, 2011, Sheryl Gay Stolberg of the New York Times asserts, "Now President Obama says his views on same-sex marriage are 'evolving,' and as he runs for re-election he is seeking support from gay donors who want to know where he stands." June 29, 2011, President Barack Obama's news conference in the East Room, Chuck Todd asks if Barack regards marriage as a civil right, but never gets an answer. He is told, essentially, that, unlike with health care, the states, and not the federal government, has the sole authority to legislate marriage. Next, Laura Meckler attempts to clarify the President's position:

> Meckler: And I'd also like to follow up on one of your earlier answers about same-sex marriage. You said that it's a positive step that so many states, including New York, are moving towards that. Does that mean that you personally now do support same-sex marriage, putting aside what individual states decide? Is that your personal view?
>
> Obama: I'm not going to make news on that today. Good try, though.

At the very end of her turn, one more try to hack through the Obamafuscation:

> Meckler: I'm sorry. I know you don't want to say anything further on the same-sex marriage issue, but what you said before really led me to believe that that's what is in your personal mind. And I'm wondering what's the distinction you're drawing.

> Obama: Laura, I think this has been asked and answered. I'll keep on giving you the same answer until I give you a different one, all right? And that won't be today.

How did the self-serving and self-protective President come across to those watching his arrogant, elusive demeanor? Mark Halperin spoke for millions when on the Morning Joe Program the next day he was tricked into expressing his opinion on live television that Barack had behaved as "kind of a dick." And Halperin did not mean Dick Chaney.

While not calling Obama a "dick," Jane Hamsher, the founder of the ultra-liberal blog firedoglake.com, also vented her frustration with him, exposing ways that Barack has used, abused, and berated his supporters through self-serving double speak and deceit. In her September 17, 2010 blog "Obama Mocks Public Option Supporters," for instance, she excoriated Barack for the duplicity and arrogance he exhibited regarding his health care program, saying that Obama was belittling his supporters and forgetting the pre-election commitments he had made to them. As many others before and after her, she referred to Barack as "egotistical" and "thin-skinned." Ms. Hamsher stated flat-out that Barack Obama would cease telling his advocates to "get over it" and make nice with them as soon as the 2012 election season begins.

Hamsher, a Democrat's Democrat, then railed against Barack's hypocritical tax policy on the December 6, 2010 PBS Newshour: "But the problem is, is that that's what he tells America that he wants. So, you have got this problem, this dissonance between what he's saying and what he appears to want. And people are very confused and they're very frustrated. I would like him to be honest." Those confused and frustrated people also included a large swath of Obama's own political party. In fact, on December 9th, only three days after Jane Hamscher's broadcast complaint, House Democrats held a caucus in which a majority voted against the president's tax plan.

What Machiavellian trick did Barack Hussein Obama pull out of his kufi cap in an attempt to defend himself against the uprising? He called upon his dearest friend, Bill Clinton, to save the day. Not only did he drag a none-too-reluctant-to-bathe-in-the-limelight Clinton in front of the television cameras, but Barack literally left Clinton to deal with reporters during the subsequent press Q and A. Just one day earlier, Obama's National Economic Council director Larry Summers had declared that passage of the tax cut bill was so essential that failure to enact it would place the country in jeopardy of a double-dip recession. So, what emergency was pulling the intrepid president away from defending the critical legislation that he had proposed? Afghanistan? Iraq? The Middle East Peace process? A nuclear meltdown? Not quite. Barack Obama begged off the stage with the announcement, "Here's [stammer] what I'll say: I've been keeping the first lady waiting for about half an hour. So I'm going to take off." To which Bill Clinton replied, "I don't want to make her mad; please go."

Bill must have been familiar with Michelle as depicted in an April, 2007 washingtonpost.com blog that mentioned Maureen Dowd's opinion that Michelle often teased Barack in public in an attempt to make him appear more likeable, but with the result that he merely looked emasculated and childlike.

That Barack tries to control the public political scene with unwavering, part-time dedication to the office of president is obvious. Not so transparent is that Obama Machiavellian control tactics also extend to his intimate personal relationships with political rivals. In *The Audacity of Hope*, he tells how, after being elected to the United States Senate, he met George W. Bush for the first time at a get-acquainted session for new legislators. In an expression of camaraderie, Bush laughingly notes that he and Obama had debated Alan Keyes as the two briefly ambled along together. Barack recalls that he draped his arm over Bush's shoulder and that such an action might have been unsettling to the Secret Service agents.

Draping your arm over someone's shoulder puts you in a position, literally, to steer them around. Since Obama is six feet, one inch and Bush is five feet, eleven inches, Barack's gesture enabled him to further reduce the president's stature relative to him—a brand-new senator. Obama tried a similar strategy to manipulate the five feet, seven inch Hillary Clinton, but Hillary saw through it. When Barack and she inadvertently met at Reagan National Airport during the 2008 primary, the two began criticizing the campaign slights of the other. According to *Game Change*, Obama put his hand on Clinton's shoulder, causing her to bristle. The action so irritated her that later she complained that Barack had violated her "personal space" and had "a lot of nerve" for doing so.

Hillary Clinton did not fall for the Machiavellian tactics of Barack Obama, perhaps because at some level of her consciousness she correctly perceived them as a variation on the Alinsky art of interpersonal manipulation. Since Hillary, herself, was an Alinsky acolyte, she knew that Obama's behavior conformed with Saul's admonition to carefully and strategically use disingenuous nonverbal and verbal communication and relationships to deceive people. I must add, parenthetically, that Barack also follows the Alinsky tradition when he uses demonization, sarcasm, and humor to disparage his rivals, political and otherwise.

The dynamics of his family of origin and the conditions of his birth virtually preordained that Barack would have identity problems. We already have discussed the profoundly troubled relationship between Stanley Ann and her father, and suggested that the precipitous sexual liaison that led to Barack's conception probably represented an acting-out of Stanley Ann's own father-based identity conflict. It is unlikely that Obama's mother was ready to raise a child. As noted earlier, Stanley Ann once had asked a schoolmate when the friend would be "sending back" her newborn brother, presaging the apparent ease and frequency with which she later would abandon her own male baby, Barry.

Perhaps Barack senior compensated for his wife's tenuous maternal attachment by being a proud and dedicated father. You can answer in the affirmative if you believe that a man with an infant can be interviewed for a Hawaiian newspaper and forget to mention that he was either a dad or husband, abandon his child days before the child's first birthday, rejoin his son only once thereafter and then merely for a couple days, and have a close African friend comment that he never knew that Barack senior had a child in the USA. Dana Chivvis of Aol News Surge mentioned that Harvard historian Caroline Elkins referred to our president's father as a "serious, fall-down alcoholic" when she spoke with Obama biographer David Remnick, and Chivvis, herself, noted that Senior earned the moniker "Mr. Double-Double" to describe his habit for ordering Scotch big-time. (We see here that Mr. Double Double sired Mr. Triple Double with Junior substituting double standards, double speak, and double binds for Senior's four measures of Scotch.)

The author Barack Obama explains that during his childhood he saw only white family faces and was raised in environs almost totally devoid of authentic black culture. Lack of exposure to the grittier aspects of "real" black experience only exacerbates Barry's preoccupation with skin color and racial identity conflicts. Attempting to compensate for the racial void, Stanley Ann inadvertently abets the identity problems by filling her son's head with super-heroic images of blacks, unfettered by any reality constraints, and confounded his black racial identity with the unfortunate reality of his being the son of a milky white mother. In *Dreams*, Barack describes Stanley Ann as advocating the view that black people benefitted from a "great inheritance" and "special destiny." He alleges that she described Harry Belafonte as the world's most handsome man. Barack says that these positive mental images contrasted with negative ones evoked in him when he witnessed a photograph of a black man trying to peel-off his black skin in a self-abusing attempt to lighten himself.

The revelation supposedly occurred when the 9-year-old Barry, living in Indonesia, discovered a *Life* magazine wherein a black man allegedly had paid for a skin-lightening chemical treatment that disfigured him. In typical melodramatic racial hyperbole, Barack, the adult, remembered Barry, the child, thinking that skin lightening was irreversible and that "thousands" of black people perform the lightening. He added that at the time of the original event he felt his neck and face flush with heat, his stomach knot, and his vision blur.

Interestingly, Obama perceived the man's trying to whiten his skin, simultaneously, as being irreversible and abortive attempts that could result in happiness or disfigurement, perhaps an unconscious allusion to his own fear and revulsion about accepting the white in himself. Although

Obama's reference to the magazine article makes for compelling reading and might even help to sell a book, in 2007 when the *Chicago Tribune* researches *Life* magazine, as well as *Ebony*, they find no such traumatizing article in the archives. Once again, we see Barack Obama projecting his inner emotional turmoil outward, setting up a straw man target for identity-related rage.

Our fearless leader's callous disregard for the will of the American people could not be missed when on August 20, 2010, he submitted to the United Nations Human Rights Council for their review a State Department Report on Human Rights that specifically mentioned the Arizona immigration law that he opposed. No matter that a Gallup Poll conducted at the end of April 2010 revealed that 51% of our citizens who knew about the law favored it and only 39% opposed. Once again, the Mexican and liberal vote clearly proved more politically valuable to the president than was during the right thing by the nation as a whole. This was merely another example of how intermingled race and self-interest regularly determine Obama's decisions and actions.

Parading before the world all that he considers wrong with America is a tried and true Barack Obama strategy intended to raise his stature with America's "people-of-color" detractors, overseas and within the United States, while at the same time enlisting support that he hopes will empower him to bully our nation into accepting whatever he knows is best for us. Expertise in lifting himself up by putting America down is a natural consequence of Obama's education at the foot of such raceketeers as Frank Marshall Davis, the pornographic novel writer and white hater of Barry's youth, and the Reverend Jeremiah Wright of Obama's adulthood, a mentor whose orientation is obvious to all. It does not hurt that he chooses a wife as skilled as he in both defiling and exploiting America.

Self-enhancing race manipulation has been a cornerstone of Michelle Obama's personality. When on February 19, 2008, the then 44-year-old Michelle says "For the first time in my adult life, I am proud of my country" anyone with half a cerebrum realizes that she is equating America's worth with the extent to which she personally profited from our country's largesse. But, given the history of her racial remarks, there must be a latent subtext such as: For the first time in my adult life, I do not feel a smoldering contempt for white America. Does anyone think for a moment that Michelle Obama never in her adult life had been proud of black America? Not proud of black professionals, black civil rights, black sports, or black entertainment figures? Her statement of February 19th reveals much more about her racially balkanized view of our country than about her gratitude for its essence. No coincidence that she symbiotically marries a man who confidently quotes every black civil rights pioneer, but who stammers and, sputters in failing to recall just how many states comprise the United States. If I were Michelle Obama-like, I would say that her husband's duping of the America occasions the first episode in my adult life that I have not been proud of my country.

The *New Yorker* magazine creates a firestorm when in July 2008 the cover depicts Barack and Michelle in black radical attire, fist bumping. That one picture says more than my ten thousand words. No, I do not mean that the Obamas are unadulterated anarchists. I mean that the caricature does what caricatures do: it exaggerates obvious features of husband and wife. The cover symbolizes the Machiavellian Barack Obama who panders self-servingly to the black electorate by getting involved in the Gates controversy, and the Machiavellian Michelle Obama who self-servingly acknowledges the value of America only after feeling confident that she will become First Lady.

The Psychopath

Since Barack Obama, obviously, is not an axe murderer or other felon, where is the psychopath in him? Consider first that, by its very nature, psychopathy is the least transparent of the dark-triad traits. One cannot help readily noticing the nose-in-the-air and pontificating narcissist Obama. His Machiavellianism is equally obvious, apparent in wealth and power grabs, abetted by his conspiring with like-minded elitists, as revealed by nationally syndicated newspaper columnist Michelle Malkin who chronicled them in *Culture of Corruption: Obama and His Team of Tax Cheats, Crooks, and Cronies*. But like all psychopaths, the psychopath Obama conceals his unpopular thoughts and emotions, fearing that they will lie bare his vulnerabilities and sinister intentions.

You might recall that in his *Dreams* book, Barack said flat out that he deliberately studied "the white man" to determine his weaknesses so as to use that knowledge against whitey. Obama no doubt vowed that he would not leave himself open to someone's using a similar strategy against him. Hence, his meticulously choreographed identity manipulation from adolescence through the present, that has enabled him to hide from America most of what he does not want us to see. Only by doing so has Barack been able to accede to the world's most powerful position without having demonstrated previous achievements that warranted the ascension.

Given the expert applications of his psychopathic strategies to date, I only can conclude that Obama's political career has something in common with Osama Bin Laden's 9/11 attack—through dumb luck both psychopaths succeeded far beyond their wildest dreams.

In the psychopathy realm rather than in the peacemaker arena, Barack Hussein Obama truly deserves a Nobel Prize. And it is for that reason that no one ever will know more than the tip of the behind-the-scenes psychopathic machinations that has facilitated the evolution of Barry into President Barack. However, I can mention a few facts.

Not surprisingly, Obama's obsessive-compulsive identity management and manipulations are keys to his psychopathy. Recall that as a child, he tries to delude others into believing that he is the son of a Luo prince and that to this day he maintains a paranoid-like delusion that he is an everyday black man, his genetic endowment notwithstanding. Putting on the face of a prince, a black, or a black prince is an epiphenomenon though, a surface manifestation of the psychopathic process writhing within the black and white soul of Barack. He is not the "comfortable within his own skin" brother that the press has concocted; he is pathetically alienated from himself, and he maintains his personal deception by identity-oriented manipulations.

One of the big identity manipulation lies that Obama tries to perpetrate is that, because he has a family that includes several groups, he knows all about race and is uniquely qualified to treat all men (and women) as brothers (or brothas). In *The Audacity of Hope*, for instance Barack states that he never permitted race or tribe affiliation to determine his relationships.

The choice of the term "tribe" is interesting, given that Kenya, the African nation that Obama calls home, is the world's hotbed of tribalism, racial and ethnic murder, rape, intimidation, and prejudice. Barack's statement, however, raises a more fundamental question: Does coming from a multi-ethnic or multi-racial family, most members of which you never or rarely met, make one more tolerant of differences? Not any more so than coming from a multi-ethnic or multi-racial neighborhood makes one more tolerant of differences. In fact, being from such an environment can have the opposite effect, causing differences to be exaggerated, resulting in intra- and inter-familial blood feuds. Just as familiarity often breeds contempt, sometimes a so-called melting pot of diverse ingredients is actually a simmering cauldron of contention, ready to boil over at the slightest provocation.

The shamelessness of Barack's attempts at electorate identity brainwashing is highlighted by Maria Gavrilovic of CBS News in May, 2008 who reports a Kissimmee, Florida speech in which Obama, when talking about his family, had the unmitigated "audacity of hype" to tell a largely Hispanic audience: "You've got my sister; she looks like Selma Hayak. I don't know if you've seen her. She looks Latin." No matter that Obama's half-sister, Maya Soetoro-Ng, is white and Indonesian: not quite Latin. (Someone should tell Barack that "people-of-color" do not all look the same.) And, as for the resemblance between Maya and the stunningly beautiful Selma Hayak, I can only say, "audacity of hype" dos.

Barack Obama insulates himself from recognizing his identity mendacity by employing the psychopathic defense of isolation which permits one to separate ideas from each other and from their associated feelings so that the psychopath can maintain contradictory positions unhesitatingly. Endowed with this magical power of personality, Barack not only can say that he is black rather than biracial, but also can maintain a self-deception that permits him to make promises that he has no intention of keeping. Can anyone forget Obama's vow that he "will not sign any non-emergency bill without giving the American public an opportunity to review and comment on the White House website for five days" and that lobbyists "won't find a job in my White House." Obama rationalizes around these lies by employing a variety of Bill Clintonesque "That depends on what the word 'is' is" strategies, providing excuses for the non-transparency of his legislative bills and lobby-oriented baggage of his appointees. The young Barry prides himself on being able to outthink and outtalk his dear, old granddad. The adult Barack goes on to professionalize his skill, becoming a lawyer (You know, a person who can demand that you answer their questions but never answer yours) and a politician (a person whose greatest skill often is a superlative capacity to say one thing along the eastern border of their philtrum and the opposite along the western border in order to manipulate all listeners).

In interpersonal relationships, the psychopathic defense of isolation morphs into a related defense called "splitting." People are split off into rigid, dichotomous groups of good guys and gals versus bad guys and gals. For Obama, this, of course, means that the bad mostly will be populated by whites and Barack detractors, and the good, by blacks and Barack advocates. To Olympian proportions, Obama relentlessly demonizes George Bush as an incarnate devil, responsible for every conceivable atrocity. At times, whole swaths of white America are demeaned as well, including the entire state of Kansas that has a "potential for unblinking cruelty." And who can forget our esteemed president during his campaign lumping together white residents of "small town" Pennsylvania and the entire Midwest of our nation who "get bitter, they cling to guns or religion or antipathy toward people who aren't like them or anti-immigrant sentiment or anti-trade sentiment as a way to explain their frustrations." Note that Obama gets so crazy with his splitting defense that he cannot even censor his thought processes sufficiently to enable him at least to qualify his criticism to say that only "some" white Kansans and "some" small town Pennsylvanians and Midwesterners conform to his hateful characterizations.

From time to time Barack Obama breaks out his I-am-the-good-guy identity, and if you stick with me you, too, will be good. To do so, he sets up an evil identity target, real or imagined, frames the debate in an obviously one-sided way, and then goes we, we, we, we all the way home. For instance, on September 6, 2010 at the Milwaukee Area Labor Council's annual LaborFest celebration, Obama makes identity the centerpiece of his speech. First, he seeks to elicit identity support for himself by screeching,

"**They** [emphasis added] talk about me like a dog." Then he creates an enemy-of-the-people phantom identity, a mythic scapegoat that he can knock down, saying, "And when times are tough, it can be easy to give in to cynicism and fear; doubt and division—to set our sights lower and settle for something less. But that is not who **we** [emphasis added] are . . ." Of course, Obama, unwitting creator of his namesake Obamafuscation process, never gives any hint about *who* would give in to cynicism, fear, doubt, and division. Seven months later, on April 19, 2011, he is at it again. This time in a Town Hall speech at Northern Virginia Community College in Annandale, Obama makes "the wealthy" his foil, claiming that they would heartlessly promote their own financial welfare over the needs of impoverished seniors, education-starved children, and medically unprotected "millions." After enumerating the helpless and the needy in order to tug at the heart strings of the assemblage, Obama follows up with his trademark "that's not who **we** [emphasis added] are" refrain.

Obama rails against business people, calling them fat cats. The fat cats are business men and women who earn six figure or more salaries, unfunded by the U.S. taxpayers. As a result, the fat guys and gals create everything from new computers and their software to novel life-preserving surgeries and medications. When salary, benefits, and time on the job are factored in, many public school educators also make far in excess of $100,000 per year. Some deserve what they get and more, but some have no interest in teaching, teach poorly, work 6 hours a day, 180 days a year, take every possible sick day every year, and cannot be fired. Moreover, citizens pay for each and every dollar that incompetent educators suck out of the educational system. There are plenty of exploitative, scamming business people and private sector professionals who make high salaries, but we can withhold our investment in their fraudulent money-making endeavors, and they have no tenure! By contrast, the often sycophantically Obama-loving public sector double and triple dips from the governmental trough with impunity.

Barack Obama despises the wealthy because he has lived a life of abject poverty; never mind that he attended silver spoon institutions from grade school through graduate school. In 2002, when the Obama family raked in an adjusted gross income of $259,394, Michelle complains that they need to make more money, so she takes a job managing community-oriented programs for the University of Chicago Medical Center who pay her what she likely felt was the paltry and humiliating salary of about $102,000. In 2004, Michelle alone rakes-in about $122,000. Then in November of the year, Barack is elected to the United States Senate and, viola! four months later, in March 2005, his wife's compensation rises to about $317,000. For 2005, the Obama's adjusted gross income is $1,655,106. Coincidentally, in February 2006, two months before 2005 income taxes have to be paid, Michelle's not really black knight in shining armor gallops onto the scene, saving The University of Chicago Medical Center's new pavilion construction project by requesting a million tax payer dollars for it. Legislator psychopathy?

Before you decide, consider the case of Barack Obama's staunch supporter and convicted felon financier buddy, "Tony" Rezko. In addition to getting the big University of Chicago payoff that year, 2005 also is the year that Barack and Michelle just have to have that house. You know, the Georgian revival mansion at 5046 South Greenwood Avenue in the ritzy Kenwood section. What to do? How about Tony? I bet he has some good advice. Yes, I know that he is being investigated by that overly zealous U.S. Attorney, Patrick Fitzgerald, but Tony's been such a muffin to us. Besides, didn't I just read that the Chicago Tribune called Tony Rezko one of Governor Rod Blagojevich's most trusted confidants? No. I am sticking with Rezko; "I can no more disown him than I can disown the black community. I can no more disown him than I can my white grandmother. I can no more disown him than I can my mentor, Reverend Jeremiah Wright."

Tony Rezko, in fact, did do as the Obamas wanted, proving that Barack not only is comfortable in his own skin and super cool, but also an outstanding judge of character. Because 5046's seller made the Georgian revival mansion sale contingent on unloading an adjoining parcel of undeveloped land, Tony "stepped up" to purchase it as a favor to our future president. Rezko and the Obamas closed their sales on the very same day, and in January 2006 when Barack wanted a larger side yard, he bought some of Tony's parcel. Two thousand six, no doubt, turned out to be a Sinatra-like very good year for Barack; not so much for Tony Rezko who was indicted on fraud charges before he could sing his next "Auld Lang Syne."

Hilary Clinton noticed the Obama-Rezko psychopathic alliance, exposing it during the Democratic presidential debate sponsored by CNN and the Congressional Black Caucus Institute on January 21, 2008 when she asserted that while she was challenging the Republican agenda Barack was ". . . practicing law and representing your contributor, Rezko, in his slum landlord business in inner-city Chicago."

In becoming president, Barack employs a "You scratch my back and I'll scratch yours" strategy by finding a few good men with whom to partner. You recall that Obama has made government sponsored green initiatives a cornerstone of his environmental policy. And, where there are government sponsored programs, there are opportunities to reward supporters. Who better to reward than Steve Westly, a man who had helped fund the Barack Obama campaign since 2007. According to a late March 2011 ABC news radio online.com .blog, "By Election Day, Westly has joined the elite circle of 'bundlers,' the candidate's top group of fundraisers who used their connections to gather more than $500,000 for Obama's campaign." Just so happens that Mr.Westly, a California venture capital magnate, also is favorably and financially oriented toward green initiatives. ABC explains this by saying that Westly visited the White House to lobby for a green energy "opportunity." Afterward, in 2010, he becomes a Secretary of Energy advisory panel member and allegedly used his website to publicize his company's Obama administration connections. The ABC piece goes on to say that Westly's group received a $465 million dollar loan for the Tesla electric automobile company, a $700,000 Philadelphia recycling project grant, a $20.4 million bio-refinery grant, and $25 million to develop a sweet sorghum-based diesel, and the White House indicates their intension to provide $7,500 incentive to consumers who purchase electric automobiles.

So, what motivated the Barack Obama-Steve Westly alliance? Was it selfless love for America and for the well-being of planet earth? Or was it a self-serving mutual admiration dyad wherein Barack regarded Steve as a "good guy" for furthering personal prestige and power, and Steve felt similarly?

In addition to dichotomizing humanity into good versus evil, the psychopath is a consummate interpersonal manipulator. We already have noted how Barack's family members, such as his grandmother, and friends, such as Reverend Jeremiah Wright, are scapegoated when Obama needs to talk himself out of unfavorable identity indictments. Even in college he takes advantage of a "buddy" whom he double-speaks into lying on an apartment contract. In a typical self-protective ploy, Barack refuses to sign the lying contract himself, but unhesitatingly lives in the fraudulently acquired apartment until he was through with it.

Obama didn't have to sign a fraudulent contract to move into the White House either, but he knew that the citizenry held him to an implicit contract, demanding that he afford equal treatment to people of every race and creed. This presented a problem, however, since equal treatment could jeopardize his quest to become a black racial hero. As usual though, Barack had an identity-oriented plan: Choose cabinet members, czars, czarinas, and other foils to implement race-based policies so that Obama takes the credit for successes and projects the blame for failures. Whenever Barack needed a racial stand-in, he would stick in his thumb and pull out a plum.

Sweet Michelle has been Barack Hussein's favorite stand-in plum for the "make me look authentically and swaggeringly black by pandering to the raceketters" campaign. Consistent with that role, for a May 2011 White House poetry and prose celebration, she showcased a radical bimp rapper, "Common" whose real name is Lonnie Rashid Lynn. Given her affection for black children, Michelle must have selected him for his role model qualities. Neil Munro from the *Daily Caller* transcribed one of Common's raps, "A Letter to the Law" that proselytized and glorified bimps, guns, violence, assaults on police, and anti-white and anti-George W. Bush rhetoric.

After Lonnie Rashid Lynn has yuked it up at the White House poetry and prose celebration with Michelle and Barack, Common might be available to speak at your local boys' club, girls' club, or Parent-Teachers Association.

If you imagine that I am being purely facetious or sarcastic, don't. On May 11, 2011, abclocal.go.com reported an Associated Press posting entitled, "White House defends invite to rapper Common." The piece cited White

House spokesman/fall guy, a.k.a. Jay Carney, as follows: "Carney says Common has earned praise for being a socially conscious rapper. He adds that Obama appreciates Common's work trying to get children in their Chicago hometown interested in poetry." So, given the President's endorsement, those interested in scheduling Common for a night of childhood enrichment can contact the Obamas at 1600 Pennsylvania Avenue NW. General Comments: 202-456-1111; Switchboard: 202-456-1414; FAX: 202-456-2461; TTY/TDD Comments: 202-456-6213; Visitors Office: 202-456-2121.

Should you be surprised that a radical black militant is invited to represent the White House and the black community, and to teach children the fine art of poetics? Probably not, since the Obama presidency literally begins with an assault on white America in the guise of religion, spearheaded by black Reverend Joseph Lowery. The slanderous, rhyming minister of malevolence pits God and all of non-white humanity against the Caucasian devil by concluding his presidential inauguration benediction saying, "We ask you to help us work for that day when black will not be asked to give back, when brown can stick around, when yellow will be mellow, when the red man can get ahead, man, and when white will embrace what is right." As any self-respecting "religious" demagogue would, Lowery then incites the crowd to scream, "Amen!" YouTube videos document how tickled Barack is at the minister's loving, humanitarian, rhetorical witticism.

Obama illustrates how the proof of the racial divisive pudding is in the repeating of it when he selects the black educator Charles Ogletree as a member of the presidential "black advisory council." (You guessed it; there is no white advisory council.) Like Lowery, Ogletree preaches that contemporary 21st century white Americans have been incorrigible, inveterate racists, biased against each and every minority. Lowery, the cutie, might encourage Ogletree, the toughie, to assert that "Everyone is grand but the white man."

Although the supply is virtually inexhaustible, one last example of Obama's anti-white foils coalition—Special Advisor for Green Jobs, Van Jones. Van, the man, sees Caucasians as deliberately trying to poison all other races: "The white polluters and the white environmentalists are essentially steering poison into the people-of-color's communities because they don't have a racial justice frame." Amanda Carpenter of the Washington Times tells us that "Mr. Jones signed a statement for 911Truth.org in 2004 demanding an investigation into what the Bush Administration may have done that deliberately allowed 9/11 to happen, perhaps as a pretext for war." (Sounds a lot like the Jeremiah Wright rant asserting that white America created and disseminated the AIDS virus as a genocidal attack on African Americans.) Van Jones also produced anti-white, anti-American CDs, one "starring" the convicted police murderer Mumia Abu-Jamal. Powerline Blog quotes some lines from one little ditty as follows:

> American way manufactured by white folk in office, by these rich men here to mock us. The United States; a piece of stolen land led by right-wing, war-hungry, oil thirsty . . . and when it's all said and done still can't [garbled] the wrong place cause they got people-of-color playing servant to do that shit for them; mother fuckers ready to wipe out soft targets on territories harboring terrorists?

Fortunately, the White House's meticulous vetting process discovers Van Jones' hateful orientation and comes out fast and strong against it. Well, not quite. Try Fox News commentator Glenn Beck; were it not for him, Mr. Jones would still be on the Obama payroll. While the administration did not ask Van to leave, according to Fred Barbash of Politio.com, the chairperson of the White House Council on Environmental Quality that employed Jones received his resignation, and responded that he had been hard worker and an advocate for energy efficiency. Barbash comments that ". . . There was no accompanying explanation on the unusual timing of the announcement, shortly after midnight on a Sunday morning before a holiday [Labor Day]."

Barack Obama addressed the racially-charged matter by saying, "   ." Sorry, try as I could, I found no comment from the commander-in-chief. I did find plenty of Barackisms in support of Henry Louis Gates junior, but then, of course, you knew that.

Since Barack's inauguration, the administration has referred to our president as "no-drama Obama." The term clearly is intended to be a high compliment: Obama the cool, Obama the unflappable, Obama the intellectual. In truth, the phrase "no drama Obama" better summarizes his isolation of affect psychological defense mechanism for all that is non-racial.

The public got their fill of Barack's vapid emotionality and disingenuous identity during the Gulf Oil Crisis. Peter Wehner of *Politics Daily* underscored the Machiavellianism and the psychopathy of Barack when he wrote that during the catastrophe many formerly supportive commentators came out against his "bloodless, distant, and uncaring" approach. Wehner felt that Obama then responded to the criticism by "casting about for a new persona" and showcasing contrived emotionality.

On the other hand, "no drama Obama" also aptly describes the controller lurking within the dark-triad of Barack's personality, the mini-him who keeps his foot on the neck of anyone who might say anything to undermine the psychopathic president's authority, standing, or wishes. Barack Obama harbors a life-long delusional-like belief that Herculean emotional restraint enables him to understand and control himself and the entire interpersonal field. A small dose of reality testing and a few moments of neuropsychological study, however, would disclose to him that virtually nothing of social consequence can be understood or controlled without the joint application of intellect and genuine emotion. Barack Obama, faker par excellence, no doubt can simulate superficial elements of a "kick ass" persona, such as the facial expression and the vocal timbre. After all, Barry Barack Hussein Soetoro Obama, master of disingenuousness, has been faking an all-black identity since childhood. But, as the 2010 election has proven, sooner or later people will tear back the opaque, black curtain and see a naked black and white Obama as he really is.

CHAPTER 4

Barack Hussein Obama:
Disingenuous, Elusive, and Protean

Munchkin minions from the Land of Ahhs genuflect before him, while the Great and Powerful Barry Barack Hussein Soetoro Obama hides behind the curtain of his pseudo-black identity. He fears nothing but facts and reality. Just as his racist African grandfather worried that his son's union with Stanley Ann would "sully" the Obama bloodline, Barack recoils at the thought of sullying his public persona with inconvenient, uncomfortable truths that reveal who he really is.

Obama withheld his birth certificate for two and one-half years, not because he was born oversees, but because he feared that its release would focus attention on objective details of his past that he could not obscure.

For one thing, the birth certificate causes one to think about the president's parents as a married couple. The slightest additional investigation then inevitably leads to the further correct conclusion that Barack was born "outside" of a proper marriage. Obama implicitly expresses fear of such disclosures about his parents, and, therefore, about himself, when, in *Dreams*, he wrote that "In fact, how and when the marriage occurred remains a bit murky, a bill of particulars that I've never quite had the courage to explore." Several writers state unequivocally that Barack senior was married and had a child in Kenya when, within a couple months of their initial introduction, he impregnated eighteen-year-old Stanley Ann. For instance, Peter Firstbrook, author of *The Obamas*, refers to Barack junior as, "illegitimate." One of the President's image advisors should remind Barack junior that the black illegitimacy rate currently is about

70 percent, that in 21ˢᵗ century America there apparently is no shame in being "authentically" illegitimate, and that if the facts show him to be so, his in-the-hood street cred actually might be enhanced.

The Obama cover-up has not been limited to details of his family background, either. Barack has withheld concrete information that would allow others to evaluate his own personal accomplishments. While eager to verbally disseminate his micro-managed legend, the erudite, silver-tongued Obama has refused to disclose his school records because authenticated transcripts would show him to be a "pale" reflection of his hyped reputation. Barack managed to publish only one article at the Harvard Law review, an inconsequential six page summary, that he attempted to hide, in which he concluded that a fetus should not be able to file a lawsuit against his mother. (Proof of the "truth is stranger than fiction" adage. For the details, see Ben Smith & Jeffrey Ressner.) As a community organizer, Barack Obama produced nothing substantial and enduring. As a state legislator, Barack was mediocre at best, and as a federal senator he spent most of his time campaigning for higher office and voting "present." Obama, the unifier had one of the most partisan voting records in Congress, and, in fact, literally was given the title of the most liberal senator of 2007.

While Obama has been accreting bits and pieces of his dark-triad personality since childhood, the elements coalesced around Barack Hussein, the president. On the eve on his presidential inauguration, when bipartisanship would augment his power, Barack was all for bipartisanship; just listen to how he tried to play John McCain and the Republicans at a January 19, 2009 dinner:

> Thank you, John, for your service to America and the service you will continue to render in the months and years ahead. And I'd like to close by asking all of you to join us in making this bipartisan dinner not just an inaugural tradition, but a new way of doing the people's business in this city. We will not always agree on everything in the months to come, and we will have our share of arguments and debates. But let us strive always to find that common ground, and to defend together those common ideals,

for it is the only way we can meet the very big and very serious challenges that we face right now.

His handling of the national debt shows the double speaking Obama in all his duplicitous splendor. Jake Tapper's January 5, 2011 blog reminds us that on March 16, 2006 the then-Senator Barack Obama voted against raising the national debt ceiling saying,

> The fact that we are here today to debate raising America's debt limit is a sign of leadership failure. Leadership means that "the buck stops here." Instead, Washington is shifting the burden of bad choices today onto the backs of our children and grandchildren. America has a debt problem and a failure of leadership. Americans deserve better. I therefore intend to oppose the effort to increase America's debt limit.

Fast-forward to April, 2011. Obama the senator is now Obama the president; the national debt is his responsibility. Suddenly, the "right thing" has rotated 180 degrees. Increasing the debt no longer is a sign of leadership failure. Increasing the debt is a leadership imperative, literally a matter of America's survival. Since the Obama handlers know that president watchers recall Obama's senatorial vote against raising the debt, could this be the time for Barack to stand up like a man before the national media, admit that his 2006 vote was misguided, and take the lead in forging a bipartisan consensus? Not really. Rather, Obama punts to his PR guy, Press Secretary Jay Carney, who on April 11, 2011 handles the messy matter via a press briefing mostly in a back and forth with Ben Feller of the Associated Press.

> Feller: A couple questions on the spending debate. I want to come back to this quote that then-Senator Obama had in 2006, when he voted against extending the debt limit, and he called it a sign of leadership failure in terms of potentially raising the limit, and it's a sign of the country's financing the U.S. government's reckless fiscal policies. Now, of course, he and the administration are saying it's urgent to extend that debt limit again. Can you explain, since this is back in the news, why that is not hypocrisy?

Carney: What I can tell you, Ben, is the President, as David Plouffe said yesterday, regrets that vote and thinks it was a mistake. He realizes now that raising the debt ceiling is so important to the health of this economy and the global economy that it is not a vote that, even when you are protesting an administration's policies, you can play around with. And you need to take very seriously the need to raise the debt limit so that the full faith and credit of the United States government is maintained around the globe.

So Carney says that Plouffe says that Obama says that he made a mistake. Barack has his turn "playing" by protesting George Bush administration policies, and that is okay for Barack Hussein, but for others playing by protesting is inane.

Carney: The consequences, as Secretary Geithner and many others, including the Speaker of the House, Senator Minority Leader, Congressman Ryan have pointed out, the consequences of not—of failing to raise the debt ceiling would be Armageddon-like in terms of the economy on—the impact on interest rates, on job creation, on growth would be devastating. Others outside of government, including former Treasury Secretary Henry Paulson, S&P chief economist David Weiss, for example, said that it could cause significant and long-lasting financial and economic disruption. JPMorgan Chase head Jamie Dimon said, "If anyone wants to push that button—i.e. fail to raise the debt ceiling, which I think would be catastrophic and unpredictable, I think they're crazy."

To vote at odds with what Barack wants is Armageddon-like and crazy. There's no crying in baseball and there's no voting according to conscience, if your conscience is inconsistent with Obama's conscience.

Carney: The point is that the President, through his actions both in the first two years in office when he demonstrated through the way he created the health care recovery—rather the health care act, the Affordable Care Act, with its deficit reduction built into it, through his signing—or rather his agreement on Friday to enact the deepest discretionary spending cuts in history, has shown that he is committed to deficit reduction. And we do not need to play chicken with our economy by linking the raising of the debt ceiling to anything. We should do that right away.

Feller: He cast that vote five years ago and issued those strongly stated views, and as recently as earlier this year, I believe, Jake asked your predecessor about this and we didn't hear that it was a mistake. When did the President come to realization this was a mistake?

Carney: Well, we asked him and he made clear that he now believes it was a mistake. And he understands that when you're in the legislature, when you're in the Senate, you want to make clear your position if you don't agree with policies of the administration. But there are many other ways to do it and—I would say. And also, there is the fact in this case that the efforts to link this to the President's commitment to deficit reduction are unnecessary precisely because he has demonstrated his commitments so clearly, and will again on Wednesday when he lays out his vision for long-term deficit reduction.

In 2006, there was only one way for Barack Obama to make his position clear when he disagreed with Bush Administration policies: by voting against raising the debt ceiling; now there are many ways to express disagreement. And, oh by the way, "When did the President come to the realization this was a mistake?" Carney, of course, never answered Feller's question that underscored how three months earlier the president had said nothing about having made a mistake when he was questioned by Jake Tapper.

Three days after Press Secretary Jay Carney had run interference for him, Obama held his own press conference to address the deficit in-vivo. The *Wall Street Journal*, in their Review and Outlook section on April 14, 2011, commented, publishing a story entitled, "The Presidential Divider, Obama's toxic speech and even worse plan for deficits and debt," claiming that Barack's statements were replete with blistering partisanship and multiple distortions. The piece commented that the Obama's presentation was designed to "inoculate the White House from criticism that it is not serious about the fiscal crisis, after ignoring its own deficit commission last year and tossing off a $3.73 trillion budget in February that increased spending amid a record deficit of $1.65 trillion. Mr. Obama was chased to George Washington University yesterday because Mr. Ryan and the Republicans outflanked him on fiscal discipline and are now setting the national political agenda . . . The speech he chose to deliver was dishonest even by modern political standards."

Once again, we find the double speaking President testing the wind before deciding to comment about an issue of critical national import. And, once again, he chooses divisive, inflammatory self-serving language, framing his remarks to curry favor with political supporters rather than to resolve a looming national, even worldwide, financial crisis.

Obama's health care reform was another one of Barack's, "I will do what I want now and later will sweet talk my way into making what I did palatable to those who resisted." You no doubt recall that few, if any, legislators had a chance to study, or even to read, the bill before the President forced a vote on it. As Nancy Pelosi advised, the new legislation would be explained to the people after it became law.

Barack the reformer asserted that public funding of elections was best for our country until he decided that it was in his personal interest to oppose it. Barack the straight-talker had the "audacity" to speak out against the Iraq War, but not the temerity to admit that the John McCain-inspired Iraq surge worked. He did not hesitate, however, to campaign for a surge in Afghanistan, since Obama needed to gerrymander "tough guy" into his identity during the election in order to answer the criticism that he was unqualified to be commander-in-chief. Since becoming responsible for our nation's security, Barack has managed to so alienate himself and his administration from the military that he and his vice president had become a laughing stock among the troops—officers and enlisted. You surely recall that Obama sacked Afghan war commander General Stanley McChrystal when *Rolling Stone* magazine disclosed that McChrystal and his aides were mocking the military incompetence of Joe Biden and Barack Obama. Why would they question the capabilities of a president who repeatedly has referred to U.S. Navy corpsmen as, "Navy corpse men?"

Yes. That's right—Navy corpse men. Check out for yourself the fact that on February 4, 2010, at the National Prayer Breakfast, Barack related a heroic story about a "Haitian navy corpse man" whom Obama tried to beatify as a patriotic guardian of truth, justice, and the American way by interjecting the race mongering Machiavellian message that black immigrants—legal or illegal—are noble and grand. Once more, Barack Obama proved that his default mentality is not the promotion of American ideals but racial demagoguery, pure and simple.

For the first twenty-one months in office, our dark, but only half-black, manipulative president proceeded to attempt to ram through each and every personal agenda item while thumbing his nose at anyone who opposed him. There was essentially no bipartisanship for proposed initiatives. There was only the crassest backroom politicking in decades, none of the transparency that the candidate had promised. Barack Obama did not focus like a laser beam on the economy and he did not keep the unemployment rate under eight percent as he promised to do in return for passage of the economic stimulus package.

Within two years of Obama's election, the Democrats suffered the most crushing defeat that either party had experienced in the United States House of Representatives, "the People's House," since 1948. The citizenry had voted resolutely and overwhelmingly to repudiate the formerly invulnerable Barack Obama. And if you doubt for a moment that the Republican sweep was directed at Obama and his tactics, you need only consider that a 2010 Harris poll conducted two weeks before the election reported that 67% of their sample rated the president's job performance negatively. This was the same Barack Obama who had received the most positively-biased media and general social treatment of any presidential candidate in modern United States history.

Why the fall from grace? The answer is: the electorate needed two years to get to know the true occult identity lying behind the identity façade that is Barack Obama. Research tells us that persons with dark-triad personality characteristics often are perceived as "charming" when first encountered, that only when their manipulative and exploitative behaviors become obvious are these charlatans seen for whom they truly are.

Geraldine Ferraro was close to correct when she said that Barack Obama never would have been the 2008 Democrat presidential candidate had he not been black. She missed the important caveat that he also needed to be unknown. It was essential that the electorate did not know Obama, the charlatan, the candidate who offered nothing special except his bogus black identity. It was essential that the electorate did not know that Obama was alienated from himself and from mainstream America—black and white.

Barack Obama's alienation from America was expressed throughout his *Dreams* book. Since his father was African, Barack's connection to the United States came exclusively through his mother and her family. Grandfather Stanley and Grandmother Toots had been raised in Kansas, the state that Barack globally dismissed as a land of "conformity and suspicion and the potential for unblinking cruelty." He wrote of his grandmother's parents as being from "Scottish and English stock" and of his three-week trip to Europe, a land that one would expect him to regard as the land of his ancestors. Predictable, this was not so. Instead, Barack said within a few days after beginning his trip that he knew that he had "made a mistake," feeling that Europe was not his, that it was "someone else's romance." He offered the vague rationalization of his "history" as the barrier that prevented him from connecting with the entire European continent.

By contrast, Barack Obama disclosed a fanciful reverie that he had entertained as he prepared for his first touchdown in Kenya, saying ". . . I smiled with the memory of the homecoming I had once imagined for myself, clouds lifting, old demons fleeing, the earth trembling as ancestors rose up in celebration."

Clearly the birthers have been mistaken all along. Obama was not born an alien to America; he simply indoctrinated himself into becoming alienated from America, from his white lineage, and from both of their European roots. Instead, he emotionally invested in all things African and Afrocentric, as well as in the Black Liberation Theology taught by his "uncle," Reverend Jeremiah Wright.

Superficial and tenuous emotional investment in traditional America explains how the Ivy League Barack Obama can misspeak that there are "57" states in the United States and that our country is protected by Navy "corpse men." Barack Obama did not naturally absorb much of "white" American culture, the way non-alienated Americans, black and white, do as a matter of course, although he did artificially suck up his version of "black" culture, American and otherwise. It was precisely the disingenuousness of Barack's bogus black acculturation that former Black Panther Bobby L. Rush addressed during the 1999 U. S. House of Representatives Democratic Primary Election when he said that "Barack Obama went to Harvard and became an educated fool. Barack is a person who read about the civil-rights protests and thinks he knows all about it."

According to Krissah Thompson of the Washington Post, in May 2011, Cornel West, an Africa American Studies (What else?) professor at Princeton, who has released rap albums "referred to Barack as a "black mascot [perhaps now we know who talks about Barack "like a dog"] of Wall Street oligarchs and a black puppet of corporate plutocrats." Thompson specifically quotes West's not-black-enough indictment of Obama: "I think my dear brother Barack Obama has a certain fear of free black men . . . It's understandable. As a young brother who grows up in a white context, brilliant African father, he's always had to fear being a white man with black skin. All he has known culturally is white."

Ken Hutcherson, a black, former NFL linebacker, shared Rush's and West's disdain for Obama. Per onenewsnow.com, in July, 2009, he also disparaged Barack's black credentials, saying:

> But I guess we . . . have to ask, Even though he is black because his father was, what is his "black experience"? He doesn't have any. He was raised by a white mother and a white grandmother, so this man has about as much black experience as my Doberman Pinscher and I guarantee [that] my Doberman Pinscher doesn't have any.

Barack Obama did not invent the dark-triad. Some would say that many of today's most powerful politicians and captains of industry exhibit a similar composite narcissism, Machiavellianism, and sociopathy. But Obama is unique in the way that he melded his dark-triad personality with his conflicted racial identity and conflicted racial preoccupations within the context of the racially obsessed and racially conflicted United States of America. Because Barack knew that he had to be black to win elective office, he enacted a masterful no-holds-barred campaign to conflate, confound, and manipulate all things with all things racial. The strategy worked in large measure because the McCain campaign permitted racial word play to disable them. From the onset of electioneering, McCain promised not to make race or personality an issue and he stuck to it; he did not realize then that race and a dark-triad, disingenuous personality were mostly what Barack was "advertising" to manipulate the electorate.

Given his profoundly conflicted racial identity and the irresistible power of his repetition compulsion, Obama naturally stumbled into his racialized political persona at first. After he realized what he had going for himself, however, he deliberately, masterfully honed his method. At that point, there was no stopping this Machiavellian; Barack Obama became undisputed king of self-serving racial doubles: double standards, double speak, and double binds.

CHAPTER 5

What Made "President" Obama Possible?

Few Americans knew or cared about Barry Barack Hussein Soetoro Obama prior to July 27, 2004 when he delivered the Democratic National Convention Keynote Address at the Fleet Center in Boston. (And few really know him now). However, by the conclusion of his speech, we should have seen Obama for the dark-triad personality that he is, since he spent the first 16 percent of the speech talking about himself—an unprecedented self-serving, narcissistic high-jacking of a gathering intended to elevate John Kerry. The televised convention enabled Barack Obama virtually to quote from his *Dreams* memoire, and thus provided a new venue in which to distribute his black identity mendacity to an unwitting United States citizenry—another preemptive self-defining political move of epic proportions.

Barack pushed all the right buttons that day, but he did not create the buttons; he merely exploited an American psyche prepped by decades of racial doubles propaganda. White and black America had been fed a steady diet of double standards invariable stacked to favor black people. For instance, racial "experts" had explained that blacks cannot be racists, since racism is a quality of the white power structure. Raceketeers had used double speak to maintain such absurdities, manipulating language to the extent that whites even were pressured not to utter certain words. Regardless of context or intent, words as profane as "nigger" and as mundane as "articulate" became off limits to whites, but not to blacks. And double bind situations were created in which whites were backed into no-win interpersonal contexts wherein raceketeers could bombard them with conflicting overt or implied messages that white people could neither resolve, nor even question. The most powerful of these double bind messages has been one in which a raceketeer asserts that a white person cannot address "black issues" because "You don't know what it's like to be black." This same raceketeer then has been able to launch into a prejudicial diatribe about how all "white folks" think and feel.

The "I know all about you but you can never know anything about me" approach is just what we need to enable honest, respectful racial dialogue. One cannot help wondering whether raceketeers have as required reading the April 2008 San Francisco fundraiser speech of Barack Obama wherein he stereotyped every small town white American by saying, "They get bitter, they cling to guns or religion or antipathy to people who aren't like them."

The racial doubles are means of thought and behavior control, a primary purpose of which is to emasculate and manipulate white Americans in order to empower professional raceketeers, black and white. By skillfully employing the doubles, raceketeers direct their spotlight, illuminating anything that in any way can be construed as white bias against blacks while casting a dark shadow to obscure anything that in any way can be construed as black bias against whites.

I must underscore that the doubles are endemic to contemporary American culture and media; they are not the exclusive purview of black or white racializers. It is not just many black Americans who accept Barack's racial identity double speak; many whites are on board with both feet because 21st century Americans have been conditioned to accept racial doubles as natural and noble.

Where are the doubles? Let's see.

Race Schism

Racialized standards, favoring blacks, are present across cultural platforms. Biased pro-black race mentality, in fact, is institutionalized. We already have spoken about the racializers and raceketeers—black and white—who feed on racial contention by attempting to ferret out and broadcast any real or imagined hint of white advantage over blacks. Equally important, African American social groups tend to be racially insulated, organized under the title "black" or some variation thereof. They have structures and processes specifically created to exclude whites, encompass all domains of human endeavor, and frequently have national, state, and local chapters. A self-imposed "us and not them" racial schism social structure, in fact, is readily apparent in virtually every facet of black life, from cradle to grave. For instance, there is a Black Mothers Breastfeeding Association and a Black Funeral Directors and Morticians Association. Of the innumerable extant black racialized social groups, consider just a few of the many genre:

National governmental organizations, such as the Congressional Black Caucus.

State governmental organizations, such as the Black Mayors Association

City governmental organizations, such as the Pasadena Black Municipal Employees Association

Citizen protection organizations, such as the National Black Police Officers Association and the Black Firefighters Association

Pride Organizations, such as Miss Black America

Political associations, such as the Black American Political Association of California

Labor organizations, such as the Coalition of Black Trade Unionists

Business organizations, such as The National Black Business Trade Association

Professional organizations, such as the Association of Black Physicians

Scholastic organizations, such as the Association of Black Collegians

Sororities and fraternities, such as the Delaware Association of Black Greeks

Educators' organizations, such as the National Alliance of Black School Educators

The above list surprises no one, since we hear references to black-only groups every day. The White House has a black-only dedicated group too—the Office of African American Media.

Mind-numbing, socially sanctioned racial conditioning, in fact, is at the heart of the issue. All races and all social groups accept the institutionalized racial preferences schism, so long as it benefits blacks. To really appreciate the malignant influence of the black-only mentality, read the above list again, substituting the word white for black; see how that makes you feel.

Of course, there are no socially sanctioned white only counterparts to the aforementioned black-only organizations. For that reason, throughout this discussion when racial preference is afforded blacks, from time to time I will explicitly or implicitly cue the reader to imagine a situation of racial reversal of the extant pro-black situation, to imagine society's outrage if whites, instead of blacks, were being given segregated preferences.

Each and every above-listed organization is a hypocritical slap in the face of Martin Luther King junior and a desecration of the equal rights amendment. However, the Congressional Black Caucus undoubtedly is the most disturbing of the abominations. The federal government, the institution expressly created to represent all United States citizens, has been co-opted into a split-off, secret black society that commiserates in racially segregated, smoke-free rooms. Of course, that's not the only place that the CBC congregates. In hustling to promote his bid to win a U.S. Senate seat, Barack jumped at the chance to attend the Annual Conference of the Congressional Black Caucus. Christopher Anderson describes that event by invoking a conversation between Jeremiah Wright and the author, Manya Brachear, during which Jeremiah spoke of Obama's experience at the Caucus. In Wright's opinion, it was a "meat market;" women were "hitting" on the future president, "talking about giving him some pussy," despite knowing that he was married. The Reverend felt that the CBC amounted to "a non-stop party, all the booze you want, all the booty you want. That's all it is." Spoken like a true reverend?

How can the fun-loving, wild and crazy Congressional Black Caucus aristocracy justify its just black folks insularity? Double speak and double standards. The black flawmakers, I mean lawmakers, pretend that they must squirrel themselves away in their clubhouse to discuss issues "unique" to their black constituencies. If so, maybe they would accept into the fraternity a white man who, himself, represents a large black community. Maybe not. Commenting on this issue, Perry Bacon junior wrote in the July 20, 2010 Washington Post that Representative Steve Cohen, white Democrat from Tennessee, petitioned to join the CBC because two-thirds of his constituents are black, but Cohen was refused membership. Guess the African American citizens from his Memphis district do not need advocacy.

As noted earlier, racial double standards can only be maintained through racial double speak. In the past, it was blacks who accused whites of duplicitous racial communication, saying that white people engaged in "code talk" in which overtly innocuous language obscured vicious racial bias and manipulation. Now the tables have turned.

Another Washington Post journalist, Eugene Robinson, a black man, indicted Joe Biden for calling Barack Obama "articulate" during the Democratic Presidential campaign. Robinson began his article by asking,"What is it, exactly, that white people mean when they call a black person 'articulate'?" He ended with, "Articulate is really a shorthand way of describing a black person who isn't too black—or, rather, who comports with white America's notion of how a black person should come across." I guess that explains why, being black, Michelle Obama can refer to her father and paternal grandfather as articulate, and Barack, despite being only half black, gets a full pass to call his daughter articulate, but that I never should call a black person articulate. Will the word police grant me permission to refer to a black man with a speech impediment as "inarticulate"? By the way, would someone tell Eugene Robinson that "white people" come in as many shades and use language as individually as black people do.

If I ever believed that all "black people" simply were too forthcoming, principled, and too racially brave to stoop to the white man's semantic mendacity, black Reverend Michael Eric Dyson, professor of sociology, disabused me from my naïve misconception. On NPR's Radio Times show, he explained that black people understand "racial politics," including the fact that Barack cannot talk honestly and openly about certain issues (a racial coward?); rather, the president does a "wink wink" at black America while double speaking white America to win and maintain his political offices. This is a variation on the tune that Jeremiah Wright sang when after the "God damn America" sermon hit the airwaves he was interviewed by Bill Moyers and said that the black community knows that Obama is doing political double speak, saying what white America wants to hear but siding with the black liberation street. BET's "Cousin

Jeff" Johnson of Rap City and Jeff Johnson Chronicles spoke similarly to the Associated Press in July 2008. In reacting to the AP report, MSNBC.com on August 1, 2008 posted a photograph of smiling Barack Obama with rapper, Ludacris, after their November 29, 2006 meeting, along with an undated discussion of the "dilemma" that the association posed for the then presidential candidate. The piece mentioned how Barack had heaped praise both on Ludacris and Jay-Z as "great talents and great businessmen" in a July, 2008 Rolling stone magazine article. It also addressed a recent Ludacris rap release, *Obama is Here*, annotated and partially reproduced below:

> Said **I handled his biz [supported Obama]** and I'm **one of his [Obama's] favorite rappers . . .**
> Hillary hated on you, so that **bitch** is irrelevant . . .
> Paint the White House black and I'm sure that's got **'em terrified [race baiting]**
> McCain don't belong in any chair unless he's **paralyzed**
> Yeah I said it cause Bush is **mentally handicapped**

Masterful ! In 50 words, Ludacris—Isn't he?—manages to malign women, the handicapped, the aged, and whites. So, along with the anarchist Lonnie Rashid Lynn, you can call me "Common," we have a second rap star, Ludacris, that Barack Obama can present as a favorite rapper and laudable role model for black children "coming up."

To be fair, however, the MSNBC posting did note that "Obama, usually a Ludacris fan, was quick to distance himself Thursday. 'While Ludacris is a talented individual, he should be ashamed of these lyrics,' Obama campaign spokesman Bill Burton said in an e-mail statement. He also called the song "outrageously offensive."

Here we find Barack Obama, the man who later would personally and publically speak out loud and proud in defense of both Wright and Gates, deferring to a "spokesman" to condemn what surely was race-inspired hate talk against Clinton and McCain. Should we expect any less of a double speak response from Barack, the master of Obamafuscation? It is perfectly consistent with Obama's dark-triad personality: using a "spokesperson" to implement a double speak strategy permitting Barack to benefit two ways: mollifying outraged whites and wink-winking at smirking black raceketeers, extremists, and racists.

MSNBC provided the smoking gun reference, a July 2008 Associated Press story concerning BET's "Cousin Jeff" Johnson of "Rap City" and "Jeff Johnson Chronicles." Jeff allegedly said that blacks and hip hop types know that Obama must play double speak word "**games**" [emphasis added . . ."for **political purposes**," [emphasis added] . . . and . . ."separate himself from anything controversially black." Johnson also referred to non-verbal codes, such as a shoulder brushing gesture, that were "**silent nods** [emphasis added] to the black community, and especially the hip-hop generation."

After all the black attention, emotion, and double speak devoted to the word "articulate," the award for hypocrite of the year, hands down, goes to African American and Assistant House Minority Leader James Clyburn, Democrat from South Carolina. At the time, the country was reeling from the horrific Tucson, Arizona attempted assassination of United States Representative Gabrielle Gifford, the wounding of 13 others, and the death of 6 more. Immediately, consistent with the "no crisis should go to waste" philosophy of Barack Obama's right-hand man, Rahm Emanuel, several democrats blamed Republicans for the massacre. Sara Palin, a central target, spoke out, defending herself. Clyburn, in turn, counterpunched with the "a-word," saying "You know, Sarah Palin just can't seem to get it, on any front. I think that she's an attractive person; she is articulate. But I think intellectually, she seems not to be able to understand what's going on here." So, unlike the innocuous way that the word usually is applied to blacks, James Clyburn unequivocally used "articulate" in a double speak, white-demeaning manner, calling Palin both articulate and stupid. I am not sure, but I think I heard Reverend Michael Eric Dyson applauding in the background.

If erudite words, such as "articulate" are so adroitly manipulated by raceketeers, one should not be surprised that vulgarity such as "nigger" would be seized upon with gusto as just the vehicle for lording it over white people. Take, for example, an episode of *The View* televised on July 17, 2008, right after broadcast of a recording in which Jesse Jackson had said he would like to cut Obama's nuts off because "Barack . . . he's talking down to black people . . . telling niggers how to behave." Whoopi Goldberg repeatedly used the word "nigger" in a back and forth with Elisabeth Hasselbeck, as the latter tried in vain to argue that that despicable word should never be used by anyone of any race. After being shouted down and frustrated by Goldberg, Hasselbeck broke into tears.

Was "breaking," humiliating, and intimidating the white Elisabeth Hasselbeck exactly what the black Whoopi Goldberg had intended? I don't know. I do know that many raceketeers use the word for just those purposes, as endorsed repeatedly during Todd Larkin's video documentary entitled, *The N Word*. Interestingly, in that very film, Whoopi claimed that never in her life had anyone used the epithet against her. And, in the same documentary, actor and reputed former Black Panther acolyte Samuel L. Jackson said this:

> I have to let people know that . . . I'm an actor, I'm a nice guy, and there are a lot of things that we can get along with. But the first thing you need to know about me is . . . I'm a nigger. And they look at me like, what? And I go. I'm not just, you know, a really nice colored fella. I'm a nigger. And they go, "What? Sam, I really don't understand".

> I'm one of those guys you really, really, really don't want to mess with. So . . . I've done things that, you know, people go to prison for, I guess, or, I'm really, you know, not gonna just punch you in the face. I'm going to do some niggerly shit to you [Big laugh from sweet Sam].

Let's try that again, imagining a hypothetical white actor whom I'll call Dewey Hatum.

> I have to let people know that . . . I'm an actor, I'm a nice guy, and there are a lot of things that we can get along with. But the first thing you need to know about me is . . . I'm a skin-head. And they look at me like, what? And I go. I'm not just, you know, a really nice white fella. I'm a skin-head. And they go, "What? Dewey, I really don't understand".

> I'm one of those guys you really, really, really don't want to mess
> with. So . . . I've done things that, you know, people go to prison
> for, I guess, or, I'm really, you know, not gonna just punch you in
> the face. I'm going to do some skin-head shit to you [Big laugh
> from Dewey].

How would black and white moviegoers react to Dewey? How would
American race monitors react? You know. No one would patronize
anything associated with Dewey. The movie industry would drum him
out of the business. Federal, state, and local law enforcement would launch
intensive investigations into Dewey Hatum's self-alleged crimes. Barack
Obama, Eric Himpton Holder, Jesse Jackson, Al Sharpton, the NAACP
and hundreds of others would appear on every media venue across the
nation; they would be on Hatum, as Marines used to say, "like stink on
shit."

Jackson's remarks once again lay bare the double standards, double speak,
and double binds of racial discourse in contemporary America. Here
is a black man with assets in the tens or hundreds of millions boasting
that he has committed race-based felonies. He does not worry about
being prosecuted because he knows that blacks can say such things with
impunity; whereas, if a white person said anything remotely like that,
the Justice Department immediately would launch an investigation. By
saying "the first thing you need to know about me is . . . I'm a nigger,"
Jackson not only tries to intimidate white people, but also lets them know
that he does not want to be judged by the content of his character, but by
the color of his skin. Finally, with his, "I'm really, you know, not gonna
just punch you in the face. I'm going to do some niggerly shit to you,"
he is double binding his white "friends" or "acquaintances" in that they
are unlikely even to want to discuss anything remotely race-oriented with
him. In essence, they are at the mercy of whatever he decides about them
racially. Maybe Eric H. Holder junior should do a how-to-facilitate "rap
on race" dialogue with Brother Jackson.

In part, because of role models such as Whoopi and Sam, use of the word
"nigger" is so pervasive that entering it into the Amazon.com book search
engine produced 2,640 titles during 2011. A recent non-fiction entitled
Nigger, written by Randall Kennedy, a black man, dedicates 208 pages to

tracing the origins and uses of the term. After meticulously considering the pros and cons, he concludes:

> Still, despite these costs, there is much to be gained by allowing people of all backgrounds to yank nigger away from white supremacists, to subvert its ugliest denotation, and to convert the N-word from a negative into a positive appellation. This process is already under way, led in the main by African American innovators who are taming, civilizing, and transmuting "the filthiest, dirtiest, nastiest word in the English language." For bad and for good, nigger is destined to remain with us for many years to come—a reminder of the ironies and dilemmas, the tragedies and glories, of the American experience.

To Kennedy I say, "masterful rationalization," enabling you to avoid the wrath of black raceketeers who never will surrender nigger as an offensive weapon. White supremacists don't need to use the word to spread their poison. The only white supremacists with any visibility capable of spreading significant racial hatred via the word nigger are the ones captured on dusty old newsreels. Randall and all Americans know who uses the word and why.

In the 1950s when America's city streets echoed with African American, American Irish, Italian, Jewish, Polish, Puerto Rican, Chinese and other accents, many people were super-sensitive to ethnicity. Then, slurs such as nigger, honky, pig-shit Irish, dago, kike, spic, and chink could be heard on a daily basis. As acculturation proceeded, however, all but one of those aspersions faded into the past. Why? Because no one had a vested interest in keeping them alive. Not so with the word nigger.

Instead of spending his time trolling the educational archives for historical information about the word nigger, Harvard Law School professor Randall Kennedy should have grabbed his pipe, a little Cherry Blend, and a footstool, and sank comfortably into his easy chair to watch *The View*. Whoopi and Elisabeth provided a naturalistic experiment into what the word nigger means today, and how it influences race relations. When the debate began, Hasselbeck no doubt was convinced that she could talk rationally with Whoopi; after all, they had been congenial colleagues for years and common sense seemed to support the notion that civilized people should speak respectfully. Whoopi, obviously, had other ideas.

Whoopi Goldberg, Samuel L. Jackson, and racketeers everywhere emerged victorious over Elisabeth Hasselbeck, since she disintegrated into tears. But the victory was pyrrhic. Whoopi taught Elisabeth a thing or two. She taught her the futility of a sympathetic white person's attempting to be reasonable with some black people about racial matters. Elisabeth learned firsthand about double standards and double speak. Elisabeth was backed into a double bind corner such that anything she said dragged her deeper into the mire. Whoopi framed her version of black reality and then demanded that Elisabeth "listen" to it. What Goldberg failed to recognize is that many thousands of white people usually supportive of blacks were not only listening but carefully watching. Hasselbeck and those whites learned that day to be, in Eric H. Holder junior's words, racial cowards, best served by avoiding interracial discourse and by letting blacks continue to rant their customary racial monologue.

Black on Black Identity Slavery

Black racketeers confidently tell white people how to act because they believe that they can speak for their "brothers and sisters." Despite regularly stating that "the black community is not monolithic," black identity slave masters regularly draw their authority from rigid, monolithic, uncompromising views that they impose regarding what it means to be authentically black. T.J. Holmes was toeing the color-line definition when he assessed Barack's "brotha" status via the "swagga" criterion.

Even the most powerful "black" men suffer disquiet when another black raises black identity issues. Consider how our insecurely half-black president handled the matter during the January 23, 2008 presidential campaign debate sponsored by CNN and the Congressional Black Caucus. When Joe Johns, an African American moderator, reminded Obama that Toni Morrison had called Bill Clinton America's first black president, Barack stammered, ultimately doing the kind of humor-disarming double speak advised by Saul Alinsky, saying "I would have ta, you know, investigate more, you know, ah Bill's dancing abilities and, you know ah, some of this other stuff before I accurately judged ah whether he was, in fact, a brother."

[The silver-tongued, supercool Barack sounded rather "inarticulate" and flustered in that black racial identity exchange.]

African American spokesman Al Sharpton and African American commentator Tavis Smiley apparently had not read Alinsky's *Rules for Radicals* book, for they did not use humor, but instead got down and dirty about racial identity on Sharpton's February 23, 2010 radio show. During that program, Smiley began by attempting to defend his agenda for black identity, but he was subjected to a withering black identity assault by Sharpton to which Tavis capitulated, sycophantically kowtowing several times to the extent that he literally and dutifully interjected his "love" for Sharpton. Tavis knew that big Al was in the racial identity driver's seat and that, for the moment, he had to go along for the ride. That Smiley allowed himself to be intimidated by Sharpton is all the more alarming when one considers that the previous year—April, 2009 to be exact—*Time* magazine chose Tavis as one of the one hundred most influential persons in the world (Rose, 2009).

Professional black men in the community sometimes suffer success guilt that renders them particularly vulnerable to bimp identity tutoring from the street. Consider John A. Rich M.D. who wrote an insightful, useful book entitled, *Wrong Place, Wrong Time*. Prompted by his experiences as an emergency room physician treating young black man gunshot and stab victims, Rich launched a series of interviews to better understand the whys and wherefores of the assaults. In the end, he reached the obvious conclusion that violence was not the "fault" of the victims so much as the result of systemic community failure, especially parenting failure.

Having begun his endeavor trying to inform about hostile behavior, however, Dr. Rich revealed that he, himself, received some tutoring in the fine art of bimp behavior. On the February 9, 2010 "Morning Edition with Steve Inskeep" radio show, Rich "confessed" that because he was raised by a dentist father and school teacher mother, his experience was "just different" from the experiences of his black patients. For that reason, the physician teamed up with Roy Martin, a black man who had served time in prison for gun violence. So far, so good. Reasonable to find someone to supplement one's own lack of knowledge or perspective. However, John Rich goes on to tell about learning bimp-oriented behavior such as "checking" someone, meaning to "aggressively correct him," if you believe he has disrespected you, such as, when Martin wanted to check a cook who he perceived was "preparing their food with a dirty spatula." (Was the spatula dirty? Who knows.) Rich mentioned that, "Roy turned to me and said, why didn't you cuss him out? And, I was, maybe at that moment, being more timid than I should have been. On the other hand, Roy's reaction was, you need to be really aggressive." Here we find the black physician accepting that he is too timid and needs to change, rather than the black ex-con accepting that he is too hostile and is the one who needs to change. Later in the conversation, Dr. Rich says,

> Well, in that same day, actually, a group of young men walked past us and Roy locked his eyes on them and watched them go past, and they did the same to him. And I said, what was that about? And Roy explained to me, you know, I have an eye problem—that is, when people look at me, I look right back at them and hold it to let them know that I'm not the one you mess with.

When Steve Inskeep made the obvious observation that "if kids want to stay out of trouble, they should stay out of trouble and maybe not stare at people on the street," John Rich did not straightforwardly acknowledge the apparent, commonsense wisdom contained within the advice, but instead, answered enigmatically. Rather than explicitly agreeing with the interviewer, the session ended with Rich stating, "And when people say to me, isn't it just a case of bad kids acting badly, I think it's an opportunity for us to educate them about these wounds of trauma and that by addressing the wounds of trauma, we can make a difference."

The ending struck me as more double speak than straight talk, more concern about not being seen as a white "collaborator" than a professional who must take the lead in decoupling black identity from bimp behavior. I could not help wonder whether Dr. John Rich's own fear of raceketeers, racial guilt, or insecure racialized identity—his own not-black-enough concerns—are standing in the way of his ability to say what needs to be said unambiguously to the young black men who are destroying their own lives and those of their black communities.

Of course, not all black men roll over when black raceketeers try to dictate how they should think and act. Ron Chrisite takes the offensive in his book *Acting White* in which he asserts that ". . . this racial slur [acting white] has become so entrenched that seemingly any African American who attains corporate success or political cachet becomes the target of black-on-black attack, accused of betraying his race in favor of 'white America'."

We all know, too, that one need not be either a corporate or political success to be mocked as acting white. For instance, Barry Obama did not hesitate to ridicule a not-stereotypically-black-enough African American fellow student at Occidental College when he wrote in *Dreams from My Father*:

> "Hey, guys," Tim had said, waving cheerfully. He turned to me. "Listen, Barry-do you have that assignment for Econ?" Tim was not a conscious brother. Tim wore argyle sweaters and pressed jeans and talked like Beaver Cleaver. He planned to major in business. His white girlfriend was probably waiting for him up in his room, listening to country music. He was happy as a clam, and I wanted nothing more than for him to go away. I got up, walked with him down the hall to my room, gave him the assignment he needed.
>
> As soon as I got back to Reggie's room [Reggie, of course, is black], I somehow felt obliged to explain "Tim's a trip, ain't he," I said, shaking my head. "Should change his name from Tim to Tom."

Barry, then soon to be Barack, did not comment on Tim's dancing abilities, but I bet he had an opinion about them. Obama made a special point of mocking Tim's Beaver Cleaver diction. As most Americans realize, Beaver Cleaver, of *Leave It to Beaver* fame, had represented the 1950s ideal of the white family and white personality. (Interesting that in *The Audacity of Hope*, the Beaver-obsessed Barack Obama used a *Leave It to Beaver* reference as an obvious compliment to the family of his wife, the Robinson family. Just more Barack double speak.) For Barack and racializers, Beaver is the goofy and phony white person, emblematic of the uncool, Caucasian buffoon. Just the kind of insult, they think, that can be used to embarrass any self-respecting black man into submission, into following the raceketeer-endorsed tough black man stereotype that they promulgate.

Equally revealing is that Barack managed to mention that Tim's "white girlfriend" was probably listening to "country music" as she waited for him to return. This was one more attempt to slander Tim by alluding to the stereotype that portrays "real" black men as mocking white sissified country music. The son of a black father and a white mother characterizes a black man dating a white woman as acting white. Obama, of course, would not stoop so low as to risk sullying his blood line by getting serious with a white woman, himself, for fear of causing his racist black grandfather to roll over in the grave. But Barack Obama claims he was tempted, at least once.

In *Dreams*, Barack relates an incident wherein he was talking to Auma, his Kenyan "half-sister," about romances when she mentioned how their shared "old man" had ruined his life. During the dialogue Barack interjected, "Well . . . there was a woman in New York that I loved. She was white. She had dark hair, and specks of green in her eyes. Her voice sounded like a wind chime. We saw each other for almost a year."

Some who have read Barack's story about this "woman in New York" regard it as pure fancy. They claim that none of Obama's friends at the time had ever met or even heard about the mystery woman. In any case, Barack described his breakup with wind chime voice, saying that it happened when he took her to a "very angry play, but very funny. Typical black American humor" during which "everybody was laughing and clapping and hollering like they were in church." When the play ended, wind chime complained that black people are consistently angry and that anger is unproductive. An argument ensued, wind chime cried, said she could not be black but only be herself, and the relationship apparently ended there

Phew! Close call. Lucky for Barack that his profoundly conflicted black racial identity conflict came to the fore, motivating him to successfully repulse the advances of wind chime voice. He had been able to intimidate his mother into renouncing her race, but not the mystery lady from New York. Had he gotten too serious with her, he might have been exposed to and poisoned by all manner of namby-pamby white habits. He might have wound up talking like Beaver Cleaver! He might have wound up listening to country music! Barack Obama, the first almost-black American president, never would have been elected had he stated acting white.

In fact, despite his relentless efforts to fulfill the rigid pro-black stereotype, as I noted earlier, the acting white aspersion has been directed toward Obama, himself, many times. During a "BookTV Afterwords" discussion, hosted by Janet Linehart Cohen, a multi-racial woman, Ron Christie, author of *Acting White: The Curious History of a Racial Slur*, reminded us that Jesse Jackson was one of those who had impugned Barack that way. Christie explained, too, that Malcolm X, an Obama raceketeer favorite, disparaged Martin Luther King junior as acting white. Moreover, Ron Christie cited multiple incidents during which he, himself, was excoriated for not adhering strictly enough to the identity slave master script of how a "real" black man must think, feel, and act. Most notably, Christie described his encounters with black, Southern California Congresswoman Maxine Waters.

First, a little recent history on Ms. Waters courtesy of Michelle Malkin, Asian American author and Creators Syndicate columnist with a national following. Under the heading, "Maxine Waters: Swamp Queen" on April 27, 2011, Malkin wrote:

> Confirmed: "Drain the swamp" is Washington-speak for "Let it fester." While House ethics watchdogs dither, it's shady business as usual for ethics scandal-plagued Democratic Rep. Maxine Waters.

> Last summer, the House Ethics Committee charged the entrenched California congresswoman with three violations related to her wheeling and dealing on behalf of minority-owned OneUnited Bank in Los Angeles. The panel accused Waters of bringing discredit to the House for using her influence to seek and secure taxpayer-subsidized special favors for the failing financial institution.

As he told it to Ms. Cohen, then, Mr. Christie met the "swamp queen" in 1991 when he was 22 years old and an intern/legislative aide for Tom Campbell, his local Congressman. At the first encounter, Maxine entered the Veteran Affairs Committee room in which Christie was sitting. According to him, shortly after that first, brief, serendipitous meeting and greeting, Waters called Ron Christie to her office, challenging why he would work for "Republicans" and accusing him of being an Uncle Tom. He said that was the first of a series of short uncomfortable interactions whose emotional tone never improved, including a time when Maxine chastised him for his service to George Bush and Dick Chaney. In recalling the event, Christie asked parenthetically, "Does it mean that you are inauthentically black if you are working for the President of the United States?"

Maxine Waters' efforts to intimidate Ron Christie represent the mere tip of a professional rackettering iceberg. Ninety percent of black-on-black racial identity intimidation is enacted far below the surface: in the most frigid, darkest depths of the sub-cultural sea, a region never penetrated by the light of day.

Let me be clear about one thing, however: I am not suggesting that one needs to be famous in order to be a race-based identity hit man, or to be in a formal one-down power hierarchy position to be a race-based identity scapegoat. Even black family members have been known to turn on each other for acting white. That is just what happened to a young black patient of mine.

Through extraordinary effort and self-sacrifice, schooling and hard work, Tanisha had fought her way out of Chester, Pennsylvania, one of the poorest, most crime-ridden small cities in our nation. She had a good, but not great, job, and she was lovingly and capably raising her children as a single mother. Sadly, when I met her, this courageous young woman had been battling a life-threatening illness for years. As a result, she expected to lose her employment and feared that her home would be next. While exploring her options with me, Tanisha maintained heroic emotional control until access to family support was mentioned. At that point, she disintegrated into heart-wrenching sobs, explaining that each time she had achieved a success, she became estranged from another family member until, finally, there was no one left with whom she spoke. She said that her family of origin, who remained in Chester, had developed the group conviction that Tanisha believed herself to be "better" than they, and they disparaged her as, "She thinks she's white." At that point in the narrative, Tanisha abruptly stopped crying, looked me straight in the eyes, and said, "I just want to do the right thing."

CHAPTER 6

From the Slavery of Servitude
to the Slavery of Attitude

So exhilarating to exert such total control over an entire race that you can tell them how "real" black people are—how to think, feel, and act. No wonder that there is no shortage of raceketeers. Black leaders choose to say that the black community is not monolithic when it suits their arguments, yet black demagogues are quick to Uncle Tom or acting-white any African American who opposes them. They drag out their not-black-enough mantra whenever convenient, but mostly when jealous or competitive of another African American. They imply: You better play the game according to my rules. Don't mess with me. I'll reduce you to a nobody—a non-black. Those who resort to racial shunning, in general, are the very persons who never question the racial identities of crotch holding, misogynistic, white hating rappers, but do not hesitate to disparage educated blacks, especially black professionals, as being racial counterfeits. Theirs is the most stereotyped of the racial stereotypes. Among the countless accomplished victims of the acting white and not black enough slanders are eminent persons such as entertainment star and philanthropist Bill Cosby, United States Secretaries of State Colin Powell and Condoleezza Rice, Supreme Court Justice Clarence Thomas, and United States Congressman from Oklahoma, J. C. Watts.

When black raceketeers turned their venom on Watts in an attempt to tutor him in the fine art of toeing their racial line, he did not hesitate to tell it like it is, calling the aggressors "race-hustling poverty pimps." You no doubt noticed that all the aforementioned targets except one had been Republicans. But don't think that Democrats are safe when black racial identity powerbrokers are on the prowl. Artur Davis, a black Representative from Alabama, the only Democrat audacious enough to resist a Congressional Black Caucus voting mandate, was chastised by Jesse Jackson who issued a blunt black identity smack down, saying "'You can't vote against healthcare and call yourself a black man."

Since powerful, high-profile African Americans are targeted by raceketeers, a working class man has little chance when he falls within their sights. That is what happened to black vendor Kenneth Gladney who in the spring of 2010 was distributing free "Don't Tread on Me" flags at Russ Carnahan's town hall in South St. Louis County at a pro healthcare rally when he was physically assaulted by two men. Presumably because Gladney was on the "wrong side" on the issue, he received no support from the NAACP, despite requesting it. Instead, the NAACP staged a press op against him in which a black official derided Gladney, saying

> Back in the day, we used to call someone like that, and I want to remind you, uh, when this incident occurred, I was really struck by a front page picture of this guy, which we called, a Negro, I mean that we call him a Negro in the fact that he works for not for our people but against our people. In the old days, we call him an Uncle Tom. I just gotta say that. Here it is, the day after a young brother, a young man, I didn't mean to call him a brother, but on the front page of the Post Dispatch, ironically, he's sitting in a wheelchair, being kissed on the forehead, by a European. Now just imagine that as a poster child picture, not working for our people.

There was a time when no American wanted to be stereotyped, but, as Michelle Obama's "You don't get any blacker than me" signifies, that time has passed. Her statement also attests that, like her husband and the NAACP official quoted above, she holds rigidly dichotomized good-bad racial stereotypes. Since Michelle undoubtedly perceives herself as elite, she must feel entitled to determine the stereotype—to decree who is and who is not authentically black.

African American Larry Elder, radio commentator and author, quotes Debra J. Dickerson, African American Salon columnist and author, regarding black racial identity mind control that she resisted when a member of the Harvard Law School Black Law Students Association (BLS) as follows:

> When I joined the BLSA . . . I found an air of perpetual grievance and mindless opposition that often struck me as a pose . . . You'd have thought blacks were still hanging from trees the way some of the BSLA members carried on. Worst of all, to disagree was to bring down the wrath of the BSLA in-crowd. Was I supposed to stand up to whites, but let blacks jerk me around? To be sure, most blacks sat silently at BLSA meetings; it was impossible to know what they were thinking. They weren't the problem. The BSLA politburo, the blackest of the black, were the ones who did most of the talking.

In this case, at least, Debra Dickerson had the grit and guts to resist black identity slave masters and to be her own person. On the other hand, in a January 22, 2007 *Salon* article subtitled, "Barack Obama would be the great black hope in the next presidential race—if he were actually black," she sang her own not-black-enough song about Obama and wrote her own racializing anthem:

> To say that Obama isn't black is merely to say that, by virtue of his white American mom and his Kenyan dad who abandoned both him and America, he is an American of African immigrant extraction.

Dickerson went on to say that while Barack is not authentically African American, "Obama, with his non-black ass, is doing us all a favor" by his political prominence.

Four years after the above quoted article, Ms. Dickerson vented about racial identity again—this time for the *Atlantic Monthly*, January-February, 2011—amounting to a blistering indictment of the financial crisis and of Barack Obama's hypocritical role in it. She seemed especially incensed with his failure to identify with struggling African Americans, as implied by her using the term, "homey," roughly meaning, "my hometown black brother."

Classless society my aunt Fanny. What we have here in this country can only be described as a plutocracy: entitled, incompetent, untouchable, and bankrupting us peons with its decadence. I'd like to hear you talk about that, Mr. President, because the feeble "deficit of trust" line in your last State of the Union address didn't go very far. Name some names, homey.

Once again, we see how real African Americans express their ambivalent acceptance of Obama's not-quite authentic African American identity, continually reminding Barack that he must prove himself. Having been a combatant in a racial identity guerilla war at least since adolescence, there is no reason to expect that a truce will be declared for Obama. That is why everything the racial identity obsessed president says and does must pass through his racial identity filter, and why he never will be able to govern in a manner that promotes the welfare of our entire nation in a colorblind manner.

What qualities do the black elite consider when they judge another African American on the elitist blackometer? In addition to Barack Obama's dancing criterion, one would expect T. J. Holmes' swagga, and, perhaps, love of NBA basketball to be defining characteristics of who is and is not racially pure. Whatever the black slave masters decide, their intention is to promote a stereotype in their own image and likeness. If they like something, it has to be genuine black.

To stereotype a person racially is to frame that person as an appendage of a racial group, not as an individual. Those who set racial standards are those who control the community. Accordingly, each everyday black person who succumbs to their black identity slave master develops an external racial locus of control in which black individuals must look outside themselves to be told how to think, feel, and act. The person cannot be spontaneous. He needs experts to advise him about what genuine black behavior is in any new situation, and he needs experts to continually update him about the black behavior de jour.

First-tier racial identity slave masters are ones who succeed not only in lording it over other blacks, but also in selling their "positive" black stereotype to the white community. Many white people are eager consumers of these stereotypes. We already have mentioned Kyra Phillips, T.J. Holmes' newscaster partner, who quivered with delight when he tutored her about black identity. And if you excuse Kyra as young and foolish, consider Cokie Roberts, the not-so-grand dame of ABC's *This Week with George Stephanopolis,* who, in 2008, when talking about strategies the presidential candidates could adopt for choosing a vice presidential running mate cackled, "Look. Obama's in a much happier position here. All he really has to do for vice president is to pick a boring white guy and there are tons of them. They're everywhere." Cokie showed that she not only had bought into the "hip black guy" stereotype, a favorite of black identity slave masters everywhere, but also combined it with the liberal, feminist, upper-crust gero-blanco-misandrogenistic attitude that regards older white men as angry, vapid anachronisms. Was she also implying something about her staid, boring white columnist husband, Steven V. Roberts?

How about Michael Moore, another raceketeer of the first order. His 2001 book, *Stupid White Men,* believe it or not, was not autobiographic, but evangelistic. It did include an inane thirty page chapter entitled, "Kill Whitey" in which he blamed whites for every social transgression since expulsion from the Garden of Eden while excusing and exalting everything black. Was the manuscript a not-so-indirect expression of fully justified self-loathing presented by a white man with the girth and grace of a lumbering, landlocked walrus?

Racial Stereotypes:
The Negative of the Positive

In America, everybody wants to be hip, cool, and swaggaing. What's wrong with promoting a "positive" black stereotype? Black can feel special. Vulnerable whites can soothe their racial self hatred and raise their righteousness quotient by embracing and celebrating pro-black identity dimensions blessed by racial identity slave masters. A favorite raceketeering strategy is first to talk about historical injustices suffered by blacks and about past negative black stereotypes as counterpoints to justify and to advocate for current positive black identity stereotypes.

"Racial profiling" is proffered as ipso facto proof of white racism's unfair negative black stereotypes. As the argument goes, no one could fail to recognize the explicit bias of policemen who stop more black than white automobile drivers, a notion sarcastically dubbed as, "driving while black." On the other hand, the evangelists who crusade against racial profiling fail to see that "affirmative action" is nothing less than racial profiling. One obvious difference between racial profiling and affirmative action is that the former has a negative black outcome and the latter, a positive black outcome. Purely on the basis of skin color, blacks are treated poorly with racial profiling and given preferential treatment with affirmative action. Another obvious difference is that driving while black stops can be explained by the principle of parsimony; given that a relatively greater percentage of blacks are incarcerated for crimes and a relatively greater percentage of blacks injure or kill police, police should proceed accordingly.

Racial profiling and affirmative action also differ on another fundamental level. Whereas the negative racism of racial profiling harms blacks, it does not really improve any situation for whites. By contrast, the positive racism of affirmative action helps blacks precisely by harming whites, since educational and employment opportunity is, in fact, a zero sum game that we will discuss later. For instance, both the public and private sectors provide a very limited number of desirable educational and employment positions. To make skin color a major determinant of selection is to make a mockery of the very notion of equal opportunity. More fundamentally, the racial profiling versus affirmative action issue lays bare a pervasive race-based bias favoring blacks that I call "positive racism".

It does not take a Ph.D. in psychology to realize, however, that one group, in this case the raceketeering black group, ballyhooing positive racial advocacy or stereotypes encourages racializing and stereotyping of all kinds across the entire racial continuum. For every action there is an equal and opposite reaction—reciprocal racializing or reciprocal racism. Positive black racial advocacy and stereotyping encourages racial filtering of human behavior and prompts other races to react defensively. The fact is so transparently true that in *The Audacity of Hope* Barack Obama wrote about it by citing an interaction he had had with a white, liberal, Democrat Illinois Senate colleague. On that occasion, when a black member was ranting that the elimination of his favored program would be racist, the white, liberal colleague leaned over to Barack saying "You know what the problem is with John? Whenever I hear him, he makes me feel more white."

Despite the obviousness of the points made above, exaltation of "positive" black advocacy and of the "positive" black stereotype circulates through American society. Popular media, especially, is inclined to pander to contemporary slave masters of black identity. There is a subculture of black and white opportunists ready, willing, and able to seize upon the latest edition of real blackness to raise their own power, prestige, and wealth. The advertising industry knows that promoting the sanctioned black identity greatly improves their chance to be noticed by the approximately 12 percent black demographic in our country and by large swaths of pandering white Americans who need to prove how accepting they are of African Americans. Anyone with two eyes readily will notice the racial double standards rife in television commercials whenever blacks and non-blacks, especially whites, occur in the same advertisement. Invariably, the white person is portrayed in a one-down position—as daft, depraved, or degenerate. Just what poses as a positive black stereotype and how non-blacks are put in their places are dictated by whatever commanding officer raceketeers are pushing at any given point in time.

Volumes could be written on this subject, but I will limit myself to four examples, merely to make my point. Consider a classic racist Snickers candy bar commercial involving Mr. T., so egregious that it was precipitously removed from circulation. In the 2008 ad, Mr. T literally crashes his car completely through a house, drives beside an exercising white man, and yells, "Speed walking. I pity you fool. You are a disgrace to the man race. It's time to run like a real man." T then rips out a machine gun and starts shooting at the white walker with Snickers projectiles. In the last frame, the self-satisfied black shooter gloats and the Stickers slogan "Get some nuts" appears on the screen. Black slave master-endorsed black identity stereotype: black men are so damn tough.

In a United States Post office commercial about mailing packages that circulated in June 2009, a chubby, nerdish white man stands on a scale holding a box to be mailed. The implication of this scene is that the fat man had been weighed earlier and that his original weight will be subtracted from his weight while holding the box to determine the cost of postage. At the white man's left side, in a controlling position, is a normal-looking black man and to the right is a white woman, serving as a prop. The overweight white nebbish pleads, "This is humiliating!" while the black man commands, "Stand still!" Black slave master-endorsed black identity stereotype: black men are in charge.

Since the pro-black stereotype has to assert African American dominance over people of all colors, a 2009 Southwest Airlines commercial provides an eastern touch. Here an Asian man asks a black woman to dance and she replies, "Show me what you got." At that point, the Asian explodes into a few deft dance steps. However, within seconds he loses control, crashes into the band's percussion section, stands up, and looks sheepishly into the camera. Black slave master-endorsed black identity stereotype: Only black men can dance.

Finally, a coup de grâce commercial that completes our look at positive black stereotypes. This little number premiered in 2008 under the auspices of hotels.com. It showed an enormous black man ensconced in a white tub with bubble-bath-like bubbles coating him. At the foot on the tub are two kneeling men—one white and one Asian. The white and Asian men are leaning over the tub at the feet-end of the naked black man, and they are blowing into the water through straws, thus explaining all the bubbles. The black guy literally looks down on the two blowers and says, "But this doesn't guarantee that you will get a deal," apparently meaning that their effort at "blowing" him is insufficient, at which point both begin to blow furiously faster and harder. Then the White guy coughs, apparently having aspirated some of the filthy bath water.

The frequently televised commercial struck me as so extraordinarily bizarre and so demeaning that I felt compelled to search for its genesis. I found my answer at urbandictionary.com that identified a practice called "ballcuzzi." The top two citations under the item were:

> 1) Place your nuts in a bowl of warm water. Then have a girl put
> a straw into the bowl and blow bubbles under your balls. Rubber
> ducky is optional of course.

2) When a male or something with nuts submerges their testicles into a cup of warm water while their partner blows profusely through a straw that has been inserted into the cup creating a Jacuzzi affect.

Given the apparent roots of the hotels.com commercial, this ad wins the prize for the most crude, degenerate race-based item ever to appear on conventional television. Black slave master-endorsed black identity stereotype: black men are destined to rule the world—subjugating, demeaning, and emasculating whites, Asians, and all other varieties of men everywhere. How long would the commercial have been aired if the man in the tub had been white and the Asian's blower partner had been black?

Racing toward a Dead End

The black identity slave master's attempts to promulgate what he regards as positive or race-enhancing stereotypes is merely a specific instance of self-interest in the guise of general raceketeering chauvinism. To solidify his own position and justify his own existence, a raceketeer must keep the black community race-preoccupied and race-discontented. He tries to convince "his" people that he, and only he, knows how to promote African American welfare and to keep whitey at bay. Relentlessly focusing attention on race, the charlatan superficially appeals to black pride and black fear when he truly seeks only to enhance his own power, prestige, and profit.

Any and all issues are candidates for raceketeer manipulation. Problems or failures by any black at any time must be attributed directly to white racism. The higher profile the affected person or issue, the better. All Americans are aware of, and many of us joke about, how raceketeers predictably burst on the scene: first responders claiming, underscoring, and advertising that the extant black problem is a direct result of current "white racism," and tying to it every other racial incident since our Paleolithic ancestors swaggaed out of Africa. (Interesting, isn't it, that most of those race mongers are quick to assert that the children of illegal aliens should not suffer due to the misconduct of their parents, but that all white people should be blamed for offenses committed by Caucasian ancestors or non-ancestors with whom they share nothing more than skin color.)

Since long before he cast his first "present" vote, Barack Hussein Obama, political superhero and raceketeer extraordinaire, has had legions of advisers cautioning him against foolhardy racialisms. He knows that he should heed their warnings and he wants to, God bless him. Barack knows that he wins elections not on his accomplishment but due to his awe-inspiring double speak. Taking an obviously racial position can be so disturbingly transparent, so hard to talk your way out of. Unfortunately, the racial identity repetition compulsion can be overwhelming. You recall how Obama stepped right into it concerning the July 16, 2009 Henry Louis Gates junior fiasco. How could Barack resist? On one side, a nobody white policeman; a white cop has got to be racist times two. On the other side, Obama's buddy, Henry, a man nationally recognized as having spent much of his life ferreting out all real and imaginary black slights by whites, by policemen, and by white policemen.

The black and liberal communities were watching; their future political support of our first almost-black president could have been on the line. Barack had been called acting white, not-black-enough, and an Uncle Tom in the past, but not this time! Barack not only asserted that the white policeman "acted stupidly" in answering a citizen call about a possible house break-in, but, true to his racial identity conflict, he insinuated himself personally into the highly racialized event, saying that if he, himself, were profiled "as a black man," he would be shot trying to enter his own home, the White House. Now that statement certainly should have pleased race mongers everywhere!

In contrast to the Gates controversy, Barack Obama did manage to refrain from any personal involvement in the New Black Panther Party (NBPP) voter intimidation case. No righteous indignation when in 2008 at a polling place in a predominately black Philadelphia neighborhood, threats of violence were being leveled **in support of Obama's election to the presidency.** Barack's racial identity repetition compulsion demon did not stir; it snored contentedly. After all, doesn't the historical record indicate that prior to the Voting Rights Act, some white people had denied voting rights to some blacks, and that some had used voter intimidation?

Besides, there are so many more whites than blacks in America; a few disenfranchised Caucasians would not materially affect the outcome of any election. Obama could pass on this "trivial" incident of race-based voting-oriented threat. Blasé Barack was the same Barack Obama who on July 20, 2006 stridently spoke out in the Senate saying, "Mr. President, I rise today, both humbled and honored by the opportunity to express my support for renewal of the expiring provisions of the Voting Rights Act of 1965 . . . We need to make sure that **minority** [emphasis added] voters are not the subject of deplorable intimidation tactics when they do get to the polls."

Barack perhaps felt that he could count on his black attorney general, Eric Holder junior to "do the right thing" by white voters. After all, as the nation's chief law enforcement officer, Holder did have responsibility for the NBPP voter intimidation "issue." Unfortunately, although the stalwart of racial justice enthusiastically has embraced his United States Justice Department duty to defend the rights of "all people-of-color," regardless of color, with white people, not so much.

On July 8, 2010, Deroy Murdock, an African American journalist who, like most African Americans, is clear-eyed and courageous enough to recognize the reality of racial oppression even when whites are the victims and blacks are the aggressors, reported in the *Washington Times* that voters on Fairmont Street in Philadelphia had been intimidated at their voting precinct. Two New Black Panther Party members, outfitted in military garb and one "wielding a 2-foot-long night stick" had planted themselves less than fifteen feet from the poll. According to Murdock, from time to time, one or both confronted whites with racist remarks such as, "Cracker, you are about to be ruled by a black man," or racist slurs, such referring to them as "white devils." The panthers also disparaged an African American couple who had come as poll watchers, calling them traitors to their race. Amplifying on the latter intimidation, Delroy Murdock said,

> At an April 23, 2010, Civil Rights Commission hearing, Chris Hill, an eyewitness, explained under oath that he spoke with the male Republican poll watcher inside the precinct. "He was definitely shook up," Mr. Hill testified. "And he told me that he was called a race traitor by [King Samir Shabazz] and that he was

threatened if he stepped outside of the building, there would be hell to pay."

Murdock concluded his report by saying that after federal prosecutors successfully litigated the New Black Panther incident against King Samir Shabazz, Jerry Jackson, and another actor, Malik Zulu Shabazz, Barack Obama's Justice Department political appointees overruled, dismissing all charges except one against King Samir Shabazz. The one conviction that they let stand was that "King" should not brandish a weapon at a Philadelphia poll, the restriction being in force until November 15, 2012. Are we to assume that he is permitted to use weapons of intimidation after that date?

We should not be surprised that the racially obsessed and black preoccupied, dark-triad President Barack Hussein Obama and his lackey, Attorney General, Eric Himpton Holder, would not vigorously enforce the voting rights of whites. The situation is just one more example of how Obama's personality psychopathology literally has colored his presidency.

Fortunately, the NBPP intimidation case was so blatant a malfeasance that some white officials felt compelled to stand-up. J. Christian Adams, a trial attorney for the voting section of the Department of Justice, resigned from his position to protest the way the case had been mishandled by Obama's "Justice" Department. He had been particularly offended by being ordered to ignore a Civil Rights Commission subpoena to testify.

Christopher Coates, head of the voting section of the Department of Justice's Civil Rights Division (CRD) and initial lead investigator of NBPP case, did appear before the commission on September 24, 2010. At the hearing, he testified under oath, "I had people who told me point-blank that [they] didn't come to the voting rights section to sue African American people." Coates did not equivocate in his condemnation of the Obama-Holder hypocrisy, double standards, and double speak approach to equal justice under the law. Coates reminded the committee that prior to 2006 the CRD never had filed even a single case under the Voting Rights Act that litigated black responsibility for discrimination against white voters.

The 2006 case in question, United States vs. Ike Brown and Noxubee County, was successfully adjudicated in favor of the white voters on August 27, 2007, but only after relentless and intense opposition by career personnel within the Voting rights section of the CRD, opposition that continued even after the case was closed. Coates said that the chief of the CRD complained to him that the Ike Brown decision had been opposed by black civil rights organizations and that the opinion had caused "problems" in the relationship between the division and black civil rights advocacy groups. Loretta King, an African American woman who had been appointed by Obama as Acting Assistant to the Attorney General for Civil rights, that is, as assistant to Eric Holder, told Coates that she did not support equal enforcement of the Voting rights Act, and she criticized the filing and prosecution of Ike Brown. Coates contended that animosity toward the Ike Brown decision among career and executive CRD personnel, along with pressure from the Legal Defense Fund of the NAACP, a group "close to the Obama Administration's management team, resulted in "gutting" the case against the NBPP. Coates' essential message was:

> It is my opinion that this disposition of the NBPP case was ordered because the people calling the shots in May, 2009 were angry at the filing of the Ike Brown case. The anger was the result of a deep-seated opposition to the equal enforcement of the VRA [Voting Rights Act] against racial minorities and for the protection of whites who have been discriminated against.

As I repeatedly have shown thus far, there always are black people with the fortitude to oppose racial double standards and the Ike Brown and NBPP cases were no exceptions. Coates mentioned that when he was having trouble finding professionals willing to participate in both cases, "A young African American who worked in the Voting Section paralegal" volunteered to do so. You will not be shocked to know that the volunteer and his mother who also worked at CDR were "harassed" by a CDR attorney, administrative assistant, and a paralegal co-worker. Can you say, "Uncle Tom?"

Voting rights is the heart and soul of our democracy, but sports are America's passion, and sports had played a leading role in tearing down racist barriers to black opportunity. Today, approximately 78 % of the National Basketball Association players are black, whereas the 2010 U.S. Census reports that the African American population comprises about 12.4% of our nation. [We will return to this issue later.] For 2009-10, the average NBA player yearly salary earns about 5.5 million dollars, and LeBron James allegedly rakes in 14.41 million for the season.

Basketball, then, is a bastion of black privilege? Is this a self-evident fact that that even a raceketeer must acknowledge? Not so fast! Enter Jesse Jackson, nutcracker sweet, who in July 2010 played the basketball race card. (Jesse, can you believe it?) Jackson excoriated Cleveland Cavaliers owner Dan Gilbert for referring to James as "disloyal" and "a coward" when the superstar took the A-Train to Miami. Jesse indicted Gilbert as treating LeBron as something that he owned, somebody in plantation servitude, and a "runaway slave." Jackson would be just a laughable, absurd man, if he were not so pathetic. He is half-living proof that when a person thinks only about race, all he sees is race.

Not to be outdone by basketball, football "stepped-up," proving that it has racketeers who can run with the best of them. On the cusp of spring 2011, the National Football League Players Association and the league owners were embroiled in a do or die power struggle. Emotions ran high, just the stimulus for instigating a little slave trade talk. Adrian Peterson of the Minnesota Vikings took the field on offense, claiming that the owners were treating the penurious players of the nation's favorite, second favorite, or third favorite pastime in a manner that indicated, "It's modern-day slavery, you know?" Of course, that got attention. Steven Smith's March 15, 2011 post referenced Doug Farrar, a white man, from Yahoo Sports:

> Peterson's remarks were later removed from the Yahoo! Sports post. The interviewer, Doug Farrar, said he believed that Peterson did not literally mean to compare the NFL's contentious labor dispute with the institution of slavery.

Scrubbing that inconvenient remark from his website revealed Farrar's wise discretion. He was not about to be associated with the racist comment, probably for fear of somehow being scapegoated as a racist, himself. So, a white man who had nothing to do with making the slavery remark felt so nervous about it that he was compelled to cover for the black man who, in fact, had made it: the doubles by proxy.

Steven Smith's post also proved an assertion that I had made previously when I said that there always is a brave black person or two who recognizes the doubles game and who often speaks up. In this case, the man was "Ryan Grant of the Packers [who] tweeted that he 'totally' disagreed with the comments, adding that there is 'actually still slavery existing in our world. Literal modern day slavery. That was a very misinformed statement.'"

And, oh by the way, nbcsports.msnbc.com on January 22, 2011 noted that "Incentives and escalators have pushed [26-year-old] Adrian Peterson's 2011 base salary to $10.2 million." Slavery never paid so well.

After the aforementioned two stories, I suppose we all could use a good laugh, so here are two compensatory, counterbalancing anecdotes for comic relief: first one from television.

On July 27, 2006, comedian Stephen Colbert traveled to the Washington office of Eleanor Holmes Norton, D.C. representative, who then had been in the position for eight terms, to interview her for his "Better Know a District" segment of The Colbert Report. The prickly, uptight representative scowled from the "get go," as they say in the hood, and remained feisty throughout the entire session. But Norton bared her fangs and spat her deadliest venom whenever she perceived, or misperceived, a race-oriented issue.

For many years, Washingtonians had been lobbying for state-equivalency in that they wanted to be granted two U.S. senators. In his characteristic fashion, Colbert started ribbing Norton about D.C. not being a state. He then asked whether Eleanor had been born "in the district' to which she replied, "Born right here." Colbert rejoined, "Then you can never be president . . . Because you have to be born in the United States." That was all the honorable rep needed; voice drooling with acidic scorn, she commenced challenging Stephen Colbert's background with questions like, "Where did your ancestors come from?" After the representative mocked his French ancestry, Stephen deftly sidestepped the marauding Norton, asking about her involvement in supporting minority hiring for federal jobs. When she gave her opinion, Colbert replied that he does not see "color" when he looks at people, a comment that, obviously, offended the race-preoccupied representative. Launching her attack like a bat out of hell, she spat, "You don't see my color? I'm black!!" Following a short-lived sparring match, during which Colbert added that he, also, has defective "gaydar," he spoofed his own sexuality. Continuing with the subject of gender, Stephen acknowledged that Eleanor Holmes Norton had helped write the Carter Administration's sexual harassment guidelines, followed by the tongue-in-check question, "Then why are you undressing me with your eyes, congresswoman?" Once again, Norton's blood began boiling, and, when a raceketeer's emotions are stoked, racialized thoughts are not far behind. She told Colbert that he flattered himself, that she merely saw him as a "plain vanilla man" to which he quipped, "French vanilla." Like ex-Mayor Ray Chocolate-City Nagin, Representative Holmes cannot even think about food without dichotomizing it along color lines.

Actually, as the counterpart to vanilla, the thinly veiled euphemistic code word "chocolate" has extraordinary appeal for black raceketeers; in a racist context, chocolate has a superficially sweet, innocuous connotation. But, like unadulterated chocolate itself, the word has extraordinarily bitter implications. The racist use of "chocolate," in fact, is rancid, repugnant, and recondite, amounting to little more than doubles inter-racial communication. Those who speak in a chocolaty, racialized way think in a chocolaty, racialized way and vice versa, resulting in an alienating, negative spiral. Moreover, the racialized talk of prominent persons percolates throughout our culture, promoting and reinforcing racialized attitudes in the general population. Persons with less intelligence, less education, and less emotional and behavioral control incorporate their leaders' superficially innocuous remarks into their own compromised personalities, frequently acting out in ways harmful to themselves and to their communities.

Ray Nagin's genteel term, "chocolate," also was included in an episode described by Larry Elder with regard to Natalie Hopkinson, an African American reporter for the Washington Times. Elder explained that when Hopkinson had purchased an expensive home in a mostly black section of Washington, she was rabidly defensive about the racial character of the area. He quoted her as saying:

> We damn sure are not about to let white folks buy up all the property in D.C. . . . Many whites want to help out, too, [presumably meaning that whites could help revitalize Washington as a whole rather than her new neighborhood] and their privileged status can only improve the city's prospects. But this is a Chocolate City.

Natalie Hopkinson went on say, "Segregation now! Segregation tomorrow! Segregation forever!" Oh, sorry! That was not Natalie. That was George Wallace, Alabama 1962.

As ridiculous as the Colbert television show and the vanilla and chocolate issues are, nothing can compare to the following incident from the world of publishing.

Graduation 2010. Time to care enough to send the very best. Hallmark greeting card corporation cites their slogan as their creed. Good try Hallmark, but apparently not good enough in Culver City, California, population about 39,000. A "you made it" graduation card mentioning "black holes" that for the previous three years had been suitable for mailing to young ones standing at the threshold of their future finally is exposed for the racist propaganda that it is. Just in time, members of the Los Angeles NAACP discover that the "talking" greeting card, intended to be humorous, actually is an intolerable racial slander. In one part of the message, the race police hear, "And you black hoes, you are so ominous. Watch your back." Leon Jenkins saw through the not so thinly disguised white code talk, saying "That was very demeaning to African American women. When it made reference to African American women as whores and at the end, it says 'watch your back.'"

Naturally, the local television station just had cover this story, calling Hallmark who claimed that the card had been intended to emphasize graduates' power to conqueror the universe, including black holes. Miriam Hernandez on March 10, 2011, reporting for KABC7 Eyewitness News, said that the NAACP members, nevertheless, remained adamant in their opposition. She explained as follows:

> "The intent here is to say that this graduate is not afraid of anything," explained Hallmark spokesman Steve Doyal.

But that's not what some people heard.

"You hear the 'r' in there. 'Whores,' not, 'holes.' The 'r' is in there," said Minnie Hatley of the Los Angeles NAACP.

Hallmark sent Eyewitness News a transcript of what the card says, but Hatley says that the actual audio raises questions.

"It sounds like a group of children laughing and joking about blackness, again," said another NAACP member.

Hallmark is now notifying all of its stores to pull the card. Walgreens and CVS are doing the same.

"In any situation where there is a circumstance that we need to be sensitive to, we try to learn from that experience," said Doyal.

However, NAACP members say they do not want to see the card on store shelves ever again.

Michael Eric Dyson undoubtedly knows about the black holes/black hoes incident. He can point to Hallmark as one more racist organization, one more example of devious white folks' white "code talk," and one more justification for him and other raceketeers to continue to promulgate retaliatory racial double standards, double speak, and double binds.

For Every Action There Is an Equal and Opposite Reaction

How do raceketeers market their doubles so widely and so effectively? We already have talked about institutionalized race schism that organizes and promotes black social groups insulated from white America. But racketeers know that a mind is a terrible thing to waste, so they indoctrinate their children early and often for fear of creating a world in which people are judged by the content of their character rather than by the color of their skin. Recruiting and training as many acolytes as possible, and using the black label as an inducement is job one. Educational institutions of all types promote formal and informal black "studies" from kindergarten through graduate school. Consider course offering within the Department of Black Studies, University of California Santa Barbara listed below:

LOWER DIVISION
1. Introduction to Afro-American Studies
1H. Introduction to Afro-American Studies—Honors
3. Introduction to African Studies
4. Critical Introduction to Race and Racism
5. Blacks and Western Civilization
6. The Civil Rights Movement
7. Introduction to Caribbean Studies
14. The History of Jazz
15. The Psychology of Blacks
33. Major Works of African Literatures
36. Afro-American Oral Traditions
38A. Introduction to Afro-American Literature (Part I)
38AH. Seminar on African American Literature (Part 1)
38B. Introduction to Afro-American Literature (Part II)
38BH. Seminar on African American Literature (Part II)
45. Black Arts Expressions
49A. Survey of African History
49B. Survey of African History
50. Blacks in the Media
55. Race and Space
58. Education and Inequality
60A. Survey of Afro-American Religious Traditions
60B. Religion in Black America (Part II)
90. Sophomore Seminar

UPPER DIVISION
100. Africa and United States Policy
102. Black Radicals and the Radical Tradition
103. The Politics of Black Liberation The Sixties
104. Black Marxism
106. Women and Politics of the Body
118. Comparative Rebellion
122. The Education of Black Children
124. Housing, Inheritance, and Race

125. Queer Black Studies
126. Comparative Black Literatures
127. Black Women Writers
128. The Black Experience in Southern California
129. The Urban Dilemma
130A. Negritude and African Literature
130B. French African Literature
131. Race and Public Policy
133. Gender and Sexuality in Black Studies
134. African American Language and Culture
136. Black Feminist Thought
138. African Religions in the Americas
142. Music in Afro-American Cultures: U.S.A.
152. Music of the African Diaspora
153. Black Popular Music in America
160. Analyses of Racism and Social Policy in the United States
161. "Third World" Cinema
162. African Cinema
169AR. Afro-American History
169BR. Afro-American History
169CR. Afro-American History
170. Afro-Americans in the American Cinema
171. Africa in Film
172. Contemporary Black Cinema
174. Plantations to Prisons
190. Senior Seminar in Black Studies
191. Senior Seminar in Black Studies
192. Community Studies and Outreach Initiatives
193. Seminars In Black Studies.
195A-B-C. Honors Thesis Seminar in Black Studies
197. Research Seminar
198. Readings In Black Studies
199. Independent Studies in Black Studies
199RA. Independent Research Assistance in Black Studies
GRADUATE COURSES
206. Graduate Proseminar
501. Teaching Methodology in Black Studies
596. Directed Reading and Research

What does one do with a Black Studies major, other than continuing racketeer propaganda and racketeer recruitment? Maybe the overemphasis on Black Studies is one reason that of the four African Americans to date who have won Nobel Prizes, one has been for Literature (Toni Morrison, 1993) and the other three were for Peace (Ralph Bunche, 1950; Martin Luther King junior, 1964; and Barack Obama, 2009). Given the bogus, disingenuous nature of Barack's award, we probably should only consider three prizes to have been given, so not to cheapen the genuine achievements of the other three black recipients. I have no doubt that African Americans are capable of winning Nobel Prizes in physics, chemistry, physiology or medicine, and economics. They merely need an environment free of racialized distractions to generate increased African American interest in science and other race-neutral avenues of endeavor.

The Black Studies movement in its myriad forms apparently is insufficient to satisfy the racialization power lust of racketeers. A rather meager number of non-blacks submit themselves to the Black Studies indoctrination process. Because the twelve percent that comprises the African American U.S. population does not always provide them a strong enough power base, racketeers sometimes need an additional strategy to work their black magic. Divide and conquer works well.

A little double speak goes a long way. What if racketeers focus exclusively on black people when there is an advantage to framing things that way? You know, sufficient numbers, votes, laws, financial contributions to issues that race mongers see as favoring African Americans. When any of the aforementioned resources are lacking, however, talk not about black versus white but "people-of-color" versus white. A stroke of genius, worthy of a Nobel Prize nomination in non-science, people-of-color means everybody in the world except white people. You know, all but the colorless people. If the people-of-color tactic doesn't work, nothing will.

We will return to the concept people-of-color later but, for now, consider that regardless of the contempt with which they hold "white folks," black racketeering Americans know that, at least for the present, the United States still is a white majority country. Maybe a little guilt will help to seduce some colorless ones to jump on the black bandwagon. Accordingly, as Whoopie Goldberg et al. prove, no self-respecting black racketeer ever hesitates to remind whites either of extant racism or the "legacy of racism." Schooled in Black Studies and all things racial, racializers can take one back to the dawn of time, enumerating each and every insult and cruelty that whites have ever committed against blacks or any person-of-color. It's as if white people invented brutality and slavery.

CHAPTER 7

Racial Atrocities: Equal Opportunity Abominations

We all learned early about the slave trade and white racism; in fact, we have heard about them in one way or another virtually every day of our lives. Admittedly, the fact that we have heard about it so much does not in any way mitigate the inhumanity of what happened to black people. I will neither attempt my own version of double speak to minimize what had occurred in America, nor claim that we currently live in a "post racial society." I do, of course, have an agenda here that will be transparently clear in a moment.

Slavery and Racial Cruelty

I am no historian, but I do know that the Egyptians of Africa, one of humanity's oldest societies, pioneered slavery. The Hebrew bible documents the Israelis' Egyptian enslavement. Yet, when its fortunes improved, Israel, too, was not above taking slaves of their own. Babylonians, Greeks, Romans—slave masters all. Slavery is as old, and, unfortunately as "natural," as civilization itself.

But all of this, if you pardon the expression, is ancient history. The American enslavement of blacks also is history—18th and 19th century history—about which raceketeers remind us continually. White Americans did not invent slavery. White Americans did free their slaves at the cost of the proportionally greatest death toll ever suffered by our people. No living white American ever held a slave; a very large majority of white Americans do not even have an ancestor who held slaves. What about early

21st century black slavery and racial cruelty? Where is its home? Certainly, neither the United States nor modern day Europe. Africa, in fact, is the center of contemporary black slavery and violent black oppression.

Many African nations have inflicted the most inhumane mistreatment on their own people and on their neighbors. Just since 1990, in addition to the black on black slave trade there has been black on black warfare raging across the continent, ravaging the populations of Angola, Burundi, Central African Republic, Congo Brazzaville, Democratic Republic of Congo, Guinea, Ivory Coast, Kenya, Liberia, Rwanda, Sierra Leone, Somalia, Sudan, and Uganda. According to the Crimes of War Project, a group created to raise public awareness and to mobilize the international communities against warfare, modern Africa's armed conflicts have been especially tragic and vicious. The project characterized the military campaigns as "remarkable for the brutality of the tactics (ranging from mass murder and ethnic cleansing, to amputation, starvation, forced labour, rape and cannibalism) used by belligerents to secure their strategic objectives." Since I do not want to dwell on this very disturbing topic, I will limit myself only to a couple detailed examples.

Barack Obama euphemistically has admitted to "tribalism" in what he refers to as his ancestral home, Kenya. The U.S. Department of State, however, did not mince words. In their "Trafficking in Persons Report" released in June 2009, they described the Kenyan slave trade as follows:

> Kenya is a source, transit, and destination country for men, women, and children subjected to trafficking in persons, specifically conditions of forced labor and forced prostitution. Within the country, Kenyan children are forced into domestic servitude, commercial sexual exploitation—including involvement in the coastal sex tourism industry—and forced labor in agriculture (including on flower plantations), fishing, cattle herding, street vending, and bars. Traffickers—who gain poor families' trust through familial, tribal, or religious ties—falsely offer to raise and educate children in towns, or to obtain women lucrative employment. Trafficked Kenyan adults are exploited in involuntary domestic servitude and forced prostitution. . . . Children from Burundi, Ethiopia, Rwanda, Somalia, Tanzania, and Uganda are

subjected to forced labor and commercial sexual exploitation in Kenya.

If any African country should resist subjugating its people, that country surely is Liberia, since it was founded by freed slaves from the United States and the Caribbean and has been emancipated for over 163 years. However, the trafficking report employs the same diplomatic language to describe Liberian slavery as Kenyan slavery.

> Liberia is a source, transit, and destination country principally for young women and children subjected to trafficking in persons, specifically forced labor and forced prostitution. Most trafficking victims originate from within the country's borders and are forced to work as domestic servants, street vendors, or beggars supporting religious instructors, or are subjected to forced prostitution. Traffickers operate independently and are commonly family members who may promise poorer relatives a better life for their children. Children sent to work as domestic servants for wealthier relatives are vulnerable to forced labor or commercial sexual exploitation. Victims of trans-border trafficking come to Liberia from Sierra Leone, Guinea, and Cote d'Ivoire and are subjected to the same types of forced labor as internally trafficked victims, and are also found on rubber plantations and at alluvial diamond sites. A small number of men, women, and children from Liberia are trafficked to Cote d'Ivoire, Guinea, and Nigeria.

Barack Obama indicted the entire state of Kansas as a land that with the "the potential for unblinking cruelty." Unfortunately, some parts of Africa have more than cruelty **potential**, most shockingly in the form of "muti," African witchcraft ritual human sacrifice. On April 2, 2002, the BBC reported a tragically gruesome incident from the Thohoyandou area of South Africa involving South African Helen Madide, her toddler, and the child's witchdoctor father:

> "He began to tell me stories. His ancestors said that he must kill me and the child so that he can be rich," Helen told Nobody's Child, a BBC documentary on the investigation into the London boy's death.

111

"He showed me the path and forced me to go along that path. He was pushing me and demanding me to go whether I like it or not. He said he was going to kill the baby first while I see the baby, then secondly he will kill me."

Although Helen tried to escape, Mabuda caught her and forced her to hold Fulufhuwani's legs while he cut the child's throat.

"When the child was dead, he started to cut all those pieces, the hands, the legs and even the sex organs," Helen says.

Limbs from children, primarily the sexual organs, are said to be the most potent. These are sometimes taken from live victims because their screams are thought to enhance the power of the medicines.

Because Helen Maddie's story is so horrific, one might be tempted to rationalize it away as an isolated event, perpetrated by one deranged person. But that would be a mistake. Many equally abhorrent slaughters, often conducted by bands of murderous men, have been reported. Mike Thomson, also of the BBC, spoke of an April 2007 homicidal rampage in eastern Congo. Here, too, a woman, Zawadi Mongane, and her baby were spotlighted, as the mother agonizingly told that she hanged her baby rather than to watch him be butchered by rebel soldiers, as "dozens" of other people had been.

The tragic Congo situation was graphically described on Radio Times, June 8, 2011, when Marty Moss Coane interviewed Jocelyn Kelly, Director of Harvard's Women in War Program, and Tony Gambino, past Director of USAID for the Democratic Republic of Congo. In the course of the "Rape and War in the Congo" discussion, the participants spoke of massive violence, especially rampant rape, mostly directed toward the citizenry, rather than toward soldiers. In fact, Mr. Gambino asserted that the modal "military" confrontation usually involves little more than posturing in which two groups of marauding male combatants confront each other, the weaker readily withdraws, and the victors descend on the closest village to torture, pillage, and rape. It was noted that Eastern Congo is regarded as the "rape capital of the world," a country in which rape is committed with impunity, and that "during a one year period, nearly 400,000 women were raped—that's an equivalent of almost one rape every minute." When Marty Moss Coane tried to rationalize the sexual brutality by alluding to the notion that rape is a regular feature of war, Ms. Kelly disputed the implication, saying that wars do occur in which rape is not normalized as an expected outcome of military strife.

The brutality suffered by Africans at the hands of Africans sometimes is unequivocally racial, as in the genocidal campaign conducted against albinos. Jeffrey Gettleman of the New York Times, in what must be nominated as the most understated title in the history of journalism, penned, "Albinos, Long Shunned, Face Threat in Tanzania," a piece published on June 8, 2008. In it, he details the living hell experienced by people due only to their having white skin. Gettleman relates that within the year nineteen albinos literally had been butchered for their body parts that eventually were sold for their supposed magical properties. He notes that the barbarism also is practiced in Kenya and Congo, citing how a Kenyan albino woman "was hacked to death in late May, with her eyes, tongue and breasts gouged out" and how Congo witch doctors had sold albino skin, much as one might sell an animal pelt.

Naturally, conventionally white, Caucasian, Africans also have been targeted for torture and slaughter. South Africa is a case in point; the brutality system is honed so finely that black murderers even have a rap for it—"Shoot the Boers," with Boer being a Dutch name for farmer. (At the time of this writing, *The Star* in Johannesburg, South Africa has published that Julius Malema, president of the African National Congress Youth League, is on trial for inciting racial hatred. So, we see the kind of "training" being provided to some black African youth.) Aidan Hartley of the Daily Mail writes on September 10, 2009 that white farmers were being systematically exterminated. He notes:

> There are no official figures but, since the election of Nelson Mandela in 1994, farmers' organisations say 3,000 whites in rural areas have been killed. The independent South African Human Rights Commission, set up by Mandela's government, says the number is 2,500. Its commission's report into the killings does not break down their figures by colour; but it says the majority of

attacks in general—i.e. where no one necessarily dies—are against white people and that 'there was a considerably higher risk of a white victim of farm attacks being killed or injured than a black victim.' It states that since 2006, farmer murders have jumped by 25 per cent and adds: 'The lack of prosecutions indicates the criminal justice system is not operating e effectively to protect victims in farming communities and to ensure the rule of law is upheld.' But among the casualties of the violence are white farmers, whose counterparts in Zimbabwe are singled out for international press coverage; here in the 'rainbow nation' their murders, remarkable for their particular savagery, go largely unreported.

As mentioned above, in addition to South Africa, Zimbabwe also had conducted a reign of terror against white farmers. With the blessing of President Robert Mugabe, rampaging bands of armed Zimbabwe blacks invaded white properties, murdered or beat the inhabitants, and stationed themselves on the land. In 2000 there were approximately 4500 white farmers in Zimbabwe; as of June 1010, there were about 400. By March of 2010, almost 20% of the country's population needed food relief. Commenting on the food crisis, on August 12, 2010, AllAfrica.com observed that "President Robert Mugabe launched the fast-track land reform programme in 2000, which redistributed more than 4,000 white commercial farms to landless blacks, which set in motion a decade-long economic malaise from which the country has yet to emerge."

Economic-based violence also has been at the heart of the Somali piracy enterprise, wreaking havoc along the coast of Africa. As the government collapsed in the 1990s and the country slipped deeper and deeper into anarchy, marauding bands of armed "fishermen" started attacking merchant ships and their crews. Reuter.com disclosed that the piracy had evolved into an operation that provides local employment and investment opportunities. The piece said that pirates created a virtual business that includes offering investment opportunities to locals. One "entrepreneur" was quoted as saying, "Four months ago, during the monsoon rains, we decided to set up this stock exchange. We started with 15 'maritime companies' and now we are hosting 72. Ten of them have so far been successful at hijacking." A happy 22-year-old female investor touted the value of the enterprise, boasting that after a mere 28 days in the exchange she had pocketed $75,000. She then added that more cash would be coming her way, since she had "invested" an ex-husband's rocket-propelled grenade as her contribution to a recent piracy.

The bottom line to all of this is to say the obvious: Literally, since the dawn of time there has been a black devil for every white devil, and Africa is not the Promised Land. Afrocentric raceketeers and flat-out black racists never would admit those facts, of course. Bill Cosby, however, was not afraid to speak the truth. At the 50th Anniversary commemoration of the Brown vs. Topeka Board of Education Supreme Court Decision in 2004, he addressed black Americans as follows: "We are not Africans. Those people [at this point in his presentation Cosby was talking about young Americans whom I have called bimps] are not Africans; they don't know a damned thing about Africa. With names like Shaniqua, Shaligua, Mohammed and all that crap and all of them are in jail."

"Afrocentric" black Americans suffer from shared delusional disorder when they gush over their wonderful motherland. The truth is that the overwhelming number of black Americans would be infinitely worse off in Africa today, much more likely to be living in poverty, disease, and warfare. For instance, the Transparency International Global Coalition Against Corruption website reveals that 24 of the 60 most corrupt countries in the world are black countries.

Scott Johnson knows. On February 14, 2009, he penned a *Newsweek* article entitled, "Fleeing From South Africa: Fourteen years after apartheid, why are the best and the brightest leaving Africa's most successful state?" with the additional subtext: A razor-wire fence in Yeoville, South Africa, a common sight due to an increasing crime rate." Commenting that one readily could appreciate the mass exodus occurring in neighboring, poverty stricken Zimbabwe, he noted that the flight from South Africa, the continent's most developed and wealthiest country, seemed puzzling. Scott said that 20% of the white population had left since 1995, and that the number of black South Africans eager to leave their homeland had doubled. The fundamental reason for the Diaspora was explained as follows:

The primary driver for emigration among all groups, but especially whites, who still retain the majority of South Africa's wealth, is fear of crime. With more than 50 killings a day, South Africa has one of the highest per capita murder rates in the world. The same goes for rape—ranking the country alongside conflict zones such as Sierra Leone, Colombia and Afghanistan. Future Fact polling indicates that more than 95 percent of those eager to leave South Africa rate violent crime as the single most important factor affecting their thinking. Lynette Chen, the ethnic-Chinese CEO of Nepad Business Group, is the only member of her family left in South Africa. Her parents departed in 2002 after being carjacked—twice. Her brother, also a victim of crime, followed suit shortly thereafter. "They're always getting homesick," she says. "But they won't come back unless the crime is reduced."

While there can be no excuse for slavery perpetrated by any people against any people, contemporary black Americans have made the best from their tragedy. In that respect, they are no different than the progeny of Irish who fled their country to avoid famine, or of Jews who fled to escape the Holocaust. The ancestors of present day Blacks, Irish, and Jews all suffered horribly, but their descendents have flourished in the "New World," not because of what their homelands were, but because of what America is.

Racial Crimes in Contemporary America

We do not live in 18th or 19th century America, and we do not live in 20th or 21st century Africa. When it comes to race relations, the contemporary United States is far better than those times and places. But racial atrocities continue in our country. Some unspeakable crimes are committed by white people who truly deserve to be called devils. That was so regarding the gruesome murder of James Byrd junior, a 49-year-old black man who was dragged to death in Jasper, Texas on June 7, 1998 by three white men, two of whom were Ku Klux Klansmen and members of a supremacist prison gang. Eleven white jurors elected a black foreman and together they rendered three guilty verdicts—two death penalties and one life in prison. The life sentence allegedly was selected because one murderer, Shawn Allen Berry, confessed one day after the crime and ultimately convinced the jury that he went along with the others only because he feared that he, too, would have been killed if he had not.

The James Byrd junior murder was an especially vicious example of extreme white on black violence, white animals acting out their depravity. But was it typical of interracial violence? Not really. According to the Bureau of Justice Statistics of the United States Department of Justice, on average, blacks murder whites at a rate 277 percent higher than whites murder blacks. We all know the groups who are not likely to be perpetrators of violent intra—and inter-racial crime: Regardless of race, women, men over 50, the highly educated, and persons in responsible occupations rarely commit violent assaults or murder. Bimps, black and white, overwhelmingly are responsible for violent crime, whether the crime is directed toward black people or white ones. The white assassins of James Byrd junior were no less bimps than is any inner-city black "gangbanger."

Although the "unblinkingly cruelty" of white interracial horror is understandably highlighted by our society, in general, and by the media, in particular, there often is deafening silence when black bimps slaughter whites. The media falls all over itself in asserting that a given black on white assault was just "a random act of violence." When, on rare occasions, the press grudgingly concedes that a black on white "race crime might" have been committed, they assert that an investigation needs to be done, and they never report on the incident again. Whites victimized by blacks have no Jesse Jackson, Al Sharpton, NAACP, or Congressional Black Caucus to take up their cause. White victims have not one of the hundreds of black racial advocacy groups ready, willing, and able to scream or threatened their own violence if "justice" is not forthcoming. One does not see or hear white mobs wailing, "No justice, no peace" or "Burn, baby burn." Our society respectfully remembers Rodney King, but gives not a second thought to his counterpart, Reginald Denny, the white man who four black assailants dragged from his truck beating him nearly to death and leaving him severely brain damaged. Moreover, unlike the Rodney King riots, after O. J. Simpson was acquitted, there were no white on black assaults and no raging fires sweeping through California cities.

I must underscore that violence against any single white victim is not perpetrated by "black people." Violence is perpetrated by one or more criminals who happen to be black. On the other hand, no criminal should be allowed to hide behind a shield of racial protection. For a time during the 1990s, one would hear the term "black predators" to describe black persons who attacked citizens, black and white, for no better reason than to rob them of their sneakers, jackets, or gold chains, sometimes killing them in the process. Raceketeers rose to the defense of the black criminals, asserting "They're not predators! They're our children!" The parents or other supporters of the ruthless white savages who murdered James Byrd junior also could have opposed their being called predators, but that would not change the fact of their predation. One must invoke the most extreme form of double speak to deny that people of any race who prey on others are anything other than rank predators.

Double speaking and hiding behind a racial shield is precisely what the predatory Jenna Six ultimately did. You, no doubt, recall at least something of the case, since raceketeers everywhere—that, of course, included Jesse Jackson and Al Sharpton—rushed headlong into the fray. I will not bore you with the specific details of the case, since most people do not care about the specific facts, preferring instead to allow their racial affiliation to guide them. There are certain "tidbits" of information, however, that are indisputably true: The day after a black student had sat under a tree at Jena High School in Louisiana, two nooses hung from that tree. As expected, the black community expressed outrage and racial conflict ensued. Over three months later, Mychal Bell, a black student, and five or six of his black friends ambushed Justin Barker, a white student, beating and kicking him into unconsciousness. When the assailants were apprehended, black raceketeers sprang into action and charges against the Six were reduced. On June 26, 2009, the assault case finally was concluded after the attackers admitted that their assault on Barker was unprovoked. CBS news stated that an attorney read a statement in court saying, "To be clear, not one of us heard Justin use any slur or say anything that justified Mychal Bell attacking Justin nor did any of us see Justin do anything that would cause Mychal to react." Of the six defendants, only Bell was charged as an adult, and he was so because his rap sheet revealed that he had been found guilty of four previous assaults. Predator?

Sympathetic racializers no doubt will justify and even lionize the Jena Six as racial heroes who stood-up for black people. That Justin Baker was brutalized unjustifiably means no more to them than does the unconscionable maiming of Reginald Denny—whitey got put in his place. In a February 7, 2008 follow-up of Jena, the Chicago Tribune reported that the previous day, nineteen-year-old Bryant Purvis, one of the Six, was arrested on a new, unrelated aggravated assault charge, this time in his new residence, Dallas Texas. The article went on to say that "Purvis' arrest is the latest in a series public embarrassments for the Jena defendants, who last summer attracted the sympathies of more than 300,000 petition signers and donations of more than $500,000 to their legal defense fund." Finally the Tribune proved my point about racial shields and racial heroes by recalling that on October 18, 2007:

> Purvis and another Jena defendant, Carwin Jones, posed like rap stars at the Black Entertainment Television Hip Hop Awards in October, where they presented a music award and received an ovation from the audience. Jena defendant Robert Bailey Junior posted pictures of himself on a MySpace page with a wad of $100 bills stuffed in his mouth. And questions arose over the accounting for some of the donated legal funds controlled by the Jena 6 families after they declined to say how they were spending the money.

Although the episodes involving Justin Baker and Reginald Denny no doubt were black on white racial atrocities, others make them seem like misdemeanors. As has been my pattern, I will cite only a few.

In the winter of 2000, two women and three men, all white and in their twenties, were tortured, sexually abused, raped, and finally murdered by two gun-toting black men, also in their twenties, in a ghoulish nightmare that persisted for three hours. The atrocity, now referred to as the Wichita Massacre, rivaled the ruthlessness and barbarity of the Rwanda genocide. The victims were H.G. (the only survivor and hence the anonymity), Jason Befort, Bradley Heyka, Aaron Sander, and Heather Muller; the murderers were Reginald Carr and Jonathan Carr, brothers. The ordeal began after all five of the victims were forced into a bedroom closet at gunpoint. Stephen Webster in the July 16, 2002 issue of American Renaissance described a brief segment of the massacre like this:

The Carrs first brought out the two women, H.G and Heather Muller, and made them have oral sex and penetrate each other digitally. They then forced Mr. Heyka to have intercourse with H.G. Then they made Mr. Befort have intercourse with H.G, but ordered him to stop when they realized he was her boyfriend. Next, they ordered Mr. Sander to have intercourse with H.G. When the divinity student refused, they hit him on the back of the head with a pistol butt. They sent H.G. back to the bedroom closet and brought out Miss Muller, Mr. Sander's old girlfriend. H.G. testified she could hear what was going on out by the wet bar, and when Mr. Sander was unable to get an erection one of the Carrs beat him with a golf club. Then, she says, the Carr brothers "told [Aaron] that he had until 11:54 to get hard and they counted down from 11:52 to 11:53 to 11:54." The deadline appears to have brought no further punishment, and Mr. Sanders was returned to the closet. The Carrs then forced Mr. Befort to have intercourse with Heather Muller, and then ordered Mr. Heyka to have sex with her. H.G. says she could hear Miss Muller moaning with pain.

The Carrs asked if the victims had ATM cards. Reginald Carr then took the victims one at a time to ATM machines in Mr. Befort's pickup truck, starting with Mr. Heyka. While Reginald Carr was away with Mr. Heyka, Jonathan Carr brought H.G. out of the closet to the wet bar, raped her, and sent her back to the closet. Reginald Carr returned with Mr. Heyka, and ordered Mr. Befort to go with him. Mr. Heyka was put back in the closet but said nothing about his trip to the ATM machine. Mr. Sander asked Mr. Heyka if they should try to resist, assuming they would be killed anyway, but Mr. Heyka did not reply. While Reginald Carr was away with Mr. Befort at the cash machine, Jonathan Carr ordered Heather Muller out of the closet and raped her.

By 02:07 on the morning of December 15, the Carrs apparently had reassured themselves as to their manhood. They did not need to swagga anymore. The fun was over; it was time to move on. The brothers required both a car and a truck to transport their victims to the slaughter. Once again, I defer to Stephen Webster:

After a short drive, both vehicles stopped in an empty field. Reginald Carr ordered H.G. to go sit with Miss Muller in Mr. Sander's car. A moment later, she saw the men line up in front of the Honda. In her testimony H.G. said, "I turned to Heather and said, 'They're going to shoot us.' "

The Carr brothers ordered H.G. and Miss Muller out of the car. Miss Muller stood next to Mr. Sander, her former boyfriend, while H.G. stood beside her boyfriend, Mr. Befort. The Carrs ordered them to turn away and kneel in the snow. "As I was kneeling, a gun shot went off," says H.G. "[Then] I heard Aaron [Sander] . . . . I could distinguish Aaron's voice. He said, 'Please, no sir, please.' The gun went off."

H.G. heard three shots before she was hit: "I felt the bullet hit the back of my head. It went kind of gray with white like stars. I wasn't knocked unconscious. I didn't fall forward. Then someone kicked me, and I had fallen forward. I was playing dead. I didn't move. I didn't want them to shoot me again."

As H.G. lay in the snow, the Carrs drove off in Jason Befort's pickup, running over the victims as they left. H.G. says she felt the truck hit her body, too.

"I waited until I couldn't hear any more," she says. "Then I turned my head and saw lights going. I looked at everyone. Everyone was face down. Jason [Befort] was next to me. I rolled him over. There was blood squirting everywhere, so I took my sweater off and tied it around his head to try and stop it. He had blood coming out of his eyes."

Wickedness such as the Wichita Massacre might lead one to agree with people who oppose calling the likes of the Carrs predators. Given the depravity and bestiality of the murderers, predator, in fact, is too civil a word for them.

Stephen Webster notes that prosecutors did not seriously pursue the possibility of the atrocity as being a hate crime; instead, it was declared to be a "random act of violence." In my opinion, even Webster, may have overlooked something regarding the racial hate character of the crime. While he did observe that "Jonathan Carr wore a FUBU sweatshirt, a brand popular with black rappers that is said to stand for 'For Us, By Us' some blacks wear FUBU clothing as a statement of black solidarity if not outright rejection of whites" Stephen then commented, "It is true that Reginald Carr had a white girlfriend, and it may be that the race of the victims was unimportant to him." To my way of thinking, having a white girlfriend does not in any way reduce the likelihood of a hate crime. Black bimps often use white women as trophies indicative of their power. You may recall, for instance, that Denise Brown, sister of Nicole Simpson, testified to having been at a dinner when O. J. grabbed Nicole's crotch and said, "This is where babies come from, and this belongs to me." As the illustrious Orenthal James did, many, if not most, black bimps with white women demean, control, and abuse them as a piece of property—as slaves.

In the end, the Carrs were convicted of first degree murder and sentenced to death. But it was not "only" the death of the four friends and the near death of the fifth that led to the conviction. Webster explained that the brothers had attacked two other white people that month, robbing and pistol-whipping a 23-year-old man on December 7th 2000, and murdering a 55-year-old woman on the 11th. As expected, the death sentence of the Carr brothers is being appealed.

The second contemptible black on white atrocity occurred in 2007. On Saturday, January 6, to be specific, in Knoxville, Tennessee, Christopher Newsom, a white 23-year-old carpenter, and Channon Christian, his white 21-year-old girlfriend, a, sociology major at the University of Tennessee, drove to a local restaurant. After dinner they boarded Channon's Toyota 4-Runner, expecting to visit a friend and to watch a movie together. Tragically, that trip was cut short when the two were hijacked at gunpoint and driven to a rented house in the neighborhood. Then began one of the most horrific, satanic crimes imaginable, perpetrated by five blacks: Eric DeWayne "E" Boyd, 34, Letalvis "Rome" Cobbins, 24, George Geovonni "Detroit" Thomas, 27, Lemaricus Devall 'Slim' Davidson, 28, reportedly the leader of the murderers, and Vanessa Coleman, 18. According to James H. Lilley,

While Channon was forced to watch, her boyfriend was raped prison style and then his penis was cut off. He was later driven to nearby railroad tracks where he was shot and set afire. But Channon's hell was just beginning. She was beaten; gang raped repeatedly in many ways, had one of her breasts cut off and bleach poured down her throat to destroy DNA evidence-all while she was still alive. To add to Channon's degradation the suspects took turns urinating on her. They too set her body afire, apparently inside the residence, but for some reason left her body there-in five separate trash bags.

And what did law enforcement decide about the nature of this abominable, animalistic slaughter? Knoxville Police Chief Sterling Owen, IV reportedly said, "We have no evidence to support the fact that this crime was a race crime. It appears to have been a random violent act." Sure it was random; just an average everyday misunderstanding by inhumane white-hating black racists, I guess. According to James H. Lilley, when interrogated by detective Nevil Norman of the Knox County Sheriff's Office, GeorgeThomas spat, "Fuck that white girl, she don't mean nothin' to me."

For his part, Thomas was sentenced to life without parole, as was Cobbins. The ringleader Lemaricus Davidson received the death sentence while Eric Boyd got off with only eighteen years. The latter had convinced the jury that he did not participate directly in the crimes, but aided Davidson after the fact. The sole female of the ring, Vanessa Coleman, was ordered to serve fifty-three years in prison. She had been declared a "facilitator" in Channon Christian's rape and murder, but not to have played a significant role in the atrocities committed on Christopher Newsom.

The final heart-rending black on white racial crime is actually a series of ruthless assaults—all against white victims. The first occurred after Dominique Wilson, a six feet, seven inch black man, broke into in a center city Philadelphia home in October 2008. He viciously attacked a 29-year-old male and repeatedly raped the man's girlfriend. During the rapes, Wilson forced the man to watch helplessly. According to Mensah M. Dean of the Philadelphia Daily News, at one point during the nightmare, the boyfriend prayed aloud, hoping to dissuade Wilson from continuing the rapes. Instead, the criminal shouted, "Bitch, what's he doing? Tell him to shut up." At another point, Wilson commanded the man and woman to have sex in front of him, but they successfully resisted. The ordeal concluded with Dominique Wilson's robbing the couple and fleeing.

The second attack happened in December when the same predator broke into a University City apartment. There, with a knife and gun, Wilson confronted two University of Pennsylvania co-eds, binding them and repeatedly raping one who noted later that he reeked of body odor. Once again, the invasion ended in robbery.

Dominique Wilson's next atrocity occurred during February 2009, in off-campus apartment in Lock Haven, Pennsylvania. Wilson was familiar with the area since he had been on the University basketball team. The Lock Haven crime lasted four to five hours during which all three of the female victims were assaulted and two, repeatedly raped.

The Lock Haven crime resulted in Dominique Wilson's undoing. On June 8, 2010, Jim Runkle of lockhaven.com described the trial, writing:

> Wilson took the stand in his own defense, claiming he has never met the victims and was never in their house. Wilson claimed that a man named "Jonathan," a drug dealer from Williamsport to whom Wilson owed several thousand dollars in drug debts from a few years ago, planted his semen in the victims.
>
> But all three of the victims also took the stand, describing the ordeal in detail while identifying the defendant as the assailant.
>
> Wilson said he came to Lock Haven from Philadelphia in 2003 to enroll at Lock Haven University, and played for the basketball team until being kicked out of school for "minor" incidents in 2005.
>
> He said he then lived at 525 W. Church St. from 2005 to 2007, admitting that he paid for his rent and other bills by selling "narcotics," specifically marijuana.

He said he then returned to his parents' house in Philadelphia until January 2009, when he moved to the Fallon Hotel, Apt. 206, because a local girl told him he was the father to her child.

But the jury did not swallow Wilson's story, finding him guilty on thirty-seven counts. Neither did Clinton County Judge Craig Miller who sentenced the rapist to 79 to 196 years in prison.

Given that university students were victimized, the Philadelphia crimes generated considerable publicity and discussion. One forum, topix.com, listed a contributor response from "Madblackwoman" as:

> you people are just sick. yall are so hype to find a person to take the fall. It really don't make no freak'n sense leave that young man alone don't have no proof, however want him prosecuted. I really hope yall are right about this situation, if not thats really disappointing, putting that boy through that much stress, making racial remarks. I'm going to need all yall to grow up and think before yall speak

Madblackwoman probably did not bother to read the November 4, 2010, *Philadelphia Daily News* article that, in describing the trial, underscored the callousness of the rapist and the trauma-inducing nature of his crime:

> A young woman told a Philadelphia jury yesterday that after she was raped repeatedly, her attacker went to her kitchen and helped himself to a dish of pesto chicken from the refrigerator.
>
> After returning to the bedroom and eating the chicken, the woman said, accused rapist and home-invader Domenique Thomas Wilson wiped his hands on her naked body and spanked her bottom.
>
> Wilson, 25, then used duct tape to bind her hands and feet behind her back, the woman told the jury on the third day of Wilson's trial in the Common Pleas Court.
>
> "I thought this is how I'm going to die," she said, weeping.

The court had decided to conduct one trial for both of Domenique Wilson's Philadelphia crimes.

On March 10, 2011, ABClocal.com reported that Wilson was convicted and sentenced to 84 to 230 years in prison. Wonder what Madblackwoman thought about that.

If you choose to dismiss the vicious, bestial attacks mentioned above as extraordinary outliers, I leave you with one last "garden variety" black on white assault. This everyday type event happened in Seattle and was reported by cbsnews.com on December 17, 2010. During the evening rush hour on November 19, 2010, pregnant, white 17-year-old Jessica Redmon-Beckstead and her white boyfriend were riding on a Metro bus that stopped to admit more riders. Among those new passengers were black Ayana Sharee Cain, nineteen-years-old, and her three black 16-year-old and one black 14-year-old girlfriends. Within half a minute, one of the five tried to snatch the MP3 player that Jessica and her friend were listening to, and, when the couple resisted, the five attacked, beat and kicked them. The report noted that:

> Redmon-Beckstead says she turned around again and was struck in the eye and began bleeding profusely. It wound up requiring six stitches to close, authorities say.

> Jessica mentioned twice that she was pregnant and said she didn't want to fight them, but says one of them made the comment, "Well, nobody hit her in the stomach."

> Investigators add that, as the attack was occurring, three of the girls stole items from the boyfriend's pockets.

All five of the predators were described as having had prior arrests. The incident garnered media attention only because it could not be ignored—scores of citizens had witnessed it firsthand and Jessica was pregnant. If either of those conditions had not obtained, not one news pixel would have been devoted to the crime. On the other hand, if even a single, marauding white predator had assaulted a black, female teenager without provocation, whether the black girl was pregnant or not, the cameras would have been rolling, the Jessie Jacksons, Al Sharptons, and NAACPs would have been pontificating, and the city fathers and mothers would have been promising a thorough, comprehensive review of racial injustice in Seattle, if not in Washington state.

Crime and Punishment
of Dostoevskian Proportions

Earlier, I briefly and generally mentioned that black on white crime is exceedingly more common than vice versa. Citing data drawn from FBI and Justice Department surveys, Patrick J. Buchanan, journalist, politician, and commentator, provides the following fine grain estimates:

> Blacks commit more violent crime against whites than against other blacks. Forty-five percent of the victims of violent crime by blacks are white folks, 43 percent are black, 10 percent are Hispanic.

> Blacks are an estimated 39 times more likely to commit violent crime against a white person than vice versa, and 136 times more likely to commit robbery.

> Black-on-white rape is 115 times more common than the reverse.

> Blacks are seven times as likely as people of other races to commit murder, eight times more likely to commit robbery and three times more likely to use a gun in a crime.

In *Reload, Rethinking Violence in American Life*, Christopher B. Strain states that during the 2000 to 2005 period, Center for Disease Control statistics reveal death by firearms rates per 100,000 as follows: 8.8 to 9.2 for whites, 7.5 to 7.8 for Latinos, and 18.4 to 19.3 for African Americans. That is, blacks were at least twice as likely to use guns than were the others. Equally disturbing, he cites "two psychologists" whose study of 1998 projected that for each school killing there were "7000 serious injuries, 28,000 thefts, 44,000 physical altercations, and 500,000 reports of bullying in American schools. These numbers, of course, reflect reported incidents of violent behavior; the actual number of incidents was presumably higher." Given those statistics, one should not be surprised at the pathetically poor school performance of many inner-city black children whose education is undermined by the bimp subculture that dominates their neighborhoods.

Because only persons capable of the utmost "courageous" racial honesty can tolerate accepting the aforementioned statistics, I am not going to attempt to convince anyone of their validity. If you think that the aforementioned crime rate data are racially biased, maybe you prefer the ones published by the NAACP:

> African Americans now constitute nearly 1 million of the total 2.3 million incarcerated population.

> African Americans are incarcerated at nearly six times the rate of whites.

> One in six black men had been incarcerated as of 2001. If current trends continue, one in three black males born today can expect to spend time in prison during his lifetime.

> 1 in 100 African American women are in prison.

> Nationwide, African Americans represent 26% of juvenile arrests, 44% of youth who are detained, 46% of the youth who are judicially waived to criminal court, and 58% of the youth admitted to state prisons (Center on Juvenile and Criminal Justice).

> 35% of black children grades 7-12 have been suspended or expelled at some point in their school careers compared to 20% of Hispanics and 15% of whites.

As alarming as the NAACP stats are, once again, virtually all pertain to blacks caught and/or convicted of crime, not to all of those who have committed crime.

Raceketeers who scrutinize the black statistics know that black criminals and black communities are the biggest losers in the crime game. So what do raceketeers do? Instead of taking charge of the mean streets, they use the stats to complain about racism, blaming every white person and institution under the sun for what really is an abysmal failure of black leadership. The white government, the white police, the white educational system, perhaps even white crayons are responsible for the black crime that occurs mostly in black inner-cities with black mayors. It is so convenient to accept racial credit for every success no matter how meager, and to be absolved for every failure no matter how egregious. For instance, when on Martin Luther King junior Day, January 16, 2006, Ray Nagin squawked that his town needed to remain a "chocolate city." New Orleans had been ruled by black mayors since 1979, had the third largest metropolitan black population by percent, and the absolute highest crime rate in the nation. Right, Ray, you and your black mayor predecessors have done well by your chocolate, vanilla, and other-assorted-flavor citizens.

Ray Nagin undoubtedly knew that Louisiana was number one in 2010 murders and number three in overall crime. New Hampshire, the sixth most "vanilla" state had the lowest crime rate in our nation. In fact, for the benefit of Ray and raceketeers everywhere, below is a table of the crime statistics relative to the percent of white citizenry in the whitest states. Because the numbers are based on 50 states plus the District of Columbia (that is treated here as a "state" merely for illustrative purposes), the leftmost column ranks the state from 1 to 51 in terms of the percentage of white citizens, such that, 51 is the whitest state and 1 is the least white state. Similarly, the rightmost column ranks the state in terms of safety, such that 51 is the most law abiding state and 1 is the highest crime state.

Whitest		Safest
43	New Hampshire	51
44	South Dakota	42
45	Utah	39
46	Wyoming	45
47	North Dakota	48
48	Maine	47
49	Vermont	49
50	Idaho	46
51	Montana	44

As is obvious, there is an extraordinarily strong, positive correlation between the number of white citizens in the state and the crime rate; the greater the number of whites, the safer the state. Yes. I know that correlation does not equal causation, but such a strong correlation cannot be dismissed. I also can hear some of you thinking aloud that poverty, not race, is the primary cause of crime.

When I was a child, one often would hear a hypothetical morality discussion about being poor and being criminal framed as, "Is it wrong for a man to steal a loaf of bread to feed his starving family?" In 21st century America, perhaps the question would be, "Is it wrong for a man to steal a high definition television to entertain his entitled family?" Since today, with rare exceptions, our society provides adequately for the basics of life, one can not equate being poor with being criminal, particularly with being violently criminal. Monetary poverty does not make people vicious; it is neither a necessary nor a sufficient condition for aggressive crime. While monetary poverty exists in every corner of the earth, poor people in other lands rarely slaughter and victimize the citizenry the way that American bimps do. Not monetary poverty but personality poverty is the single most important factor determining who does and does not become a criminal, and, more than anything else, personality depends on the family and the immediate neighborhood in which a child develops. So now the bottom line question: Why is black bimp crime out of control?

CHAPTER 8

Roots:
Origins of Black Male Identity

Like Bill Cosby, I lived in mid-20th century Philadelphia, a city that had some mixed neighborhoods and some that were ethnic, religious, or racial ghettoes. In that era, local government was controlled almost exclusively by whites, from city hall to the local police precincts. Since affirmative action programs and a few special opportunities for black people literally just began, African Americans had not yet received any significant benefits from them. Yet, white and black families did not differ appreciably in their capacities and behaviors necessary to nurture young children; mothers and fathers knew their responsibilities and, by and large, did their best to fulfill them. Despite being victimized by segregation and racial bias, black adult males did not routinely abandon their children and black adolescents did not routinely slaughter each other on the streets.

In contrast to the days of my childhood when blacks often were second-class citizens, over the last twenty or more years, many of our largest cities have been governed by African Americans. For instance, Philadelphia has had black mayors for 17 of the last 25 years, and black police commissioners for 13 of the last 23 years as well as for all years since 2002. Across America, trillions of dollars have been poured into crime prevention and law enforcement, mostly in metropolitan areas with large black populations. And, the result?

In January 2009, City Journal reporter Heather Mac Donald addressed the issue. Citing Northwestern University's James Alan Fox and Marc Swatt, she enumerated the following: From 2002 to 2007, the overall number

132

of homicides by black males increased 43 percent, and the number of gun homicides, by 47 percent; whereas those crimes by white males of the same age group fell slightly. Moreover, during the three decade period investigated by Fox and Swatt, at its maximum point (1991), the rate for 18 to 24 year old white males was 32 homicides per 100,000 persons, as opposed to the maximum (1993) 320 homicides per 100,000 persons for black males of the same age cohort.

In addition to citing the statistics, Ms. Mac Donald exposed the racial double standards and double speak hidden within the data. Referring to the maximal black versus maximal white rates, she explained:

> Even this apparent ten-to-one disparity between black and white homicide rates doesn't tell the full story. Fox and Swatt include Hispanic homicides in the white rate, though they do not disclose that they are doing so (both the inclusion and the silence about it follow FBI practice). Hispanic crime rates are between three and four times that of whites—meaning that if one excluded the Hispanic homicides from the white rate, the black-white differential would be even larger than ten to one.

Not unexpectedly, the rise in black criminality tracked closely with the disintegration of the black nuclear family. In 1944, "racist America" had a black illegitimacy rate of about 11%. In the intervening years, from then until now, as America became increasingly proactive in combating prejudice, we paradoxically have "progressed" to the point that during the presidency of Barack Obama we witness a 70% black illegitimacy rate and a prison population that is 43% black, whereas African Americans comprise only about 12 percent of our citizenry.

Many have tried to offer a comprehensive, research-based explanation for the decline of the black family and the rise of black criminality. My goal here is much more modest: I simply present for your consideration anecdotal information suggesting that that the inner-city black male persona, and the forces that have created and sustained it, are same forces that are destroying the black family and decimating black men.

Peter J. McCusker

Black Enough?

In the 1960s, the Yardbirds, an English rock group, sang, "Turn, Turn, Turn," resurrecting an old biblical injunction advising us that there is a time for virtually everything. Consonant with that advice, there was a time for a vigorous black civil rights movement, a struggle that truly did make America a better place for all its people. Back then, in your face advocacy and black self assertion sometimes was a necessary ingredient in the struggle. Excessive violence did occur sometimes but, true to its creed, most civil rights activities were relatively nonviolent.

The civil rights moment needed to be vigorous and relentless because American society had been complacent in its racial hypocrisy, and progress toward equality was moving at a snail's pace. To keep the movement on course and on time, civil rights activists had to continually remind blacks that they deserved respect and whites, that they were responsible for racial injustices and for correcting them.

Over the years, assertive actions by black and white civil rights groups and lawmakers eventually resulted in formal and informal legislation and popular acceptance of the need to be true to the words of our Declaration of Independence that all men really are created equal. Because blacks had been oppressed and discouraged, civil rights advocacy targeted self-esteem as critical to African American progress.

"Black pride" became a mantra designed to lift up blacks and to restore their confidence. Anyone who viewed it objectively saw the initial idea as a necessary, salutary strategy during an age epoch of rampant racism and marginalization. Over time, however, raceketeers co-opted and corrupted the black pride ethos, even creating a black power salute that is a knock-off of the Nazi sieg heil. Militants, such as Stokely Carmichael and Willie Ricks, turned the socially constructive notion of black pride, a notion embraced by all Americans, into a black racist campaign hell-bent on "burn baby burn" whose major goal was intimidation and destruction. Instead of endorsing a treat-everyone-equal attitude, black power created and proselytized their own "positive" stereotype of what a "real" black person needed to be. In truth, however, the stereotype promulgated a negative black self-identity in that African Americans were mostly defined as the opposite of European Americans. Black identity remained yoked to white identity, not free to pursue any and all opportunities for personal enhancement. Raceketeers assumed the role of black identity slave masters, supplanting the white plantation slave masters of the previous century.

Raceketeers: Bernie Madoffs of the Black Community

Bernie Madoff duped the Jewish community regarding financial resources by appealing to their religious identities. He presented himself as one of their "own," appealed to their trust in his expertise, and encouraged them to invest their finances with him. Raceketeers do the same. They communicate: I'm a nonpareil black man; I'll lead you to the Promised Land; invest your self-concepts to me. Raceketeers then patiently and relentlessly exploit the community, working toward a day when they, too, can enrich themselves to the extent that they can afford a palatial home as grand as Barack Obama's.

Many black identity carpetbaggers immigrated into poor black neighborhoods disguised as preachers, the Reverend Jeremiah Wrights of the community. Others—black and white—got their start in academia. Professors of paranoia convinced black citizens that the deck was stacked against them and that they could not cope. The message was: Racist white America owes you; make them pay; don't work for a pittance; accept welfare. In time, a self-fulfilling prophecy ensured that many blacks did fall further and further behind in their capacities for fulfilling employment. Meanwhile, some "mental health specialists" disseminated their own destructive messages, pronouncing, for instance, that "black rage" was a natural, inevitable consequence of white on black prejudice.

When the welfare state collapsed under its own weight, America was forced to expect more from African Americans, and, more important, they were forced to expect more from themselves. Accordingly, today blacks work in every field of endeavor; it no longer is surprising to encounter a black physician or black engineer. This, of course, is not to say that the employment situation is "good" for blacks, just demonstrably better than it was under the "welfare state."

Despite the fact that African Americans have been slowly clawing their way up from low paying jobs, as Barack Obama's appeal to dancing and T. J. Holmes comment on "swagga" show, definitions of black identity remain entombed in the era of the black power movement. Cobbs and Grier, two African American psychiatrists of the 1960s, wrote that *Black Rage* was the expected outcome of racism, and, by implication, the responsibility of white, not black, Americans.

By 2010, things are little changed: The black intelligentsia continues to find any and all excuses to justify black anger and failure. In *Handbook of African American Psychology*, black editors Neville, Tynes, and Utsey assemble a collection of papers that differ around the edges, but at their hearts are implicit or explicit assertions that African Americans are justified in their distrust of, even rage toward, European Americans, that all black deficiencies are rooted in white racism, and that black accomplishments have been heroically attained despite interference from "white folks." For instance, like Reverend Jeremiah Wright, Thompson and Alfred advocate BLP [black liberation psychology]:

> Black people do not seek out acceptance from Whites; neither are they mystified with some quixotic notion of harmony that ultimately means a compromising of their selves, their groupness. They achieve harmony from within the group, and from this place there likely will be conflict and turmoil that can lead eventually to the regard they deserve as a people.

Having staked out a separatist-paranoid agenda, as all paranoids do, conforming social scientists orient their selves toward gathering proof to justify and to sustain their convictions. Sometimes the effort requires considerable overreach. The poster child of this absurdity is the delusional proposition wherein whites, but not "people-of-color," are said to engage in "racial micro-aggressions," usually characterized by very brief, very subtle, hostile looks, comments, or actions toward non-whites. Of course, to cover their tails, the proponents of this theory note that the racial micro-aggressions also can be acts of omission, such as not being as friendly to a person of color as one would be to a colorless white person.

Some anthropologists, too, seek fame and fortune by appealing to real or fictional white racial animosity. John L. Jackson junior is one of these who took up the Cobbs and Grier mantle by penning a book called, *Racial Paranoia*. Now I certainly do not begrudge him his title, since, I, obviously, have made a thousand indirect references to racial paranoia myself. It's just that, as expected, he uses the term to condemn whites and to rationalize away the shortcomings of blacks. Often he cites racial-micro-aggression-like scenarios in which whites initiate a hateful action and blacks react with "justifiable" paranoia:

> This book tries to explain why race, especially in the form of racial paranoia, is so hard for all segments of America to shake. It is about the suspicions black people have to beat back whenever, say, an idle white salesperson takes a few seconds longer than needed to furrow his brows and sigh himself into unenthusiastic response.

As a non-black, I must confess that white salespersons just fall all over their selves with giddy, ecstatic anticipation whenever I walk into a store. Sometimes I have to separate three, four, or five of them as they, with glowing countenances, relentlessly compete to satisfy my every whim. It can be rather embarrassing.

Having subtitled his book *The Unintended Consequences of Political Correctness*, one of Jackson's major points is that old, in-your-face white racism might have been preferable to what he believes is the new covert white racism. He contends that contemporary white anti-black attitudes drive African Americans to become more paranoid than ever—Cobbs and Grier times two. Jackson attempts to concretize the thesis by referring to the black comedian Dave Chappelle who he suggests "walked away" from a $50 million television contract solely because a white crewmember had reacted in a manner that Chappelle regarded as a possible racial put down. Specifically, Dave Chappelle just had completed a comedic skit wherein he was a wealthy black airline passenger who had been asked which meal he would like and who feared that choosing chicken would reinforce a black stereotype. While walking off the set, "Chappelle says that he glanced over at one of his crewmembers and felt disturbed by **the way** [emphasis added] this person, a white man, was laughing at his racial caricature . . . There is only a **hard-to-pin-down suspicion** [emphasis added] that Chappelle feels while deciphering the **lackey's wordless laugh** [emphasis added]."

If sociologists, psychologists, and anthropologists cannot resist the temptation to blame whites for microagressions and to pardon blacks for anything and everything, we certainly should expect no less from a civil rights attorney. And that is what we get from Michelle Alexander in her *The New Jim Crow*. While she rightly acknowledges that blacks are the major victims of black crime, she chooses to minimize this, to focus instead on black male incarceration as a racist plot to disenfranchise and sideline her people. Ms. Alexander emphasizes that drug-related crime is the primary cause of black male imprisonment, as if it were no big thing. She does not entertain the thought that drug-running causes myriad problems for the offender, the offender's family, and the offender's community, and that many, if not most, of the runners have multiple, sundry offenses, that they usually are convicted by majority black juries, and that most black (and white) criminals of all types never are even brought to trial, let alone imprisoned.

Let's assume that Michelle Alexander's implicit request for drug crime leniency is enacted. Would we expect the black community to reap rich rewards? With a diminution of enforcement, drug trafficking presumably would increase in the "hood," and, with it, all the gang banging and turf warring appertaining. Given the lax laws, more inner-city black males likely would gravitate toward drug dealing and away from school, traditional work, and other socially prescribed pursuits that benefit them, their families, and their communities. In short, drug crime leniency would be more destructive to black safety, self-esteem, motivation, and initiative than welfare ever was.

All the aforementioned illustrates how well-educated, well-heeled raceketeers play word games to achieve personal fame and fortune and to demagogue mostly the black, and partially the white, communities. The examples show the obvious: that when you trade in race, you can always find racism. The Dave Chapppelle saga is particularly transparent. True to the black comedy tradition, without race, Dave has little to say. Here is a man who lives by the sword and dies by it. He cultivates an exquisite sensitivity to anything that can be gerrymandered into being racial for the purpose of exploitation. He creates a "funny" skit, blames a white man for the lackey's wordless laugh, and then, almost literally, tries to make a federal case out of it. Enter the erudite Mr. Jackson who attempts to elevate Chappelle's paranoia via a polished, published intellectualization that he hopes will garner him a few bucks. The circular, self-reinforcing racial capriciousness of institutionalized raceketeering would be worthy of another Dave Chappelle skit, if it were not so tragic.

Now, I am no comedian, but I do have a punch line to the Chappelle charade. On July 22, 2011, Dave took the stage for the 15th Annual Summer Groove in Hollywood, Florida—an event for and by African Americans with an overwhelmingly African American audience. So how did Dave Chappelle do? By all accounts he was irritable, petulant, and defensive. Rumorfix.com described him in an article entitled, "Dave Chappelle Apologizes for Meltdown," and PerezHilton.com called his piece, "Dave Chappelle Booed Off the Stage at Miami Charity Show!" Even Roland Martin, black racketeer and CNN commentator, acknowledged the fiasco. Alex Alverez on RolandMartin.com claimed that Martin's tweets referred to Chappelle's stand-up as "disastrous" and "shitty." On a CNN July 26, 2011 segment, Roland excused Dave, however, saying that the comedian just "can't tolerate heckling."

A certified public account who cannot tolerate heckling: that I can understand. But a stand-up comedian who cannot tolerate heckling? That's a bit like a Florida roofer who can't stand the sunshine, or a rock musician who can't stand loud sounds. Maybe John L. Jackson junior should reconsider the role that the white "lackey" stage crewmember played in Dave Chappelle's having walked away from his alleged $50 million television contract.

In contrast to Chappelle, Chris Rock showed that he can give it and take it when stand-up gets hot.

Chris Rock and Role: Bimps in the Hood

In 1996, Chris Rock toured the United States in the now famous *Bring the Pain* show with the both controversial and celebrated skit, *Niggas vs. Black People* in which he crudely, but convincingly, described elements of

139

a personality type very similar to what I have called "bimps." Although Rock's routine focused on niggas and black people, however, I contend that white people also can be bimps. I suggest an analogy between professional basketball players and bimps. Whites can and do play in the National Basketball Association, but the modal NBA player is black. Similarly, there are plenty dark-triad personality rural and urban white people, but the modal bimp is black and inner-city. So, mindful that Rock's criticisms of "niggas" apply to some whites, too, let's review in detail the underlying uncomfortable, inconvenient truths contained in Chris Rock's skit.

In *Niggas vs. Black People,* Rock repeatedly operated counter to the first commandment of black-white communication: Blacks should never speak honestly and openly about black deficits, black divisions, or "dirty little secrets" (F. James Davis, 2001) when non-blacks can hear. He, of course, knew that his racial courage would engender criticisms so, when he made cutting remarks, he often incorporated his rejoinders into the skits. For instance, Rock ended a segment on bimp criminality saying that "niggas" ruin black peoples' good times with their violent behavior and added, in his comedic way, that he did not buy some African Americans' attempts to blame him or the media for exposing black criminality.

Chris Rock's attack on bimp lawlessness had a clear and strong pro-African American community stridency. He wanted everyone to know that he had had enough of watching his people being victimized by thugs who care about no one by themselves, complaining that blacks must continually fear neighborhood "niggas" breaking into the houses.

Similarly, Rock zeroed-in on bimp double speak in which bimps narcissistically mug for applause and sanctimonious preach to the masses about how wonderful they are. He decried the bimp need to be praised for simply doing the right thing, suggesting that some bimps want "a cookie" when they behave properly, such as when they assume responsibility for their children or manage to stay out of jail.

Rock also tapped into the discrepancy between the ethics of everyday blacks who assiduously labor to make a better life for their families, and bimps who only want to "get over." He underscored that while many blacks are "bustin their asses" working one or more jobs, "niggas" are worried that their "welfare" payments might be reduced and are raising "nine kids on welfare." Using blunt language, Rock advised nine-baby mommas to "just stop fuckin."

Finally, Chris Rock emphasized two systemic problems at the root of bimp subculture—disdain for academics coupled with hyper-masculine swagga attitudes that infect the "hoods" in which they live and that help perpetuate the dark-triad personality legacy. Rock maintained that some "niggas" take perverse pride in "not knowing" academically-oriented "stuff." He advised that persons in black neighborhood should hide their valuables in books, since "books are like kryptonite to a nigga." Chris lamented that African Americans post-high school graduates returning to the inner-city often are treated with suspicion and envy while returning convicts are lionized as heroes.

Chris Rock's fame and comedy permit him to make his points about mainstream, constructive black culture versus the bimp street mentality that threatens it. Others are equally adamant, but struggle to be heard. Referencing his own struggles that ultimately resulted in earning a Ph. D., African American physicist Gary M. Stern, in *Black Issues in Higher Education* January 1997, argues for promoting science education among black youth. Like many other black educators, he celebrates the science enthusiasm of elementary school black children, but laments the attitude of older ones. In Stern's words, "It's not hip for a Black kid to show interest in science."

I would add that science and academics have been crowded out by activities involving hyper-masculine swagga. Clive Lewis, another concerned black man, in *The Telegraph* newspaper August 10, 2007 agrees, saying "Black boys and young men desperately need a greater diversity of images and portrayals, showing that black men can be, and are, successful in a wide range of careers including business, teaching, the law and health care." A comprehensive piece by black Harvard professor Pedro Antonio Noguera in *Motion Magazine* May 13, 2002 also said it well, emphasizing that African American males are expected to "excel in sports, but not in math or history" and, in large part, blaming identity-oriented expectations and a relative absence of role models for those attitudes. The Professor observed that

Even when there are a small number of Black males who do engage in activities that violate established norms, their deviation from established patterns often places them under considerable scrutiny from their peers who are likely to regard their transgression of group norms as a sign of "selling out."

So, we see Noguera pointedly raising black identity as pivotal for academic and vocational success, just as I have earlier.

To summarize, identity problems can be internal and/or external. The internal issue concerns young, academically-oriented African American males who experience unwarranted guilt about their own not-black-enough self image, and the external issue is that those same students, and others, often fear social censure that follows if they step outside of non-socially prescribed roles.

Here's a novel thought: Instead of relentlessly pressuring the so-called not-black-enoughs and so-called Uncle Toms—persons like Bill Cosby, Colin Powell, Condoleezza Rice, Clarence Thomas, and J. C. Watts—African American and Caucasian racial identity slave masters might consider directing their animus toward the black and white bimps who drag our country down.

CHAPTER 9

The Incontrovertible Reality of Race Need Not Be a Really Big Thing

David Chappelle and Chris Rock exploit race, but they did not make race the attention magnate that it is. Human nature did that for them. No matter what double speak some social scientists might throw at you, you know that even toddlers who never have heard a word about race or racism "notice" the race of a person at the racial extreme; that is, a person whose physiognomy and pigmentation makes him look extraordinarily white, black, Asian, and so forth. But that same child also notices a person of any race who is extraordinarily thin, fat, big eared, or big nosed. Race attracts our attention for a fleeting moment, but socialization primes us to linger on race or to move on from it. When raceketeers and mass media—black and white—drone endlessly about race-specific negatives or positives, race continually is fore grounded and reinforced as something critically important that people need to attend to. Only extraordinary citizens can resist succumbing to the constant barrage of race propaganda.

Our race conditioning explains some puzzling social realities. For example, we have been led to believe that segregation is the province of "ignorant" people, that education facilitates racial integration. Perhaps we should recall the higher education of Michelle Robinson Obama. As mentioned earlier, during post-secondary education, the future first lady preferred to separate herself from the white student body, seeking out whites only for opportunistic purposes. She was not the aforementioned extraordinary person capable of resisting our racializing society. Michelle enthusiastically embraced the racializing raceketeers, became a race cadet of the first order, and worked vigorously to earn each and every black patriot merit badge.

Neither was Miss Robinson extraordinary in having been exploited by the purveyors of black-oriented racism. Raceketeers always have targeted African Americans in higher education, since they have the "good sense" and big bucks to enrich the demagogues.

Michelle Robinson's future husband also was on the receiving end, as much as on the giving end, of education-oriented racialization. One can hear the ghosts of Barrack Obama's past: Frank Marshall Davis seeking to instill racial identity fear, telling the teenager "You're not going to college to get educated. You're going there to get trained. They'll train you to want what you don't need. They'll train you to manipulate words so they don't mean anything anymore. They'll train you to forget what it is that you already know. They'll train you so good, you'll start believing what they tell you about equal opportunity and the American way and all that shit." Then there is Bobby L. Rush, mocking the racial identity of the adult Senate candidate by saying that "Barack Obama went to Harvard and became an educated fool. Barack is a person who read about the civil-rights protests and thinks he knows all about it."

In short, The United States President and First Lady are The Stepford Husband and Wife of racial identity, dutifully executing routines programmed into them by raceketeers and our racializing society. Having fallen under the sway of race-based thought, they embraced the cult and evangelized the message.

Social conditioning also accounts for the absurd racial double standard and racial double speak immediately after Barack's presidential election. You recall that initially many talking heads heralded a new day in race relations, given that Obama won forty-three percent of the white overall vote and even won the overwhelmingly white majority state of Iowa. The knee-jerk response was that the white vote signified at least a temporary movement toward a "post-racial" America.

Nobody thought anything of the fact that 95 or 96 percent of black voters voted for Barack Obama. Whites had changed; ergo, racism had improved. Blacks remained prisoners of their own race paralysis, but this "positive" black racism was just fine. As we all know, however, even this benign revisionist thought threatened raceketeers. Fearing that white post-racial behavior would mean loss of special race-based black privileges, they mounted and continue to mount a relentless campaign to mock the notion of significant change in white America while Uncle Tomming any black who dares say otherwise.

With affirmative action as a measure of their righteousness and their ticket to government funding, educational institutions from preschool through post grad have sought to perform conditioning of a racially "salutary" variety. Somewhat paradoxically, this has meant policies such as those that encouraged the creation of black-only student groups, ones Michelle and Barack just adore. These groups further integration? Oh, sorry. Lapse of thought. Black-only student groups are "positive" racial separatism while white-only ones, if they did exist, would be virulent separatist Nazism. Separatist black behavior, "good;" separatist white behavior, "bad." If you doubt this, consider what happened at a mid-sized state school in Pennsylvania.

On December 2, 2010, Angus Johnston of StudentActivism.net, who describes himself as "a historian and advocate of American student organizing" wrote in his blog:

> Early this week my Google search results started lighting up with hits on an old post on White Student Unions. It took me a while to track down the source, but I eventually did—it turns out that someone was posting flyers at West Chester University advertising a meeting of a new white student group on campus.

> West Chester, outside Philadelphia, is a public university of twelve thousand students. Its student body is about 85% white. As photos of the flyers circulated on Twitter, WCU students were upset and annoyed . . . but also skeptical.

> As it turns out, they were right to be. University administrators have announced that there is no White Student Union forming on the campus, and that the flyers were a hoax. The intent, they say, was **"to draw anti-racists together"—it was a case of good intentions gone awry**. [emphasis added]

145

> The identities of the students who posted the flyers have not been released, and **the university plans to take no disciplinary action**. [emphasis added]

> It's worth noting, by the way, that **White Student Unions are pretty much entirely mythical** [emphasis added]—whenever they've been proposed, to my knowledge, they've been nothing more than provocations from one side or the other. **I know of no instance in which students have established a WSU as an actual, functioning organization**. [emphasis added]

Johnston's blog powerfully illustrates some of my major points. First, the mere thought of a white student union is worthy of print space—horrifying to the racialized national consciousness. (Since the United States Census Bureau projects a non-white country beginning in about 2042, maybe someday equal opportunity will include whites having their own student union.) Second, lies, double standards, and double speak are justified to rally the troops, but only when the purpose of the rally is to promote a black agenda, never a white one. Third, posting a flyer encouraging white unity is, at minimum, worthy of scrutiny by Big Brother's Ministry of Truth and for possible retaliatory action by the thought police. Fourth, to search for a white student union is as patently absurd as is searching for the fountain of youth. And finally, Johnston, who specializes in American student organizing, has no knowledge of any white student union. When it comes to the educational conditioning of positive black racism and negative white advocacy there is no doubt that raceketeering philosophy rules the day.

How about religion? Surely religion is the one area that must be free from divisive conditioning enacted through racial double standards, double speak, and double binds. Many white churches expend intense effort to welcome blacks. One successful campaign made its way into *Time* magazine on January 11, 2010 in the form of David Van Biema's article, "Can Megachurches Bridge the Racial Divide?" Van Biema told the story of Willow Creek Community Church, a 23,400 congregation under the leadership of Bill Hybels, its founder and senior pastor. As the result of over a decade long effort, Willow Creek raised its minority membership from virtually zero in the mid-1970s to about twenty percent currently.

Hybels reportedly "re-engineered" Willow Creek to favor minorities, especially blacks. Among the changes were to institute: Bridging the racial divide small group meetings, "larger race-oriented seminars and reconciliation-themed book clubs," a yearly staff bus trip to "bloodstained civil rights pilgrimage sites," and an annual two-day Martin Luther King junior celebration, completed with an eighteen minute multimedia tribute.

Larry and Renetta Butler, a black couple, acknowledged the effort. Renetta explained that the pastor rarely presented a sermon without acknowledging race-oriented features. She spoke of having led five of the racial reconciliation group meetings. Ms. Butler recounted an anecdote from one particular 2001session, the program's first session, during which "a well-meaning white woman" asked, "Do you people want to be called blacks? Or African Americans? I never know what to call you people." Renetta and her brother, also a member of the group, were offended, telling the lady that such talk was "holding them back," making them feel "not included." Not unexpectedly, the woman began crying in frustration and embarrassment (Sound like Elisabeth Hasselbeck?) then asked what she "should" call them.

"You people," often mentioned by blacks as offensive, is emblematic of the racial chasm—racial double standards, double speak, and double binds. Maybe "you people" results from several factors. First, one never can be sure what some race-preoccupied, race hyper-sensitive blacks want to be called. Second, given the frequently observed automatic African American penchant for calling each other "brotha' and "sista," many whites feel a chilly breeze and associated "distance" flowing between them and any black with whom they interact. Third, as mentioned previously, some neutral, or even complimentary, words, such as "articulate" are verboten to white people. Last, there is an equivalency between whites using "you people" and blacks, even phony, half-black ones like Barack Obama, who stereotype Caucasians, such as by referring to multi-state whites by using the collective word, "they" as in, "So it's not surprising then that **they** [emphasis added] get bitter, **they** [emphasis added] cling to guns or religion or antipathy to people who aren't like them or anti-immigrant sentiment or anti-trade sentiment as a way to explain their frustrations."

I have a suggestion for David Van Biema: Write a thorough report on the extent to which black religious institutions are reaching out to whites, and include how welcoming the congregations are. African American Larry Elder provides an example of the relative lack of African American acceptance of whites into their churches, saying

> One white lady wrote to black columnist Larry Meeks about her experience when she attempted to attend a black church in her neighborhood. A lover of gospel music, she could hear the music in her home that came from a nearby church every Sunday. She said that before she even sat down, an usher rudely demanded what she was doing there, and told her that she should go to another church—meaning a white church. She left—hurt disappointed, and embarrassed.

> Meeks responded, "Church racism is a dirty little secret that religious people try to hide and pretend does not exist. Minorities love to fault whites for their racism, but many minorities are guilty of the same behavior.

Wonder if Larry Meeks' gospel-music loving white lady watched "The View" wherein Elisabeth Hasselbeck was excoriated for advocating respectful race-oriented dialogue and integration. They might have had something to discuss between themselves.

Van Biema also provides a little additional perspective on the entire race-church affair, referring to Michael Emerson, whom he describes as a race and faith specialist from Rice University. The latter instructs us that "the proportion of American churches with 20% or more minority participation has **languished** [emphasis added] at about 7.5% for the past nine years." David Van Biema might inform Emerson that people attend same-race churches for the same reasons that they patronized same-race barber and beauty shops; they sometimes prefer affiliating with those who share their experiences and values—plain and simple.

The affiliation tendencies of people are similar to their attention-orienting tendencies, then. Most individuals naturally are drawn toward persons that they regard as most similar to them, and away from those whom they see as excessively different. Here, too, no amount of social science double speak can get around those basic facts. And here, too, society determines whether people mindfully or mindlessly make the determination as to who is and who is not similar to them. Social conditioning is key.

Consider how whites and blacks are socially conditioned about race these days. Virtually all of the race-oriented "propaganda"—from white and black sources, explicit or implicit—directed toward whites is propaganda promoting white acceptance of blacks, white guilt for what "white folks" have done to blacks, and white responsibility for making good toward blacks. Virtually all of the race-oriented "propaganda"—from white and black sources, explicit and implicit—directed toward blacks is propaganda promoting blacks as special, exclusive, and entitled to get from white folks all that white folks owe blacks. Should we be surprised that white majority settings are more likely to include blacks than vice versa? Next time you see video of an entertainment venue featuring a big-time black performer make note of the number of whites in the audience, and next time you see video of an entertainment venue featuring a big-time white performer make note of the number of blacks in the audience. Do the same for virtually any large social gathering and you will see what I mean.

School lunchrooms are not much different. This, of course, has been a particularly touchy subject given the history of segregated eating facilities in bygone days, and I understand the effort to ensure that blacks are treated fairly. Anyone with two eyes, however, knows that despite educational institutions having stood on their heads trying to get the races to sit together at lunch, the project has been an abysmal failure. And any raceketeer readily can give a positive black racism rationalization as to why. Take, for example, Beverly Daniel Tatum, African American president of Spelman College, an "historically black" [so goes the jargon] liberal arts school for women in Atlanta, Georgia, who wrote *Why Are All the Black Kids Sitting Together in the Cafeteria?* Predictably, this woman, who has spent her whole adult life obsessing about and writing about black race advocacy, concludes that black-initiated (but certainly not white-initiated) segregation is not only desirable but necessary. While her argument and conclusion are as expected, I must admit being surprised by the Amazon. com product description of her book:

> Anyone who's been to a high school or college has noted how students of the same race seem to stick together. Beverly Daniel Tatum has noticed it too, and she doesn't think it's so bad. As she explains in this provocative, **though not-altogether-convincing book**, [emphasis added] these students are in the process of establishing and affirming their racial identity. As Tatum sees it, blacks must secure a racial identity free of negative stereotypes. The challenge to whites, on which she expounds, is to give up the privilege that their skin color affords and to work actively to combat injustice in society.

"Though not-altogether-convincing?" What a bold move by Amazon. com; perhaps an oversight. If this ever gets out, I am sure that the National Association for the Advancement of Raceketeers (NAAR) will mount a spirited protest campaign that eventually will result in a new, more complimentary product description being placed on the Amazon website. When the new summary is written it certainly will not mention the fact that when black and white students do voluntarily eat at a table together, one invariably finds more blacks being welcomed to sit at majority white dining tables than vice versa. This occurs because, in general, a white majority tends to be friendlier to blacks than the converse. What a bold thing for me to say! Maybe I can get a job writing product descriptions of raceketeering books at Amazon.com.

Social programming directs us to overstate the importance of race, to communicate about race with double standards, double speak, and double binds, to promote pro-black and anti-white racism, and to make natural human attention and affiliation inclinations seem immoral or evil. Maybe it is time to retool the social programming. To begin, we need first to admit and then to accept that whether it is students at a lunchroom or commuters waiting at a bus stop, there is nothing inherently wrong with wanting to be with people like yourself, so long as that does not infringe on the freedom, safety, comfort, or access of anyone else. Next, we need to stop advocating pro-race for any race and stop talking in ways that elevate any group based on their racial heritage. And, finally, we need truly to look at people based on the content of their character, not the color of their skin; that is, we must look at individuals, accepting them for the unique persons they are and avoiding typing them as Uncle Toms, not-black enough, white trash, or any of a million other racialized epithets.

Imagine a white American man who has absolutely no Chinese language facility, sitting alone in a train station in Beijing. Imagine a black American man at the other end of the train station, also alone, and similarly limited in his ability to speak Chinese. If they happen to meet at that time and place, are they more likely to regard each other in terms of their similarities or their differences? If they happen to meet in the USA after having watched a video of Reverend Jeremiah Wright's raceketeering rant, are they more likely to regard each other more in terms of their similarities or their differences? If Barack Obama owns up to his biracial status, and at every public forum whenever someone characterizes him as black, he corrects them by saying that he is black and white, might this help begin to dampen black-white balkanization and facilitate dialogue on racial reconciliation?

Barack will follow my implicit advice when hell freezes over. He is who he is, a man who has lived a racial lie at least since adolescence. We need authentic black persons to speak authentically, people who are all around us, but who usually have no forum to express their thoughts. Tim Scott, Congressman from South Carolina, is a case in point. Scott is an individual who is proud to be black, but who does not think black; he has the integrity to think Tim Scott. According to ABC News' Cullen Dirner in December 2010, when Scott was invited to join the Congressional Black Caucus, he replied, "While I recognize the efforts of the CBC and appreciate their invitation for me to caucus with them, I will not be joining at this time. My campaign was never about race." Although Diner solicited a response from the CBC, he noted that "So far the Congressional Black Caucus and has not returned messages from ABC News."

Tim Scott exemplifies one who has risen to Eric Holder junior's literal challenge to be racially brave, although I do not for a minute think that Holder wants intrepid honesty when intrepid honesty challenges black advantage. Someone should inform Eric that black people are the ones who need the most racial courage because of pressure from profiteering

151

black demagogues who attempt to talk for them. This is just one more social conditioning stress that weighs heavily on African Americans. When raceketeers try to double speak blacks into believing that they must toe the racial line in order to be genuinely black, they actually are not empowering blacks, but are undermining their independence and self determination—infantilizing them.

Racial Identity: Looking Within Versus Looking Without

Psychologists have shown that that our personality strength usually is enhanced by an internal locus of control (ILOC) which basically means that the individual looks within himself to evaluate circumstances and to decide what is right and wrong for him. Conversely, personal power usually is diminished by an external locus of control (ELOC) that directs one's attention to what other people believe is proper. Sometimes locus of control is global (GLOC), influencing large swaths of thought and behavior, and sometimes it is specific (SLOC), limited to a given situation. The final LOC dimension is temporary-permanent. In short, there are three interrelated dimensions relevant here: internal-external, global-specific, and permanent-temporary, and all three affect a person's independence and self-esteem. Those contingencies might play out like something this:

Internal Locus of Control

Permanent-Global: I always am primarily responsible for my success.

Temporary-Global: While I am out of town, I am responsible for my success.

Permanent-Specific: I always am responsible for learning new skills.

Temporary-Specific: While my supervisor is on vacation, I am responsible for learning the new material that will be presented at the staff development seminar.

External Locus of Control

Permanent-Global: All of my success always depends on my following the advice that I find in black-oriented media.

Temporary-Global: While I am acclimating to my new neighborhood, all of my success depends on my following the advice that I find in black-oriented media.

Permanent-Specific: My emotions at work always depend on my following the advice that I find in black-oriented media.

Temporary-Specific: While I am acclimating to my new job, all of my emotions depend on my following the advice that I find in black-oriented media.

Black racial identity slave masters attempt to inculcate in their victims a global-permanent-external locus of control (GPELOC) where racial identity orientation is concerned. They think they know what basic black is and they are intolerant of exceptions. Of the possible combinations then, GPELOC is the most inimical to an individual. In matters of race and racial identity, such persons are little more than puppets in the hands of racial Machiavellians and other demagogues.

Given that they continually are under withering assault from their would-be racial identity slave masters, only the strongest, most determined African Americans are able to maintain a global-permanent-internal locus of control (GPILOC) regarding race and racial identity. Those with a GPILOC are persons who always say what they believe, regardless of the pressures that invariably are exerted against them. More common are individuals with a specific-temporary-internal locus of control (STILOC) who, while often intimidated by raceketeer-determined standards, find the strength at certain times or situations to speak from their hearts rather than to toe the raceketeer line.

Fortunately, few people are so passive as to fall into the GPELOC racial category, although that person would be a raceketeer's dream—someone easily, readily and totally subject to racial manipulation. On the other hand, when it comes to racial identity, an ELOC is common and, in and of itself, can wreak havoc because racial identity based on ELOC is capricious, subject to the racial thought or behavior du jour that has been determined by raceketeers. A person with any degree of ILOC is a raceketeer's worst nightmare. Those with a racial ILOC identity have the courage and determination to resist the relentless, ubiquitous social conditioning that permeates our society and that promotes a mindless acceptance of the divisive overt, covert, subtle, and blatant racial cues that assail us every day.

There is an added bonus for communities that foster an ILOC rather than ELOC for racial matters: Prejudice tends to decrease under the former condition and to increase under the latter. Lisa Legault, Jennifer Gutsell and Michael Inzlicht (2011) of the University of Toronto Scarborough demonstrate in two studies that external efforts to impose non-prejudicial thoughts and behaviors usually fail. In fact, coercion may even increase racial bias. By contrast, when persons are helped to see the value of equality and, critically, to choose that route volitionally, they are much more likely to behave non-prejudicially. The results of this study support earlier general LOC research showing that when authorities attempt to manipulate subordinates into doing the "right thing," persons previously inclined to perform the desired behavior frequently reject it, presumably in an attempt to maintain their independence (Ryan & Deci, 2000).

In addition to illustrating the importance of ILOC, studies such as those conducted by Legault et al. and Ryan and Deci inadvertently provide insights into the ways that racial propagandizers and raceketeers pervert LOC regarding race. Professional raceketeers know how to market their pro-black product, rarely telling listeners what they specifically should do to be genuinely black, but, rather, talking about what garden variety "real" black men or women do—only implicitly advising the "right" personal identity choices. Identity manipulation is the keystone. In fact, race mongers emphasize that people who freely choose raceketeer-scripted behaviors not only are authentically black, but authentically and righteously black.

In short, raceketeers attempt to delude blacks into misperceiving ELOC-induced choices as independently-initiated ILOC decisions that naturally, definitively differentiate black people from white ones. These racial identity slave masters promote separatism by demonizing whites and minimizing any movement toward inter-racial reconciliation. The race mongers want all Americans to ignore the fact that anti-black racism has slowly but inexorably receded. They broadcast any real or imaginary white racism to justify evangelizing their version of pro-black identity propaganda. Because of raceketeers' repetitive, strident screeching, pro-black advocacy that once had been necessary has evolved, over time, from being stirring, to familiar, to monotonous, to just plain irritating and self-defeating.

Barack Obama succumbed early to raceketeering propaganda that defines black identity as the obverse of white. In fact, the President has made the dichotomous black versus white mentality a centerpiece of his being. That is why he could not bear to check the black AND white blocks on his 2010 census form, as the instructions permit. Over his lifetime, Obama developed a rigid specific-external locus of control (SELOC) where racial identity is concerned. At least since adolescence, in his own mind, he undoubtedly has questioned whether he is acting white, black enough, or Uncle Tom. Barack's private, inner racial turmoil increased and became more publically observable when he left the protective Hawaiian womb, exposing himself to professional black race mongers who literally leveled (and continue to level) not-black-enough and Uncle Tom criticisms toward him.

Once the identity conflict was thoroughly established, the repetition compulsion took over so that now we see the otherwise overly careful, mindful Dr. Barack Obama degenerate into the impulsive, mindless Mr. Barack Hussein Obama whenever his black identity or allegiance is threatened. That, for instance, is what happened during the 2009 Henry Louis Gates, Black Studies professor, versus James Crowley, white police officer, affair.

It is a bit frightening to contemplate a president with half-black skin so fragile that he must scan the environment to ensure that he is "acting" racially pure. As everyone knows, the young set the cool agenda in our country, and, in the black community, inner-city males—mostly bimps—represent the gold standard. Today, Obama must swagga, swoon over basketball, and acknowledge being impressed by rappers, such as Ludacris and Common.

155

Where will Barack's inner-city, adolescent-inspired black allegiances lead him tomorrow?

The major challenge for Obama, and for people like him, is that, similar to other psychological sensitivities, their race-oriented external locus of control becomes more intense and expands its sectors of influence over time. The external focus begins with swagga, basketball, and rap and spreads from there. Originally, those with a racial specific external locus of control (SELOC) attend only to obvious racial stimuli, such as to real racial hate crimes, but the more they look for race, the more they find it. In the United States, social conditioning encourages this racialization "creep" for blacks and whites, so that a Hallmark card about black holes is perceived as about black whores, and NGR on a license plate becomes a racial slur against African Americans. Both subtle and obvious social cues promoting white racial guilt and excusing black racial rage adds to the toxic mix, reinforcing racial paranoia on both sides. In this atmosphere, the black versus white race-obsessed Barack Obamas among us find justification for framing virtually anything as racial, for attributing anything negative to the race demonized as opposite to theirs, and for attributing anything positive to their own race.

America cannot expect its profoundly racially conflicted President to encourage the citizenry to develop an ILOC in racial matters. So what can individual black and white citizens do to promote their own racial ILOC as a first step in addressing the unique 21st century racial divide that confronts us?

We all need to pay attention to the ways that we frame situations racially—positive and negative. The obvious must be understood at a gut-level, not just at an intellectual level: Because someone is of a race different from you does not mean that race is the reason for their behavior when that behavior is different from yours. If a person can dance, it's not because he is black. If a person is mathematically-oriented, it's not because he is Asian. If a person is a gang-banger, it's not because he is black, and if a person is dismissive of non-whites, it's not because he is white. We also must consider the attributions that we apply to others. Psychologists know that all people often exhibit an actor–observer bias such that we attribute our own positive qualities to permanent aspects of our character, our negative qualities to transient situational factors, and that we regard others in the opposite ways. Thus, actor-observer bias causes us to believe that the positive characteristics of others are situational and passing and their faults are inherent and permanent. Finally, we must accept that there is nothing wrong with wanting occasionally to be with people of our own race; that is it no different than sometimes wanting to be with someone who attended our high school. As mentioned earlier, the challenge for America is to decenter from race, so that own-race does not automatically, uncritically signify someone who is like us, and other-race does not does not automatically, uncritically signify someone who is not like us. NEWSFLASH: Black people and white people can be brothers and sisters!

Blacks and whites should not be passive or compliant in the black-white dialogue. They can and should advocate their own opinions and do so in their own language, language that is concrete specific and respectful. The biggest difference between blacks and whites in racial communication is that while black grievances have been aired loudly and relentlessly, white grievances have been whispered and episodic. Overt white advocacy has been relegated mostly to white extremists with their hate-filled agendas. Average white citizens, understandably, have distanced themselves from the bigots. But in doing so, they have overreacted, pretending that they are unaware or undisturbed by the anti-white racism espoused and enacted by some blacks and by some disturbed whites as well. Without a socially acceptable venue for expressing their legitimate racial grievances, white Americans have had to siphon off the associated resentment through surreptitious means and behind closed doors. Society does not grant white people the right even to be racially "irritable," but is sympathetic and welcoming to black "rage." It is for that reason that the New Black Panthers can arm and station themselves at polls, intimidating white voters in word and action while the threatened whites do not even rate protection from the United States Department of Justice.

Language That Sustains the Racial Divide

To talk about race one needs to use language and, sadly, in race-obsessed America, language is structured to promote racial division rather than unity. The process of discourse is constrained. Raceketeers set the race language agenda, decide what can and cannot be said during the discussion, and how the dialogue, or, more likely, black raceketeering lecture and monologue is "executed." Black advocacy is black patriotism. White advocacy is white racism.

Because of raceketeer influence, the prevailing American ethos dictates that only blacks can be considered racial experts, and black race experts are ubiquitous. More black race experts means more racial focus on issues important to blacks and more attention to racial incidents involving blacks. Thus, blacks are always on the racial offensive. The converse applies to whites who always feel under racial assault, and, therefore, always are on the defensive. To be defensive is to avoid or to attack the source of assault. The more whites avoid or retaliate, the more black raceketeers say, "I told you so," and the prognosticating, pontificating race mongers increase in stature, influence, leadership, and assertion in their racial crusade. Whites, in turn, become even more defensive and reactive, and the downward spiral continues.

As mentioned earlier, black demagogues attempt to discredit white input by saying "You don't know what it is like to be black." On the other hand, everyday black individuals who honestly listen to white racial complaints and honestly share their own racial concerns often are shunned and spurned as Uncle Toms. White people are expected to refrain from racial bias; told that "Blacks are people just like you." But that is not how whites are treated by some blacks. Whites can't dance, jump, or swagga. Popular black parlance includes words that specifically exclude whites; who are neither "brothers' nor "sisters." A black African man could fly into JFK from Kenya for the first time, step off the plane, and instantly be regarded as a brother by many members of the black community, whereas a life-long white neighbor, based solely on the color of his skin, never would be viewed as a brother—mostly due to social racial conditioning. When whites say that no one should employ racially incendiary and dehumanizing names such as "nigger" they are told: "No. Blacks can speak this way." Some blacks delight in shocking and silencing whites with provocative street lingo, such as the word "nigger." Racial laws and mores are so twisted that the Supreme Court has decreed that if a black is called nigger by a white person and kills that white person, the curse is considered to be a "mitigating circumstance." In essence, our culture tells whites: Don't even try to see yourself as similar to blacks. If you try, we will use it against you, embarrass you, or worse! Clearly, we must address the double standards, double speak, and double binds of language in detail before we can begin to talk honestly and to constructively approach fundamental issues militating against reconciliation.

On a March 28, 2009 CNN Newsroom segment, T.J. Holmes, the black swagga man, was conducting an interview with Marc H. Morial, president and CEO of the National Urban League, during which Morial was asserting what he believed the national government and Barack Obama needed to do for black Americans. At the time, a few white talking heads had been complaining loudly about that issue, saying that African Americans should take personal responsibility for their own situations and not depend so much on government. Very tentatively and apologetically, Holmes raised that extant, obvious issue, to which Morial responded with a brief, token, platitude-like admission that self determination was important. He then expounded on his original point with even greater specificity, indicating that every level of government—from local to national—should "step up" to help blacks. Holmes permitted Morial's points to go unchallenged, almost as though the newsman's original question was a pretext for advertising the National Urban League platform. The interview then ended with Holmes sheepishly commenting "Thanks my brother," as if to say, "Don't think I was challenging you; I was only doing my job." How often have you heard a reporter end a session with "Thanks my brother?" Would Holmes have taken an apologetic tone and have ended an interview with a similar comment had Morial been white?

Brother is a mind-control strategy, nothing more than a short-hand term for "black enough." As everyone knows, by definition, black Uncle Toms are not brothers and are specifically derided that way. Our society must ask whether the essence of the worth, dignity, and identity of an African American should be reduced to a "black enough" race metric. Is black enough the litmus test of a black person's being? Must everyday blacks continually obsess about defining themselves negatively—as the extreme converse of white? Does being white automatically decree that a Caucasian American cannot be a brother, a role model, or a confidant to a black person?

In his *Dreams* book, Barack Obama repeatedly spoke about his search for an identity to enable him to live life as a "black man." What does that mean? You can live life as a hermit, a world trekker, or a priest because those lifestyles rigidly are defined by what you do—explicit behavioral scripts that you must follow in order to meet the definition of what that kind of a person is. Skin color, however, never defines what you do or who you are; when skin color does, it is playing to the stereotype and is inimical to the player. Only trivial, superficial preferences, attitudes, and behaviors differentiate white groups from black groups, such as when blacks are portrayed as enjoying gospel music and whites, country music. Raceketeers—black and white—are the primary actors who reinforce, underscore, and promulgate the racial stereotypes of their choices. No matter what double speak they throw at you about wanting to forge a color-blind society, they are the primary ones with a vested interest in keeping the races separate and distinct.

Because of social and cultural pressures exerted by the black and white subcultures, raceketeering messages have succeeded more with black people than with white ones. Divisive messages permeate the black subculture with race-alienating talk regularly practiced everywhere from barber shops, to churches, and schools. Black comedy without race talk is called silence. Sports are arenas to show racial allegiance. Basketball, of course is king. If a city has a mediocre or losing basketball team and a gymnastics team of gold medal quality, no self-respecting black would stoop to talking about the latter. Many blacks are taught to embrace Islam primarily because some consider Islam to be a black or "people-of-color" religion, and Christianity, white. It is no coincidence that Islam in the inner-city mostly calls its adherents "Black" Muslims. In an environment wherein race is everything and unanimity of race-oriented opinion is the only opinion tolerated, positions become mandatory "black think" and mandatory "black talk." There is not enough diversity of discourse openly expressed in many black communities to enable whites to see blacks as rational and approachable when there is a racially-oriented difference of opinion. Raceketeering blacks see any space between black people as a threat. The loudest most aggressive and/or most connected black voice is the one that rules the black community. The Al Sharptons determine the black agenda, talk, and silence; they decide what blacks should think and say. Mind control extends to prohibitions against letting whites perceive any dissention in the black position—everything must "stay in the family." No airing of "dirty linen" or "dirty little secrets."

Once the race-specific language police have been mobilized, they expand the range of their territory beyond person-to-person dialogue. Any word or words can be assaulted by their swat team. The Culver City NAACP black holes/blackhoes fiasco is not an isolated event, despite its absurdity. Moreover, blacks are not the only ones on the prowl for pseudo-racist language that even can include initials or word fragments. Consider, for example, how a white woman responded when she received her new license plate. According to CNN Headline News in July 2008, Alice Kunce became offended after discovering that she had been assigned Arkansas plate 018 NGR. Why? NGR to her meant "nigger." And Arkansas? You guessed it; they withdrew the entire NGR series, perhaps replacing it with the WTRSH series.

Maybe Ms. Kunce was wise to renounce her plate. The national landscape is littered with the bones of very powerful but racially misspeaking white folks. To reiterate a few well known ones: There's Geraldine Ferrarro, who felt that Obama never would have been nominated president had he been white; Joe Biden who considered Barack clean, articulate, and bright (Should he have said: dirty, unintelligible, and dim?); and Bill Clinton who regarded the Barack story as a "fairy tale." Less attention was given to Dan Rather who stated that Barack "couldn't sell watermelons if . . . you gave him the state troopers to flag down the traffic." Made almost apoplectic from the ensuing outrage, Rather quickly rationalize his remarks, saying

> I was talking about Obama and health care and I used the analogy of selling watermelons by the side of the road. It's an expression that stretches to my boyhood roots in Southeast Texas, when country highways were lined with stands manned by sellers of all races. Now of course watermelons have become a stereotype for African Americans and so my analogy entered a charged environment. I'm sorry people took offense.

Dan Rather was scrambling to avoid the fate suffered by other commentators who stumbled into the racial buzz saw, such as Don Imus who in April 2007 was fired from both a lucrative radio and television program after crudely referring to the Rutgers women's basketball team as "nappy-headed hoes." While I do not condone his language and have no trouble with his firing, I do have a couple points to make. First, his grooming, language, and bearing suggest a white man with an extraordinary need to swagga. White man, swagga: A clear contradiction, bordering on delusional. How to accomplish this impossible dream? I've got it: Talk bimp! Now, unfeminine equals nappy-headed. Girl equals hoe. A stroke of pure genius. (Through such cool-speak Imus seeks to attain the same level of instant street cred that Barack Obama so painstakingly cultivated when running for elected office in the black community.) If you doubt what I say about the nappy-head incident, refer to the Urban Dictionary that explains the Imus slander as follows:

> Although mainstream media dubbed it as a racist remark it is really used as a more general term to describe broke-down bitches of all races. Misunderstanding that by using the term "Nappy Headed" Imus was merely making reference to the players unkempt appearance not to their black heritage and that with the word "ho" he was simply making reference to them as women and not prostitutes.

I, for one, can appreciate the social conditioning power of lingua-bimpa, since I have witnessed its power in the most unexpected places. Take, for instance, Avalon New Jersey, an upscale beach town with a black population that city-data.com claims is one-tenth of one percent. On a visit there, I noticed a store called *She Be Surfin*, obviously a surf shop for women. Intrigued, by the in-the-hood name that be so out of character with the setting, I asked the owner about it. She answered that it be the brainchild of her husband who once saw a truck with the signage, "He be landscaping." What a be-utiful advertising strategy!

Talking Up Racial Barriers

The definition of race is the soft underbelly of racial conflict. Raceketeers must know who is and who isn't a brotha in order to pretend to advocate for them and against non-brothas. Whoever controls the definition of race has an almost insuperable verbal and practical advantage over all competitors.

There was a time when white raceketeers ruled the day in defining who was black. Those white racists, mostly, but not all, Southern, wanted to marginalize, control, and disenfranchise blacks. One drop of black blood was the definition that they used to oppose black access to equal rights and full citizenship. F. James Davis, retired black professor of sociology at Illinois State University, explains the situation of pre-20th Century America as follows:

> The nation's answer to the question 'Who is black?" has long been that a black is any person with any known African black ancestry. This definition reflects the long experience with slavery and later with Jim Crow segregation. In the South it became known as the "one-drop rule," meaning that a single drop of "black blood" makes a person a black. It is also known as the "one black ancestor rule," some courts have called it the "traceable amount rule," and anthropologists call it the "hypo-descent rule," meaning that racially mixed persons are assigned the status of the subordinate group.

In 21st century America, black raceketeers have replaced white racists as the ones most interested in categorizing people as black **versus** white. If acting white is a crime requiring "black folks" to be monitored and maligned for any and all infractions, then the race police have to know how to decide whether someone is black. Barack Obama cited dancing abilities, since everyone knows that only black people can dance. F. James Davis seems to have given the matter a touch more attention. In his 2001, tenth anniversary edition of *Who Is Black?* Davis talks about longstanding conflicts within the black community about skin shade, underscoring the intra-race skin bias that has plagued black solidarity. He explains how the "one-drop rule" contributed to the in-fighting. He reminds us that segregation pushed virtually all mixed race persons into black neighborhoods where many were scapegoated by their "all-black" neighbors on a too-light to be black basis. Davis cites numerous examples of extreme skin-based prejudice by some blacks against their too-light skinned mono-racial black, bi-racial black, or multi-racial black neighbors. One especially pitiful situation involved a multi-racial young woman living in a black community in Iowa. According to F. James Davis:

She aroused hostility because of her ambiguous appearance and long hair. She tried to be a "good black" but was not accepted. When she tried to date black men, one angry black woman told her, "Leave our black men alone!" At age nineteen, she was raped and severely beaten by a group of young black males because she did not "fit in." As they beat her face, the attackers said they would break her nose because it was "too white."

Given the malignancy of the "how much black is black" preoccupation, African American leaders mounted a strenuous, relentless campaign to have the one-drop rule repealed. Well, not quite. Raceketeers wanted one-drop to be the law of the land in perpetuity. Like the word "nigger," they embraced one-drop, reasoning that more "blacks" in the population meant more power for them. It was not until the late 1980s that a significant, concerted effort coalesced around petitioning the federal government to have the category "multiracial" added to the 1990 census, and that effort came not on the initiative of the black leadership, but of the Association of MultiEthnic Americans, an organization that had just been created in 1988. Speaking of the initiative, F. James Davis noted a blistering assault on the proposed change from . . ."the NAACP, and other black organizations. The issue had become very political. The Congressional Black Caucus, and Democrats in general, opposed this addition, assuming that a multiracial category would reduce the size of the black community and divide it." I guess the Congressional Black Caucus had been ignorant of divisions created by vicious accusations of acting white or not-black-enough and its accompanying violence endemic in the "hoods."

Mind and language control begins with the "one drop of blood" philosophy and with other manipulative ways to define what is race and who belongs in what category. The social attitude that permits one drop leads inexorably to all manner of racial double standards, double speak, and double binds. It is the attitude that allows Emperor Obama with impunity to claim that he is black and never to say that he is white. The thought and language that results in one drop-induced blindness also grants implicit permission for sociologists to say that blacks cannot be racist, that whites should never call blacks "articulate," that legislators can pass laws that discriminate for blacks and against whites, that whites, but not blacks, are culpable for "micro-racist comments," and that blacks are correct to dismiss whites as not knowing what it is like to be black while presuming they know what it is like to be white.

We all have heard of the power of number control: how easy it is to lie with statistics. Word and language control is infinitely more powerful, and even better when statistics and language control are combined. Racial demagogues not only determine who is black and how black, they also masterfully expand or contract word definitions, concepts, and dialogue to suit their purposes. For instance, sometimes racializers argue that African Americans need some resource or other special consideration because blacks are underrepresented, as in a job sector like engineering. Other times, they assert that African Americans need some resource or other special consideration because blacks are overrepresented, as when legislators demand a black-only Congressional Black Caucus because their constituency is largely or totally black.

Changing definitions, concepts, and dialogue related to race-oriented issues also enables raceketeers conveniently to omit counting black Hispanics when complaining that there are not enough blacks in Major League Baseball, to conclude that the overwhelmingly favorable black racial imbalance of National Basketball Association is just fine, although there are not nearly enough black coaches, and to inflate the need for black-friendly legislation and laws by including black Hispanics in those black numbers.

Raceketeers, then, combine their selectively chosen numbers with their selectively defined words to argue for whatever special consideration that is on their agenda. Let's think about that strategy by focusing again on baseball and basketball.

Many race mongers express alarm that Major League Baseball begins 2011 with blacks constituting "only" 8.5 percent of the MBL rosters, and whites, about 64%. [According to the Associated Press, Hispanics comprise about 27% of Major League Baseball, and of course, the 8.5 figure for blacks does not address the black-Hispanic issue, but we will let that ride.] The 2011 National Basketball Association rosters, by contrast, have 78% blacks, and whites, about 17%. So, with the white population accounting for 74.5% of the general population, we have whites underrepresented by about 10% in professional baseball and by about 57% in professional basketball. Blacks, on the other hand, with 12% of the general population are down by 3.5% in baseball and up by 66% in basketball.

America expresses stunned disbelief that African Americans have "slipped back" in baseball. However, slamonline.com, that I use for the basketball racial demographics comments that "Richard Lapchick, the author of this [racial ratios] research, has shown that the NBA is leading all other major sports as **the most uniquely diverse professional sport**." [emphasis added]

Is there anything left to say?

CHAPTER 10

People-of-Color

One drop of blood is a satisfactory strategy for swelling the numbers within the black constituency, but raceketeers hit upon a far better idea. What if there was a way to unite all the people on earth as one massive counterpoint to whites? Presto! People-of-color (POC). The concept POC makes the aforementioned opportunistic racializing "add or subtract strategy" easy, understandable, natural, and even noble. POC are poor, dispossessed, and historically exploited by the evil white man. Black Americans share the history of white exploitation too. Could any alliance be more justifiable? If an almost-black president cannot find enough black cabinet members and black "czars," to pander to him, he can select a so-called person of color who shares his disdain for whites and get credit for it, double credit if the POC is a woman. I, for one, ". . . would hope that a wise Latina woman with the richness of her experiences would more often than not reach a better conclusion than a white male." Don't you agree?

POC-seeking raceketeers have been especially keen to recruit any non-white of notoriety, and to apply pressure to have the person call himself black. The situation with Tiger Woods was particular egregious. In April, 1997 on the Oprah Winfrey Show, Woods was asked if he was bothered when people refer to him as black, to which he replied, "It does . . ."I'm just who I am," whoever you see in front of you." [How very unlike Barry Barack Hussein Soetoro Obama.] Tiger explained that as a young boy he coined the word "Cablinasian" to celebrate his being Caucasian, Black, Indian, and Asian. Seem harmless enough? Not to some black opinion makers who were incensed. Gary Younge, black newsperson of the Guardian

Newspaper, quoted Mary Mitchell, black newsperson of the Chicago Sun Times, as writing:

> When Tiger admits having a problem with being referred to as an African American, it is as if he thumbed his nose at an entire race of people . . . His actions are as conflicting as they are confusing. On the one hand, Tiger Woods gladly accepted the mantle of hero. On the other, he wants to transcend race, at least the African American part of it.

I am always bemused by African American intelligentsia who double speak the definitions of black and person of color (POC) to their advantage. These race-obsessed individuals often are the very same people who, in other venues, when it is to their advantage, claim that race is not monolithic, that people-of-color are not of one mind, or even acknowledge that the very concept of race is elusive. Writing in the journal *Canadian Psychology* in 2009, in an article entitled "Psychology without Caucasians" Thomas Teo of York University addressed the race issue from a scientific perspective, advising:

> Clearly, the terms Black and White are nonsensical from a biological perspective, are embedded in racialized and racist traditions, and are incorrect in terms of their representations. These terms are not sustainable for the long term, but there exists a difference in the pragmatics of language that is relevant to these terms. Although linguistic pragmatics is not a justification for the usage of everyday terms in academic contexts, I suggest keeping the terms Black and White in North America in quotation marks or in Italics—when they are introduced as political categories without biological meaning. This makes them equal to the term Caucasian (both are nonsensical) but different in terms of their application: white and black are understood as socially constructed categories that have no natural representation . . . My concern is that the historical conditioning of thinking in races, including the thinking in Caucasians, will prevent a critical understanding of one's biological ancestry that includes shifting practises of migration and intermarriage, but also notions of identity.

In short, Teo regards black and white not as dichotomous biological categories, but as political concepts. His statements are consistent with two critical ideas. First, the similarities among people are infinitely greater than their differences. Second, demagogues who segregate human beings into racial camps do so to suit their own narrow purposes, most often in a self-serving, disingenuous way. If not black enough, everyone certainly is human enough.

Ideas such as those detailed above muddy the racializing waters—inconvenient, uncomfortable truths. If the American citizenry accepts the validity of race as explained here, raceketeers cannot merely count every black head as someone inherently different from every white head. The POC concept is just one more way to divert our attention to skin and away from the real, fundamental social issues that affect all Americans. Racializers don't want to deal with authentic social issues, such as socioeconomic need, because discussions of socioeconomic need necessarily would include whites and necessarily would exclude most middle class blacks and other middle class POC, diluting the raceketeer power base.

People like Teo threaten raceketeers, because, if he is correct, there is nothing about being black that automatically entitles a person in 21st century America by reason of skin color alone, to any special privilege or to any special consideration. If there are special privileges to be granted, the privileges must be apportioned on a race neutral basis. Sometimes blacks will be overrepresented in the group receiving special consideration and sometimes they will be underrepresented. Black NBA players do not need food stamps, but many white Appalachians do. White college professors do not need state-funded medical care, but many inner-city blacks do.

How does this apply to multiracial POC? Where do they belong on the racial ledger? Barry Obama heard from one such person when he attended Occidental College, and, as he is wont to do, he used the experience to justify his already preconceived, malignant notions of race and racial identity. In *Dreams from My Father*, when reminiscing about his adjustment to school, he wrote that his black experience was more like that of suburban African Americans rather than inner-city ones. Reflecting on black authenticity or lack thereof, he spoke of Joyce whom he had asked about the Black

Student Association. "Good-looking" Joyce replied that she was not black, but "multiracial" with an especially "sweet" Italian father and a mother who was part African, French, Native American, and who knew what else. She tearfully asked Barack why she must choose between the races and then continued, "It's not white people who are making me choose. Maybe it used to be that way, but now they're willing to treat me like a person. No-it's black people who always have to make everything racial. They're the ones making me choose. They're the ones who are telling me that I can't be who I am."

Several lines later, Obama refers to himself with the disparaging term, "half-breed" and alludes again to his profound racial conflict. He makes clear that he cannot merely follow his heart and just be himself—all of himself, black and the white. Rather, Barack allows racial purity to dictate his own sense of self worth, rejecting racially "unclean" blacks and other "unclean" people-of-color in the process. While admitting to being "hard" on Joyce and other blacks who deviate from the Barack Obama-sanctioned definition of basic black, he rationalizes that he needs to "put distance between them and myself" for fear of being a racial "sellout." He then justifies, as well, his friendships with campus radicals of all sorts.

Barack Obama, People-of-Color, and Racial Identity Bondage

To read *Dreams from My Father* in its entirety is to discover that, like Mary Mitchell, Obama has no sympathy for multi-racial POCs who refuse to call themselves black—who refuse to alienate themselves from the totality of their being in order to please black raceketeers. Our race-conflicted president, in fact, frequently does what many nervous people do when everyone is watching him; he jokes.

We already have mentioned that during the Democratic primary, Obama joked about the skin credentials of his Democrat nemesis, Bill Clinton. True to his character, Barack also joked disparagingly about the skin credentials of his Republican rival. At the White House Correspondents' Association dinner of May 9, 2009, Obama made fun of multiracialism quipping, "In the next hundred days, our bipartisan outreach will be so successful that even John Boehner will consider becoming a Democrat.

After all, we have a lot in common. He is a person of color, although not a color that appears in the natural world." The extent of Obama's neurotic skin-oriented repetition compulsion became even clearer about two years later when, on March 12, 2011 at the Gridiron Dinner, Barack returned to his not-so-funny reference to Boehner. After winning the Speaker of the House position a few months earlier, John Boehner had become choked with emotion as he reflected on his childhood working class struggles. The robotic Obama, however, no friend to genuine non-race-based emotion, saw this as an opportunity to mock John for both his skin color and for his sincerity, saying that the Speaker of the House's "unusual skin tone" really was "rust" caused by his tears.

Given that Barack Obama, student of all things racial, learned his evangelical speaking style at the feet of black minister Jeremiah Wright, perhaps he learned his comedic style from black comedian Wanda Sykes who at the May 2009 Correspondent's Association Dinner earlier in the night said that Obama was receiving much positive attention at the time but that if he missteps, the black community will abandon him asking, "What's up with the half-white guy?"

Déjà vu. As has happened his whole life, a black person reminds Barack that his racial cred is provisional and considerably less than skin deep. No wonder he cannot tolerate any racial identity ambiguity. For the president, black is black and white is white; he continues to frame the interpersonal world as he did as a child, transfixed by archaic mental images of his "pitch black" father and "milky white" mother. By choosing Wanda Sykes to perform, he perhaps unconsciously attempts to assuage his own race-conflicted ego and to titillate the racializing blacks and the race-pandering, swagga-loving whites in the audience. The performance undoubtedly is the most racialized display at a formal White House affair since the ante-bellum period ended.

Barack Obama, the NAACP, the Congressional Black Caucus, and raceketeers, black and white, express scant respect for the integrity of multiracial people as multi-racials. To them, multi-racials constitute merely one more group to exploit for their own narrow, misguided black advocacy and black identity purposes. Multiracial people who advocate against race consciousness are no friend to race-based divide and conqueror black-oriented coalitions.

The Hood and People-of-Color

Exploitation that begins at the top inevitably works its way down to the street. Non-black, so-called people-of-color, regularly are targeted by marauding black bimps. For instance, on June 29, 2008 Jennifer Miller of the Daily Local in West Chester, Pennsylvania authored "Chef: Blacks Prey on Hispanics." Her article concerned the nearby community of Coatesville, a town 48 percent black and 11 percent Hispanic. She wrote that:

> The Coatesville Police Department continues to receive reports of black city residents robbing, assaulting and raping Hispanic immigrants, according to Police Chief William Matthew.
>
> Matthews said African Americans are targeting Hispanics who are vulnerable. The victims do not speak English and often do not report crimes to the police out of fear their immigration status will be questioned, he said.
>
> African Americans are responsible for robbing, assaulting and raping Hispanics, as well as invading their homes, Matthews said. "A segment of our community—the African American community—is preying on them."

Preying? Did he say preying? If you think that Chief Matthews is just another white, racist law enforcement officer, demeaning and scapegoating innocent black kids, you are mistaken. Matthews is black, and presumably proud to be so. Equally important, he is a man with the integrity to speak the truth, even when the truth is uncomfortable for him.

South Philadelphia High School, approximately 70 percent black and 20 percent Asian, also captured local headlines in December 2009 when Asian students boycotted classes, protesting years of verbal and physical abuse at the hands of the black majority. On January 26, 2010, Dale Mezzacappa of Metropolis, a Philadelphia-based website and newsletter, reviewed the incident, noting that a group of mostly African American students rampaged throughout the school, down the halls and burst into classrooms, ultimately assaulting at least 30 Asian pupils. In response, fearing for their safety, approximately 50 of the Asian students refused to attend school. With the support of their community, the pupils requested to meet with the African American Philadelphia School District Superintendent, Arlene Ackerman, and asked that she guarantee their safety.

According to Mezzacappa, the Superintendent not only refused to meet with the Asian pupils but also "appeared to take sides rather than try to get to the root of the problem," suggesting that the Asians had started the trouble by having attacked a disabled black student earlier in the week. Weeks passed before Ackerman finally met with the aggrieved pupils. Dale Mezzacappa further explained that Superintendent Ackerman

> . . . created a group of mostly African American "student ambassadors" who were not involved in the violence, and said their voices were missing from the discussion. She said the schools were being asked to solve societal problems. She blamed the situation on the media and on the advocacy groups who were advising and supporting the Asian students. She suggested, without any evidence, that perhaps "gangs" were involved.

The unsympathetic and racially defensive remarks from Arlene Ackerman apparently were par for the course. G.W. Miller, III, Temple University professor and journalist, had tried to alert the public about South Philadelphia High School Asian abuse in an article he posted in September 2009. Three months later, he wrote,

> After 26 Asian students were assaulted at South Philly High in December, dozens of Asian students boycotted classes for more than a week because they didn't feel safe at the school on South Broad Street. They said that Asian students had been randomly attacked for years and neither the school administration nor the district did much—if anything—to help.
>
> When the Asian students returned to school—after a week of intense media coverage detailing the abuses suffered by these

teens—LaGreta Brown, the recently appointed principal at South Philly High, brought students together in the auditorium.

"The newspaper is full of lies," she told the assembly, according to students who attended the meeting.

The principal claimed that the media blew the stories of violence against Asian students out of proportion to sell newspapers and draw viewers to their broadcasts. They did not report the full story, she asserted. There was not a race problem at the school, she told the students; rather there was an undercurrent of violence that exists in the city.

In short, she deflected all criticism and responsibility, which has been the district's consistent approach to this issue.

Racially-biased black superintendent and black principal united in their denial of African American racial aggression and bigotry, blaming two amorphous entities, the newspapers and the city. Asian students paying the price. Big surprise.

Jenna Sommerkom, a white 2006 English as a Second Language coordinator at Southern High, knew firsthand the harassment and indignities suffered by Asian students. Namely, Asians were being targeted relentlessly at least three years prior to their boycott. Susan Phillips of Whyy.org explained that:

> . . . two or three times a month, she [Ms. Sommerkom] witnessed major assaults in the hallways on foreign-born students. But she says school administrators and security staff did not respond to her pleas for help.

> "That was the biggest source of assaults; you had students who would cruise through the floor between classes, just punch somebody or clock a small Asian girl and then run. You would ask someone for their badge and they would verbally abuse you and run."

> Sommerkorn says the Asian students were terrified of entering the cafeteria, and often asked to eat in her classroom. She quit after just 8 months on the job.

The Asian abuse fiasco so alarmed the educational community and legislators that an effort was launched in March 2011 to reinstate the "safe schools advocate" that the previous governor, Ed Rendell, had discontinued. Think about that. Did you need a safe schools advocate in your school in order to keep students from race-based brutality? The need for a safe schools advocate is yet another example of the bimp over academics orientation of inner-city schools. How can people-of-color, black, or white pupils learn in an environment so malignant as to require a corps of adults whose sole purpose is to maintain racial peace?

F. James Davis, the black sociologist whom I cited earlier, spoke of the torment experienced even by some of the most successful bi- and multi-racial blacks. He noted that Halle Berry "reported being called such epithets as 'Zebra' and 'Oreo' when she was at school and since." He said that Renee Tenison, Playboy Playmate of the Year for 1990, protested that she would not deny her white ancestry, and that Chelsi Smith, Miss USA 1995,

> when asked how it felt to be the first black to win, replied that she is both black and white. This rejection of the one-drop rule set off a flurry of controversy in the black press, which usually portrayed Smith's stance as a threat to black unity.

Fortunate for humanity, responsibility-denying racially-challenged inner-city school officials and other Barack Obama types are starting to be counterbalanced by racially courageous persons with a vested interest in the welfare of all POC and of all Americans.

On June 11, 2008, black NPR talk show host Michel Martin emceed a round table with three multiracial persons: Elliott Lewis, author and television freelance journalist; Fanshen Cox, host of Mixed Roots, a film and literary festival specifically designed to discuss multiracial issues; and Paul Foreman, a 19-year-old University of Pomona student whose parents are longtime friends of Ms. Martin. All three expressed frustration with the life-long need to explain themselves to others racially, yet all expressed conditional hope for the future.

Lewis, who had written a book called *Fade: My Journeys in Multi-Racial America*, said that he agreed with a psychologist with whom he had spoken who had suggested that persons of the baby boomer generation are much less accepting of biracial and multiracial identity than are younger persons. He noted that: "One of my earliest experiences in the whole racial identity formation game came when I was somewhere between 10 and 12 years old and my mother, she comes from a large family of 10, so she was taking me over to introduce me to this one particular uncle, who was dark skinned. You know, when she introduced me, and said, you know, this is your uncle so-and-so. He looked at me, didn't say a word and instead, turned to my mother and said, where did you get this white boy from?" Elliot Lewis claimed that many multi-racials are "bothered" when asked, "What are you [racially]?" feeling that the questioner is uncomfortable with deciding how to categorize non-black, non-white people.

Ms. Cox stated that she has trouble classifying herself, adding "I tend to answer for the day, for the moment that they ask me. Right now I'm calling myself black and white. In college I was black. In high school I was mixed. So it really depends on my mood for the day." Tellingly, however, she later said that, " In college, when I was confronted with the 'What are you?' question by a black student, and actually asking me whether I would join the black student union, and I said, well, no, because I'm Jamaican and Scottish. And he said, 'You're black.' And it was something about the conversation we had there, and the impact of his words and also my father, who identifies strongly as a black man, that I suddenly felt a responsibility towards the black community. That suddenly I was accountable."

The youngest member of the panel, Paul Foreman, did not want to have to be accountable, however. He felt that, "It can be a little frustrating. It's strange having to sort of explain my entire family history when I'm asked a simple question, and I wish I had something more easy to identify as. Just to say, this is what I am." [Sounds like Tiger Woods on the Oprah Show.] Obviously wanting to maintain an internal locus of racial control, he later asserted, "For a long time I tried to convince myself that my identity has nothing to do with how someone else sees me. My parents took that opportunity, took many opportunities, to educate me about, first of all, the fact that I can define my identity as a multiracial person, as a black person, as a **white** person. [emphasis added] It's nothing I should have to defend."

Although Foreman was the most explicit about it, all three of Ms. Martin's discussants were talking about racial locus of control, desiring an internal locus and feeling societal pressure toward an external locus. All wanted to be themselves and not to submit to anyone else's definition of who they are or how they should be. Two provided direct examples of racial pressure, both coming from black people: a dismissive, demeaning attitude by Lewis' black uncle and "You must choose or you are a traitor" coercion of a black college student peer. It is reasonable to speculate that the lifelong weight of having to submit to racial identity games and to racial identity coercion played significant roles in Mr. Lewis's writing a book about multi-racism and Ms. Cox's creating a website devoted to it.

Although understandably still tethered to and preoccupied with race, Lewis and Cox soldier on, freedom fighters in the vanguard of a counterattack against racial divide and conqueror social forces. They have managed to achieve half-freedom so far. I hope someday soon they will achieve complete liberation. The youth of Mr. Foreman gives him a reasonable chance.

If he eventually breaks free, Foreman should have a sizable number of cohorts. Tamela Edwards, an African American newscaster, who hosted a 6ABC series with a segment called, "Parenting Across the Color Line" asserted that "Experts now advise kids be raised as bi—or multi-racial" rather than having them chose one race over another with which to identify. Ms. Edwards' also presented an African American professional representative from Children's Hospital of Philadelphia, Marissa Coleman, who seconded the motion, pointing out that "It does not insult one culture and it's a more accurate reflection of who that child is" to identify himself/herself as bi-racial or multi-racial rather than as mono-racial.

CHAPTER 11

Forces That Maintain the Racial Divide

We all know how we arrived at this point. The historical record is clear: 18th and 19th century blacks ruthlessly abducted from African and enslaved by 18th and 19th century whites, servitude, the Emancipation Proclamation, the Civil War, segregation, the civil rights movement, Brown versus the Board of Education, and so forth. But what maintains our black and white racial identity bondage in the 21st century?

We could approach this issue in the conventional way, by speaking about institutionalized racism, "micro racial transgressions," and everything in between. If so, we basically would be following the same archaic black and white raceketeering script that has taken us nowhere. Instead, I will take a different tack, discussing what whites and blacks jointly contribute to the uncomfortable stasis that persists in American race relations. We have spoken directly about some of this and alluded to some. Since I am white, I, obviously, approach race from a white perspective. But, because an honest white perspective rarely is communicated, I hope to have something meaningful to offer. I do not pretend to know what "blacks" sincerely think and feel, but neither do Al Sharpton, Jesse Jackson, NAACP President and CEO Benjamin Todd Jealous, nor does any black or white racial expert. I do not even pretend to know what "whites" sincerely think and feel about race. I do firmly believe that there is no one black or white perspective on race, that intra-individual psychological influences play a crucial role in our racial attitudes, and that there is a social-media complex that relentlessly assails all of us with destructive, manipulative racial messages. For instance, think about the implications of Barack Obama's having been asked about Toni Morrison's referring to Bill Clinton as the first black president. What intra-individual and societal mental processes underlie such a question? What does that vacuous question mean? What does the question say, rather than ask? What personality dynamics cause Obama to answer by manipulatively joking about Clinton's dancing style? Understanding such social-media and intra-individual psychological influences helps prepare us to anticipate and enact changes required to make constructive inter-racial dialogue possible.

Unintended Consequences of the Civil Rights Movement

The Rise of Black Raceketeers

Previously I made several points about the civil rights movement: that, at the time of the movement, in your face black advocacy was a necessary response to the hypocrisy of the unfulfilled American creed that "all men are created equal;" second, that promotion of black self-esteem and black pride were self evident imperatives to be encouraged; third, that pressure by black civil rights groups and white sympathizers led ultimately to formal and informal legislation and popular white acceptance of the need for blacks to be treated in ways consistent with the literal wording of the Declaration of Independence; and, finally, that over time raceketeers co-opted and corrupted the black pride ethos, turning it into an excuse for black militancy and for defining black negatively, as the converse of white. Black militants declared war on white America, doing their best to indoctrinate black youth with their destructive, hateful, racist ideologies. As Barack Obama's mother, Stanley Ann, complained to him, black extremists characterized all whites as racists.

Black raceketeers—militant and non-militant—learned quickly that they could control the black community by declaring themselves the guardians of black identity by which they yoked blackness to anti-whiteness. These identity slave masters grew in fame and fortune in direct proportion to their abilities to squelch any black individuality that contradicted the black identity party line. Raceketeers could not acknowledge improvements in black-white relations, because to do so would be to undermine their own prestige and power. Rather, they had a vested interest in the opposite: to find any "injustice" any "inequality," to magnify it, to underscore it, and to advertise it as broadly and relentlessly as possible.

In short, some blacks who ascended into leadership positions during the height of intense inter-racial conflict have been so richly rewarded as guardians of the masses that they still cannot relinquish their privileged positions. Like third-world rebel soldiers who refuse to lay down their arms when the war is over, they do not want the people to return to normality. Normality is the enemy of those profiteering from chaos.

Unlike the third world, however, America is savvy enough to recognize and to oppose unwarranted, blatant racial warfare. Raceketeers know this well and have adjusted their tactics accordingly. The old hostile, blatant, 20th century anti-white militancy mostly has been replaced by a business-like approach to racializing. In 21st century America, racializers have instituted a sophisticated program to recruit and to train their foot soldiers through education and marketing. Black Studies is a cornerstone of this strategy. I looked for but could not find a reliable statistic on the number of blacks who, when given the chance, enroll in Black Studies and/or major in Black Studies, but the number undoubtedly is very substantial. Every Black Studies major is a student who is not majoring in a non-racialized curriculum, and who will be looking to perpetuate the Black Studies racializing tradition for their entire lives. (Michelle Obama, of course, minored in Black Studies.) One should not look for a Black Studies major to find a cure for cancer or for fossil-fuel-based pollution.

With an army of race cadets to implement their strategies, raceketeer executives, such as Al Sharpton Jesse Jackson, and Benjamin Todd Jealous, enrich themselves: raising and investing their funds, joint venturing with like-minded "race is everything" types, and marketing as broadly and ubiquitously as possible. For instance, while Al Sharpton has been incredibly successful in hiding his net worth, on August 6, 2010, in a Washington Post op-ed piece, Larry Elder, black radio commentator and author, quoted the Village Voice as saying that the Sharpton family lives in an "enormous Brooklyn mansion." Jesse Jackson, however, has been around too long to hide. He was outed by Mychal Massie, a black columnist and former business man, who on September 16, 2003 wrote in wnd.com a commentary entitled, "Jesse Jackson—for blacks or himself?"

Mr. Massie commented on Jackson's "plush lifestyle," featuring limousines, special stock market holdings, "three lavish homes . . . first class travel,

180

private schools and the best universities for his children." The blogger wondered aloud whether big business was doting on Jesse to "assuage" its own guilt. He spoke of wealthy, pandering, colluding Jackson "sycophants," and he ended his piece by asking Americans, "How much longer will you sit quietly by, fully cognizant that your country is being torn away from you by thieves and vandals?"

Although relatively little of substance is known about new president Benjamin Jealous' private finances or ambitions, his NAACP's strategies are part of the public record. Their website is instructive of their current approach to acquiring wealth and spreading their influence. As black adults drifted away, the organization has morphed into "a civil rights organization for ethnic minorities in the United States," no longer limited to "colored people." What a wonderful way to extend influence and to fill coffers. So, while black bimp youth terrorize non-black ethnic minorities, the NAACP solicits support and funds from the self-same people-of-color.

A casual glance at the NAACP website is most revealing. What do you think an organization devoted to the advancement of all people, except white people, reveals as the most prominent permanent feature of its home page? Okay. I'll let you guess. Multiple choices are such fun. Is it: a) treat all people with dignity and respect, b) treat all people-of-color with dignity and respect, c) treat all black people with dignity and respect, d) treat all black women with dignity and respect, or e) none of the above. The answer is "e," but gosh, oh gee, that was a tough one. Let's try another series of answers to our question: They are: a) obey the law, b) stay in school, c) don't sell or use drugs, d) stop shooting guns within 1000 feet of a school zone, or e) "Fathers, live with and take care of your children," or, whoops, I've used up all the mandatory "a" through "e" multiple choice answers. Oh well, you probably already guessed that the correct response, once again, would have been, "none of the above." Rather, the most prominent permanent feature of the NAACP home page as of February 2011 is a GET INVOLVED textbox whose first line contains a glaring dollar sign and DONATE NOW, both printed in oversized font and uppercase letters.

Those sympathetic to the NAACP likely are thinking now that the organization needs money to do their charitable, laudable work. In that case, I suggest that the number one "business" of the NAACP business, like every other business, is to make the organizational hierarchy fat and happy and to stay in business, in their case. mostly through black identity slavery But what credibility do I have? I am just a colorless white man, willing to defer in this matter to an African American who has followed the NAACP for much of his life. That man, Roderick Raynor "Rod" Paige, seventh United States Secretary of Education and first black Secretary, was cited by freerepublic.com on July 17, 2004 as saying:

> I have a message for the NAACP's Julian Bond and Kweisi Mfume, who have accused black conservatives of being the "puppets" of white people, unable to think for ourselves: You do not own, and you are not the arbiters of, African American authenticity.

> I am a lifelong member of the NAACP. I have a great respect for the organization. Its historical leaders, all visionary thinkers, have been responsible for helping to advance the struggle of African Americans over the past century, making our nation a more equitable and race-blind society. Sadly, the current NAACP leadership has managed to take a proud, effective organization in a totally new direction: naked partisan politics, pure and simple.

The NAACP and raceketeers everywhere malign the Roderick Raynor Paiges of the world, because people like Paige not only threaten the establishment today, but also its propagation. Race mongers have created what they correctly perceive as a very lucrative, successful black enterprise. To them, racketeering is a family business that they wish to pass on to the next generation, ensuring that the racial reconciliation that Martin Luther King sought will forever remain his dream and not America's reality.

"It's Our Turn" Mentality

If the first unintended consequence of the civil rights struggle was to create a corps of black elitists determined to exert hegemonic control over the identities, thoughts, feelings, and behaviors of the black citizenry, the second has been that black elitist corps' success in inculcating an entitlement mind-set into the consciousness of many black Americans. The elitists teach that African Americans are justified in doing "whatever," because whitey has been "getting over" for 200 years. By buying into the it's-our-turn-philosophy, blacks can feel justified in making any demands, or in doing anything, from expecting special recognition and special privileges, to outright antisocial activity. For instance, on October 27, 2008, Dawn Turner Trice, black columnist and commentator, wrote in the *Chicago Tribune* that, "police departments around the country are gearing up in case Obama doesn't win. The thinking is that because of the historic nature of his candidacy, there may be riots if supporters feel the election was stolen." Note the word "stolen," suggesting that 2008 was an "our turn" moment—that if the "black" man lost, the election had to have been stolen from its rightful African American owners. And, if the black man lost, people, especially white people, should expect a violent response.

It's-our-turn also must have played a role in Barack Obama's White House decorating decisions in 2009. Newsweek.com reported on February 21, 2009 a story about the bust of Winston Churchill that had been delivered to the White House after the September 11, 2001 attacks on our nation. Tony Blair, no doubt, felt that the man who led the British through their darkest hours aptly represented the grim, relentless determination that Americans needed in our time of trial. Churchill, perhaps more than anyone else, symbolized the oft-repeated "special relationship" that binds the United States to the United Kingdom. But the United Kingdom is a predominantly white country and Winston Churchill was not black. Obama wanted his bust to be one of Martin Luther King junior. Now don't think for a minute that Barack Hussein ever would entertain the thought of having Churchill in the same room with King. White with black? No way. Proselytizing racial coexistence is not a consistent, prominent feature of the Barack Obama dark-triad, good-bad splitting personality mentality. No. Obama had to send that Winston bust back where it belonged—to the British embassy. The English were not pleased. *The Daily Mail* ran the headline: "Churchill out, Martin Luther King in: First glimpse at President Obama's revamped and thoroughly modern Oval Office."

Snubbing a beloved white leader is nothing new for almost-black and for fully black racializers, though. The president simply was being true to his raceketeering roots. Martin Luther King junior's turn had to come at the expense of Winston Churchill.

Just as Winston could not be permitted to share a space with Martin inside, George Washington needed to sequestered, in fact, entombed for a South Caroline rally, so that King could be celebrated in an unsullied manner. John O'Connor of *The State: South Carolina's Homepage* reported on January 18, 2011 that the NAACP nailed a State House statue of Washington into a coffin-like enclosure to hide it during the annual, outdoor Martin Luther King rally that Monday. Now why would they do that? According to O'Connor:

> A three-sided structure that covered the front and sides of the statue was intended to display a rally graphic and serve as a photo-and-television backdrop for the event's speakers, said S.C. NAACP executive director Dwight James. **However, the graphic was not finished before the rally and could not be put in place** [emphasis added].

> Photos from the event showed a three-sided box with Washington's statue visible only from behind the stage. "What we had constructed was a background with a graphic to be placed on it," James said. "We weren't trying to obstruct anything."

> King Day organizers have built similar structures around the statue **dating back at least to 2007,** [emphasis added] according to The State newspaper's archives.

> Most State House rallies, including Saturday's anti-abortion rally, use the statue as an unobstructed backdrop.

Barack Hussein Obama and the NAACP prove once more their all-or-nothing perspectives on race and racial identity. Whites have had their chance; they need to get out of the way now and watch blacks swagga. And watch they do. Aspiring black race cadets in training also watch.

The feeling of "our turn" enabled Kanye West to snatch the microphone from Taylor Swift's hand at the September 2009 MTV video awards ceremony, since Swift is white and West was advocating for Beyoncé, a black woman, because, according to West, "Beyoncé had one of the best videos of all time." Our-turn accounted for Whoopi Goldberg becoming incensed in February 2011 when she incorrectly assumed that she was being snubbed in a *New York Times* article by Manohla Dargis and A. O. Scott that had mentioned a few black Oscar winners, but not Goldberg. According to Marc Schneider's AOL Original posting of February 14, Goldberg "misfired" in feeling "disrespected" by the *Times* article. He reported that it was not Whoopi's "turn" to be irate, since Dargis and Scott were focusing on an entirely different time period in their article: black Oscar winners since 2002, whereas Goldberg's award was earned in 1990.

Black political hacks exploit our-turn to win elections. The most infamous of these is the unbelievable story of Washington D.C.'s Marion Barry. *New York Times,* Times Topics, updated March 2, 2010, recounted his exploitations.

The piece reminded us that in 1990, during his third term in office, Barry was videotaped smoking crack, subsequently spent six months in prison, and in 1994 was re-elected mayor by his black constituents. Barry rewarded his beloved district by presiding over its demise; his tenure "was marked by huge deficits and dysfunctional agencies." But Marion refused to capitulate; after all, it was his turn. In 2002, he ran for City Council, relenting only after "the United States Park Police reported finding small amounts of crack cocaine and marijuana in his illegally parked car." Two years later, that's right, Barry won re-election to City Council. The *Times* summed up Marion Barry's career with the statement: "Over the years, Mr. Barry's public life continued to suffer from steady brushes with the law, including failed drug tests, a conviction for failure to pay taxes, probation violation, traffic offenses and, in July 2009, a charge that he was stalking an ex-girlfriend. (That charge was later dropped.)" Mercifully, perhaps temporarily, Marion Barry's political turn ended in March 2010 with his being accused of corruption in a unanimous censure by the Council of which he was chairman, and the Council's request that Marion be subjected to federal investigation.

If Marion Barry's turn at political entitlement was the most outrageous, Charlie Rangel's has been the most long-lived. Founding member of the Congressional Black Caucus, Rangel was elected to the United States House of Representatives in 1971, replacing Harlem dandy Adam Clayton

Powell junior who repeatedly had been accused of corruption in office. Ironically, Rangel initially had campaigned on a stop corruption platform, only eventually to be convicted of malpractice himself in December 2010. By a 333 to 79 vote, Charlie Rangel was censured by The House for financial misconduct. Fox News' Chad Pergram and The Associated Press reported that Rangel's offenses included: failing fully to pay his New York and Federal Income Taxes for seventeen years (despite having been chairman of the powerful House Ways & Means Committee: the committee responsible for writing tax laws), accepting corporate funding of his two trips to Caribbean conferences, using congressional letterhead and congressional staff to attempt to influence businesses to fund a City College of New York center being named after Rangel, and establishing a Harlem campaign office in the building in which he lived, despite having signed a lease forbidding non-residential use. What other malfeasance has remained undetected?

Star Parker, an African American columnist and commentator, posted a blog on November 20, 2010 entitled, "Why corrupt Charlie Rangel was re-elected." In it, she noted, "Charlie Rangel, convicted of 11 ethics violations—the most ever found against any member of Congress—was resoundingly re-elected November 2nd, getting 80 percent of his district's vote." She added that, of the Congressional Black Caucus' 41 members, 37 of 37 incumbents were reelected, and of the 4 seats that had been vacated, all were won by new black Democrats. Ms. Parker implicitly indicted the one-sidedness of the electoral process by mentioning that, on average, Black Caucus members won 75 percent of the votes.

Reading, Writing, and Raceketeering

The third unintended consequence of the civil rights movement concerns the subversion of education processes and institutions in order to promote what some see as a pro-black agenda.

There was a time, of course, when the education of black Americans was a disgrace. Some African American children received no schooling at all; many others went to inferior buildings with inferior materials and inferior teachers. The most assertive, sustained advocacy was essential to provide even a small modicum of educational adequacy. White racism was the primary cause—pure and simple.

Through exposes, protests, and legislation, things slowly improved. This is not the place to argue whether or not "institutional racism" has been totally eliminated or managed to the extent that education is completely fair. If there are institutional barriers today, however, I firmly believe that they are more related to poverty than to race, and that they impede the schooling of poor white children, as well black. Yet, raceketeers continue to play racial "games" with education. Of the hundreds, I'll mention only two.

The April 19, 2010 issue of *Time* magazine sported the major headline: "Should Schools Bribe Kids? A major new study reveals an uncomfortable truth—it can work (if it's done right)." On the cover was a broadly smiling Norman Rockwellesque white girl, pencil in hand, writing on a piece of paper. In a school bag draped over the back of her chair was a folded test, topped with an enormous "A+" grade. On the corner of the girl's run-of-the-mill school desk was a foot-high stack of dollars and other bills lay scattered at her feet. The cover sure seemed to advocate the "pay me and I will excel" philosophy.

Open the cover and what do you find? Photographs of children participating in a money-for-schooling program pioneered by Roland Fryer junior, a black Harvard economist. The children? There were eighteen shown, and all were black. Speaking of school-initiated "bribes," the article mentioned that

> In recent years, hundreds of schools have made these transactions more businesslike, experimenting with paying kids with cold, hard cash for showing up or getting good grades or, in at least one case, going another day without getting pregnant.

Can you tell me why the article had a white girl on the cover and only blacks inside? I suggest that a program paying children of any color for schooling is intrinsically offensive to most Americans, that the cover was a veritable whitewash designed to displace blame racially in an attempt to make the unpalatable, palatable. Maybe this visual cover version of the education-oriented racial doubles has some redeeming value, but I fail to see it. I believe that it just rates a grade of "D" for deception.

Society does "profit" when children excel scholastically. We all reap benefits when the brightest of the bright are given the enriched educational experiences that they need, such as those executed under the Advanced Placement (AP) umbrella. So what about AP and race? What if there are not "enough" qualified African American children to satisfy an explicit or implicit quota in an AP class? Neal Conan of the NPR radio show *Talk of the Nation* found out on April 25, 2011 in his interview with Junia Yearwood, a retired, apparently black, AP English teacher.

Ms. Yearwood spoke with Mr. Conan about an op-ed she had written for the *Boston Globe* that recounted race-based problems with Advanced Placement at her school. In this case, it was not that qualified black students were being excluded, however, but that unqualified ones were being admitted artificially, dishonestly raising the numbers of minority students—to their detriment and to the detriment of those who were truly AP qualified.

> Conan: And I just wanted to clarify one point, Junia Yearwood. You say administrators were primarily interested in making, forcing, as you say, a lot of these kids to go to A.P., register for A.P. classes, in order to make their numbers look good, in order to say, look, we have lots of minority students in these A.P. classes, not just white kids and Asian kids.
>
> Yearwood: Exactly. The pressure was not just from the school's administration but from the city. They picked up on the campaign for increase in the numbers in A.P., from my perspective. This is my opinion, okay? That's the only reason that so many of my kids were forced to be in A.P. or school at that time and still is; wasn't placed at an underperforming school. But our A.P. classes and numbers tripled, I would say, in two or three years. Now, how could that be?

Putting children from any race into a class for which they are unprepared undermines their self-esteem and confidence—a recipe for failure that is not done with the students in mind, but to empower adults, in this case racializing adults, to achieve their own self-serving ends. Believe me, there are plenty of black children capable of legitimate A.P. African Americans do not need and do not benefit from educational double standards.

If educators are willing to lie in a bogus attempt to place unqualified black children in AP, would they be willing to conduct a no-holds-barred, self-serving cheating campaign across an entire school-district? Well, you guessed it; the answer is a resounding "yes."

Huffpostaolnews' Dorie Turner documented such an outrage on July 16, 2011 in "Atlanta Schools Created Culture Of Cheating, Fear, Intimidation." According to her report, Atlanta permitted institutionalized standardized test cheating from at least 2001 to 2011. Almost half the district schools participated, and, in some cases, teachers literally changed students' test papers, replacing incorrect with correct answers. Some staff members accused high-level administrators of orchestrating the scam. Ms. Turner stated that Atlanta might be required to return "hundreds of thousands of dollars in federal funding that they received for good test performance" and that "at least one member of the Atlanta school board wants to reclaim tens of thousands of dollars in bonus money that former Superintendent Beverly Hall received for the high test scores."

On February 20, 2009, David Gargione speaking for the American Association of School Administrators had explained that Hall, a black Jamaican, began her tenure as Atlanta School District chief in 1999, just before the cheating campaign began. Gargione, however, had not come to bury Hall; he was there to praise her, crowning Beverly as 2009 United States' "superintendent of the year." At the same venue, Dan Domenech, Executive Director of the American Association, said of Beverly Hall, "Throughout her long and successful tenure in Atlanta, Hall has accomplished significant gains in student achievement."

Student achievement surely played the dominant role in Hall's receiving the 2009 commendation. Similarly, Georgia Governor Sonny Parker, on August 24, 2010, announced that the state had won Barack Obama's "Race to the Top" due in large part to the Atlanta record of illegitimate standardized test score improvement. The illicitly earned award promised

$200 million dollars in grants for Georgia schools. With so much on the line, the Superintendent allegedly shrugged off initial accusations of a cheating offensive that almost exactly tracked her superentendency, suggesting instead that the accusers sought only to disparage the district's outstanding test score progress. As evidence supporting the allegations piled up, however, Hall backtracked. Ms. Turner wrote the following regarding the change in Beverly Hall's rendition of events:

> "To the extent that I failed to take measures that would have prevented what the investigators have disclosed, I am accountable, as head of the school system, for failing to act accordingly," Hall wrote. "If I did anything that gave teachers the impression that I was unapproachable and unresponsive to their concerns, I also apologize for that.

In Atlanta, as in Philadelphia, then, the first response of a black superintendent under fire is not only to deny personal responsibility but also to blame others. Moreover, the superintendents both serve school districts with large black majorities, meaning that black students are the primary victims of self-serving adult actions masquerading as concern for those same black children.

If the Atlanta and Philadelphia scandal perpetrators intend their actions to be benign forms of educational double standards in support of African Americans, I advise them to think again. Like all other students, black students at do not need scams; they need honest, quality assessment and instruction. Many African American educators agree. Consider Dr. Walter E. Williams.

Williams, an independent, authentic black man, has lived a life of courageous opposition to raceketeers' supposed pro-black educational advocacy. For instance, on January 4, 1974, when a professor at Temple University's School of Business Administration, Dr. Williams wrote a memorandum to the faculty that began:

> It has come to my attention from several sources that some minority students are being treated differently in the School of Business than are their majority counterparts. The allegations

> and rumors assert that in some classes minority students are receiving grades higher than merited by academic performance. The alleged reasons for this behavior on behalf of my colleagues varies from those having to do with fear to those having to do with "compensatory" treatment. Aside from moral indignation that could be made, I have some observations to make on an academic process that I fear is widespread on Temple campus.

Williams went on to articulate his specific concerns. He spoke in support of unbiased preadmission testing of minorities. On the other hand, the Professor adamantly derided the department's giving credit for "courses with little content, double standards in grading, incomplete or withdrawal grades for failing work, and withdrawal from college disguising flunking out of college," saying that such practices are "clandestine and dishonest and more importantly harmful to black students and black people." Dr. Williams' final and most powerful indictment involved the inimical affects that "double standards" have on black students themselves:

> a: the benevolent paternalism of white faculty members tend to generate "hustler" attitudes among black students.

> b: fraudulent grading denies black students measures of their relative competence.

> c: it fosters superiority attitudes among white students and tends to reinforce stereotypical view held of blacks.

> d: it undermines the effort and merit of those minority students who receive honest grades.

> e: regardless of the intent of double standards in grading, it plays into the hands of the most racist elements in our society for there is no more effective way of destroying the credibility of academic accomplishments by blacks.

Why should we listen to what Walter E. Williams has to say? Because he has lived a life consistent with his words.

Williams was not raised silver-spooned, as Barack Obama and Eric Himpton Holder were. The above quoted excerpts come from Dr. Williams' autobiography, *Up from the Projects*. Walter fought for everything that he has accomplished. Born in 1936, he received no affirmative action; rather, he stared unblinkingly into the eyes of American society when anti-African American racism was common. Despite this, he did not succumb to black racial identity slave masters. Through it all, Walter E. Williams maintained an internal locus of control. He knew the reality of his situations, and he needed neither patronizing special privileges nor raceketeers to tell him what to do in order to achieve his educational and vocational aspirations.

Educational Raceketeering—as all raceketeering—traffics in reality distortion, leading inexorably to problems for individuals directly affected by the raceketeered practice, and for society, in general. As noted above, educational advocacy often has little to do with the intellectual success of African American children per se; rather, its primary purpose is to further raceketeers' own power, prestige, and profit by pretending to advance a pro-black agenda. Sometimes pro-black excuses function as racialized weapons to advance a racializing educator's career.

Pro-black educational advocacy was the ostensible reason for principal pressure applied at the predominately black (86 percent) Thomas Mifflin Elementary School in Philadelphia. Maryclaire Dale of the Associated Press chronicled the dispute in "Lawsuits: Whites told they can't teach blacks." According to the May 18, 2011 article, four white teachers contended that black principal, Charles Ray III, created a racially hostile work environment, treating the aggrieved whites in a biased manner by making them read an article asserting that whites could not adequately teach blacks, ". . . reprimanding them, randomly changing their room assignments, and letting black teachers ignore rules that their white counterparts had to follow." He allegedly directed a supervising teacher to check line teachers' personnel files, and even was accused of having the line teachers' personal lives investigated. When they filed a grievance against him, Ray III reportedly "retaliated" against the white teachers.

Here we find yet another example of racial double standards and double speak. If we accept that white teachers cannot teach black children, should we believe that black teachers cannot teach white ones? How about Indians, Chinese, and Native Americans? Should every racial and ethnic group have its own cadre of teachers and human services providers? The absurdity of white teachers being unqualified to teach black students reminds me of the 1970s debates in psychology as to whether a white psychologist could treat a black patient. Of course, no one then or now ever questioned whether a black psychologist could treat a white patient.

White Man's Laws Do Not Apply

The fourth unintended consequence of the civil rights movement has been the most pernicious, opening the door for some aggressive black males literally to take over the streets of inner cities that have substantial black populations. For years, the raceketeers had given black youth a green light to "stick it to the man," so long as "the man" meant the white man. Violent African Americans learned to count on a sizable collection of Al Sharptons—black and white—to excuse virtually any crime committed by poor, fatherless urchins who had been abandoned by white racist America, left to fend alone on the "mean streets" of urban ghettos. You've no doubt heard of the birth of the blues; well, this was the birth of the bimps.

Black raceketeers had not figured that, once created, the bimp subculture would expand to fill the disciplinary void. Acceptance, and even encouragement, of black adolescent disrespect for white authority aligned synergistically with commonplace adolescent rebellion. Since black kids spent more time with blacks than with whites, their disrespect and disdain for authority eventually affected their intra-community relations as much as their relations with "the man." Black authorities fared little better than white authorities in their inability to rein-in aggressive black youths. Over time, the most violent young bimps started lording it over black authorities, driving them and the general black citizenry behind closed doors, cowering in their homes to avoid barrages of gunfire echoing through the hood.

I must reiterate what I have said before: Violence is not black. White people and people of all races have the capacity for and do commit the most wicked, heinous, aggressive acts. In his book, *Reload, Rethinking Violence in American Life*, Christopher Strain acknowledges this. Equally pertinent to my point, Strain, a white man committed to doing his part to oppose violence, admits that he, himself, struggles with his own hostility-oriented impulses. He speaks of the enjoyment that he has derived from guns and other violence-related pastimes, saying

> Nor do I think that violent video games, movies, or TV shows are morally reprehensible, at least not solely because of content . . . I have gleefully and unapologetically played such games as Grand Theft Auto, Vice City, Max Payne, and Unreal Tournament—a first person shooter that rewards "head shots—for hours on end. I have watched Pulp Fiction more times than I care to admit, and whatever guilt I have felt in watching the Ultimate Fighting Championship has usually faded after the first flurry of bare-fisted knuckle blows.

Whether you find Strain's "confession" refreshing or abhorrent is for you to decide. The important issue for me is that many normal, everyday men, and a sizable number of women, have violent-aggressive impulses that need to be, and usually are, sublimated or otherwise held in check. I believe that the excessive, overt, real-life, acting out of violence in the black community is a direct result of the rise of a bimp mentality and lifestyle that uses race to rationalize their predation. Bimps are given the implicit, and sometimes explicit, message that society-based bias means they will never "make it" in America if they are not aggressive, and that aggression is not so bad as long as it is directed away from those endorsing it.

Rappers regularly sing the praises of bimp subculture, spreading the word far and wide. Thus glorified, the hyper-masculinity and rebelliousness of gangbangers appeal to many black and white male teens, although most embrace the behavior in its mild, swaggaing form, rather than in the overtly murderous incarnation. Again, I repeat that one need not be black, or even be from the inner-city, to be tepidly or virulently bimp. All that is required is that you hold your crotch, promote racial discord and/or misogyny, care about no one but yourself, and act out your rawest extant impulses. Once you begin this narcissist, psychopathic behavior you be on your way to bimphood. Should you aspire to a higher calling, choose an institution of higher education where you can learn Machiavellian tactics that facilitate the development of a full-fledged, soft-core, dark-triad personality structure. Work hard, pander to anyone with money and power, network relentlessly, and you have a fighting chance to become president of the United States.

Bimps of Soft-Core and Hard-Core Varieties

At the extreme, "bimp" is merely a synonym for one variety of narcissistic-psychopathic criminality. I cited black and white bimps earlier when talking about vicious, racially-motivated murderers. But any lesser anti-social or asocial person who adopts a stereotypic gangbanging persona—social boars, bullies, braggarts, and others—qualifies as a garden variety bimp.

Some everyday blacks and whites think that persons with a mild to moderate bimp orientation are kind of cute and sassy. After all, a bimp without swagga is no bimp at all. The supporters reinforce bimp mentality by buying morally and sexually obscene rap records. It's just so titillating to witness an adolescent male giving free reign to raw "sensual" impulse. Conventional social mores are so yesterday, so boring—as boring as white, middle-aged males, even ones who became president despite being swagga-challenged. A bimp can tell it like it is. They not be restrained by dumb-ass social conventions. They be singin straight-up, straight-up, like the following lines from Lil' Jon's "Push That Nigga, Push That Hoe":

> Lame ass niggas get da fuck out da club pussy ass niggas
> get da fuck out da club hoe ass niggas get da fuck out . . .
> Yall ain't nuttin but some hoes Yall ain't nuttin but some hoes

Buoyed by adoration from the teeming masses, even the mildest bimps eventually become emboldened enough to progress from lyrics to actions. Think again about Kanye West's outrageous racialized interruption of Taylor Swift's speech at the 2009 MTV Video Music Awards. If a multi-millionaire on stage with everything to lose thinks nothing of bimping it up before millions of viewers, can we expect any less from fatherless, uneducated, "penniless" boyz n the hood?

It's the penniless part of the fatherless, uneducated, penniless triangle that raceketeers talk up. Lack of economic opportunity, not enough basketball courts, inadequate books and schoolrooms, and other such nonsense is just the platform from which racializing groups proselytize, distorting and exaggerating reality to bolster their claim of needing more money and more social influence. They know just what to do to stop the slide of the young African American male into a black hole. Sorry, can't say "black hole." I mean "abyss," an abyss created by racist white Americans.

African American racketeers broadcast poor, helpless black people propaganda as part of their effort to keep the community under their thumbs via an external locus of control. Moreover, society, at large, colludes, reinforcing the inadequacy messages. Although people of all races find solace in projecting blame for their limitations, only blacks are given a green light to do so. White people have no trouble finding external excuses; they say: I didn't succeed because people treat me unfairly, since I'm chubby, I'm skinny, I'm too tall, I'm too short, I am bald, I have bushy hair. But if you are black, you have every white excuse times two. For African Americans, the scripts go something like this: I didn't succeeded because people treat me unfairly, since I'm chubby, I'm skinny, I'm too tall, I'm too short, I am bald, I have bushy hair, I'm chubby and black, I'm skinny and black, I'm too tall and black, I'm too short and black, I am bald and black, I have bushy hair and I'm black. And unlike whites, who typically are derided for their external projections, black projectors readily find sympathetic black and white listeners who lend credence to their racialized excuses, making African Americans less likely to resist projecting and less likely to begin developing an internal locus of control.

The "you can't make it in conventional white American society and it's not your fault" messages have a counterpoint—the "positive" black male stereotype. Consistent with the bimp persona, the positives are mostly of the hyper-masculine, hyper-aggressive types. Those who epitomize the stereotype aspire to the NBA, the NFL, and the rap music hall of fame. In the media, they see wealthy, high-profile sports and entertainment brothas ostentatiously showing off their bling, tattoos, and fast cars, and decide, "That's for me." Naïve about the odds against their making it in sports and entertainment, they orient themselves away from school and associated activities, disparaging such pursuits as effeminate. Contrary to the stereotype, however, some black adolescents can't jump, can't play sports, and can't dance. Where's their chance for bling? Simple: Gangbanging. Gangbanging requires no extraordinary strength, coordination, agility, or skill of any kind. And hyper-masculine, hyper-aggressive gangbangers demand and get respect, coercing it from their neighbors. No one dares to diss a gangbanger.

The unintended legacy of the civil rights movement, then, was to create an army of raceketeers and race cadets whose mission has been to keep the racial pot roiling, to amplify black-white tensions or inconsistencies, and to mute black-white agreements and consistencies. A cutesy soft-core bimp culture has been reinforced by blacks and whites alike, making hyper-aggressive, narcissistic, psychopathic-like personality characteristics appealing to many black and white teens. Just as natural disasters attract looters like spilt sugar attracts ants, the soft-core bimp ideology caught the attention of the frankly psychopathological who developed it into organized, hard-core criminal bimp activity with the law-abiding black community as its bulls eye.

As the bimp mentality grew in power and scope, the exploitative, the angry, and the exploitative and angry have taken over inner-city black communities in the same way that the Taliban took over Afghanistan. Like the Taliban, raceketeers and bimps try to make people perform prescribed rituals and to refrain from proscribed ones. Sometimes the black raceketeers and hard-core bimp Taliban clap their hands and the people fail to perform. When that happens, the black Taliban feels very disappointed, pouting and complaining that nonperforming people must be infidels—Uncle Toms—who merely pose as faithful. The racial Taliban then symbolically or literally execute the non-believers.

A relative absence of sustained, society-wide opposition to bimp behavior implicitly sanctions its associated quasi-criminality or frank criminality. Lacking adequate moral or legal restraints, bimps have created their own subculture, complete with uniforms, publications, and music. Wikihow. com advises us:

> You probably think that gangsta clothings is just baggy clothings, blings, baseball hats, etc. But there's more, there's a wide variety of gangsta fashion; there's casual-hip hop, straight-up gangsta, pimp-gangsta, preppy gangsta, skater thug, emo gangsta, Mexican gangster/cholo and lastly, but not least, Vietnamese gangstster style.

Goggling "gangsta publications" in February, 2011 yields 185,000 references. Relevant periodicals have titles such as: Downlow Magazine, Gutta World, Murder Dog, and Six Shot. Bimp music "song" labels include, "Swagga Like Us," "That's Gangsta," "Who Shot Ya," and "Why We Thugs."

Just innocent adolescent rebellion. All kids go through a brief "difficult period," right? Not when episodic antisocial gangsta rap words become consistent illegal actions. The misdemeanor youth rebellion of yesteryear—slashing tires and ripping antennas from cars—has been supplanted by "sophisticated," organized anarchy. It is a criminal bimp subculture, intent on honing dark-triad skills and alliances. The adherents do whatever they can to achieve distinction and prestige within their communities. Bimp capabilities are cultivated, intentionally and thoroughly, much as normal people develop school-oriented, music-oriented, or vocationally-oriented ones. This is not just a random collection of kids; they are Lord's Resistance Army-like or Somali pirate-like cadres with underworld mentalities. Like violent third-world insurgency "soldiers," bimps require supportive, accepting, or passive local citizenry to cover for them. Bimps depend on a "They're not predators, they're our children" black community philosophy and Al Sharpton-like raceketeers to cover for Jena-Six-like crimes and worse.

On February 23, 2011, Kare11.com reported an incident of bimp mob violence that occurred in Golden Valley, Minnesota four days earlier. Fifty "kids" attacked a Holiday convenience store, stealing merchandise and assaulting the cashier. Shortly after the mob raced from the store, a shooting occurred nearby, injuring two.

But Minnesota has not invented bimp mayhem. Such incidents occur across many large urban centers. Since I am familiar with Philadelphia, let's focus on it to illustrate the problems.

Cbs3.com on June 2, 2009, spoke of a "South Philly rampage," with assaults and robberies. The report noted:

> Police are searching for a group of teens who went on a destructive
> rampage in South Philadelphia early Sunday morning. Dozens of

teens apparently arranged to meet near South and Broad Streets at about midnight before embarking on an evening of destruction. Police said several of the teens hijacked a Liberty taxi cab near 12th and South Streets, crashing it into a car and a light pole near Fitzwater Street. Two people inside the car and the cab driver were treated for minor injuries. Near the scene, police said a paralegal with the Philadelphia District Attorney's office and another person were pulled from their vehicle and assaulted. The suspects apparently struck the paralegal numerous times before fleeing with her purse. The mayhem continued at a Sunoco A-Plus mini-mart at Broad and Christian Streets as the teens ransacked the business, pilfering and damaging an estimated $3,000 in merchandise.

The South Philly attack appeared to be of the "flash mob" variety, meaning a coordinated assemblage of people who quickly join together to perform some specific action, often bimp criminality, and then quickly disperse. Since then, Philadelphia regularly has experienced this variety of mass chaos. Consider just a few more of the many other flash mob rampages that could be cited all of which were organized and executed by bimps.

On March 23, 2010, Shai Ben-Yaacov of why.org had been the person writing about a relentless campaign of intimidation and violence through which bimps controlled city streets. His article explained the "particularly disturbing" incidents perpetrated by flash-mobbing preteens and teenagers, especially a so-called game of "Catch and Wreck," in which an innocent victim is "chosen at random" and pummeled." According to Ben-Yaacov,

> Two recent assaults on the Market Frankford El involved young teenagers ambushing middle-aged men, laughing and photographing the action. What all the incidents have in common is that they seem to involve young people engaging in violence as recreation.

> The other curiosity about the attacks on El platforms is that the victims in the incidents are brothers.

> Bill Costa is 47 years old and small in stature: about 5'5. He was attacked on the El platform at Bridge Street in Northeast

Philadelphia—by about six kids roughly ages 10 to 15—while he was on his way to a computer class in Center City.

"And as I passed by them, the one kid tripped me, and the other kid pushed me," Costa said. " And I almost fell onto the tracks. I hit my head on the cement, and I broke my finger when I hit the ground.

Bill's attack came on March 3rd, the same day a flash mob swarmed the gallery in Center City, causing widespread damage to retailers and knocking over passersby. He believes the kids who attacked him were on their way to that melee.

"They were saying they were going down town to 'rock it out.' And I don't know what that means, but I don't think it means play music. I don't think that's what they meant."

Bill's brother, Joe, is taller: about 6'1. But he's 57, and his wobbly gait hints at his past drug and alcohol abuse. He lives in Parkside in West Philadelphia—he says he moved there because it's close to the drug rehab center he now goes to. He says most of the time, he eats at a homeless shelter.

Joe was attacked at the 60th Street station on March 4—the day after Bill's attack.

"And I got to the turnstile, and that's the last thing I remember. Somebody hit me with something . . . a board, something . . . and I went down on my knees, and next think I know, there's just eight kids, six guys, two girls just wailing on me."

Actually, Joe doesn't remember that part. He says he didn't actually see any of his assailants. After the attack, someone nearby told him there were six boys and two girls. The man wouldn't identify himself because he lived in the neighborhood, knew the kids, and feared retaliation.

In both Joe's case and Bill's, the kids took pictures with their cell phones.

Sarah Bloomquist and David Henry of abclocal.go.com issued a written report on July 5, 2010 about how "an unruly crowd" assembled at midnight in South Philadelphia after the Independence Day celebration, resulting in a "chaotic scene." ABC local did not elaborate on the chaos, but Rob Taylor of red-alerts.com did. Noting that the police and traditional news organs were trying to soft pedal the mob violence, he asserted, "But word games only help police statistics (We only had 7 flash mobs this year, out of 16 riots! We're doing great!) not the people assaulted, robbed and worse by the lawless and violent youth culture of Philadelphia. Judging from the video and witness statement much of the violence was racially motivated." In fact, on the ABC Action News 6:00 P.M. broadcast, a witness had been interviewed who claimed that he observed people, including an Asian man, being punched in the face for no apparent reason.

The Associated Press, on July 12, 2010, chronicled still another incident of semi-organized chaos in an article entitled, "Black Greek Organizations Not Welcomed in Pennsylvania." Reportedly, after midnight, about 20,000 people massed within just eleven blocks of a South Philadelphia shopping area, resulting in a situation so chaotic that the police had to close off the area, because they feared that the community would be "overwhelmed." The atmosphere of threat continued into the evening when a large fight erupted during which one man was stabbed in the abdomen and another in the forearm.

How unfair for Philadelphia to be unwelcoming to a rowdy crowd of 20,000 swarming within an eleven block area of a shopping district. Maybe the city's previous experiences with similar mobs affected their attitude.

The final flash mob incident that we consider occurred in suburban Upper Darby, a small mixed-race town bordering West Philadelphia which is almost completely African American. On June 28, 2011, Paul Jones of the Philadelphia Inquirer described how 30 males, some preteens, descended on the local Sears Roebuck store en mass in a grab and run frenzy. Of the 16 apprehended suspects, not one was from Upper Darby—all were from adjacent West Philadelphia. Upper Darby Chief of Police, Michael

Chitwood, expressed his opinion that social web sites and/or cell phones were used to organize the onslaught.

Flash mobs garner attention because they are so obvious and relatively infrequent. In contrast, most everyday inner-city violent turmoil, like a Stealth bomber, slips under our radar. Perhaps not coincidentally, the day before the Upper Darby Sears Roebuck assault, Mike Newall and Allison Steele, also of the Inquirer, wrote an article entitled, "32 people shot in 3 days of Philly violence." Although flash mobs were not responsible for the carnage, the lawlessness was pure bimp and may have whet the appetites of the flash-mobbers. According to Newall and Steele, from the 24th through the 27th of June, 2011 Philadelphia police reports documented 32 wounded citizens: 20 shootings, 6 deaths by firearm, and 1 death by stabbing.

Philadelphia, the 4th blackest city in the USA, is not alone in bimp atrocities that regularly occur in every major population center in our nation. Consider metropolitan Chicago, with a black population second only to metropolitan New York, where in 2009 there were 460 homicides compared to 149 military battlefield deaths in Iraq and 317 in Afghanistan. Reflect on the fact that in 2010, black congressman LaShawn Ford joined with his white colleague John Fritchey to call for the National Guard troops to patrol the streets of Chicago because by April 26th, one hundred seventeen Chicagoans already had been murdered in the city (including seven on one night alone), with most killings occurring on the predominantly black, south side (Gordan, 2010).

I strongly suspect that prior to reading the above, many of you did not realize the extent of the bimp-executed, organized, mass violence rampant in our cities. In any case, consider this: Most crime never goes reported. Ask inner-city black women what it is like to live their lives in bimp-dominated neighborhoods, constantly fearing for the safety and welfare of their children and of themselves.

Even wealthy, famous black women suffer from marauding, malevolent, male bimps. For instance, *Mercury News* reported on March 5, 2009 that Chris Brown had been charged with a felony assault against Rihanna, repeatedly punching, choking, and threatening to kill her. Two years later, *TMZ* noted that Brown wanted Rihanna's support to lift the court restraining order against him. Not everybody was buying what Brown was selling, however. For instance, Kiernan Maletsky of westword.com wrote a piece entitled, "Chris Brown is an ass who doesn't deserve another chance." He was incensed that Brown's career had not suffered, that "plenty of people have apparently forgiven Brown," referring to him as "a violent idiot." Maletsky's frustration is understandable; however, the public, at large, rarely recognizes the double standards and double speak that forgives swagging bimps.

Infrequently, raceketeer leaders do grudgingly acknowledge the devastating affect that bimps have had on black neighborhoods, but they then make only half-hearted, inconsistent moves to correct the problem. When, in rare circumstances, the black racial identity slave masters are proactive, they frame their efforts in racially divisive ways. Cases in point are anti-black violence campaigns. We all have seen these: television cameras, newspaper coverage, banners, marches, speeches, and pledges. Sometimes bling masters from the NBA, NFL, and entertainment world make brief cameo appearances, smiling broadly and speaking sternly to the adoring throng. The masters are "giving back," a double speak mantra among many high-profile, successful blacks. (At this point, although it defies proper writing convention, I simply cannot resist an aside: If these benevolent blingers are sincere, I suggest that all the give-backers sign binding legal contracts designating an automatic 30% of their pre-tax income to restoring black families and black communities. Hell, I'm only half as black as Barack Hussein Obama, and I promise, here and now, that if I am awarded the average annual NBA salary of $5.356 million dollars, I will sign the contract, tighten my belt, and live on the remaining yearly salary of $3,213,600.)

After the media leaves, what enduring effort sustains the antiviolence campaigns? Nothing. And what has been the implicit message of anti-black on black violence campaigns? Rapper Sister Soleja, bimpess maximus, explicitly explained why the campaigns are called anti-'black on black" violence, rather than anti-violence, in a May 13, 1992 *Washington Post* interview with David Mills:

I mean, if black people kill black people every day, why not have a week and kill white people? You understand what I'm saying? In other words, white people, this government and that mayor were well aware of the fact that black people were dying every day in Los Angeles under gang violence. So if you're a gang member and you would normally be killing somebody, why not kill a white person? Do you think that somebody thinks that white people are better, or above dying, when they would kill their own kind? [The rapper, obviously, sees whites and blacks as of two different "kinds."]

Souljah was being true to her creed. Mills mentioned a rap "song" the bimpess had written that some people actually paid money to buy. Not quite a lullaby, the *Washington Post* quoted this part:

Souljah was not born to make white people feel comfortable. I am African first. I am black first. I want what's good for me and my people first. And if my survival means your total destruction, then so be it. You built this wicked system. They say two wrongs don't make it right, but it damn sure makes it even.

As expected, Barack Obama's Uncle Jeremiah Wright has had something to say about black on black aggression: No, not to stop it, only to redirect it. Ministers-best-friend.com quotes him as asserting, "Black men turning on black men—that is fighting the **wrong enemy** [emphasis added]. You both are the targets in an oppressive society that sees both of you as a dangerous threat."

Black on black violence, no. Black on white violence, go. Attack or kill whitey and be a black freedom fighter. People espousing this hateful garbage are accessories to the regular black on white slaughter that occurs every day on the streets of 21st century America. For this, there is no march. For this, there are no cameras. For this there are no racial advocates. For this there is no outrage demanding the filing of a case by the Office of Special Investigations in the Criminal Division of the U.S. Department of Justice.

Talking about black on white urban genocide would embarrass white officials and subject them to accusations of racism by Jesse Jackson, Al Sharpton, Benjamin Todd Jealous, and raceketeers of all types. Thus, even though journalist David Mills exhibited a touch of Eric H. Holder junior's elusive "racial courage," he softened his piece by referring to little Miss Souljah as "a woman of poise and intelligence;" saying that "She attended Rutgers University between 1981 and 1987, majoring in history, though she didn't earn a degree" and quoting her publicity material as mentioning that "She has lectured in South Africa, Europe and the Soviet Union." If Souljah has lectured, we witness another selection of black and white markets for bimp-inspired black racism and violence. Would the good sista have been a welcomed lecturer in South Africa, Europe and the Soviet Union, if she had been a white supremacist, advocating their brand of racist poison?

CHAPTER 12

Popular Media:
American Pravda

Government officials avoid speaking about the corrosive effects of raceketeers and bimps on the black and white communities because, like the NAACP hierarchy, most government officials operate primarily out of self interest. They have nothing to gain by causing "a fuss," and everything to lose—a cushy job, excellent salary, gold plated medical and dental care, every paid holiday imaginable, liberal vacation time, a retirement plan that just won't quit, and the opportunity to rake in millions in any number of post-government consulting and lecturing jobs. Moreover, established raceketeers have friends in very high places, all the way up to the Oval Office. Raceketeer guys can get downright nasty when you air their "dirty linen" in public. Government officials would rather let popular media do that investigational stuff and leave stagnation to the government where it belongs.

In one respect, news organizations in America share the same avowed underlining journalistic philosophy as *Pravda*, the principal news organ of the old Soviet Union. Russian N. K. Mixajlovskij (1842-1904) explained the dual meaning of the word "pravda" by saying, "'truth' and 'justice' are called by the same word, and fuse together in one great unity." Truth and justice, isn't that what journalists are talking about when they regularly refer to freedom of the press as the cornerstone of our political system? Usa.usembassy.de apparently agrees, noting that:

> The U.S. media today is frequently known as the Fourth Estate,
> an appellation that suggests the press shares equal stature with the

other branches of government created by the Constitution. The press, or "Fourth Estate" plays a vital role as a guardian of U.S. democracy. That role is guaranteed by the First Amendment to the U.S. Constitution, adopted in 1789, stipulating that Congress not enact any laws abridging freedom of the press.

Truth and justice. Is that what America gets from the 4th Estate where race and race relations are concerned? What about race and government? How do the guardians of democracy handle race when the American presidency, the position that they regularly describe as the "most powerful office in the world" and the keystone of our entire governance, is on the line?

On July 20, 2010, Matt Lewis of Politicsdaily.com commented on a *Daily Caller* expose' regarding the "Journolist," a "listserv where hundreds of liberal journalists and academics collaborate and share information." (One must wonder why the expose conveniently appeared two years too late to have any meaningful impact on the presidential election. But, at least, the truth eventually was disclosed.) The Politicsdaily article said:

Today's column reveals that in 2008, several liberal journalists on the list were overtly discouraging others from covering the Rev. Jeremiah Wright story—his incendiary remarks were an embarrassment for the Obama presidential campaign—and, in at least one case, plotting to undermine the reputation of conservative journalists

Arguably, this is the most disturbing section from the story:

In one instance, Spencer Ackerman of the Washington Independent urged his colleagues to deflect attention from Obama's relationship with Wright by changing the subject. Pick one of Obama's conservative critics, Ackerman wrote, "Fred Barnes, Karl Rove, who cares—and call them racists."

Later, the *Daily Caller* quoted Ackerman as writing:

I do not endorse a Popular Front, nor do I think you need to. It's not necessary to jump to Wright-qua-Wright's defense. What is necessary is to raise the cost on the right of going after the left. In other words, find a rightwinger's [sic] and smash it through a plate-glass window. Take a snapshot of the bleeding mess and send it out in a Christmas card to let the right know that it needs to live in a state of constant fear. Obviously I mean this rhetorically.

The bogus neutrality of the "body journalist" was shamefully on display at the May 9, 2009 White House Correspondents' Association dinner, the one during which Wanda Sykes wondered about whether Obama eventually would be seen for the "half-white fella" that he is, and during which Obama made fun of multiracialism. In his remarks to the Association, Barack, with pubertal-like giddiness, boasted to the sappy-eyed press corps, "Most of you covered me; all of you voted for me." Har, har. Making light of media bias. That's almost as funny as his demeaning jokes about multi-racialism and the Special Olympics. Mr. Obama, that night, your patron saint and Machiavellian mentor, Saul Alinsky, must have been smiling down on you from his exalted throne in the sky.

As the *Daily Caller* expose' implies, press bias during the election was so egregious because journalists feared that any objective assessment could reveal that Barack Obama was totally unqualified to be president. Journalists had to support him because they thought: First, that he was an almost-black man; second, that "white folks" would never vote for an almost-black man if they had all the facts about him; third, that the press didn't want to be blamed if an almost-black man was not elected; and, finally, that the press did not want to be "on the wrong side of history." Given the 2008 election results, media types instinctively knew that many "black folks" and other "people-of-color" would vote for Obama even if he wore a Black Panther outfit and screamed, "Burn, baby burn."

The Media confidently believed that they knew what was right for America, and didn't want to muddy the electoral waters by providing objective, valid information to the racist white populace. The unseemly media colluded with the unknown, and perhaps unknowable, candidate, canonizing and then evangelizing him as a political savior. Even as recently as 2010 the author Jonathan Alter continued the messianic propaganda by titling his Obama book: *The Promise*. The fact that Barack was almost black surely was the central motivator of the pandemic of outrageously irresponsible behavior from all sectors of the popular media. However, this was identity politics, not only based on the candidate's race, but also on the identities of the journalists themselves: media types infatuated with their own elitist perspicacity.

Racialized identity and elitism also figured in a March 2011 National Public Radio fiasco. Repeatedly, I have said that one need not be black to be a raceketeer; all that is necessary is a racially obsessed, sanctimoniously elitist orientation, in the Barack Hussein Obama tradition. Take, for instance, National Public Radio executive Ron Schiller, a white man, caught in a sting operation by two persons posing as members of a Muslim Brotherhood affiliate who indicated their willingness to donate five million dollars to NPR. Using Obama language, Schiller pandered to his potential benefactors by looking down upon the groveling white masses from his exalted throne and pronouncing:

> The current Republican party is not really the Republican party. It's been hijacked by this group; that is, not just Islamaphobic but really xenophobic. I mean, basically, they are, they believe in sort of white, middle American, gun totting—I mean, it's scary. They're seriously racist, racist people . . . Well, to me, this [Egypt uprising of February 2011] is representative of the thing that I, uh, I guess I am most disturbed by and disappointed by in this country; which is that the educated, so-called 'elite' in this country is too small a percentage of the population, so that you have this very large, uneducated part of the population, that, that carries these ideas.

Also like Barack Obama, when caught, Ron Schiller lacked the integrity to own up to his racialized double standards. Instead, he reverted to double speak that is the touchstone of raceketeers everywhere:

> While the meeting I participated in turned out to be a **ruse** [emphasis added], I made statements during the course of the meeting that are counter to NPR's values and also **not reflective of my own beliefs** [emphasis added]. I offer my **sincere** [emphasis added] apology to those I offended.

Let's see if I have this straight, Ronnie. You were tricked into speaking extemporaneously, thus revealing your unedited, authentic convictions. But we now should believe your post hoc statements, since you in no way have been influenced by the firestorm of negative popular opinion that has burnt you to a crisp. And, of course, we do accept that you were insincere then, but "sincere" now.

Okay, one last point after this discussion of NPR, Obama, and his cohorts: there were a couple faint shafts of light in the darkness of the media coverage of the 2008 presidential election. First, on November 24, 2008 (a convenient 20 days AFTER Obama had won) Jake Tapper of ABC News posted the following blog:

Halperin Decries 'Disgusting' Pro-Obama Media Bias in Election Coverage

Via Politico we hear that at a recent conference, Mark Halperin—of Time and ABC News—decried the media coverage of the 2008 race. "It's the most disgusting failure of people in our business since the Iraq war," Halperin said. "It was **extreme bias, extreme pro-Obama coverage**." [emphasis added]

"The example that I use, at the end of the campaign, was the two profiles that The New York Times ran of the potential first ladies," Halperin said. "The story about Cindy McCain was vicious. It looked for every negative thing they could find about her and it cast her in an extraordinarily negative light. It didn't talk about her work, for instance, as a mother for her children, and they cherry-picked every negative thing that's ever been written about her."

The Michelle Obama profile, however, was "like a front-page endorsement of what a great person Michelle Obama is.". . . perhaps the most unfair and negative TV ad run during the entire campaign, by either side, was the Spanish-language TV ad Obama ran against Sen. John McCain, R-Ariz, that got very little media coverage.

> Why didn't it get more coverage? If McCain had run a comparable ad—with unfair charges, **trying to exploit racial tensions** [emphasis added]—would it have been as under-covered?

Second, and more to the point, If you want a comprehensive discussion of the disgraceful 2007-2008 media fiasco that masqueraded as election coverage and its aftermath, I refer you to Bernard Goldberg's, *A Slobbering Love Affair: The True (And Pathetic) Story of the Torrid Romance Between Barack Obama and the Mainstream Media*. For a video treatment of the topic, try *Media Malpractice*, a John Ziegler documentary and official selection of the Newport Beach Film Festival.

What about raceketeers and bimps? How are they treated by the media? You know the answer: the media just fall all over themselves to accommodate. Like government officials, no media type wants his corporate offices to be boycotted with the "No fairness, No peace" chants that would erupt if they were to say something unflattering about raceketeers or bimps. Raceketeers, in fact, are provided a virtual open-door to the press to "get their messages out" to the people. Whenever news shows discuss race, the spokesperson invariably is black, because only blacks are race experts. If there is a panel, and the panel is to speak about, oh let's say white attitudes about race, one likely would find two or three black participants and maybe a token white. When a high-profile black man, such as Samuel L. Jackson, makes a racially contemptuous remark, the item typically is not aired, and, if it is aired at all, it is broadcasted sparingly at a 3:00 A.M.-like time slot. But if Don Imus is equally insensitive, the sound bite is aired continuously, critics are solicited to speak, and a special hour long prime time television report or series about white racism is forthcoming.

Having over-mortgaged their integrity, the fourth estate is deeply underwater. Once an exquisite location where only the "best" people resided, the estate now is up for a short-sale, hoping to recoup some of its losses.

CHAPTER 13

Tell Michelle

When white Americans try to discuss their honest racial opinions, raceketeers harangue them with lectures about how white people "don't know what it's like to be black in America." That statement is at the heart of doubles used to silence non-African Americans during black-white discourse. At times the strategy is wielded so blatantly and so aberrantly that even psychologists, characteristically inclined to be black apologists and white detractors, feel compelled to acknowledge the double standards, double speak, and double binds to which whites are subjected. Phillip Atiba Goff, Claude M. Steele, and Paul G. Davies did that in the *Journal of Personality and Social Psychology*, January 2008 in their article called, "The Space Between Us: Stereotype Threat and Distance in Interracial Contexts." In a series of four studies, they showed that cross-race dialogue is very threatening to white people who fear that merely conversing with blacks makes them vulnerable to accusations that they are racist. Accordingly, those people tend to distance themselves defensively from black conversational partners, with "distance" meaning literal physical distance, as well as interpersonal and mental distance.

Kenneth R. Thomas evidenced an extraordinarily high degree of Eric H. Holder junior's racial courage when in the May 2008 *American Psychologist* he took on the highly lauded concept of white micro racial transgressions that had been pioneered by Derald Wing Sue, a "person of color." Thomas pulled no punches, saying of Sue's seminal paper, "much of what is presented in the article is pure nonsense." He set the stage for his critique by quoting Sue's keystone definition, saying:

> ...racial micro-aggressions are "brief and commonplace daily verbal, behavioral, and environmental indignities, whether intentional or unintentional, that communicate hostile, derogatory, or negative racial slights and insults to the target person or group." Moreover, their article leads one to believe that these micro-aggressions are somehow unique to interracial interactions. One could question whether all or even most of the micro-aggressions described by Sue and his associates are racially motivated.

Although Thomas decimated Sue's psychobabble in a dozen ways, for our current purposes, two points are critically relevant. First, the concept of racial micro-aggressions, if widely publicized and accepted, would gravely undermine the white population's willingness to interact with non-whites. And second, to embrace Sue's assertions as valid is to regard:

> . . . people-of-color as weak, psychologically vulnerable people who are unable to respond effectively even to real incidents of "micro-aggression." White people, despite a few obligatory protestations by Sue et al. to the contrary, come across generally as being consciously or unconsciously "(a) racially insensitive, (b) unwilling to share their position and wealth, (c) believing they are superior, (d) needing to control everything, and (e) treating . . . [minorities] poorly because of their race" (p. 277)."

Seems to me, then, that only the racially micro-intelligent would accept Derald Wing Sue's racial micro-aggression concept.

The aforementioned psychological studies, and all that I know about racial double speak, lead me to conclude that when a race-mongering raceketeer whines that I do not know what it's like to be black in America, I should reply: "You are right. I don't know what it's like to be black in America. And you don't know what it's like to be white in America, especially in an America that panders to the never ending litany of complaints asserted by raceketeering people like you. I wish you could experience what it's like to hear your incessant moaning about how I don't know what it's like to be black"—relentless pro-black, anti-white propaganda not unlike the irritating beep, beep, beep of a smoke alarm whose battery needs to be changed.

White Racial Courage:
Is Anyone Listening?
Does Anyone Care?

So much proactive racial research and media attention to blacks and "people-of-color;" so pitifully little proactive attention to whites from professionals, to what whites believe and to what whites want racially. But, if you open your ears, you will find no shortage of race-oriented white opinion and emotion from everyday people, living everyday lives. Just a few of these follow.

In July 2000, *Pbs.org Online News Hour* reported about a *New York Times* series regarding the state of race relations in our country that included reader questions and comments, such as the following one from Patrick Madden of New York, New York:

> Why is the subject of race always treated as a 'white thing'? Always in an inflammatory context. Why isn't the subject of African American racism ever addressed? To me it is the most violent, virulent and prevalent form of racism in our country today. There are things that so-called 'black activists' say about white people that would get a white man put in jail, or at the very least cost his job and his career but they draw no notice by press and media, no sanction by 'responsible' Black leaders. Don't you think hatred and prejudice are all wrong no matter where they come from?

A viral email sent to me mentioned that physician Dr. Roger Starner Jones became so incensed by the situation presented to him by an African American patient that he submitted a letter to the editor of the Jackson, Mississippi Clarion Ledger who, on August 23, 2009, published it under the title, "Why Pay for the Care of the Careless?"

> During my shift in the Emergency Room last night, I had the pleasure of evaluating a patient with a shiny new gold tooth, multiple elaborate tattoos, and a new cellular telephone equipped with her favorite R&B tune for a ringtone.

Glancing over her chart, one could not help notice her payer status: Medicaid.

She smokes a costly pack of cigarettes every day and somehow still has money to buy beer.

And our president expects me to pay for this woman's health care?

Our nation's "health care crisis" is not a shortage of hospitals, doctors or nurses. It is a crisis of culture, a culture in which it is perfectly acceptable to spend money on luxuries and vices while refusing to take care of one's self or, heaven forbid, to purchase health insurance.

Life is really not that hard. Most of us reap what we sow.

Starner Jones, MD

The next series of quotes were contained in a another viral email and concerned Robert David Hall, a man who served his country with distinction, first, as a United States Marine and, later, as a Massachusetts state senator. Because his powerful blog entry is too detailed to reproduce in its entirety, what follows is a much abbreviated version, focusing only on the most relevant remarks.

First we learn a little about who Robert David Hall is:

I'm 63. Except for one semester in college when jobs were scarce and a six-month period when I was between jobs, but job-hunting every day, I've worked hard since I was 18. Despite some health challenges, I still put in 50-hour weeks, and haven't called in sick in seven or eight years. I make a good salary, but I didn't inherit my job or my income, and I worked to get where I am. Given the economy, there's no retirement in sight, and I'm tired. Very tired.

Next, a comment or two about some famous raceketeers, America, and how our country compares to a couple high-profile people-of-color homelands:

> I'm tired of being told how bad America is by left-wing millionaires like Michael Moore, George Soros and Hollywood Entertainers who live in luxury because of the opportunities America offers. In thirty years, if they get their way, the United States will have the economy of Zimbabwe, the freedom of the press of China, the crime and violence of Mexico, the tolerance for Christian people of Iran, and the freedom of speech of Venezuela.

Hall also is acutely aware of the double standards, double speak, and double binds as well as their deleterious effects on persons of all races.

> I'm tired of being told that "race doesn't matter" in the post-racial world of Obama, when it's all that matters in affirmative action jobs, lower college admission and graduation standards for minorities (harming them the most), government contract set-asides, tolerance for the ghetto culture of violence and fatherless children that hurts minorities more than anyone, and in the appointment of U.S. Senators from Illinois.

Robert expresses his acceptance of black people, in general, but does not shrink from criticizing a pretend black president who does not share his values.

> I think it's very cool that we have a black president and that a black child is doing her homework at the desk where Lincoln wrote the Emancipation Proclamation. I just wish the black president was Condi Rice, or someone who believes more in freedom and the individual and less arrogantly of an all-knowing government.

Skeptical of profiteering elitists, Hall calls them out regarding their smug, "I'm special" attitudes, expectations, and manipulations.

> I'm tired of hearing wealthy athletes, entertainers and politicians of both parties talking about innocent mistakes, stupid mistakes

or youthful mistakes, when we all know they think their only mistake was getting caught. I'm tired of people with a sense of entitlement, rich or poor.

Robert Hall's last major point underscores the way that masters of identity slavery do what Barack Obama so adroitly did during the presidential election campaigns—control discourse by controlling the definitions of who is who, what means what, where responsibilities lie, and how to make wrongs right.

> Speaking of poor, I'm tired of hearing people with air-conditioned homes, with color TVs and two cars called poor. The majority of Americans didn't have that in 1970, but we didn't know we were "poor." The poverty pimps have to keep changing the definition of poor to keep the dollars flowing. I'm real tired of people who don't take responsibility for their lives and actions. I'm tired of hearing them blame the government, or discrimination or big-whatever for their problems.

Like her husband, Barack, Michelle Obama also has lived a life predicated on racial double speak and divisiveness, including Ivy League schooling in black, self-imposed isolation at Harvard, and about 20 years religious indoctrination in bigoted black liberation theology by Reverend Jeremiah A. Wright at Trinity United Church of Christ. As I have noted previously, her February 18, 2008 comment that she was then proud of America for the "first" time in her adult life really meant that it was the first time in her adult life that she was proud of "white" America. That comment by Michelle presented a shameful lesson in racial narrow-mindedness to the men, women, and children of our country. Although I could provide many more examples of Michelle Obama's racial bias, let's consider only three.

The first is an anecdote by Christopher Anderson who mentions that Michelle and some of her white classmates at Harvard Law had volunteered to devote at least twenty hours per week to help the poor, mostly black, Bostonians. According to him,

Peter J. McCusker

Many of her colleagues who came from more affluent backgrounds were witnessing urban poverty for the first time. A few, tired and frustrated, became emotional. Michelle, who had little patience for such self-indulgent displays, waited until she was back in her residence hall to vent her frustration, "oh, puh-leeze," Michelle complained to one of her African American classmates. "Do you think these people want to hear some rich white girl crying? They've got *real* problems. Give me a break!"

Here we not only see the extent of Michelle Robinson's racial contempt, but also her lack of appreciation for white efforts to extend the hand of friendship to blacks. If this sentiment sounds vaguely familiar to you, perhaps you recall my *Dreams from My Father* quote. Barack mentioned taking his white "friend" Jeff home from an otherwise all-black high school party and, when Jeff expressed a desire to understand the "black experience," Obama responded as follows:

In the car, Jeff put an arm on my shoulder, looking at once contrite and relieved "You know, man," he said, "that really taught me something. I mean, I can see how it must be tough for you and Ray sometimes, at school parties . . . being the only black guys and all." I snorted. "Yeah Right." A part of me wanted to punch him right there.

When Barack and Michelle team-up, they double their double standards, double speak, and double bind capabilities. Their racial attitudes come straight from the *Raceketeer Handbook* that regards any positive white overture with suspicion, disdain, and derision. The tried and true formula is followed by all card-carrying members whether a law student, a United States president, or a celebrity discussant on *The View* television show.

For the second example, Michelle Robinson, the student, has morphed into Michelle Obama, the First Lady. While her station has changed, however, her personality has not.

Recall that the Haitian earthquake had struck on January 12, 2010 with devastating consequences. A country over 90 percent black, received vigorous, generous support from white Americans, and from whites all

218

over the world. By April 6th the effort to rebuild and restore Haiti had been in full swing for months. On that day, the Upper Big Branch mine in West Virginia, a 95 percent white state, exploded, immediately killing 25 and trapping 4 more, a catastrophe considered to be the worst mine disaster in more than 25 years. After a week of alternating hope and anguish, on April 13th the bodies of the last four miners were recovered. The community was exhausted and numb, just the time when presidents and first ladies usually arrive to provide solace.

But neither Barack nor Michelle Obama arrived on April 13th. In fact, that very day, Michelle almost literally flew over the West Virginia neighborhood en route to a "surprise" visit to Haiti. Was it a mere coincidence that 28 of the 29 West Virginia miners were white, and not until weeks later, in fact, did those outside of the mining community learn that a solitary miner was black? Would Michelle have delayed her Haitian trip by an hour or two in order to comfort the miners' families had the racial ratio been the converse? You bet she would have.

The final example, also taken from 2010, concerns the Gulf of Mexico calamity after the Deepwater Horizon oil rig exploded on April 20. By July, the worst of the crisis seemed behind us, so Michelle Obama staged a photo-op, encouraging Americans to vacation in the Gulf, saying at the Panama City Welcome Center, "It is vacation time. Folks are looking for things to do with their kids, and this would be a great opportunity to do a few things—help this community, send a different message about the extent of the spill, and also think long term about how the rest of the country can help this economy and the folks down here." Four days later, she and her family hustled onto Air force One to vacation in Maine. One month later still, they were off on a beautiful-people, luxurious extravaganza along Costa Del Sol in Spain about which Andrea Tantaros of the New York Daily News wrote a scathing editorial on August 7, 2010, referring to Lady Michelle Obama as a "modern-day Marie Antoinette."

The Obamas egregiously duplicitous behaviors neither escaped the attention nor the ire of everyday Americans. Scores of emails and articles have circulated through the white community, beginning in February 2008 when Michelle uttered her derisive remarks about not being proud of our country until she felt confident that her husband was going to win the Democratic presidential nomination.

As late as February 2011, the hypocrisy of our First Lady continued to inspire viral emails such as the following:

Dear American Taxpayer

For only the second time in my adult life, I am not ashamed of my country. I want to thank the hard working American people for paying $242 thousand dollars for my vacation in Spain. My daughter Sasha, several long-time family friends, my personal staff and various guests had a wonderful time. Honestly, you just haven't lived until you have stayed in a $2,500.00 per night suite at a 5-Star luxury hotel. Thank you also for the use of Air Force 2 and the 70 Secret Service personnel who tagged along to be sure we were safe and cared for at all times.

Air Force 2 only used 47,500 gallons of jet fuel for this trip and carbon emissions were a mere 1,031 tons of CO_2. These are only rough estimates, but they are close. That's quite a carbon footprint as my good friend Al Gore would say, so we must ask the American citizens to drive smaller, more fuel efficient cars and drive less too, so we can lessen our combined carbon footprint.

I know times are hard and millions of you are struggling to put food on the table and trying to make ends meet. I do appreciate your sacrifice and do hope you find work soon. I was really exhausted after Barack took our family on a luxury vacation in Maine a few weeks ago. I just had to get away for a few days!

Cordially,

Michelle Obama

P.S. Thank you as well for the $2 BILLION trip to India we recently went on. Love ya, mean it.

P.S.S. Hope you had a Merry Christmas, hope Santa was good to you? You know we also had a great Christmas in Hawaii. Thanks again.

Color Commentary about Colorless Americans

Given her sometimes apathy, sometimes disdain regarding white people, it is fitting to provide a lesson for Michelle Obama about the compassion and caring that many white Americans have expressed toward black people every second of her racially shallow life. I challenge Michelle to find equally compelling stories of black people helping whites to match those that follow. Although I could fill a computer hard drive with stories of white activism in support of African Americans, I merely will mention several to make my point.

Power of Half

Charity begins at home. At least it does if you live in Atlanta and are a 14-year-old young lady named Hannah Salwen who decided that her family did not need all the material possessions and financial resources that they had. Rather, Hannah believed that the family should down-size their house and contribute half the sale proceeds to 24 villages in Ghana. Nice thought, but who would do such a thing, especially since the Salwen's literally did not know where in Africa Ghana is? All they knew was that the people there in those villages were desperately poor. That was enough for them.

Because of her selfishness, Hanna, at age 20, was selected as one of *Glamour* magazine's 20 Amazing Young Women. In an interview with hercampus.com's Cara Sprunk on November 22, 2010, when asked what inspired her to launch her project, Hanna replied, "I was riding in the car with my dad and I looked to my left and saw a homeless man and then turned to my right and saw a man in a Mercedes. I toggled back and forth between the have and have-nots and realized I needed to do something about the injustices in the world." That was enough for her.

Goods for Good

While Hannah Salwen's humanitarian charity to black people began at home, Melissa Kushner's started on the road, in association with a 2003 United Nations sponsored trip to Malawi. According to nextgencharity. com, Melissa solicited American manufacturers, convincing them to denote over 4000 pounds of consumer goods to a community center and an orphanage dedicated to helping black children with AIDS. The trip so moved her that she not only continued the work after returning home, but also added Liberia and Pakistan as beneficiaries. In 2006, Melissa founded Goods for Good, ensuring that the needy would not be abandoned. As of 2010, Melissa Kushner's foundation provided health and hygiene, educational, and clothing products to "183 community-based organizations, orphan care centers, and public schools, which serve the needs of 54,000 orphans and vulnerable children across Malawi and Haiti."

According to the Goods for Good website, in 2010, Melissa received New York University's Robert Wagner School of Public Service Torch Award. The choice of Ms. Kusher seemed especially appropriate in that the torch, inspired by the Statue of Liberty, is used by NYU, university-wide, to represent commitment to community service.

Award for Advancing Racial Harmony

While black liberation-oriented organizations, such as Reverend Jeremiah A. Wright junior's Trinity United Church of Christ, indoctrinate their followers with racial anti-reconciliation theory and practice, America-oriented, majority white Christian organizations promote racial unity. Every year the Council for Christian Colleges & Universities (CCCU) presents the Robert and Susan Andringa Award for Advancing Racial Harmony to schools that demonstrate outstanding progress in promoting diversity, racial harmony, and reconciliation. For 2010, that school was North Park University, listed by stateuniversity.com as having a student body that is white (56%), black, non-Hispanic (9%), Hispanic (8.4%), Asian (7.4 %), American Indian/Alaskan Native (.003 %), and race unknown (16 %).

CCU praised North Park for its efforts and successes in furthering diversity by partnering with minority community and faith-based organizations. It recognized the school's sponsorship of diversity-enhancing programs such as Diversity Across the Curriculum: Developing Intercultural Competence in Students, Re-Centering: Culture and Conflict Symposium, and Chicago Latino Film Festival. Some of the educational courses noted were: African American History, Latino Religious Experience in the United States, African History, Foundation of Islam, Culture and Identity in Korea, Hispanic Feminist Theology, The Politics of Mexicans in America, and Politics of the Middle East.

Invisible Children 2008 Human Security Award

Sometimes white advocacy for blacks literally has meant the difference between imminent death and survival, and that is why Jason Russell, Bobby Bailey and Laren Poole won the University of California, Irvine 2008 Human Security Award conferred by the Center for Unconventional Security Affairs (CUSA). The commendation noted the all-white team's "dedication to empowering young people and raising awareness and support for the children of Uganda." What began as nothing more than a relatively casual film-making project ended in the initiation of "a movement that channels the creativity and energy of youth in the United States and Europe into a variety of programs that allow viewers of their films to become supporters and generate resources to provide health, safety and education for the children of Uganda."

Invisiblechildren.com explains the story like this: "In their effort to make a 2003 African-oriented film, Russell, Bailey, and Poole were appalled to discover that Ugandan children were being both conscripted into and victimized by a brutal civil war that had persisted for about 20 years. To expose the atrocity, they documented it in 'Invisible Children: Rough Cut,' a no-holds-barred expose so powerful that it mobilized our nation, resulting in the establishment of the non-profit, Invisible Children, Incorporated."

Today, Invisible Children's mission statement indicates that they are "story tellers," producing and distributing awareness-promoting documentaries about the needs of East-African children. However, Russell, Bailey and

Poole make it clear that their mission is much more than movies. Rather, they assert that:

> With the support we receive from our tours and young supporters, we are able to implement cutting edge programs on the ground in Uganda. To prioritize and understand the needs of the community, our Uganda staff is 95% Ugandan. We focus on long-term development, working directly with individuals and institutions, to best understand the needs of these war-effected areas. We rebuild schools devastated by war, benefiting over 8,400 Ugandan youth in the areas of water and sanitation, books and equipment, refurbishment of structures, teacher support, and technology and power. We provide 690 scholarships to specifically chosen secondary students and 180 full ride scholarships to University. We employ mentors that holistically oversee healthy development for our students. We have also implemented micro-economic initiatives that are impacting 360 Ugandan's in transition from internally displaced camps to their original homes as well as 13 formerly abducted child mothers who are now self-sufficient through our tailoring center that provides training in savings, investment, numeracy, literacy and health. These savings-and-loans initiatives have allowed villagers to save money and earn interest for the first time, freeing them to start their own businesses and provide for their families like never before. We believe that the problems of central Africa need to be tackled comprehensively, from peace to education. Solving them is no easy task, and it will take all of us doing all that we can to ensure it.

Ditch Cancun

Extraordinary people do extraordinary things, but many everyday white individuals do their small parts as well. Elizabeth Fiedler of why.org reported on March 31, 2009 about college students who sacrificed their spring breaks by volunteering with Urban Promise in order to make a personal difference in the lives of the citizens of Camden, New Jersey, an overwhelmingly black city rife with poverty and violence. Under the tutelage of Jim Cummings, a white man, about 200 mostly white college students spent their free time painting school buses, "fixing or cleaning up bathrooms, painting classrooms, building fences, helping get garden areas ready, landscaping projects, and putting up basketball hoops."

As often happens, those everyday college students depended on an extraordinary person, again a white man, to do their parts. The Urban Promises website identified that man as Bruce Main who has been executive director, and currently president, of the organization for over 20 years. In addition to the college volunteer program, Urban Promises was said to host "several after school programs, summer camps, employment readiness programs, entrepreneurial training opportunities, missionary internships, alternative schools for teens and the Camden Forward School—an elementary school experience for low-income families." Moreover, Urban Promise programs was said to be doing their good work now in Wilmington, Delaware, Toronto, Canada Vancouver, British Columbia, and in Lilongwe, Malawi.

Sometimes You'll Never Know Who Helps Whom

Even a single act of unsolicited kindness per year can promote one-person-at-a-time racial reconciliation and inspire those who learn about it. For the past couple years, national television news programs have broadcast a story that fits the bill. At the story's heart is a televised, face-obscured white man who distributes money to the needy during Christmas time. On December 19, 2008, Katie Couric presented brief footage of the man doing his thing. The fellow was shown giving money to black and white people, but mostly black. For example, he presented a black lady with $400 to pay her mortgage, $200 to a black man standing in a cue, and $50 each to an entire class of black adolescents. The world-wide financial crisis had begun in September 2008, and, although the generous one allegedly had lost over "40 percent "of his wealth during the previous several months, he would not refrain from his annual Yuletide charity. The news piece suggested that by Christmas Eve "Secret Santa" would have distributed a grand total of nearly $100,000.

Drugs, Sex, Rock and Roll, and Humanitarianism

In today's world, when celebrities do what superficially looks like the socially "right thing," the general public often responds with skepticism, if not outright scorn: blockbuster singer, Madonna, experienced this first hand, as did baseball superstar, Cole Hamels. Even the humanitarian pioneers Bono and Bob Geldof have had their detractors. But Bono and Geldof stand head and shoulders above virtually any entertainer in the duration and intensity of their social activism. To speak comprehensively about their pro-black efforts would be to add another full chapter to this book. So, with apologies, I merely provide an incomplete, but illustrative, timeline of their accomplishments abstracted from Wikipedia. I deliberately omit mentioning the scores of awards that Bono and Geldof have received.

Bono

1984   sings "Do They Know it's Christmas?/Feed the World" as a member of Band Aid, along with about 43 other, almost totally white, artists.

1986   sings in Live Aid and Band Aid for famine relief in Ethiopia.

1999   launches campaigns to reduce 3rd world debt, to increase awareness of Africa's problems, and to fight AIDS.

2002   encourages the United States government, in general, and President George Bush, in particular, to greatly increase financial support to Africa

accompanies United States Treasury Secretary Paul H. O'Neill on a trip to four African countries.

co-organizes DATA (Debt, AIDS, Trade, Africa) program designed to fight African HIV, AIDS, and poverty

2004   sings again on the this year's version of the 1984 "Do They Know it's Christmas?/Feed the World" release.

begins, with like-minded others, to form ONE, an organization committed to combating preventable diseases and poverty, especially on the African continent

2005   joins Bob Geldof and Bono to organize Live 8 project.

records "Don't Give Up with Alicia Keys, with proceeds going to Keep a Child Alive program for AIDS prevention and treatment in four African countries and in India.

2005   teams with his wife, Ali Hewson, and with Irish fashion designer, Rogan Gregory, to create Edun, a clothing line in which at least 80% of the garments are made in Africa.

2006   cooperates with Bobby Shriver to create Product Red, a brand licensed to partner companies. Project Red's primary goal is to help underwrite Global Fund to Fight AIDS, Tuberculosis, and Malaria in Africa.

2007   is designated a special guest editor for Vanity Fair's July 2007, "The Africa Issue: Politics & Power," employing 20 different covers and having photos of various prominent persons, rewarding them for their Africa-oriented humanitarian efforts.

2007   appears with Brian Williams on NBC Nightly News to publicize Africa's humanitarian crises.

helps facilitate the merger of DATA with ONE, resulting in a world-wide anti-poverty program with special attention to Africa.

Bob Geldof

1984   mobilizes and organizes rock stars to work for Ethiopian famine relief. Co-writes, "Do They Know It's Christmas" and performs it with Band Aid.

1985   co-organizes Live Aid concert with Midge Ure for Ethiopian famine relief.

2002   cooperates with Bono in the DATA (Debt, AIDS, Trade, Africa) program designed to fight African HIV, AIDS, and poverty

2005   creates Live 8 with Midge Ure, eight concerts distributed throughout the world to lobby for donor countries to Africa double aid from donor countries, to cancel debt, and to reformulate trade rules to favor Africa.

2007   accepts advisory position on the Africa Progress Panel, a group committed to demanding that world leaders follow through with commitments that they had made to Africa.

2008   joins forces with Bono in his ONE Campaign, a world-wide anti-poverty program with special attention to Africa.

Save Darfur and More

Bono's and Bob Geldof's humanitarian projects serve as catalysts for another famous celebrity who does not allow fear of public skepticism to deter him from doing what he feels needs to be done—George Clooney. Facesofphilanthropy.com notes that Clooney participated both in the Live 8 and in the ONE Campaign, experiences that apparently reinforced his commitment to Africa and its people. With his father, Clooney has been in the forefront of the Save Darfur Coalition since 2006, among other things, creating the film, "Journey to Darfur."

As recently as October 2010, Clooney met with President Obama to advocate for Sudan. But his pro-black campaigns have not been limited to Sudan. Among his other efforts: George Clooney has been tireless in advocating for Haiti, including having organized the January 2010 "Hope for Haiti Now" telethon. George Clooney, along with Don Cheadle, Matt Damon, Brad Pitt, David Pressman, and Jerry Weintraub created "Not On Our Watch' whose mission statement informs us that the organization works "to focus global attention and resources towards putting an end to mass atrocities around the world" by providing assistance to persons in life-threatening situations. However, two of the three countries targeted for help are African—Darfur, and Zimbabwe—with the third being Burma.

One Courageous Man, One Daunting Mission

Neither Al Sharpton nor Jesse Jackson was there, but Carl Wilkens, a white missionary, and his wife, Teresa, were during the 1994 apocalyptic genocide that ravaged Rwanda. Hutus literally were butchering Tutsis in towns and villages across the nation. The United States Embassy had decreed that all Americans should evacuate immediately, and almost everyone did.

Genocideintervention.net explained that Wilkens remained, however, resolving to rescue as many Tutsis and to quell as much violence as one person could. His first efforts were directed at successfully helping to protect Tutsi friends and neighbors. For three long weeks, he and six of them lay huddled in his home with no other goal than to survive the slaughter. Next, Carl realized that the nearby Gisimba Orphanage was in the sights of murderously rampaging militia. Intervening with the Hutu prime minister of Rwanda, he helped ensure that over 400 orphans and staff escaped massacre. After order was restored to the country, Wilkens continued to work tirelessly for the next eighteen months to do his part in contributing to reconciliation and rebuilding. For the whole harrowing story, please refer to Carl Wilkens book, *I'm Not Leaving*.

Kanye West's Favorite Racist President

In September 2005 during a NBC special to support disaster relief for New Orleans, Kanye West accused the president of racism screeching, "George Bush doesn't care about black people!" This, of course, is the very same Kanye West who, almost exactly four years later, stormed up from the MTV Video Music Awards audience onto the stage and wrenched the microphone from the hand of Taylor Swift who was about respond to having just been selected as winner in the Best Female Video category. In his racially-biased way, he disrespected Swift with the thinly-veiled slander, "Yo Taylor. I'm really happy for you, I'm going to let you finish, but Beyonce had one of the best videos of all time." So nice, though, that Kanye told Taylor that he planned to let her finish—a real gentleman.

But what of the racist, Bush? Perhaps we should let Bob Simon of CBS News tell us about Bush's racism.

On April 4, 2010, Simon presented a 60 Minutes report entitled, America's Gift: Fighting HIV/AIDS in Uganda, introducing it by saying:

> As president, George W. Bush did something momentous that few of you may know about—something so momentous that it is saving millions of lives and generating good will for America around the world.
>
> Millions of Africans who had been dying of AIDS are now living with AIDS, thanks to President Bush's program. The U.S. is providing pills to more than two million people with HIV/AIDS, people who could never afford them and who were condemned to die. The medicine not only saves their lives, it permits them to live full lives.

George Bush had launched the program in 2003 and the fruits of the initiative had grown steadily over the years. 60 minutes quoted esteemed African AIDS treatment specialist Dr. Peter Mugyenyi, as saying, "We thank, sincerely, the American people. They are the people who are saving lives. They are the people who can be proud that lives are being saved on this continent." He added that in his opinion, "There has never been a rescue mission, a mission of mercy of this magnitude that has produced such magnanimous results," and that America's standing on the African continent had been elevated greatly by the Bush-initiated program.

As early as 2008 the Bush initiative was making a profound difference in the lives of black Africans. Reporting from Dar Es Salaam, Tanzania on February 17th of that year, John Hendren noted that "President Bush may be struggling at home, but he remains surprisingly popular here in Africa, where his face adorns everything from billboards of thanks, to women's dresses, attributing his fame to the anti-AIDS campaign that had invested over $15 billion dollars to date." Hendren said that Bush intended to push to raise the financial underwriting to $30 billion by 2013. Like Dr. Peter Mugyenyi would two years later, the Tanzanian government expressed their profound gratitude to George Bush:

> Different people may have different views about you and your administration and your legacy," Tanzanian President Jikaya

Kikwete said. "But we, in Tanzania, if we are to speak for ourselves, and for Africa, we know for sure that you, Mr. President, and your administration, have been good friends of our country, and have been good friends of Africa.

That's one more lesson for Michelle Obama and for the "talented" Mr. Kanye West.

The Greatest Black Hero of All Time?

From time to time we hear the expression, "quiet hero." Well, here is a particularly quiet one, a man about whom most black and white Americans are totally ignorant: Norman Borlaug. When Borlaug died in September, 2009, there was no moment of silence in Congress for him, as there was for Michael Jackson; the flag did not fly at half-staff; President Obama did not make a speech commemorating his passing. *Time* magazine did find it in their hearts to include a 135 word tribute to Borlaug in the "Fond Farewell" section at the end of their December 2009 issue, a tribute by Bill Gates that reads:

> I never met Dr. Norman Borlaug, the Nobel Prize–winning plant scientist who did more than anyone in history to fight hunger, but I've admired him for years. When I started learning about agricultural development, his name came up so often that I felt as if he were my teacher. He began his career in the 1940s, helping Mexican farmers increase their yields almost six fold by breeding better seeds. Over the next 40 years, that success spread throughout Latin America and Asia. The Green Revolution, as Dr. Borlaug's life's work is called, cut global hunger in half. Some critics say the world's efforts to improve poor people's lives are doomed. But Dr. Borlaug is proof that large-scale progress is possible. He is a genuine hero, and his story should make us optimistic about the future.

The towering presence of Norman Borlaug has shined healing light across every region where people eat, but, in keeping with the subject of this book, I will limit myself to Africa. The best way, I feel, to do that is to quote from "Farm Journal," June 25, 2003 which implies the special affiliation, affection, and concern that Norman felt for black people.

> While poverty is still rampant in Asia, Borlaug said Africa remains the region of greatest concern. Declining soil fertility and sparse application of improved technology, coupled with the lack of roads and transport, poor education and health services, high population growth even with the spread of HIV/AIDS, has led to continued chronic hunger for 200 million people in Sub-Saharan Africa and portends an unprecedented humanitarian crisis . . . Since 1986, Borlaug has been the President of the Sasakawa Africa Association, an international Extension program to increase farm production in Africa, and the leader of the Sasakawa-Global 2000 agricultural program in sub-Saharan Africa.

Even in death, Norman Borlaug will continue to help feed Africa and the world. The United States Department of Agriculture did think enough of him to create the Norman Borlaug Commemorative Research Initiative, a cooperative effort between the department and the U.S. Agency for International Development with the primary goals of reducing world hunger and poverty. Feedthefuture.gov specifically notes that "the Borlaug Initiative will leverage one of the world's largest public research systems, spanning the USDA's research agencies, increasing its relevance and impact on problems and opportunities faced by smallholder farm families in Africa, Asia and Latin America."

One on One

What can be said after just having reviewed the humanitarian contributions of the giant Norman Borlaug? Only that sometimes the most moving stories are the least complex: One white man and one black man relating and sharing at the most fundamental level conceivable. That's what transpired in early February 2011.

According to a February 8, 2011 huffingtonpost.com article by Joedy McCready, white Tom Walter, Wake Forest baseball coach, donated a kidney the previous day to black Kevin Jordan, freshman Wake Forest outfielder. Kevin's father regarded the procedure as virtual "divine intervention" that the coach and his player were a physiological match. NewsCore observed that "Doctors reiterated Wednesday how fortunate Jordan was in finding Walter as a donor match, saying patients typically wait up to three years for a kidney donor." Ron Green junior from newsobservor.com added that one of Kevin Jordan's physicians, Dr. Tim Newell, commented that coach Walter's action was "a remarkable thing triggered by one person's generosity." And the other physician, Dr. Kirk, expressed the medical opinion that the kidney operation "should add 10 years to Jordan's life beyond what he would have had if he had remained on dialysis without a transplant."

White Poverty and White Needs

So there you have it, white people—from the most average to the most extraordinary and back again—who freely have chosen to exert special effort and to make special sacrifices that help black people; special circumstances that never will be trumpeted by wind instrument virtuosos like Jesse Jackson, Al Sharpton, or Michelle Obama.

Do I have a problem with the white people who have made the effort and who have made the sacrifices for black people? Absolutely not. In fact, I am immensely proud of them, and I believe that every single project that I mentioned above was well worth the sacrifice necessary to carry it out. On a purely statistical basis, I am sure that there are more profoundly needy black people in this world than white ones. But now the inevitable caveats: Are there no deserving white people? And where are the black people of means—black superstar athletes, entertainers, government officials, captains of industry, professionals, entrepreneurs, and everyday middle class blacks—offering support for whites where white poverty and needs are concerned?

There are white people in need; for instance rural Appalachia is one of the poorest and whitest regions in America. While few average Americans think or care about the plight of the Appalachians, the people's needs did garner fleeting attention when in February 2009 ABC's 20/20 broadcasted "Children of the Mountains Struggle to Survive" hosted by Diane Sawyer. The program chronicled the lives of four white Appalachia children—two boys, both age 18 and two girls, ages 11 and 12—as they struggled to survive in the face of grinding poverty. Among the facts disclosed during the show were that Appalachia has a poverty rate three times the national average, that the region's inhabitants have the shortest life span in America, that prescription drug abuse is rampant, and that depression, toothlessness, and major depression are endemic.

The needs of the long-term poor—black and white—undisputedly require our attention. However, what of those not chronically indigent, but acutely desperate due to unforeseen, extraordinary circumstances? More specifically, what about white people who need immediate, short-term assistance? Some Caucasians resent what they regard as double standards in the provision of help to blacks versus whites, resulting in viral emails such as the following that is reproduced just as I received it:

From: Jude Brennan

To: Undisclosed-Recipient:

Sent: Saturday, May 21, 2011 12:00 AM

Subject: Just Wondering . . .

Two Standards?

After Katrina, the media blamed the lack of response on the Bush administration's dislike of black people. Can we then conclude from the lack of media coverage and response by the Obama administration that Obama doesn't like white people?

Where are the Hollywood celebrities holding telethons asking for help in restoring Iowa and North Dakota and helping the folks affected by the floods?

Where is good old Michael Moore?

Why is the media NOT asking the tough questions about why the federal government hasn't solved this problem? Asking where the FEMA trucks and trailers and food services are?

Why isn't the Federal government moving Iowa people into free hotels in Chicago and Minneapolis ?

When will Spike Lee say that the Federal government blew up the levees that failed in Des Moines ?

Where are Sean Penn, Bono, and the Dixie Chicks?

Where are all the looters stealing high-end tennis shoes, cases of beer and television sets?

When will we hear Governor Chet Culver say that he wants to rebuild a 'vanilla' Iowa . . . because that's what God wants?

Where is the hysterical 24/7 media coverage complete with reports of shootings at rescuers, of rapes, and murder?

Where are all the people screaming that Barack Obama hates white, rural people?

My God, where are Angelina Jolie and Brad Pitt, Oprah, and Ray Coniff, Jr?

How come you will never hear about the Iowa flooding ever again?

Where are the government bail-out vouchers?

The government debit cards?

More people died in these floods then from Katrina . . . how come the media doesn't report that?!!!!!

There must be one hell of a big difference between the value of the people of Iowa and value of the people of Louisiana .

HERE'S THE REAL TRUTH:

THIS IS AN EXAMPLE OF GOVERNMENT CONTROL OF THE MEDIA, AND SOON TO BE GOV'T. CONTROL OF INTERNET, CELL PHONES, RADIO AND ALL COMMUNICATION AS WELL AS THE PRESENT NETWORK NEWS ON TV.

WAKE UP, AMERICANS . . .

Pass this unedited, un-doctored, factual information forward . . . to get Americans thinking, the media WON'T!

White people in our homeland need help sometimes. White motherlands are not totally devoid of misery, either. Eastern Europe, for instance, has been struggling. Speaking about that region, for example, on April 24, 2009 worldbank.org explained that we "now are seeing the global economic and financial crisis push almost 35 million people back into poverty and vulnerability, or about one-third of the people that had escaped from it over the last ten years." Noting at the time that 40% of the inhabitants were "poor or vulnerable," they estimated that the numbers would increase to about 45% by the end of the year, and to accelerate further in 2010.

I leave you, then, with one last issue: How much black or white political activism, or even talk, is directed toward white poverty and other needs experienced by white Americans and white Eastern Europeans? Preoccupation with black poverty and lack of concern for white poverty are two mindless features of our national consciousness. No one in my neighborhood would even think to collect clothing for impoverished whites. Yet, when leaving the gym recently, a gym racially consistent with the black-white demographics of America, I discovered a large bin in the vestibule with PPPF on it and a sign requesting that members donate their unwanted sneakers to the Perpetual Prosperity Pumps Foundation, so that they could be "recycled" to Ghana, West Africa. A worthy cause? Definitely, but must charity be so racially one-sided?

Ronald Brownstein addresses the consequences of one-sided racial concern in his May 31, 2011 National Journal article entitled, "Why the white working class is alienated, pessimistic." After pointing out that whites without a college degree continue to be the largest workforce demographic, substantially large than minorities who comprise less than one-third, he cites a Pew Charitable Trusts' Economic Mobility Project poll of the previous week. Brownstein then specifically states that when respondents were asked whether they anticipated being more financially secure in 10 years than they are presently, about 66 percent of Hispanics and 66 percent of blacks said "yes," but only 55 percent of college-educated whites, and only 44 percent of whites without college agreed.

Inter-Racial Dialogue:
A Conversation Analysis Conducted with
Eric Himpton Holder junior in Mind

Fox News, March 2, 2011, Megyn Kelly reporting. You know, Fox, the station that liberals relentlessly malign as promoting a radically conservative agenda, presented a piece entitled, "Non-profit under Fire for White Male-Only Scholarships." The show featured two discussants: William Lake, the white financial director for The Former Majority Association for Equality (FMAE), and Jehmu Greene, a black, female Fox News contributor and former director of the Women's Media Center.

Kelly introduced the story with a taped statement from Colby Bohannan, the Association's founder, who was attempting to defend the group from implicit and explicit charges of racism. Colby explained that he started his organization after becoming acutely aware that virtually all ethnicities and women had group-specific scholarships, but that Caucasian males did not. He emphasized that FMAE did not have a "racist agenda," and, in fact, accepted scholarship candidates who had as little as 25% Caucasian ancestry.

The segment then continued with Lake who immediately was challenged to justify the white and biracial male-only program. In fact, his initial defense accounted for 160, or 43%, of the 374 words that William Lake spoke during his entire time on the air, meaning that he spoke only 114 words—half as much as Greene—during his ensuing discourse with her. Moreover, Jehmu Greene, essentially, pummeled Lake with race-based attacks that consumed almost all the rest of his time. He never really had a chance to advocate for his organization. By contrast, Jehmu Greene spoke 431 words, always on the offensive, and never having to justify a single word that she said. Toward the end of the program, Megyn Kelly apparently noticed the one-sided nature of the "discussion," and promised to give "the white guy" a chance to rebut Greene; however, wouldn't you know it, time ran out before Lake could have his opportunity.

Originally, I had planned a traditional conversation analysis of the broadcast by presenting an annotated verbatim transcript of the entire news segment. That would have been the most "fair and balanced" way to treat the subject. However, Fox refused to grant me permission to do so, proving that one need be neither a racializer nor a raceketeer in order implement verbal double standards. I will address the free-speech issue in the epilogue of this book. For now, in the next few paragraphs, I merely paraphrase and comment on the FMAE as best I can, given the Fox-imposed restriction.

Megyn Kelly introduced Jehmu Greene and William Lake. She then addressed Lake, asking why he would do "such a thing" as promoting a white male-oriented scholarship, a comment that had a "you naughty boy" quality to it.

William then reiterated the FMAE rationale much as Bohannan had, but, before he had finished, Kelly interrupted, asking if he and his group were "bitter" or had "an axe to grind."

"Axe to grind" and "bitter" so early in the session, to my way of thinking, presaged anything but an unbiased evaluation of Lake's position. If Lake were black, perhaps the Association would not have an axe to grind, but an understandable, even laudable, pro-black advocacy position.

Lake, of course, was left trying to defend the very existence of his organization; at which point Megyn called upon Jehmu Greene asking whether the entire "controversy" was "much ado about nothing."

Much ado about nothing: a perfect set-up for Jehmu to set the record straight.

Greene began with a tried and true raceketeering script, giving lip-service to the fact that everybody deserves equality; then immediately implying a parallel between FMAE and white-only scholarship sham programs facetiously proposed by the College Republicans of Boston and Rhode Island a few years earlier.

Lake tried to address the issue, but could not get in a word edge-wise. Greene went on and on, suggesting that she knew what was "behind" this organization, lecturing William about organized efforts to "put down programs focused on diversity and inclusion." Jehmu sarcastically referred to white males as being disadvantaged, oppressed, and down-troddened. She then launched into a serious litany of all the advantages that white men enjoy, such as being able buy cars at a rate lower and being paid at a higher rate than blacks, so-called people-of-color, and women. By adding women and people-of-color to the argument, Greene once again was following the "unite everyone in the world against the white guy" strategy so favored by raceketters.

Why did Jehmu Greene use the all-aboard strategy? Probably because it always has worked so well. It certainly had the desired effect on William Lake who almost stood on his head, trying to distance himself from any suggestion that he favored white male privilege.

At the conclusion of the program, Greene goaded Lake with the notion that he should surrender his white male advocacy, and transform his organization into one advocating programs and scholarships that included her favored black and "people-of-color" groups. She did so by introducing the morally appealing idea of an "integrated society" rather than one full of men-only country clubs. William should have asked Jehmu to show him a listing of the latter and he should have requested a seat at the next Congressional black Caucus meeting.

When Williams Lake capitulated, saying that he agreed on the idea of an integrated America, Megyn Kelly saw her chance, suggesting that they had reached a "note of agreement" on which to end.

So there you have it. But what do you have? Was this a "fair and balance discussion?' Was this racially courageous dialogue between equals?

Perhaps I shouldn't taunt either Fox or Megyn Kelly. Both, I do believe, are about as fair and balanced as one can expect on the contemporary news scene. However, do you think for one minute that the pairing of so-called race and gender expert and Fox contributor Jehmu Greene versus a man who looked as though he is 24, and spoke as timidly as a 10-year-old was coincidental? The debate was a virtual set-up, perhaps intended to portray Lake as a stumbling, bumbling, fumbling, non-swaggaing white boy. Of course, William Lake did refer to himself as the "financial director" of his organization. A multi-billion dollar, multi-national group, no doubt.

Doubt. Actually, on its website in March, 2011, The Former Majority Association for Equality boasted: "We have reached our goal for the Fall 2011 semester, and have raised $2500 . . . Also, we have set a new goal for the Spring 2012 School Semester. We are doubling our scholarships to $1000 scholarships awarded to 5 students." No wonder Jehmu was up in arms; hell, at this rate, the Association soon will have sewn up virtually all available scholarship funds, leaving nothing for blacks, people-of-color, women, or anyone else on planet earth!

The Fox conversation illustrates the racial double standards, double speak, and double binds endemic to black-white discourse. Blacks are entitled to black-only scholarships, but there are no white people who either deserve or need special treatment. The attempt to provide scholarships for white males, and for bi-racials at least 25% white, prompts the African American, Jehmu Greene, to remind us of the civil rights struggle. Blacks can advocate for funds, but, if whites do, it's racism. A discussion of white needs devolves into a lecture by a black woman about why the proper advocacy of The Former Majority Association for Equality should not be for white males, but for blacks, people-of-color, and white females. When the "white guy" tries to explain himself, he is talked over, given half the time as the black woman, and promised, but never given, time to rebut. The session concludes with the host deciding that they had reached agreement. Perhaps she should have checked with William Lake.

Megyn Kelly's "axe to grind" comment to William Lake suggests another obvious point: That The Former Majority Association for Equality might not be a "legitimate" organization, but a clandestine pro-white, consciousness-raising advocacy group, as though such a group would be illegitimate. If Lake and FMAE are nothing more than racial saboteurs, one must ask what socio-cultural factors encourage that desperate tactic. Moreover, the notion of pro-white advocacy as de facto negativity reminds us that only pro-black advocacy is encouraged and celebrated. Even "burn baby burn" black rioting is rationalized as an understandable response to institutionalized racism. But white advocacy—even education-oriented advocacy—for white and for bi-racial males, at least 25% white, has no place in contemporary America. White male advocacy widely is regarded as mad and/or bad.

Colorless People in the People-of-Color World

Like blacks, white people, too, are responsible for perpetuating America's obsession with race. Some of the whitest whites in the outermost rural regions are as bimp as the blackest bimps in the inner-most city. Like hard-core black gangbangers, there are hard-core white bimps with dark-triad personalities—criminal or crazy—who hate and exploit blacks, whites, or both in an attempt to satisfy their own raw impulses, with no concern for anyone or anything but themselves. As with black hard-cores, hard-core white bimps are few in number, but their vicious behaviors can be most destructive to the community at large and to race relations in particular. Hard-corps white bimps—such as Aryan Nation—get no cover from the white community and, thankfully, are an endangered species. If hard-core black bimps were treated with as much contempt and opposition as the white variety are, black bimps would be on the way out as well, and law-abiding inner-city African Americans could walk the streets of their communities with a modicum of safety and confidence.

Again, as with black bimps, most white bimps are soft-core, more obnoxious and irritating than dangerous. Like their black brothas, they, too, suffer inadvertently as a result of their irresponsible and self-destructive behaviors. The bimp lifestyle is a ticket to familial, school, and occupational failure. However, the negative repercussions of a soft-core bimp orientation do extend beyond the individual, significantly undermining the community as a whole. Unable to cope, white bimps, as black ones, drain neighborhood resources and pass on their unproductive legacy to their children and to any others who model on their swagga.

Since "bimp" refers to a black, inner-city, male persona, why has it spread to white youth? Because the "white world" likes swagga as much as it likes rock and roll. Even many white adults and white media types are intrigued by the rebelliousness and sensuality of the bimp personality. Marketers go gaga over the bimp ability to attract attention. People attend to you when you wear your pants below you butt, grab your crotch, and talk in monosyllabic expletives. Marketers know that anything that attracts attention can be converted into money. To hell with the consequences of perpetuating boorish, brutish, or criminal behavior, I see an advertising and multimedia opportunity here!

So bimps get plenty of air time and a few make big bucks in the process. But bimps, youth, and the media are not the only reasons that America is unable to put race into its proper perspective.

Earlier, I mentioned that a corps of black race experts exist whose raisons d'être are to promote their own fame and fortune by perpetuating racial division and by providing cover for limitless black demands. I also said that Black Studies and social service personnel inadvertently encourage the racial divide. I noted that many black psychologists traditionally and currently imply or explicitly assert that "African Americans are justified in their distrust of, even hatred of, European Americans," that virtually all black deficiencies are rooted in white racism, and that black accomplishments have been heroically attained despite interference from "white folks."

Now is the time to show that some white social scientists collude with black ones not only in blaming whites, but actually in helping to promote white racial guilt. Don't believe it? Try this on for size. Below are excerpts from a July 2009 article from the *Journal of Counseling Psychology* by three white psychologists whose study, basically, was designed to keep the focus on white responsibility for black problems rather than helping blacks develop an internal locus of control and, thus, to foster black empowerment:

> Guilt and shame also are common reactions of White individuals to
> societal inequality and White privilege (Iyer et al., 2003; Kernahan
> & Davis, 2007; Leach, Iyer, & Pedersen, 2006; Spanierman &
> Heppner, 2004; Swim & Miller, 1999). These reactions have been

the focus of social and counseling psychology research and have been linked empirically to White privilege. In their examination of the impact of an undergraduate psychology and racism course on students' White privilege awareness, Kernahan and Davis (2007) found that White privilege awareness, feelings of White guilt, and discomfort with White privilege increased following the course. Other studies have identified a strong association between White privilege awareness and White guilt (Iyer et al., 2003; Powell et al., 2005; Swim & Miller, 1999). For example, Swim and Miller (1999) found that higher levels of White privilege awareness lead to greater levels of White guilt and support for affirmative action. Acknowledgement of White privilege also has been associated with collective White guilt, defined as feelings of group self-blame for illegitimate racial advantages (Powell et al., 2005). Among a sample of 110 White introductory psychology students, Powell and colleagues (2005) found that framing racial inequality as privileging Whites resulted in higher levels of collective White guilt relative to framing racial inequality as disadvantaging African Americans.

Maybe it's just me, but all these years I have suffered under the misconception that psychologists' interventions seek to reduce unjustifiable guilt rather than to promote it. So, if I'm reading this research correctly, "an undergraduate psychology and racism course on students' White privilege awareness" makes white students feel more guilty for racial crimes that they have never committed. I suggest that these researchers spend a little more time trying to inculcate guilt into hard-core and soft-core bimps—black and white—who drag society and themselves down instead reinforcing guilt in white psychology students who are in college, trying to raise themselves up.

Where are we now? White and black governmental officials, majority white media, majority white marketers, majority white social scientists, and the racial guilt that they help engender in the white population—all promote race preoccupation and all are barriers to black-white reconciliation. Then there is the non-social science intelligentsia. This group is composed of people who, if they ever have had any experience with black people, have met their black acquaintances at Harvard, Princeton, or the Hamptons.

The black people they know intimately have more in common with them than I do, and I have more in common with everyday black people than their black friends do. The only bimps that the white intelligentsia know are the ones slurping cocktails with them at private post MTV music awards parties—Sister Souljahs and Kanye Wests. Barack Hussein Soetoro Obama might be there. They all have swagga; they all be cool.

Do everyday white people notice double standards and double speak perpetrated by racializers, raceketeers, race cadets, governmental officials, media, marketers, social scientists and the non-social science intelligentsia? You know they do! Do they talk about it? You know they don't. But it's not that they lack the racial courage of an Eric H. Holder junior. It's the double binds. White people keep their mouths closed about race because demagogues, government, business, social science, and intellectuals will not listen to complaints by everyday white people. They are too busy listening to black advocates and too preoccupied with profiteering from the racial divide. As mentioned earlier, when everyday white people do try to speak up, they are told they don't know what they are talking about and shouted down. Even on national television, Elisabeth Hasselbecks are humiliated merely for arguing that perpetuating the word "nigger" aggravates race relations.

As is usual when white people address race in a way that is not to the liking or benefit of blacks, black advocates, who have spent their whole lives archiving racial slights, real or imagined, swoop down on them like hawks pursuing rabbits. It is not racial cowardice that keeps whites quiet; it is common sense. In inter-racial discourse, the tried and true syllogism goes like this:

Mr. Whoever is black.

You are white.

Whites who make reference to anything that can be construed as negative toward any black person are racists.

You said something negative about Mr. Whoever.

You are racist.

Whites need not address race in order to incur raceketeer wrath, however, and Mr. Black Whoever need not be an everyday person, or even a Mister. Consider Ms. Sheila Jackson Lee, black democrat from the great state of Texas, who addressed Congress on July 18, 2011.

During the general speeches timeslot, the Representative ostensibly rose to offer her views regarding the national debt, initially explaining that the legislative body should not be hasty in cutting programs. After that red herring quickly swam downstream, however, Sheila Jackson Lee launched into a raceketeering diatribe that presumably had been the real impetus for her monologue.

Representative Lee's remarks and my annotations follow:

> I am particularly sensitive to the fact that only this president, only this president, only this one has received the kind of attacks and disagreements and inability to work. Only this one. [*If she believes what she is saying, Ms. Lee must have been on an extraterrestrial junket during the George W. Bush presidency.*]

> Read between the lines. [*In other words, carefully listen to me double speak my double speak.*]

> What is different about this president that should put him in a position that he should not receive the same kind of respectful treatment of when it is necessary to raise the debt limit in order to pay our bills, something required by both statute and the 14th amendment? [*Then why did Barack Hussein Obama and all 47 of his Democrat Senate colleagues vote AGAINST raising the debt limit ceiling in March, 2006?*] Why isn't this addressed in the manner? [*Excuse me Ms. Lee, but what does "in the manner" mean?*]. It's alright to disagree on the balance budget amendment . . .

> But I do not understand what I think is the maligning and maliciousness of this president. [*Here we find an interesting*

slip of the tongue, inadvertently suggesting that Barack Obama is malicious.]

Why is he different? And in my community that is a question that we raise. [*Or rather, the tried and true race card politics that Ms. Lee promotes.*] In the minority community that is a question that is being raised. Why is this president being treated so disrespectfully? [*Consider again George W. Bush, repeatedly mocked as a buffoon.*]

Why has the debt limit been raised 60 times? [*Actually, according to Jeanne Sahadi, senior writer at CNNMoney, that is 74 times since March 1962.*] Why does the leader of the Senate continually talk about his job is to bring the President down to make sure he is unelected? It's 2011. It's not 2012. You need to play those politics in 2012. Not now. [*Sheila Jackson Lee needs a short powwow with Barack to address the relentless re-election campaigning that he had conducted over the prior three months*]

Aside from the above, anything else I know about Ms. Lee is based on what I read. But reading about her is illuminating. Joyce Jones (2011) of Black Entertainment Television writes that the Congresswoman is being sued by her former congressional aide who alleges that Sheila Jackson Lee treated her in "a humiliating manner." The piece also refers to Ms. Jackson's reputation as "the boss from hell." Doug Powers (2010) claims that on one occasion Jackson said, "Today we have two Vietnams, side by side, North and South, exchanging and working. We may not agree with all that North Vietnam is doing, but they are living in peace." Powers asserts that another time she referred to "countries like Europe." Sounds as though Sheila Jackson Lee is just the governmental representative that America needs to foster national racial reconciliation, employee-employer harmony, and international understanding.

Legislating to Exploit and Augment Lawlessness: Fudge Factor

The Sheila Jackson Lee affair illustrates how black raceketeers attempt to get their way by setting up white racism as a straw man. More important, it shows the power of anti-white, race-based advocacy in contemporary America. Permit me two more examples to make my point.

July 13, 2011, the entire United States is focused on the national debt ceiling, on what Barack Obama and his supporters warn is impending financial Armageddon if the ceiling is not raised within the next few days. However, Marcia Fudge, black congresswoman from Ohio, has something else on her mind: voter suppression.

What, you might ask, is voter suppression? In this case, voter suppression refers to the fact that about 23 states and the District of Columbia require some form of identification before an individual enters the voting booth. Such an onerous burden, one akin to "forcing" someone to show identification before renting a car, buying an airline ticket, or checking into a hotel room. Marcia Fudge and other Congressional Black Caucus members are up in arms. Requiring voter Identification could make it more difficult for illegal aliens or criminals to vote. Requiring voter identification would have compromised the good work that the Acorn organization did in abetting fraudulent voter registration in support of Barack Obama's presidential election. Voter suppression apparently does not include prohibiting armed New Black Panthers from stationing themselves outside the polls to intimidate anyone bold enough to vote against Barack. The Congressional Black Caucus remains mum on that minor voting rights issue.

So, the Congressional Black Caucus lobbies for states to rescind their "racist" voter suppression/identification laws. Similarly, the Caucus wants the "Dream Act" to be passed, an act that allows the non-United States-born children of illegal aliens to become citizens after completing two years of college or military service. If the Act does not pass, their attempt to promote it will have ingratiated the Congressional Black Caucus to people-of-color, thereby enhancing that black separatist group's power and prestige. If the Dream Act does pass, the Black Caucus can do a "you owe me one" to all the grateful new Democrats that the Act has enfranchised.

Both the voter suppression and Dream Act issues are lessons for those who seek encouragement to "do the wrong thing." Media-based legislative advocacy on behalf of the issues tells everyone that criminals can do as they please and have a fighting chance to beat our laws. Those who vote illegally can get away with it. Those who violate United States borders can ensure a better life for their children if they just hold out long enough for a change in statue. The Congressional Black Caucus is shown to be a staunch ally and advocate for law-breakers as long as the law-breakers are black or so-called people of color. The Congressional Black Caucus enhances its power, prestige, and profit while undermining the welfare of our nation.

CHAPTER 14

Barack Obama:
Epitome of Racial Hypocrisy and the Doubles

The election of Barack Obama blatantly exposed the double standards, double speak, and double binds always extant but usually occult in America for the past several decades. Obama, who has lived a life of racial hypocrisy, joined with a regiment of professional Machiavellians and raceketeers to orchestrate the biggest race-based political scam in history. I don't believe the birther fantasy purporting that Barack is not American. I have no reason to doubt that he breathed his first breath in Hawaii. But subtle realities of American culture, effortlessly assimilated by most citizens, never seeped into Barry Barack Hussein Soertoro Obama's bones. That is why he can misspeak about the number of states in our country and why he refers to a navy corpsman as a "corpse man." Only the Lord knows what other particulars of the American experience are foreign to Barack.

The man with swagga is, if you'll pardon the expression, a man with no soul. What Obama's marketing gurus advertise as cool is nothing less than a propensity for what psychologists call "isolation of affect," alienation of the man from his authentic feelings—a defense mechanism cultivated ever since Barack was Barry and when mom and dad were polar opposites with nothing between them but thin air. The emperor not only has no clothes, he has no integrity. He professes to be a racial unifier but behaves as a divider. He loves people-of-color and multi-racials, but cannot consistently embrace the reality of his black AND white genome; to do so would be to compromise his black race appeal, the main personality constituent that distinguishes him from thousands of other potential political aspirants.

Obama fits the racializing and raceketeering bill to a tee. Alienated from his authentic, biracial self, he has manufactured a what-if personality, opportunistically throwing off and putting on bits and pieces of who he really is and what he has really experienced, burnishing his dark-triad personality image to make himself look attractive to whomever he needs to manipulate. Barry Barack Hussein Soetoro Obama has played hide and seek and sundry other pretend games with his racial identity since childhood, and the games continue. For the past several years, much of the country willingly, even enthusiastically, has played Obama's games with him. So, I unapologetically ask that you and I play pretend now.

Step into my time machine; I've already warmed it up, and dialed it back to February 10, 2007. We are in Springfield, Illinois, about 15,000 of his supporters have come to hear Obama announce his presidential candidacy, a speech in which race is not mentioned once. No coincidence, Barack and his political handlers made a conscious, calculated political decision to avoid making race an issue when a general audience was listening, but to underscore his black cred when addressing African Americans.

Having lived a life created around double standards and double speak, Barack Obama is doing just fine racially until March 13, 2008 when ABC airs Jeremiah Wright's "god damn America" rant. Not a casual acquaintance, this is the guy who has mentored Barack since 1985, who brought him into Afrocentric, radical, white-maligning Christianity in 1988, who married the first couple in 1992, baptized daughter Malia in 1998 and Sasha in 2001, and whose sermon inspired Obama to entitle his second book, *The Audacity of Hope*. Reality has a funny habit of sneaking up on you. Barack Hussein Obama cannot just sidestep Wright the way he adroitly sidestepped the William Ayers controversy that hit the fan the previous month.

What to do about the good Reverend Wright? How about a speech? Verbal obamafuscation always has worked for Barack. Not only a speech. How about a "race speech?" In the Rahm Emanuel "never let a crisis go to waste" tradition, let's give a gangbusters speech that will project a heroic racial image, making lemonade from lemons. The self-serving speech, on March 18, 2008, contained the following widely reported account of the Obama-Wright alliance:

> I can no more disown him [Wright] than I can disown the black community. I can no more disown him than I can my white grandmother—a woman who helped raise me, a woman who sacrificed again and again for me, a woman who loves me as much as she loves anything in this world, but a woman who once confessed her fear of black men who passed by her on the street, and who on more than one occasion has uttered racial or ethnic stereotypes that made me cringe.

Take an episode of virulent racism and anti-Americanism and attempt to double speak it into a talking down to white folks lecture about human nature, all at the expense of the white grandmother for whom you have professed undying love and gratitude. (Where is that castrating, castigating, avenging angel, Jesse Jackson, when you need him?)

Nineteen days later, November 6th, Barack is up on the pulpit, racializing again. This is his "cling to their guns and religion" tongue lashing, indicting white, "small town" Pennsylvanians and Mid-Westerners as being bitter, religiously fanatical, and xenophobic. As a result of an ensuing uproar about the racialized nature of his talk-down to whites speech, Obama launched a marketing campaign of racial cover, including releasing a picture of himself with white mother, grandmother (the same racially-insensitive Toots that he had defiled on March 18th), and grandfather. (In addition, on Memorial Day, Barack advanced a patriotic, Caucasian-pandering sound bite, boasting that his white "uncle" [actually a great-uncle], Charlie Payne, was part of an army contingent that helped liberate Auschwitz [actually Buchenwald].)

Just when Obama is catching his breath, Jeremiah Wright appears on November 25th with Bill Moyers and says about Barack,

> He's a politician, I'm a pastor. We speak to two different audiences. And he says what he has to say as a politician. I say what I have to say as a pastor. But they're two different worlds. I do what I do. He does what politicians do. So that what happened in Philadelphia where he had to respond to the sound bytes, he responded as a politician.

This is almost as upsetting as being called Uncle Tom or not black enough. "Hey, Jerry, It's okay to mock America and whitey, but don't you diss me!!" This is an assault on Barack Hussein Obama's disingenuous persona, lifting the curtain to expose the naked great and powerful Barack. His response? Within a week, the *Atlantic* releases an article entitled, "Obama Denounces Wright."

> EARLY THIS MORNING, after a long day of campaigning, aides showed Barack Obama extended excerpts from Rev. Jeremiah Wright's jaunty and freewheeling press conference in Washington. Obama, the aides said, was **deeply, visibly angry**. [emphasis added] Two said he "insisted" that he hold a second press conference today to unequivocally denounce Rev. Wright's conduct and sever himself from Wright's fulminations. Obama did not want to let Wright hijack his campaign any longer. Five days was enough.
>
> Judging by his square jaw and his posture—rigid—and his tone of voice—elegiac and sad at points, and hard and resolute at others, Obama **felt aggrieved and disrespected**, [emphasis added] especially by Wright's implication that Obama's speech on racial politics in Philadelphia was mere politics.
>
> "I want to use this press conference to make people absolutely clear that obviously whatever relationship I had with Rev. Wright has changed, he said. "I **don't think he showed much concern for me** . . . [emphasis added] and what we are trying to do in this campaign."

The unflappable, super-cool Barack gets angry, feels aggrieved and disrespected, and decries being treated with lack of concern. When disparaging black on white racism is the topic of Wright's conversation, Barack Obama readily rationalizes and minimizes the issue, even turning on his own grandmother. But, when his identity is being challenged, Barack gets all verklempt, to use a Saturday Night Live-ism. Despite popular opinion to the contrary, the man does feel emotion—emotion when narcissistically wounded. His megalomaniacal self-esteem—especially his racial self-esteem—clearly is Barack Obama's Achilles Heel.

The dark-triad Obama personality is like a white egg that has been dipped in black food coloring. When you squeeze Barack lengthwise with stressors that many people would find onerous, he does not smudge and he demonstrates noteworthy resilience and unflappability. However, his shell is thin; tap it against a hard, race-relevant surface and it shatters to pieces, makes a gooey mess, reveals its hidden inners, and shows that, despite his protestations to the contrary, Barry Barack is as white as he is black and as volatile as he is cool.

Check the record and you will find this eggshell sensitivity whenever Obama's self-esteem and racial identity are implicated, from Reverend Wright to Professor Gates. Both the Wright and Gates incidents are the kinds of hard surfaces that crack the 44th president's thin shell because, being widely and glaringly publicized, both expose Obama's exquisite sensitivity to being racially shamed. Whenever race is on the line, the repetition compulsion kicks in and Barack's identity demons emerge from their dens, tormenting him into action. In these circumstances, this obsessively cautious individual speaks impulsively, exposing the sensitive little boy inside the swaggaing, self-assured man. Fortunate for Barack, neither all the king's horses nor all the king's men are required to put Humpty Obama back together again, usually a clandestine cigarette or two work just fine to restore his equanimity.

Machiavellian Barack and the doubles go together like peanut butter and jelly.

On the November 8, 2004 *Meet the Press* show, Obama totally and unequivocally stated that he would not be a 2008 presidential candidate, saying "You know, I am a believer in knowing what you're doing when you apply for a job. And I think that if I were to seriously consider running on a national ticket, I would essentially have to start now, before having served a day in the Senate. Now, there are some people who might be comfortable doing that, but I'm not one of those people." On the same show, about fourteen months later, Tim Russert reminded Obama of his previous statement and asked once more about his presidential ambitions. In *Game Change*, Mark Halperin and John Heileman wrote that in the first show Barack answered "absolutely" when asked if he would complete his U. S. Senate term, meaning that he would not run for the White

House in 2008, and when in the second show moderator Tim Russert explicitly asked, "So you will not run for president or vice president in 2008?" Obama replied, "I will not." Seems to me that "absolutely" and "I will not" are rather definitive, or, at least, they should be.

Barack Obama performed a similar slight of mouth trick on February 2, 2009. At the time, Tom Daschle, Obama's choice for Secretary of Health and Human Services, had been under intense fire for failing to pay $128,000 in personal taxes. Asked by reporters whether he would stand by Daschle, Barack gave a terse, "Absolutely." The very next day, the president accepted Daschle's withdrawal from consideration, saying that Daschle was an "outstanding" person who made an "unintentional mistake." Gee, I thought all mistakes were unintentional. Perhaps Obama's terse "absolutely" comment the previous day predicted how he would manipulate and spin the fiasco that he unwittingly had manufactured.

After having pretended to travel to the past that was, let's now imagine the past that could have been. What if Barack had retained Barry as a nickname, and always acknowledged, even celebrated, the incontrovertible reality of being biracial—white and black? This would have taken a large dose of Eric H. Holder junior's racial courage. This would have required Obama to put race relations and America ahead of his own self interest and personal ambition. Merely by being consistently racially honest, Barack Obama would have done what no American politician has ever done: He would have defied and undermined black and white racists; he would have served as a sterling example to all American men, women, and children; he would have encouraged biracials and multi-racials to just be themselves; and he would have redeemed his white mother and her forebears by embracing the simple reality of her heritage, of who she was, and what she stood for.

What would Barack Obama have lost by being authentic? He might have failed to earn the Democratic nomination, but, almost certainly, he would have won the Vice Presidential spot. With hard work and just a little luck, Obama could have parlayed his popularity into a future presidency, built upon a solid foundation of truth. That presidency would have offered unprecedented opportunity to move our country into the 21st century with renewed unity and greater commitment to universal civil rights and civil interracial discourse.

The Obamas would not have starved, suffered, or experience reduced opportunity or living standard had he not planted his flag on the top of the hill. And, while he will never admit it to himself, and as incredible as it sounds, America would have found someone fully capable of leading the nation had he never run for president. Even if he never had become Vice President or President, by delaying his presidential ambitions, Barack could have enjoyed being fully present with his daughters during their formative years.

Christopher Anderson reports that Obama's political preoccupations almost caused his marriage to disintegrate in 1999. Barack Obama understands fully, then, the parenting stress that the presidency inevitably poses for his family, and how it undermines his presence within the home. In fact, when writing for the *People* magazine June 20, 2011 issue, Barack Obama, himself, admits that children need fathers who are both physically and emotionally available. He knows that no father can be physically or emotionally free from the maddening, overwhelming distractions inherent to the "most demanding job on earth." In *People*, the President does note that he has not "always been a perfect dad," a personality-consistent Obamafuscation. By saying he has not *always* been *perfect* but providing no details, Barack says nothing of substance. However, the double speak serves him well since, if challenged later, he self-servingly can claim to have acknowledged his shortcomings.

Regardless of Barack Obama's racial courage or cowardice, his charitable or selfish intentions, his dark-triad personality or his impeccable character, he did not get elected on his own. For better or worse, millions of Americans bought what Barack was selling. The Obama victory said as much about my community and me as it did about Barack and his handlers. America wanted so much to get past race that our citizens played pretend with a biracial man who had no prior record of governmental accomplishment, who said the right things on the campaign trail, and who, after being elected, thought, and still thinks, that he knows more than the people who put him into office.

The black community is even more vulnerable that the white one where racial play pretend is concerned. Fox News, on February 17, 2011 interviews Herman Cain, black, 2012 conservative presidential candidate, who comments on the Gestapo-like influence of black identity slave masters over his black constituency. For example, he mentions attending his African American church and having a fellow parishioner softly, surreptitiously murmur, "I'm with you," meaning, "I support your independent-minded views." Cain thanks the man, then adds, "But why are you whispering?"

Llyod Marcus, a proud black man, who, nevertheless, describes himself as an "uhyphenated American," also is baffled by America's blind acquiescence to racial politics and to Barack Hussein. Marcus, who refuses to be intimidated by black identity slave masters, has much to say about nation-wide racial identity manipulation. On March 25, 2010, in "A Black Man, The Progressive's Perfect Trojan Horse" he writes, "The mainstream liberal media continues to portray all who oppose Obama in any way as racist. Despite a list of failed policies, overreaches into the private sector, violations of the Constitution and planned destructive legislation too numerous to mention in this article, many Americans are still fearful of criticizing our first black president. Incredible."

Like me, Herman Cain and Lloyd Marcus have learned a crystal clear lesson: Our country cannot wait for any leader of any race, especially a political leader, to do what must be done in order to consign black-white division and racial discord to the interiors of history books.

CHAPTER 15

General Racial Reconciliation Impediments and General Solutions

What can we do society-wide to address the unique 21st century impediments to racial equanimity? We need honest, authentic dialogue on both sides of the chasm. This means that black citizens must speak up, and not allow profiteering black demagogues to talk for them. Everyday blacks cannot be passive or compliant in the black-white dialogue. They should advocate their opinions, and do so in language that is concrete and specific. Everyday whites must behave similarly. The biggest difference between blacks and whites in this circumstance is that while black opinions and grievances have been aired loudly and relentlessly, white opinions and grievances have been whispered and episodic. White advocacy has been relegated mostly to white extremists with their hate-filled agendas. Average white citizens, understandably, have distanced themselves from the bigots. But in doing so, they have had to pretend that they are unaware of and undisturbed by the anti-white racism espoused by some blacks and by some disturbed whites as well. Without a socially acceptable venue for expressing their legitimate racial grievances, white people have had to siphon off the associated animosity through surreptitious means and behind closed doors. It is for this reason that, whereas pre-election polls often show strong white support for black candidates, post-election results frequently reveals a much reduced white turnout for them.

Aside from the obvious general fact that black and white extremism is destructive to blacks, to whites, and to the nation in general, what are some particular ailments attendant to the rampant racializing and raceketeering extant in our country, and what cures do they imply?

First, and foremost, racializing and raceketeering keeps skin color and skin allegiance in the forefront of our consciousness. There is an old-fashioned, but useful, concept in psychology called "cathexsis" that helps explain the significance of race preoccupation. For our purposes, cathexsis refers to the amount of mental energy invested in thoughts, feelings, and actions. Theory purports that one has only so much mental energy available to pour into any single thing at any one point in time; this accords well with our commonsense understanding that we function best when we focus intently on one major idea or task. For those of you inclined to believe in "multitasking," research consistently shows that multitasking results in less efficient and less effective results than does focusing on a singularity. In fact, studies strongly support the notion that one cannot really think about two disparate things simultaneously. Sometimes we have the illusion of doing so, when, in fact, we are rapidly shifting from one notion to the other.

So, applied to race, the concept of cathexsis indicates that the more time and energy devoted to attending to race, the less time and energy we have for more constructive endeavors.

The next fundamental impediment derives from the fact that we depend heavily and mindlessly on racializers for our race-relevant information. Since they allege to be the race experts, we defer not only to their opinions, but also to the reliability and validity of the racial "data" that they choose to promulgate. That information comes to us along a broad spectrum, from obvious racial evangelizing, as by the Al Sharptons, to subtle black and white media messages of all types. The news media condition us with information such as commentators' explanations of what is and is not swagga, and its importance. Films provide implicit information about the workings of the racial world. Case in point: Spike Lee's "Do the Right Thing." (This reportedly was the first film that Barack and Michelle attended together.) On the face it, this 1989 film pretends to offer us an opportunity to rationally evaluate non-violent versus "burn baby burn" approaches to racial division. But the movie's true message clearly is that racial anarchists and swagging, black-enough males are the heroes to be emulated. Moreover, we are given a clear message that anti-white-ism is virtuous. That people-of-color should unite against the evil, racist whites comes through loud and clear toward the end of this insufferable movie.

After burning down a white merchant's store, a black mob descends on a Korean business, intent on torching it as well. But the street-wise Korean has properly assimilated the divisive race information endemic to our culture; he knows just what to say, "I no white! I black! You, me, same! We same!"

Racialized information carpet bombing is hard to avoid in the United States. Given enough time, it pounds us into submission. Our habit of cathexsizing race and our mindless approach to race render us vulnerable to the assault. Individuals and groups must unite to disclaim and oppose all racialized information, no matter how subtle: a relentless, withering counterattack in the overwhelming force tradition of Desert Storm.

The third, fundamental impediment is the inevitable result of the first two; namely, that the more white people are assailed with interminable pro-black propaganda, the more their own racial protectiveness is reinforced. The situation is not much different than that which exists when an individual is subjected to a constant barrage of "My kid can do this and my kid can do that." Interminable testimonials are received as indigestible abominables. For every reaction there is an equal (or greater) and opposite reaction. Over time, just as an individual retaliates against a chronically child-bragging associate, whites become increasingly more protective, more oppositional, more resistant, and more determined to negate the pro-black tsunami of racialized rhetoric.

A fourth problem is that racialization directly conflicts with our ability to relate spontaneously and genuinely with each other, whether the relating is positive or negative. Being white, I honestly can consider another white person as saint or a sinner without being worried that someone will regard me as a panderer or a bigot for doing so. Never do I need to be on tenterhooks about every word that comes out of my mouth. If someone is "articulate," I can say so, and, if someone is a boor, I can say that too. When a black man and I are able to both compliment and criticize each other without either of us wondering whether the other is racist, America will have turned the corner racially. That day will not come until race preoccupation, the first problem, is under control.

Fifth, rampant racialization creates excessive, even unattainable, standards of conduct. While automatic, complete integration is an idealized goal, there is nothing inherently wrong with occasionally preferring to be with one's own race, or with periodically engaging in behaviors and activities skewed toward one's own race. These should not be regarded as signaling prejudice, so long as they do not infringe on the comfort, rights, and freedoms of people from other racial groups. That is why even blacks and whites who are friendly and treat each other respectfully at school sometimes voluntarily eat at "segregated" lunch tables. Problems arise, however, when one or both groups advertise their separateness in racialized, loud, or obnoxious ways.

A sixth problem is that raceketeering not only keeps the dividers in the forefront, it relegates unifiers to the background. Aside from actual physical intimidation, shunning and mockery are other weapons of choice, used by black identity slave masters to hustle black dissenters to the back of the bus. African American voices of understanding and moderation are muffled or totally silenced by fear of Uncle Tom and not black enough. The shunning, of course, says almost nothing about the offenders and almost everything about the thought police. Robert Kurzban and Mark R. Leary in *Psychological Bulletin*, March, 2001, commented that "people stigmatize others to (a) enhance their self-esteem, (b) enhance their social identity, or (c) justify a particular social, economic, or political structure." In other words, raceketeers shun in order to bolster their personal status and power in the community. In the rare circumstance when dissent is grudgingly tolerated, the token freedom is tempered by a stern injunction to "keep things in the family;" that is, in the black family. This is a variation on the control-the-dialogue-and-you-control-race strategy that keeps America on a racial razor's edge.

Asymmetrical language freedom is the seventh problem. The issue has been mentioned many times before, so, despite how important language freedom is for race relations, I will be very brief. The essential point is clear: there will be no genuine racial reconciliation until there is parity of racial verbal expression. The Elisabeth Hasselbecks of the world must be given a receptive forum. They are the white voices of moderation and rationality. They are the ones who want to make the effort to listen to black concerns, if only they, themselves, will be heard. When white Americans witness verbal abuse heaped upon the Hasselbecks they think and/or say, "See I told you so. Keep your mouth shut about race;" they withdraw, ceding the floor to white, racist identity slave masters, like Aryan Nation.

Shit happens. We all have heard this crude but physiologically accurate description. Vomitus happens, too. Racism constitutes part of the social shit and vomitus of our society, and it must be dealt with. Our eighth problem concerns that challenge. Each person is responsible for the effluence that issues from both ends of his own alimentary system. But none of us needs to hear every fart and retch that sounds out from every part of our country. America has sanitation squads to handle large messes. America has laws to deal with destructive racial incidents. These laws should be vigorously enforced by color-blind professionals who take on the New Black Panthers as readily as the Ku Klux Klan, and we need oversight to ensure that they do. Popular media need not advertise and reinforce every racial incident that they can drag out of the social toilet.

Growing up in Philadelphia in the 1960s, I witnessed racist mentalities rampant in both black and white communities. Most often, the mind set was subtle and relatively "harmless." Sometimes it was overt and vicious.

In the 2000s, I perceive a real and dramatic positive change in the mindset of white America. Anti-black attitudes, implicit and explicit, are a dying species. And I am not just talking about attitudes voiced among casual acquaintances in formal settings. When I am among friends and family, I detect sincere acceptance of blacks and advocacy for treating them as equals. Make no mistake (as Barack Obama would say), I am no Pollyanna. When black raceketeers say that having a "black" (read "half-black") president does not mean a post-racial society, they are right. However, I believe they are right for the wrong reason. The race merchants mean that white on black racism is alive and well, flourishing not only in the hearts of evil whites but in the fabric and structure of the United States. To my way of thinking, America has not entered a completely post-racial period because there never was and never will be such a purely post-racial period anywhere on earth, as long as raceketeers hold sway. The raceketeers, themselves, have and will continue to oppose racial harmony, since racial harmony literally puts them out of business. It also has been raceketeer racializing, I assert, that in large measure accounts for the fact that the average non-psychopathological black is less accepting of whites than is the average non-psychopathological white.

The ninth difficulty with race is our country's failure to explicitly acknowledge and to emphatically address the major perpetrators of racism and black failure—men, especially men under 30 years of age. While we do have Sister Souljahs vamping off the blood of our citizens, it is mostly the male ghouls, the bimps, that perpetuate racial discord. The obscenely high so-called black-on-black crime rate is exceeded only by the disproportionally high black-on-white crime statistics relative to the white-on-black stats. The double standard and double speak by which black-on-black violence is decried rather than black violence, per se, literally sets a dangerous standard, encouraging psychopathic bimps to attack whites and inciting white retaliation.

Men also, overwhelmingly, are the primary reason for the shortcomings of black families. Everyone has heard about the abysmally low rate of father presence in the home. "Baby mama," meaning a male-female relationship of barely sufficient duration to result in fertilization, is the standard term used to light-heartedly absolve black male youth of paternal responsibility. Disparaging women is the self-serving strategy implying that "bitches" get what they deserve. Incredibly, some females collude in their own degradation, masochistically seeking relationships with misogynistic, narcissistically-preoccupied, smooth-talking black males. They have babies, sometimes multiple babies, with the losers, thereby consigning themselves and their children to lives of poverty and pain, and perpetuating the self-defeating cycle.

White bimps are no better than black ones. Their behaviors are as egregious and as destructive. In short, because men under 30 are the primary problem, those men—black and white—must be targeted for early, intensive, corrective intervention.

By grotesquely distorting an old song title, we arrive at problem number ten: accentuate the negative and eliminate the positive. That, unfortunately, is the way race relations are treated in our country right now. The popular media and raceketeers do their best to keep it so. Organizations such as happynews.com and goodnewsnetwork.org are butts of jokes. For instance, on September 28, 2009, Raina Kelley, a black Newsweek columnist, contemptuously campaigns against any thought that America is moving toward being a more accepting society by writing, "Almost anything would be better than the 'post racial' and 'Kumbaya' crap we're being pedaled."

Without the counter-balancing effect of positive race news, America can sink into racial reconciliation despair. Without the counterbalancing effect of positive race news, merchants of inter-racial doom rule the day. But, just because we rarely hear about them, does not mean that good things are not happening every day. I have already mentioned eleven white people who have done extraordinary things to support blacks. How about two more?

On July 29, 2010, I read a piece that Thomas Barlas of *Press of Atlantic City* wrote about a Vineland, New Jersey man who was killed by a falling tree. Person crushed to death by a falling tree; that is newsworthy. But the real story had nothing to do with trees or death; it was about the life of a man, a white man who gave selfishly to black children. You see, Dominick Visconti, 61, and his white wife, Linda, devoted their lives to needy youngsters. Barlas explained:

> The Viscontis adopted six children during their 40-year marriage. One was born to a drug addict. Another was found eating out of a garbage can. And one child was adopted after the couple watched television coverage of the 1998 bombing of the American embassy in Kenya. The child, wounded by shards of flying glass, lay in a hospital bed, telling an interviewer how much he wanted to learn to read.

> "He said, 'We have to find him,'" Linda Visconti said while sitting in the kitchen of her Mays Landing Road home Thursday. "I looked at him like that was a very nice, ridiculous idea. He said, 'We have to do this.'"

> Dominick Visconti's persistence paid off, and after months of haggling with Kenyan officials, and finally getting the help of a Kenyan military official who realized the sincerity of the couple's adoption efforts, he brought the child home. Now 24, Simon still

lives in the house that the Viscontis have called home for more than two decades.

Although I am unaware of the race of all of the adopted children, at least two others are black. Writing of them, *The Press of Atlantic City* article mentions that "Ronnie, now 27, and Rhonda, now 24, came together. They are brother and sister, and were both living in squalor in Camden."

Two days later, abclocal.go.com told the story of Austin Gutwein, a white boy, who, at age nine, watched a film about African children who had been orphaned due to AIDS. The film prompted him to begin a continuing fund-raising effort that to date has collected at least two million dollars. The article noted that when Carl Taylor, white CEO of Nashville-based Synergy Production, heard Austin talk about his project, he came on board. As a result, "Hoops for Hope" was created wherein participants donate funds for the privilege of shooting free-throws.

I chose to relate the two additional stories merely because, occurring in such close temporal proximity to each other, they struck an emotional chord in me. I could have written about any one of a hundred similar stories, stories of everyday white people assisting everyday blacks. I could have mentioned how often whites anonymously volunteer to work in inner-city black neighborhood projects like Habitat for Humanity. Do Jesse Jackson, Al Sharpton, Benjamin Todd Jealous, or the NAACP know about white people such as these? Do they care?

"Non-Zero sum game," you no doubt have heard this popular phrase used to describe race-oriented issues, and this is our number eleven focus. The phrase is a favorite of racializers and raceketeers when advocating race-based affirmative actions or special favors for African Americans. The advocates suggest that resources are sufficient to implement a pro-black policy without impinging on the resources or rights available to whites, that the policy they desire merely is intended to "level the playing field." Most often such affirmative actions or special favors sail through governmental or private agency gatekeepers with nary a blink from them. One never hears the phrase non-zero sum game applied to proposed programs for needy white people. Rather, race-based programs for them, if they existed, would be called "institutional racism."

In fact, most, so-called, non-zero sum games are, in fact, racialized zero sum whereby one takes from white Peter to give to black Paul. Almost no one talks about, or even wants to hear about, these "games." However, every once and a while, the Peters speak out against the race-based double standards, challenging governmental or private agency gatekeepers who have executed the pro-black preferential treatments.

Allan Bakke, a white man, was a pioneer in the "stick up for yourself" crusade. Despite having better admissions test scores and academic credentials, he was denied admission to the University of California, Davis, Medical School twice, with "his spots" going to less qualified African Americans. Although the lower court ruled against Bakke, the Supreme Court supported him, resulting in the 1978 white equivalent to Brown vs. Board of Education. Not surprisingly, the victory was achieved only through a split, five to four decision.

Pro-black bias at white expense also was front and center when white Connecticut firefighter Frank Ricci asserted himself. After having chosen a measurement consultant to design a fair and relevant test for firefighter promotion, New Haven applied it in 2003. The test, whose specific purpose was to provide a color-blind method of selection, produced inconvenient results for the city. For the one captain's position being offered, eight of 41 (19%) test-takers were black; for the one lieutenant's position, nineteen of 77 (24%) were black. While no blacks qualified for the promotions, two Hispanics did. Allegedly dyslexic, Ricci worked his tail off in preparing for the assessment, studying well over 20 videos and taking a college level fire science course in preparation. When, citing possible anti-black discrimination, the city voided the test results, Frank Ricci and other successful test takers launched a legal challenge under Title VII and the 14th amendment, the very laws that blacks had used to their advantage for decades. As expected, the litigants lost at the local and state levels, with Sonia Sotomayor, Barack Obama's favorite anti-white Hispanic, ruling against the test passers. On June 29, 2009, the high scoring candidates did win, however, in the United States Supreme Court. The decision, you guessed it, was five to four.

If you are black, should you care about Frank Ricci and his white co-workers? I think so. Employment discrimination against African

Americans, no doubt, happens regularly. That discrimination is as wrong, but not more wrong, than what New Haven tried to do to the white firefighters. Freedom is still the freedom to say that two plus two makes four. We need to move race relations forward together, not separately. When whites know that everyone's rights are protected equally and no one is getting preferential treatment, they will be much quicker to acknowledge legitimate black claims and, even, to support them.

Number twelve. One last, but most critical point, is an amplification of an essential continuing theme asserted throughout this book. All blacks and all whites must do their best to fulfill Martin Luther King junior's civil rights advice. In this case though, I must supplement his plea for us to judge people by the content of their character instead of by their race. In addition, we must permit people to be autonomous individuals, instead of being mere appendages of a group or caste. The admonition is more than semantic. When we say that people should be judged by the content of their character, we indirectly reinforce their external local of control in the sense that the focus is on someone judging someone else by imposing a personal definition of that other person's character. When we say that people should be free to feel, think, and act according to what they responsibly regard as proper, we directly reinforce their internal local of racial control. Persons who feel, think, and act as individuals and who treat others similarly are persons disinclined to racializing, stereotyping, and discriminating. This does not mean that these internal locus of control people are less proud or less committed to their race. This does not mean that they will cease spending time and enjoying same-race affiliation activities. It does mean that they need not keep looking over their shoulders to see whether black raceketeering and/or bimping racial identity slave masters are evaluating them.

Americans, then, are assailed by social factors that both pummel and seduce us into a race-preoccupied mentality and an external racial locus of control. As with pravada, there is not much truth or justice in the United States' race-oriented propaganda. The analogy with pravada is instructive in another way as well.

Because the N.K. Mixajlovskij quote that I mentioned earlier when discussing the American media perplexed me, I asked a Russian friend about it, a friend who had lived in the former Soviet Union. Sergei said that he was unfamiliar with the truth-justice fusion, but his aside was germane to our race discussion. After reminding me that *Pravada* (truth) had been the name of the Soviet Union's main newspaper, and *Izvestia* (justice), the primary Communist newspaper, he smiled and related a popular ironic "joke" from his past: "In truth there is no news, and in news there is no truth." Obviously, this means that, in the Soviet Union, most socially and culturally sanctioned sources of information were irrelevant and misleading, and, by implication, malignant.

In matters racial, the Soviet joke sadly describes the current social, political, and media situations in twenty-first century America. Today, truth and justice aren't what journalists are talking about when they regularly refer to freedom of the press as the cornerstone of our political system. In classrooms and on streets, in truth there is very little news, and in news there is very little truth. After years of race-oriented carpet bombing, truth is an abandoned, dilapidated shell, subverted regularly to blame whites for all race-related ills and to favor blacks in those matters. Most politicians either fear challenging anti-white propaganda or contribute to it. All media know that white bashing by action or omission is a sure-fire way to sell product, to ingratiate themselves to raceketeers, to keep on-the-right-side-of-history, and to prevent some black protestors from burning down their buildings, either literally or figuratively. White blaming and bashing is espoused from the oval office, from Black "Entertainment" Television, and from websites, newspapers, and magazines throughout the nation.

Twelve is a conveniently round number, but a dozen points hardly do justice to an issue as complicated and longstanding as our troubled race relations. However, the twelve do provide one set of specific, concrete challenges that everyone can understand and everyone can do his small part to address.

CHAPTER 16

Shedding a Little Light
on Individual Mentality Regarding Race

From the outset, I said that I would not approach this book as a traditional scientific treatise, and I would not be comprehensive with references, because the people who feel most passionately about race—racializers and raceketeers—want no part of objective data or objective discourse. However, because I have been a practicing psychologist for well over thirty years, I can no more disown psychology than I can disown the white community. I can no more disown psychology than I can disown my white grandmother. The avoid-psychology spirit is willing, but the I-just-have-to-make-a-couple-psychological-points flesh is weak.

Those who take an optimistic view of human nature might be puzzled and frustrated about how simultaneously irrational and ubiquitous our racializing and racial biases are. What mental mechanisms possibly can account for the perplexing situation? Let's consider some principles of human thought and emotion that render us vulnerable to race problems, and that cause us, unwittingly, to collude with social forces and raceketeers in creating and perpetuating racial discord, instead of opposing and eliminating it. By understanding these principles, you and I have a fighting chance to assume personal responsibility for what we think and do racially.

A psychological principle already has been introduced when we spoke about locus of control (LOC). Formally, LOC is defined as a form of "attribution," meaning beliefs that we entertain about the reason for thoughts, feelings, actions, and so forth. Of course, there truly is no one reason for anything that we do, but rather, layers of reasons, some conscious and some unconscious. An attribution is mostly one primary reason that we would give or could give verbally when pressed to do so, answering questions as mundane as, "Why are you eating again?" to ones as extraordinary as, "How did you discover that chromosomes are organize helically?"

We noted that the internal-external LOC dimension has two complementary dimensions, global-specific and permanent-temporary. But while the LOC concept revealed where we locate a reason, it did not tell anything about "how" the attribution came to be. The section below briefly addresses, in outline form, the how. Since libraries are devoted to the concept of attribution, as usual, I have chosen to briefly discuss a few concepts. My goal is modest: Merely to help you begin to think seriously about the chosen psychological concepts as they relate to the genesis of racialized thoughts, feelings, and actions, and to their maintenance.

Some Cognitive-Emotional Mechanisms That Contribute to Our Racial Identity and Racial Dialogue Problems

Attention

As alluded to earlier, most of our mental functions are steered by attention: attention that can be deliberate or incidental. We must be conscious how we direct our deliberate attention, if we are to be racially fair and balanced. Those who deliberately attend to every racial situation everywhere will find plenty reasons to be prejudiced. Incidental attention, obviously, is less amenable, but not totally intractable; we manage it by surrounding ourselves, as much as possible, with information, people, and places that are open-minded and tolerant. Pro-black and anti-white raceketeer and media propaganda have a negative influence on race relations because they negatively bias our attention. The more we attend to each other as individuals and not as skin classifications, the more we can focus on what matters in our daily interpersonal relationships.

Framing

This concerns the parameters that we place around the information that we collect. For instance, if one frames meeting an individual of a different race as an opportunity to learn and to expand his own horizons, race-relevant differences will be viewed as interesting and enriching. If one frames the differences as threatening, they will only cause him to recoil and to be more convinced than ever of the superiority of his own race-different perspective.

Familiarity

An old adage advising that "familiarity breeds contempt" finds some support in research by Michel I. Norton and his associates in a Volume 92, 2007 *Journal of Personality and Social Psychology* article about which the PsyNET abstract reads:

> The present research shows that although people believe that learning more about others leads to greater liking, more information about others leads, on average, to less liking. Thus, ambiguity—lacking information about another—leads to liking, whereas familiarity—acquiring more information—can breed contempt. This "less is more" effect is due to the cascading nature of dissimilarity: Once evidence of dissimilarity is encountered, subsequent information is more likely to be interpreted as further evidence of dissimilarity, leading to decreased liking. The authors document the negative relationship between knowledge and liking in laboratory studies and with pre—and postdate data from online daters, while showing the mediating role of dissimilarity.

If merely learning more about persons of another race is not sufficient to make us "like" them, we should not expect that social "exposure" programs necessarily lead to better racial relations. Genuine liking is a laudable goal. However, we must make a conscious effort to refrain, insofar as possible, from liking and disliking games, so that we genuinely can accept dissimilarity with equanimity, always accepting without always necessarily liking.

Expectation

Liking and disliking games are not especially productive. On the other hand, because we all must struggle against the natural human tendency to see what we expect to see, in racial situations, one must have at least some positive exposure to the "other" race, if he is to have any chance to overcome prejudice. Exposure offers the possibility of acceptance without the pressure of having to like. But even the potential benefits of simple exposure can be corrupted by negative expectation—self-fulfilling prophecies wherein, having anticipated the worst in the other race, the biased one sees only the worst. The formidable challenge here is to generate positive racial expectations, conveyed subtly and gradually. One way to do so is to encourage cross-racial alliances involving brief, concrete, common goal-related activities, as when a few whites and blacks volunteer to help at church or to clean-up the neighborhood.

Cognitive Dissonance

Dissonance is the opposite of expectation—situations of conflict between what is and what we thought would be that can occur for better or worse, as when we are pleasantly surprised or sadly mistaken. In black-white circumstances, both positive and negative dissonant events need to be processed and understood because both are learning opportunities. When the surprise is that the racially "different" person turns out to be "better" than we thought, we need to have the integrity to revise our expectations of him accordingly. When the surprise is that the racially "different" person turns out to be "worse" than we thought, we can strive to understand why, and to accept the reality as being the negative differences of two individual human beings, not that of two entire races.

Recall Errors

Memory can be enemy or friend to race relations, either undermining or facilitating our inter-racial communications and efforts at reconciliation. To date, undermining has had the upper hand. Raceketeers, specifically, and society, generally, have succeeded in making America "remember" each and every white anti-black statement and action, from 1500 A.D. to 2 seconds ago, and to forget every black anti-white statement and action.

More important, the collective consciousness of the black community has been so brainwashed as to qualify as having racial false memory syndrome, remembering some incidences of "abuse" that never were. The antidote to false memory victimization is for black and white people to forget and to remember, to forget socially-fabricated racial lies and to remember their own positive racial truths.

What about authentic racial abuse that has occurred? How do we handle that?

Many of the people who disseminate and reinforce memories of past white racial injustice are the very same ones who want us to forget the offenses that blacks have perpetrated. For instance, raceketeers advocate for black ex-cons, saying that these men have "paid their debt to society" and should be "given a second chance." Maybe black and white America, as a whole, also needs a second chance, but that opportunity never will come if raceketeers succeed in their relentless exhortations for us to "remember" every white racial negative, no matter how remote in time or how trivial in content.

Downward Comparison

According to this principle, everyone needs someone to feel superior to. This is the "I may be bad off, but I'm better off than that fool" attitude. In our divided society, we, of course, racialize downward comparison: white men can't jump, but blacks can; white women can't dance, but blacks can; black men can't swim, but whites can, and black women can't eat sensibly, but whites can. Such a convenient strategy to buoy flagging self-esteem, since one can always find a racist—black or white—to agree with his disparaging view of the out group. The remedy for this is transparently easy to understand, but sometimes difficult to implement: When you have an impulse to disparage someone of another race, focus on yourself instead. Ask why you need to mock them, and I guarantee you will find some personal shortcoming fueling your bias. When you do, find a way to raise yourself up, instead of dragging someone else down.

Hedonic Treadmill

Downward comparison is externally focused, but racial discontent also can arise from what begins as an internal focus. All people tend to run on a hedonic treadmill in that we readily acclimate to our good fortunes; what had pleased us formerly soon becomes status quo and uninspiring. As a result, we fail to count our blessings, focusing instead on our discontents. In the racial domain, this means that success in race relations soon becomes status quo. What once was new and hopeful in our black versus white world becomes "no big thing." Since raceketeers and the media will be trumpeting every racial ill, those problems have no counterbalancing positives; we are left with race discouragement and ennui. Counting our racial blessings provides fuel with which we can energize further success. Let's start counting and keep counting.

Bad Is Stronger Than Good

Interference from our hedonic treadmill tendencies is merely one feature of a more pervasive human propensity that interferes with our ability to promote racial harmony. We all experience this in multiple venues throughout our lives, whether we are staring at the one "C" on an otherwise all "A" report card, or obsessing about the fact that we can't go to our luxurious spa because we have a head cold. Roy Baumeister and his colleagues illuminated the unfortunate truth that "bad is stronger than good' in *Review of General Psychology*, December 2001.

> The greater power of bad events over good ones is found in everyday events, major life events (e.g., trauma), close relationship outcomes, social network patterns, interpersonal interactions, and learning processes. Bad emotions, bad parents, and bad feedback have more impact than good ones, and bad information is processed more thoroughly than good. We are more motivated to avoid bad self-definitions than to pursue good ones. Bad impressions and bad stereotypes are quicker to form and more resistant to disconfirmation than good ones. Various explanations such as diagnosticity and salience help explain some findings, but the greater power of bad events is still found when such variables

are controlled. Hardly any exceptions (indicating greater power of good) can be found.

Taken together, these findings suggest the importance of "bad stronger than good" as a general principle across a broad range of psychological phenomena. In race relations, fear of the bad often trumps striving for the good. Some people refuse to speak up racially because they are so intimidated by the prospect of saying the wrong thing, looking foolish, or being called racist.

Bad is stronger than good implies another important issue: We need many more positive relationship and positive talk experiences to counteract the power of a few negative ones. How much? We can infer the answer from the work of John Gottman (2011) who studies happy and unhappy marriages in minute detail. Thirty-five years of research produces this most essential conclusion: for every negative mutual interpersonal experience, satisfied couples evidence five positive experiences.

If a five to one positive to negative ratio is required for harmony between two people who supposedly love each other, what should we expect for inter-racial interaction? Think about our culture with its rampant, virulent raceketeering. If anything, we hear five or ten negative to one positive media reports where race is concerned. Citizens need to counter this pessimistic racial spin that assails us. We need to look for the positives and we need to petition the media to tell us about the good inter-racial relationships and good inter-racial talk occurring every day in America.

In short, we cannot merely blame raceketeers and the media for the fact that counting our racial blessings is easier said than done. Each of us must work explicitly to address the "natural" pessimism that lurks within. Just as social support makes smoking cessation or alcohol cessation more likely, success in formulating and implementing positive racial thought, talk, and action will be more likely if we know that moving forward requires sustained effort, and if we engage with like-minded others who are determined to work vigorously to achieve our common racial-reconciliation goals.

Broaden and Build Versus Narrow and Destroy

Although bad might be stronger than good, positive definitely is better than negative in the realm of human emotion and human interaction. No one has explained this any better than the "good," not "bad" psychologist, Barbara Fredrickson. According to her University of North Carolina Positive Emotions and Psychophysiology Lab web page:

> Central to many existing theories of emotion is the concept of specific-action tendencies—the idea that emotions prepare the body both physically and psychologically to act in particular ways. For example, anger creates the urge to attack, fear causes an urge to escape and disgust leads to the urge to expel. From this framework, positive emotions posed a puzzle.
>
> Emotions like joy, serenity and gratitude don't seem as useful as fear, anger or disgust. The bodily changes, urges to act and the facial expressions produced by positive emotions are not as specific or as obviously relevant to survival as those sparked by negative emotions. If positive emotions didn't promote our ancestors' survival in life-threatening situations, then what good were they? How did they survive evolutionary pressures? Did they have any adaptive value at all?

Barbara Fredrickson developed the Broaden-and-Build Theory of Positive Emotions to explain the mechanics of how positive emotions are fundamental for survival. According to the theory, positive emotions expand cognition and behavioral tendencies. Taking issue with the view that all emotions lead to specific action tendencies, the theory argues that positive emotions increase the number of potential behavioral options. Fredrickson believes that emotions should be cast as leading to changes in "momentary thought-action repertoires"—a range of potential actions the body and mind are prepared to take.

The expanded cognitive flexibility evident during positive emotional states results in resource building that becomes useful over time. Even though a positive emotional state is only momentary, the benefits last in the form of traits, social bonds, and abilities that endure into the future.

The implication of this work is that positive emotions have inherent value to human growth and development and cultivation of these emotions helps people lead fuller lives.

Frederickson's theory and research prepare us for the distinct likelihood that honest racial dialogue will not necessarily improve race relations in the short-term, since compromise and seeing another's point of view usually does not provide the immediate tension reduction that follows when we feel we have "showed that so-and-so a thing or two." In fact, honest discourse might even cause a brief period of increased tension within and between races when each has to listen to points of view at odds with their own. But, I agree with Barbara Fredrickson that, in the long run, positive emotions win out by enabling blacks and whites to consider new ideas and, eventually, to act out new behaviors. First we broaden and build our inter-racial dialogue, then we broaden and build our inter-racial activities and resources.

Leveling-Sharpening

Consider this a kind of arithmetical-geometrical understanding of racial issues. Leveling is a process by which we look at two disparate things, focus on their commonalities, and decide that they basically are similar. Depending on our framing, we can level virtually any two items. A mosquito is like a whale: both are alive. Black Africans and black Americans are "brothers;" they both have black skin. White Americans and skin heads are racists; they both have white skin. Sharpening is the inverse of leveling. He's not a brother; he's white. He's not trustworthy; he's white. Barack Obama is nothing like George Bush: Barack is black and George is white.

So many times in this book I have tried to hammer away at the destructiveness of pro-black, pro-white, anti-black, and anti-white propaganda promulgated by black and white raceketeers and media. For their narrow self-serving ends, they seek to indoctrinate us with a sharpening mentality regarding black people and white people. They want to sensitize us to each and every racial difference and to blind us to each and every similarity. To do so, they look at group statistical differences and parade them before us: Real black people attend black-only churches. Real white people attend white-only churches.

The plane geometry of leveling-sharpening is plainly true: We need to sharpen awareness of some racial group issues and level some others. Try sharpening the intra-racial, becoming aware that just because someone is of our race does not mean that we are "just like" him. Try leveling the inter-racial, becoming aware that just because someone is not of our race does not mean that he is not like us.

Miscalculation

Miscalculation is the ubiquitous human tendency by which we mistakenly believe that we have weighed every gram and counted every bean in arriving at our "objective" conclusion about an issue, in our case, a racial issue. In everyday terms, individual black and white citizens sometimes do their best to "objectively" measure the pros and cons of their race-relevant choices. What potentially could be gained or lost by supporting or by opposing race-positive or race-negative reference group pressure? In truth, however, the objective, here-and-now choice often is neither here-and-now nor objective, but something akin to superstitious behavior that is rooted in longstanding emotional and/or cognitive calculation habits. There are so many relevant varieties of miscalculation that a hundred could be cited. I, mercifully, will not inundate you with them, just present three in outline form.

Pseudocertainty Effect

This principle suggests that we are inclined to make a risky choice when we "objectively" calculate that an outcome will be positive:

> I read the focus group report last night. If we support bill HR 323, we stand to gain 200 new black voters, and lose about 250 white from our regular constituency. I say we support the bill. We need to make gains into the black community. Losing 250 white voters is worth it.

At the same time, pseudocertainty encourages us to avoid the very same risky choice when we "objectively" calculate that an outcome will be negative:

I read the focus group report last night. If we support bill HR 323, we stand to gain 200 new black voters, and lose about 250 white from our regular constituency. I say we oppose the bill. We need to make gains into the black community, but cannot afford to lose 250 white voters to do so.

In both scenarios, the deciders can point to objective data to "prove" that they have made the correct decision despite the risks involved.

Failure to Consider Base Rate

A base rate is simply the true frequency of a phenomenon in the real world, whether the number of people in a population or the average number of hairs on a human head. Obviously, knowing the base rate is not easy for an everyday person in an everyday situation, and people rarely consider base rates when making race-oriented interpersonal judgments. What happens instead is that we have racialized thoughts and make racialized statements like: I sat next to this black (white) guy on the bus today. When I tried to make small talk with him, he just ignored me. Those people don't want any part of us." Failure to consider base rate was alluded to earlier when I said that if an individual of another race does not treat us according to the content of our character, we mis-presume that the average person of our race would have. Perhaps, had we sat next to someone of our own race, we would have found him to be no more welcoming than our "opposite-race" commuter.

Without knowledge of base rates, personal biases determine our expectations about the normative behavior of both out-groups and in-groups, and we react accordingly.

Forward Projection

The habit of forward projection is in force when we smugly, authoritatively apply old, outdated data to new situations. This is a frequent source of inter-racial paralysis when, on a group level, we cite "statistics" from decades earlier to justify our belief in current institutionalized racism, and, on an individual level, when we cite racial experiences from grade school to justify our current reluctance to participate in a university project with someone of another race. The forward projector says with a straight face: "I lived during the sixties. I know how racist whites (blacks) are. Come here. Let's review my *Time* magazine archive; I'll show you the articles and photos. No way I'm going to believe what whites (or blacks) tell me."

Concorde Effect

One last example of miscalculation: The Concorde, a super-polluting "supersonic" passenger jet jointly built by the British and French that first operated in 1969 and that last flew in 2003. The British lost tons of money on this transatlantic speed demon, but they felt compelled to fly it because they had "sunk" so much money in its development. Accordingly, the Concorde effect also is called the "sunk-cost" effect.

For our purposes, the Concorde Effect means that once a raceketeering person or group calculates that he has substantial chips on a racial issue, he must maintain his position to save face, even if, literally or figuratively, it costs him in the long run. Contemporary social institutions cannot step back from their legacy of race mongering or they risk losing whatever little credibility that they have left. The same can be said for raceketeers, racializing politicians, race-profiting media types, and even some particularly outspoken private citizens.

America needs to do whatever it can to counter the Concorde effect, such as by giving the traditional facilitators of racial discord a face-saving way to abandon their long-standing, self-serving, destructive messages without totally losing too much of their residual credibility or customary privileges.

Self-serving Bias

Thus far, I have used the term "self-serving" colloquially, never attempting to specify precisely what I meant. But since "self serving bias" is pervasive and critical in our lives and in race relations, the time has come to elaborate this psychological concept. To do so, I begin by mostly paraphrasing the report of Thomas Shelley Duval and Paul J. Silvia in the *Journal of Personality and Social Psychology*, January 2002. Contained within their work, but not specifically mentioned by them, are notions of internal and external locus of control that I have discussed at length.

Duval and Silvia explain that our self-serving explanations typically involve internal attributions for success and external ones for failure. However, while psychological studies consistently show the expected internal attribution for success, some research finds internal attribution for failure as well. The manner in which the self-serving bias plays out has major consequences for individual and group self-esteem and for racial harmony.

In essence, Duval and Sylvia assert that the self-serving bias is modulated by two psychological mechanisms—a system that sets personal standards and a system that evaluates personal responsibility. The more we focus on ourselves as the responsible agent, the more we are inclined to claim credit for success—an internal locus of control. A self focus coupled with an accompanying ability to improve prompts us to acknowledge our role in our failures as well our successes—also an internal locus of control. In contrast, when self focus is high but we believe that we cannot improve, we project blame for failure to something outside ourselves—an external locus of control.

If accurate, this research provides hope for situations wherein we attribute failure to ourselves when the failure attribution accurately reflects the reality of our personal responsibility. It is a troubling finding, however, when we accept blame for problems that we neither cause nor perpetuate. Race-oriented general social propaganda, such as media propaganda, and raceketeering, keeps black personal standards focused on being black (black enough, Uncle Tom, brotha, and so forth) and their personal responsibility system focused on blaming whites for all failures (institutionalized racism, racial micro-aggressions, employment discrimination, and so forth). For whites, race-oriented general social propaganda, such as media propaganda, and raceketeering, also keeps white personal standards focused on race (being the only non-person-of-color group on planet earth, having unfair privilege, not having to worry about violent neighborhood crime, and so forth) and whites' personal responsibility system focused on accepting blame for black failures and for white failures (not doing enough to reverse institutionalized racism, acting-out racial micro-aggressions, committing employment discrimination, and so forth). Thus, our cultural milieu reinforces blacks for avoiding responsibility and punishes whites when they refuse to accept responsibility for problems they do not cause.

Twenty-first century America, then, is structured to perpetuate destructive self-serving biases. Blacks and whites are assailed by overt and covert messages that keep race in focus. With race always on their minds, blacks develop an external locus of control for all negative things, and an internal locus of control for all positive things. Critically, messages to African Americans that they cannot control problems cause them to project responsibility, to blame whites, and to despair of being able to overcome impediments that are well within their capabilities. Locus of control social messages to whites are narrower: White people are not taught to believe that all their problems are race-oriented, but they are relentlessly given messages suggesting that they are colorless outsiders, and that they cause all problems for, so called, people-of-color. So, many racially-focused whites develop an internal locus of control regarding black problems and feel responsible for ones that they neither cause nor perpetuate.

Meta-communicative Void

Of all the psychological concepts that could be cited, the meta-communicative void constitutes one of the most critical and debilitating for race relations. By meta-communicative void, I mean the absence of honest, inter-racial, collaborative discussion about the conduct of race-oriented talk. Please note that I am *not* referring to the *content* of dialogue, but to the *process* of conversing. I am saying that all races must be able to talk across race about the specific, concrete impediments that impede their abilities to speak honestly to each other. We already have addressed some of these: such as that whites are told they have no right to give their opinions on some racial matters and that blacks are allowed, even encouraged, to use racially inflammatory words like "nigger." In fact, the notion of double bind, itself, is a meta-communicative notion, since double bind includes the idea that one is prohibited from talking about the process of conversing.

To counter the meta-communicative void, we must short-circuit an unproductive conversation in real time by pointing out and challenging that which is blocking it. Most notably, we need to explicitly identify the doubles—help our conversational partner to recognize them, and work together to reverse them. For example, if when talking about affirmative action, a black person repeatedly cites the "legacy of racism" as justifying today's special black privileges to keep the white person on the defensive and to avoid addressing discrete current conditions, the white person should cease speaking about affirmative action and focus instead on what is happening between the speakers at the moment. Applying that meta-communicative strategy to the Michael Lake-Jehmu Greene discussion, Mr. Lake might have addressed Ms. Greene as follow:

> I am trying to talk about a particular issue in effect right now in 2011—that any single white person has as much, but not greater, right to higher education scholarships as any single black person does. But every time I try to make my points about that specific here-and-now issue, you attack me, do not answer my question, do not address my points, monopolize the dialogue, speak over me, or talk about racial inequality of the past, such as how blacks and women were barred from country clubs decades ago. We never will resolve our differences if we do not listen respectfully to each others' ideas and address them specifically. I will listen quietly and attentively to you to the extent that you listen quietly and attentively to me.

Mindlessness

While the meta-communicative void, and, essentially, all the cognitive-emotional mechanisms that we have considered above, can operate as the result of deliberate or inadvertent effort, the inadvertent is particularly important, since one cannot act to correct errors that he does not recognize. Ellen Langer refers to inadvertent social thinking as "mindless." Writing in the May, 2010 *Psychology of Aesthetics, Creativity, and the Arts* journal, she, Michael Pirson, and Laura Delizonna explain mindless as they see it. Namely, mindlessness is depicted as automatic, ubiquitous, and at the heart of the how people determine "the merit of achievements, expectations of ability, and mood" in social situations.

Locus of control is implicated in the work of Langer and her associates, as well. Insights from locus of control and context-dependent studies play a prominent role in their conclusions. They underscore inimical effects on one's self concept, adaptive skills, and social relationships when global-stable locus of control (GSLOC) attributions, rooted in other times and other places, are inappropriately applied to current situations. For us, their essential conclusions are:

> While mindfully engaging in social comparisons, one does not deny the relevance of categories derived from past experience—it is only that they are experienced as flexible and permeable enough to be susceptible to change in response to newly relevant information. Mindless social comparisons, on the other hand, over utilize categorizations made in the past, keep them rigid and impermeable, making newly emergent contextual information obscured, and thus ineffectual. Mindfulness, by definition, promotes the experience of self as a continually changing subject, whereas mindlessness promotes the experience of self as a passive, stable, and reactive object.

Mindlessness is another friend to raceketeers. The identity slave mastering and anti-reconciliation propaganda machine requires a passively receptive audience. The more mindful we are, the more here-and-now and contextualized our thoughts and feelings are, the more autonomous and rational we will be about race. More mindful black and white men and women are capable of more realistic and reasonable understanding of human nature and of their own nature. They know that every single individual has a personal responsibility to do that which is within his or her own power to make race relations work. They also know that they are not responsible for every racial inequity that every same-raced person ever has perpetrated since the human species was banished from the Garden of Eden. Armed with this awareness of themselves and of the world, individuals can make reasonable commitments to racial harmony, rather than ignoring the challenge or engaging in empty talk about what would be "nice" inter-racially.

Peter J. McCusker

Caution: Human Vulnerability at Work

Barack Obama incorrectly presumed that writing *Dreams from My Father: A Story of Race and Inheritance* miraculously would overcome his admitted racial conflict and turmoil. But, of course, it did not. Similarly, my having written here about "Some Cognitive-Emotional Mechanisms That Contribute to Our Racial Identity and Racial Dialogue Problems" did not ensure that either you or I readily can overcome them. In fact, David Buss, specialist in Individual Differences and Evolutionary Psychology at the University of Texas admitted that he still struggles to overcome cognitive-emotional obstacles. In his words, "One nagging thing that I still don't understand about myself is why I often succumb to well-documented psychological biases, even though I'm acutely aware of these biases."

Buss's comment indirectly relates to the psychological notion of "working through," a term used to explain the difference between knowing something intellectually and acting upon it behaviorally. We "know" much about what is right and right for us: "I should exercise more, eat more healthfully, stop smoking, save for retirement, speak respectfully to my spouse, and treat all people the way I want to be treated." But knowing is not doing. To do things differently requires us to be vigilant, to sacrifice, and to persist. It is not so simple to move from talk to action. In order to implement significant, enduring changes in our behavior, we must work them into our lives, over time and over contexts. Working through is not easy, most often requiring a "corrective emotional experience" or two. At one time or another almost everyone has had such an experience that transforms superficial, intellectual understanding into gut level, authentic awareness and action. Imagine that your mother forever admonished that, "You don't care about anyone but yourself" and you had always responded to her mentally with a "Yeah—blah, blah, blah" self-statement. Mother's advice remained little more than background noise in your mind. Then, at age thirty-two, you have landed a coveted job, the job you have pursued for a decade, the job that you just love. As with many jobs, you have been on a probationary period and the moment of truth has come. The boss starts the review complimentarily, recites all your technical skills, but ends with, "Unfortunately, we must let you go. You do not fit in socially with us. This is a business built on relationships and, I hate to say it, but several people have told me that you only care about yourself. Sorry that the job didn't work out for you."

We all—black, white, and in-between—must work through our racial attitudes. We all need corrective emotional experiences to transform our knowledge of how we should treat each other into actions by which we do treat each other. If you sincerely aspire to treating people as individuals and by the content of their characters, be prepared for a relentless, life-long struggle of working through. You will not always succeed, but to whatever extent you do, you and our country will be the better for it.

CHAPTER 17

Obama, Identity, Race, and America

Barry Barack Hussein Soetoro Obama, Identity, and Racial Hypocrisy in America: Double Standards, Double Speak, and Double Binds opens with the assertion that I initially had considered voting for Barack Obama, but that the more I learned about him, the more I knew I could not. From that initial opening to now, I sometimes have indirectly and sometimes have directly given unelaborated rationales for my voting decision. Now is the time to be explicit and detailed.

From my perspective, the fundamental problems with Obama as president are fundamental problems with his personality. Identity is our glue and identity is our compass. To quote a colloquialism, Barack is "not glued too tight" in that his identity never has been a natural, unified constituent of his personality. His many identities are merely costumes that he puts on or takes off in attempts to manipulate his way toward extant goals. As with all people, a president must be coherent, authentic, and whole within himself, if he is to be that way with others. The failures of Obama's personality lead inexorably to the failures of his leadership and of his presidency.

Barry Barack Hussein Soetoro Obama has been Barry Barack Hussein Soetoro Obama since the 1960s, but he never really has embraced the totality of his being. Barry—the closeted white ghost that haunts the personality pantheon—is the son of an identity-conflicted, ambivalently American Caucasian mother. Barack is the son of an angry, abusive, narcissistic, anti-colonialist, alcoholic, absconding, inadequate black African father who acted superior to counter pervasive self-doubt. Hussein is an ethnic-religious alien lurking in the shadows. Soetoro also is the son of an alcoholic, inadequate husband and father who served as a colonel in the murderous regime of Indonesian dictator Kemusu Argamulja Suharto. Barack Hussein Obama is the grandson of an anti-British, white-hater who stridently proselytized his racism. All these characters have been housed within dead-bolted chambers in the biracial edifice that is the 44th President of the United States. The characters rarely interact or speak with each other, but landlord Obama can release any of them at any time onto the world stage for brief, advantageous cameo performances. The profoundly racially conflicted Obama reigns as the greatest identity quick change artist of all time. Now you know him; now you don't. Mesmerized by the contrasting milk whiteness of his mother and pitch blackness of his father, Obama never developed the capacity to see beyond race, or to regard race as anything other than a rigidly dichotomous, either-or, choice.

To be valid and useful, every comprehensive theory of personality must address identity development. And, the broad sweep of identity includes racial identity as one part. Given the history of slavery and racism in America, it is reasonable to assume that forging racial identity can be more challenging for average African Americans than for average white Americans; I understand that the journey might be torturous, and even tortured, for some blacks. Being biracial just adds another layer of complexity to the process. I acknowledge that Barack Obama could have had identity obstacles that I might not ever fully comprehend. On the other hand, Obama has lived a life of privilege, rather than disadvantage, despite his whining that scooping ice cream at Baskin-Robbins while working a high school summer job caused him anguish because it was difficult for him to "look cool" in the required uniform. Are we to believe that this is the kind of challenge that regularly confronts authentic inner-city black adolescents? Everyone forms an identity but only few, such as Barack Obama, focus on its racial component so obsessively-compulsively and manipulatively.

Innumerable blacks who have endured authentic disadvantage or who have lived genuine working- or middle-class lives have been able to put race in its proper context. Race is a part of identity, but race is never identity. Race can be an impediment to realizing one's hopes and dreams, but, as millions of African Americans prove every day, in 21st century America, race is never an insuperable barrier.

As we have seen, on occasion, not-black-enough and Uncle Tom naysayers from the African American community have used Barack Obama's "good life" background against him: proof of the salience of the following adolescent fantasy that Barack related in his *Dreams* book:

> And yet, even as I imagined myself following Malcolm's call, one line in the book stayed me. He spoke of a wish he'd once had, the wish that the white blood that ran through him, there by an act of violence, might somehow be expunged.

Despite Obama's having spent a lifetime imaging himself as a black hero, and, regardless of the number of people who share the delusion from his father that he would look great in basic black, the emperor has no clothes. Just as surely as "freedom is the freedom to say that two plus two makes four," and, irrespective of who says what to the contrary, nothing is sufficient to negate the simple, unassailable truth that Barry Barack Hussein Soetoro Obama always was and always will be both black AND white. Someday, perhaps, he will aspire to being a biracial hero.

If Barack Obama was so conflicted, how could he become president of the United States? He did so by developing intellectual and personality strengths as direct byproducts of the love and care provided to him by his white mother and her white parents. His black father gave him nothing substantial in the love or care domains. The darkness of his dark-triad personality came inadvertently. Due to their own personality aberrations, Barry's white family doted on him in ways that promoted his profound narcissism. He was smart enough to "realize," first mindlessly and then mindfully that he could use his biracial status to get what he wanted. Equally important, Barry cultivated socially winning ways in the psychopathic tradition. He knew how to say what people wanted to hear and how to pretend to be what people wanted him to be. By the time Barry became Barack, he had acquired all the skills necessary to qualify as an apprentice Machiavellian. He already had studied the masters of social and political demagoguery and interned with them whenever possible.

Obama is living proof to the wisdom of the popular saying that luck comes to those prepared to seize and run with it. Opportunities came to Barack Obama like pigeons come to popcorn, and, almost all, were attributable to his life-long, finely honed capacity to micromanage a phony black racial identity. White people have been the most gullible and quickest to embrace Obama's disingenuous persona; blacks resisted initially but, as a result of Obama's successful street cred campaign, African Americans eventually succumbed to him. Even Jesse Jackson, I am sure, is glad that he never cut Barack's nuts off; so glad that he blubbered like a baby at the Barack Obama now-you-can-refer-to-me-as-Hussein presidential inauguration.

Since to maintain his swagging and black-enough status, the not-much-of-a-player but one hell of a sports cheerleader, Barack Obama regularly broadcasts his abiding love of basketball, I now pay him the ultimate compliment: He, hands-down, is the Michael Jordan of race-based political manipulation. But, like Mike, Barack never could have done it without his teammates. As has been documented by several authors, his all-star collection of likeminded political cranks know just how to feed him the ball. Second string politicians share their insights about the way that Barack plays his game. Senators prove particularly helpful in their comments about the pretend black candidate for president. Senator Joe Biden observes, "I mean, you got the first mainstream African American who is articulate and bright and clean and a nice-looking guy. I mean, that's a storybook, man." Senate Democratic leader Harry Reid marvels at the attractiveness of a "light skinned" African American "with no Negro dialect, **unless he wanted to have one**". [emphasis added] Very perceptive, Mr. Reid, to notice how opportunistically protean the Obama persona is.

Political crank cheerleaders notwithstanding, the folks in the stands were the critical ingredient in Barack Obama's double standards, double speaking, and double binds successes. America, especially white America, was begging to be bamboozled. Once black citizens ceased their disturbing habit of questioning Obama's racial credentials, all Americans—colorless ones and people-of-color—could rally around the United States' great "let's pretend he is black" hope. Everybody knew for certain that Obama would be *The Promise, The Bridge,* and the *Son of Promise Child of Hope.* They were sure that, if just given just half a chance, Barry Barack Hussein Soetoro Obama and likeminded citizens could act as though he was anything that they wanted him to be. Most of all, the election of Barack Obama, they felt, undoubtedly would demonstrate to the world that his white supporters were neither racist nor mean-spirited, and that black supporters were both clever and capable. As for other Barack Obama-supporting people-of-color, your guess is as good as mine.

With all his racial study and racial practice, Obama should have learned by now that there never was and never will be a racial paradise, that there always will be people who perceive skin differences as too obvious to ignore and too exploitable to pass up. The same is true for any glaring individual difference, such as weight or height. Race is special in America because race has so much "baggage" associated with it, and so many raceketeers are socially and monetarily invested. Our country unwittingly has created a raceketeering-media-societal army with generals, soldiers, and logisticians, dedicated to underscoring, advertising, and exploiting any and all, real or imaginary, race-oriented differences. Accordingly, individual black and white citizens cannot look to "the system" to create a better racial world; we must take personal, individual responsibility to begin fashioning it in spite of the system. Racial reality, like Barack Obama, is not black OR white; it is black AND white. Racial reality is mottled gray. Whether we like it or not, racial reality always will be fuzzy, requiring us to search through the cultural fog in order to make our way forward together. We must find common ground wherever possible. As we trudge along, at times we will need to follow the common sense popular advice to "agree to disagree," rather than to submit to raceketeers enjoining us to "agree to be disagreeable."

The reality gaps between who Barack is, how he has been marketed, and what people think about him were implied when Bill Clinton referred to Barack Obama's story as a "fairy tale." Phony tale is a more accurate description. Starting in childhood, Obama chose his characters and wrote his script, revising it continually to add drama and continuity. He obsessively and compulsively researched raceketeers and other relevant demagogues. He read classic racist and racialized literature and interned, whenever possible, with racist or racializing mentors. Barack mastered bimp quintessentials—swagga, smokes, drugs, music, and basketball. As he "matured," Obama managed to find ways to supplement the street cred and black-enough qualities that he lacked. Presaging his future acquaintance with Latina friend, Sonia Sotomayor, Barack instinctively, correctly, believed that Michelle Robinson, a wise "nobody's blacker than me" woman who with the richness of her experiences, more often than not, would be able to seduce the African American community into accepting him. But, just to be sure, Obama joined the radical, black liberation theology Trinity United Church of Christ under the inspirational leadership of the most honorable Reverend Jeremiah Wright. By doing so, Barack not only could pretend to be a righteous Christian—a prerequisite to any in-the-hood black political success—but also to get on the good side of radical blacks, even Black Muslims, enamored with Wright's anti-white, anti-American rhetoric.

Despite a lifetime of hard work, not even Barack Obama could have made it alone. Barack's greatest political strength is that he has been a Machiavellian virtuoso, wily enough to have enlisted and to have led an all-star group of demagogue specialists. He has applied his dark-triad personality skills to fashioning a self-serving myth and to manipulating gullible people into swallowing it. As the Obama bandwagon rolled along, a few notables made half-hearted efforts to point out how naked our impresario emperor is. You remember that: Geraldine Ferraro said that Barack received special privileges because he is "black;" that Justice Samuel Alito shook his head and mouthed the words, "not true" as Barack used his first State of the Union to criticize a Supreme Court ruling on election law; that United States Representative Joe Wilson of South Carolina shouted out "You lie!" when Barack claimed his health care legislation would not mandate coverage for undocumented immigrants; and that the entire Fox News organization was frozen out of presidential interviews after what they said had hurt Barack's most sensitive feelings.

Is the Barack Obama who refused interviews with Fox News the same Barack Obama who, during the campaigned, emphasized that he would maintain ongoing dialogue with our enemies? At the Summit of the Americas on Saturday, April 18, 2009 in Port-of-Spain, Trinidad and Tobago, Barack challenged those in the United States who opposed this philosophy of open communication. As Bill Meyer documented,

> "The whole notion was that if we showed courtesy or opened up dialogue with governments that had previously been hostile to us, that that somehow would be a sign of weakness," Obama said, recalling his race for the White House and challenging his critics today.

291

Peter J. McCusker

"The American people didn't buy it," Obama said. "And there's a good reason the American people didn't buy it—because it doesn't make sense."...

"If we are practicing what we preach, and if we occasionally confess to having strayed from our values and our ideals, that strengthens our hand," Obama said. "That allows us to speak with greater moral force and clarity around these issues."

Speak with your enemies; shun your countrymen; ingratiate yourself to Fox News haters. That sounds like a wonderfully self-serving, Machiavellian recipe for political success.

One readily can appreciate Obama's cowardice where Fox is concerned, though, since he has seen his surrogates' doubles disemboweled on Fox. For instance, Greg Pollowitz of Real Clear Politics transcribed Chris Wallace slicing open the Obama terrorism doctrine as articulated by National Security Advisor, Tom Donilon on Fox News Sunday, May 9, 2011.

During the program, Wallace asked about the apparent contradiction of Obama's sanctioning the shooting of unarmed Osama bin Laden, but refusing to permit waterboarding. When Donilon attempted to side-step the issue by providing the scripted non-response that, "waterboarding is not consistent with our values," Wallace countered, "But shooting bin Laden in the head is consistent with our values?" Chris Wallace then tried once more to extract a reasonable explanation from Tom Donilon's closed-mind but only got, "I think that the techniques are something that there's been a policy debate about, and our administration has made our views known on that."

On July 24, 2011, when interviewing Treasury Secretary Tim Geithner, Wallace shifted his assault from military campaigns to budget battles. Once again, the dialogue amounted to an Obama administration bob-and-weave with Geithner providing only the Oval Office party line—evasive, double standard, and double speak answers. The Secretary simply lacked the courage and integrity to speak forthrightly about Barack Obama's fiscal duplicity. Chris Wallace, on the other hand, told it straight, reminding Geithner that Obama:

Page 292

1) failed in December 2010 to endorse any of his own Debt Commission's recommendations that would have cut 4 trillion dollars of debt.

2) presented a January 2011 State of the Nation speech that droned on for over a half-hour without a single mention of the national debt.

3) proposed to erase 400 billion dollars over the next ten years, a proposition that his Democrat-controlled Senate voted down ninety-seven to zero.

4) floated a budget sound-bite so amorphous that, when asked about its feasibility, the Congressional Budget Office answered, "We do not estimate speeches."

Why no presidential fiscal leadership?

You recall Barack's electioneering. Obama pledges to change Washington: No politics as usual. No partisan bickering. Barack Obama, Machiavellian extraordinaire, knows what he is doing. Let the senators and representatives, Democratic and Republican, fight it out. If the Democrats win, Barack boasts how he and his party stand up for principled government. If the Republicans win, Barack claims that he did what was necessary for the good of the nation and demonstrated his capacity to "reach across the aisle." Regardless of the outcome, without dirtying his hands, Obama signs "the best bill we could get," financial Armageddon is averted, and Barack takes credit.

Finances, of course, are just one small feature of the President's leadership AWOL. Barack is absent without leave in the social sphere, as well: quick to say whatever will get him what he wants and slow to fess-up when he does not "stand and deliver."

Like most dark-triad Machiavellians, Barack Obama employs Sartre-like bad faith—denying responsibility for accountable behavior whenever confronted with his duplicity. July 25, 2011 is a case in point. Barack performs his typical vote-getting, pandering prevarications when addressing a Hispanic crowd at a gathering sponsored by the National Council of La Raza, a Hispanic advocacy group. Rather than acknowledging his failure to fulfill his campaign promises about reforming immigration to favor south-of-the-border illegal aliens, Obama blames the Republicans; then he twists the knife saying, ". . . But here's the only thing you should know. The Democrats and your President are with you. Are with you. Don't get confused about that. [Applause] Remember who it is that we need to move in order to actually change the laws."

What prompts Barack to "do the twist?" Because Obama's self-esteem and racial identity are on the line. Earlier in the speech he says, "Now, I know some people want me to bypass Congress and change the laws on my own." And the crowd bursts into applause chanting, "Yes, you can! Yes, you can! Yes, you can! Yes, you can! Yes, you can!" Having had his Achilles heel laid bare, he instinctively and deftly moves to protect the vulnerability by finding someone or something to scapegoat via the doubles.

Barack Obama and his double standards, double speak, double binds machine has chosen the proper time and place to publish their phony tales. Twenty-first century America has been perfect because, after being assailed by decades of pro-black, anti-white propaganda, when it comes to race, most white Americans don't know their ash from a hoe in the ground. Many whites have devolved to an external racial locus of control, a "just tell me what I should think and what I should do" in order to be "on "the right side of history" philosophy. Others, such as those who have witnessed incidents like the View's humiliation of Elisabeth Hasselbeck, have despaired of and withdrawn from any constructive inter-racial discourse. The latter know that racial dialogue is a double bind for average whites whom raceketeers regard as having no credibility, no legitimacy, and nothing substantive to add.

Whites believe that anything they say will be distorted into a grotesque parody of what they had intended. They recognize that the Barack Obamas and Eric Holders of our country have a hidden agenda: ready, willing, and able to talk openly and freely about race for as long as it takes to get whites to capitulate to Afrocentric points of view.

If, like Barack Obama, you believe that pro-black racism is a positive force, consider what Rafael A. Javier and Mario Rendon said when endorsing the views of Michael Moskowitz, their colleague, in *Psychoanalytic Psychology*, Volume 12,1995:

> This is Moskowitz's basic point. He postulates that although the potential for racism is deep and universal, it can only become actualized in an atmosphere where stereotyping becomes a central component of the interaction:

> There is no ethnicity. There is hatred and the need to deny our own badness, and fear of our own hatred. Ethnicity and race are fantasies that we use to deny our own badness and displace it onto others, as well as to protect ourselves against the very real hatred that others may have for us.

In short, Moskowitz asserts that all people are capable of creating positive or negative stereotypes, and that stereotyping requires that one's own "good" self and good racial group are juxtaposed against another "bad" person and bad racial group—another example of the psychological defense mechanism of splitting. In the very act of stereotyping, the stereotyping person or group acts out its own anger, deriving two related benefits: Cathartic release of aggression outward, and preparation for retaliatory aggression directed toward him from the target of his angry outburst. For our purposes, Moskowitz's two essential points are, first, that anything keeping race in interactional focus—positive or negative—either primes us to stereotype or to be stereotyped, and, second, that stereotyping is fueled by anger that says more the stereotyper than about the person or group being stereotyped.

Black Identity as Lynchpin for America's Racial Future

We all have our vulnerabilities, some innate and some acquired, that militate against our health and success. Conversely, we all have strengths that can be called upon to enable us to overcome our weaknesses. The most formidable burden for African Americans has been the emotionally and socially unhealthful conditions that have persisted in black families and black communities for decades, many as unanticipated, negative consequences of the civil rights movement and other efforts to help black people. By reason of their gender and social pressures on them, black males have suffered the most from the deleterious conditions, and black males, in turn, have contributed most to perpetuating the very conditions that caused their people's original problems. Since I believe that the lion's share of intra-racial difficulties in black America and the bulk of inter-racial difficulties with white America derive from black male problems, especially black male identity problems, I emphasize them in what follows, although females, and their problems, will also be mentioned whenever they directly affect black males.

The Color of Black Identity

Black raceketeers, white apologists, and virulent racists, black and white, live and profit by defining and manipulating the definition and discourse of racial identity. They all know that identity is a core component of human personality and social relationships, and that those who control identity control both dialogue and the interpersonal field.

Case in point: Barack Obama launched his political career with the autobiographical book, *Dreams from My Father*, subtitled, A Story of Race and Inheritance. You may recall that earlier I agreed with Sharon Churcher of London's Daily Mail who called Dreams a "preemptive strike" against those who might challenge or threaten Barack's political ambitions. I added that candidate Obama, with nauseating frequency, made self-defining statements such as saying that he is "a black man with a funny name." When it comes to self-definition, Barack Obama has been at his dark-triad personality best.

Because identity is so central to human development, every comprehensive theory of personality must address it in order to be valid and useful. Of extant theories, Erik H. Erikson's is one of the most longstanding, well-respected, well-researched, and most widely taught, so I will briefly summarize and apply this "epigenetic" explanation to our discussion.

Erikson proposed that individual human development proceeds through a series of invariant stages, each stage having an optimal age-epoch during which to flower. The stages present developmental goals that must be addressed, and the ways that the goals are successfully or unsuccessfully handled have major personality and adaptive effects. Although the challenges sprout during a particular stage of development and become especially salient then, they are fundamental and remain critically important all the days of our lives. Moreover, the manner in which earlier stages are handled determines how well or how poorly we handle subsequent stages.

The first stage, the foundation of personality, begins at birth and concerns basic trust. During approximately the first eighteen months of life, the emotionally healthy child develops an implicit awareness that the world and he are "good" and relatively dependable. The world in this case is the physical and interpersonal environments that impinge upon him. He will "trust" if he is fortunate enough to live in a relatively comfortable space—temperature, noise level, et cetera—and to be "mothered' by females and males who attended to his fundamental bodily and emotional needs—safety, stimulation, et cetera.

The Eriksonian stages are framed as polarities—goal versus threat. For instance, the basic trust goal has as its counterpart the threat of basic distrust. However, please note that the theory does not propose that trust is always proper and that mistrust never is. On the contrary, Erikson says that, as we mature, we must develop the capacity to understand and to act trustfully or mistrustfully as warranted by circumstances. It is the default conditions that are critical for our personality. Individuals strongly inclined toward Eriksonian goals tend to be healthier than those inclined toward the threats. Accordingly, persons with a primarily trusting attitude usually have a strong adaptive advantage over those primarily mistrustful.

Because a thorough discussion of all subsequent epigenetic stages would take us too far afield, let me merely list them, and their rough timeline, as follows:

Age	Stage	Threat
Birth to 18 months	Trust	Mistrust
19 months to 3 years	Autonomy	Shame & Doubt
4 years to 6 years	Initiative	Guilt
7 years to 12 years	Industry	Inferiority
13 years to 21 years	Identity	Identity Confusion
22 years to 40 years	Intimacy	Isolation
41 years to 60 years	Generativity	Stagnation
61 years until Death	Ego Integrity	Despair

Even causal consideration of the above list reveals that all stages and all threats pertain to identity. For the most part, we feel best and succeed best when our identities are dominated by trust, autonomy, initiative, industry, intimacy, generativity, and integrity. The most healthful identity development is proactive identity development that enables an individual to evaluate and try out a wide range of behaviors in order to find the ones that work best for him while avoiding, as much as possible, identity threats.

Negative identity is a primary threat, a variation on the theme of identity confusion. A negative identity proceeds from a not-me mentality: a reactive, restrictive, rather than proactive and open, process. Negative identity components are the "You wouldn't catch me dead doing that" features of personality. Those with such an identity proclivity look outward to discover what they don't like in people and strive to be the opposite. I suppose that strategy works well if you live in a prison for the criminally insane, but almost everywhere else it is its own kind of identity slavery, with the proper behavior being defined by whomever controls the definition of the to-be-avoided characteristics. In the African American community, raceketeers do the defining and whatever they deem too white is just what they proselytize against. They might decide, for instance, that lacrosse is a white sport, that no self-respecting inner-city black boy should have any interest in lacrosse. Conversely, the raceketeers determine that some activities—such as basketball—are pro-black, virtually required for any male aspiring to full African American racial identity. If racializing propagandists spent one-tenth as much time talking-up the identity-enhancing value of the binomial theorem as they do basketball, perhaps we would not be able to cite the grim 2007-2008 statistic indicating a black male high school graduation rate of only forty-seven percent.

So, what happens to blacks who do not want their personality development dictated by either the negative identity, not-me criteria, or by the pro-black, that's me criteria, espoused by identity slave masters? What happens to the black adolescent boy who has no basketball skills, or the black adolescent girl who can't dance? Both often are shunned or ridiculed, such that they cease trusting themselves and others.

In the ideal course of events, identity primarily follows one's free-flowing thoughts, feelings, attitudes, and behaviors. That certainly is not to say that external factors play no part, only that the impetus should come from within while opportunities and some of the reinforcements come from without. Imagine black boy number one who tends to be curious about why things are as they are. He always wonders about weather, machines, or distances. Those things excite and attract him, and, so, he informally experiments or tinkers with them. He imagines that one day he might actually make a living performing science-like activities. That boy's identity can evolve from his proactive inclinations. By contrast, think about black boy number two. Like the first one, he is curious. But his curiosity does not power his identity. Rather, his identity has been scripted for him. Boy number two has been taught that black males do not sit around intellectually tinkering; they belong on the basketball court or rapping on the corner. Intellectually-oriented activity is, in the bimp vernacular, for pussies. Black boys, including Barry Obama, too frequently believe that authentic black identity depends on street cred, and street cred depends on following a rigid pro-black script that black identity slave masters, bimps, and the popular culture have written and promulgated throughout our society.

Since basic trust is the foundation of all stages, trust also is the foundation of identity, having the single most important affect on identity development. Trust has been the biggest loser in black-white race relations, with blacks explicitly being taught by identity slave masters that paranoia is not only appropriate but wise when dealing with white people. Accordingly, negative, not-white personality characteristics have become primary foci for black identity, especially for inner-city black male identity. With that in mind, the basic trust-identity nexus is emphasized in the rest of this section. To do so, I draw heavily on a paper by Curtis S. Dunkel and Jon A. Sefcek that they published in the March 2009 *Review of General Psychology* wherein they combined Erikson's insights with those from Life History Theory (LHT), a theory that looks at life history as a metric for explaining an individual's adaptive and maladaptive behaviors.

Identity and History: Reciprocal Influences

Life History Theory takes an evolutionary-oriented approach to identity, looking at ways that individuals apply their material and bioenergetic resources to facilitate personal adaptation, with "material" referring to such variables as time allocation and financial assets, and "bioenergetic" referring to variables such as physical energy and intellectual effort. As an evolutionary theory, LHT devotes much attention to differentiating strategies that promote an individual organism's maintenance and longevity versus those that favor the well-being of an individual's offspring. Dunkel and Sefcek, for instance, speak of two strategies: "Type I strategy represents a path of fast development and quantity in mates and offspring and Type II represents slower maturation with a greater emphasis on the quality of mates and offspring." Basically, Type I is the "slam, bam, thank you ma'am" approach to fatherhood and Type II is the one-woman, committed, devoted husband and father approach. Not surprisingly, father absence greatly increases the likelihood of low investment and low resources being allocated to children, that is, to Type I fatherhood. Citing previous research, Dunkel and Sefeck point out that

Quinlan (2003) analyzed retrospective data from over 10,000 women and found that early parental divorce was associated with early menarche, age of first sexual intercourse, first pregnancy, and shorter duration of first marriage. Likewise he found that unpredictability of parental care was associated with early menarche and age of first sexual intercourse, greater number of sexual partners, and shorter duration of first marriage. The relationship between these indicators of exposure to early stressful environments and indicators of a Type I strategy held regardless of whether the women lived with their mother or father. Likewise Chisholm, Quinlivan, Petersen, and Coall (2005) found that in a sample of pregnant women that uncertain early environments were associated with early menarche and age at the birth of their first child.

Applying Life History Theory to Eriksonian Theory, the authors postulated that a Type I fathering strategy would incite identity confusion in offspring. In light of the epidemic of father absence and indigent motherhood in the black community, one must be especially alarmed that Dunkel and Sefeck concluded:

Research has shown that role confusion is associated with low levels of parental and adolescent connectedness (Campbell, Adams, & Dobson, 1984), parental and adolescent communication (Grotevant & Cooper, 1985; Papini, Micka, & Barnett, 1989; Reis & Youniss, 2004), family cohesion (Papini et al., 1989; Mullis, Brailsford, & Mullis, 2003), parental identification (Cramer, 2001; Dignan, 1965; Knafo & Schwartz, 2004), trust and degree of parental care (Hoegh & Bourgeois, 2002), parental support (Sartor & Youniss, 2002), and authoritative parenting (Adams, Ryan, & Keating, 2000; Berzonsky, 2004; Waterman, 1993). Summarizing the research on the type of parenting related to identity confusion Waterman stated that parents whose children have role confusion are, "seen as indifferent, inactive, detached, not understanding and rejecting" (Waterman, 1993, p.62).

Type I fathers and role confused sons are at the root of the disintegration of the 21st century black family, a family that had been strong and effective during the worst days of 20th century racism. Type I fathers and role confused sons are the reasons that bimps control the streets of inner-city African American communities, that many average black people live in neighborhoods rife with fear, and that academic failure endangers the future of millions of black children who have the intelligence but not the environment in which to learn.

The sons of Type I fathers feel abandoned. They have only half the parenting resources and accompanying financial resources available to children with an in-home mother and father. Type I sons have no realistic, day-to-day model of authentic masculinity with which to identity. These boys tend to resist mothering for fear of being emasculated. They are pulled instead by pervasive hyper-masculine bimp culture and recruitment that seduce or coerce them into life on the street. With bimps manipulating and intimidating their sons and fathers absent from the home, despite their best intentions, many single-parent black mothers simply cannot provide their boys an environment sufficient to counter the destructive forces pressing on them from all sides. Because inner-city father absence is nearly 70 percent, such neighborhoods perpetuate the self-defeating Type I, bimp fathering pattern from generation to generation. Psychologists know this and are trying to sound the alarm. Below is a report of one such effort.

Black Mothers Love Their Sons and Raise Their Daughters

Mandara, Varner, and Richman, in the *Journal of Family Psychology, Volume 21,* 2010, test the validity of what they describe as "an old saying" in the African American community that "black mothers love their sons and raise their daughters." According to them, "This saying implies that many African American mothers give girls more responsibilities, monitor their whereabouts more, have higher educational expectations, and are more demanding of them than they are of boys." Mandara and his colleagues' review of relevant literature cite many well accepted findings that support the positions that they take. The authors note that black females' academic and social successes significantly exceed those of their black male counterparts,' and that ". . . men of all ethnic groups engage in more externalizing behaviors than do female adolescents, but the gender gaps in behaviors such as major and minor delinquency, violence, and involvement in the justice system tend to be larger for African Americans." They mention father absence as a major reason for black male problems which means that mothers experience increased burdens and responsibilities for how their sons are raised and how well they succeed; thus, mothering is particularly critical in black male identity formation and behavior outcomes.

In summarizing the results of their own research, Mandara, Varner, and Richman state that they found that both gender and birth order are critical for black male identity development. Later-born boys are said to argue more with their mothers, to have fewer household responsibilities, and to be given less guidance about where they spend their time outside the home. Despite what appears to be greater "freedom," the later-born boys perceive having less freedom than their siblings. Mandara and the other researchers conclude that later-born black boys generally live in less stimulating homes—having fewer books, less visits to museums, less exposure to training with musical instruments, and less extracurricular lessons in general.

Birth order, however, does not appear to meaningfully affect black boys' "externalizing behaviors," meaning mothers' reports of their sons' levels of headstrongness, antisocial behavior, and hyperactivity. Firstborn black boys are as high as their later-born brothers in externalizing, and black girls are significantly less externalizing than either group of boys.

Perpetuating or Reversing the Bimp Lifestyle

Type I, mostly bimp, fathers and "loving" but "non-raising" mothers. Boys roaming streets ruled by Type I bimps. Raceketeers encouraging black paranoia and rage, and rushing to pardon, even to condone, anti-social, destructive acting out. Government officials believing that black boys will be just fine if just a few more basketball courts are built in their neighborhoods. Television news media featuring 21st century real-life inner-city shoot-em-ups in lieu of campy cowboy shows of yesteryear. Michael Moore-like documentaries excusing perpetrators of black crime by blaming white culture. *Boyz n the Hood* and *Do the Right Thing* cinema glorifying crime and hyper-aggressive "masculinity" in the movies. Black superstars participating in five minute photo-op sessions to show that they "don't forget where they came from." These are the ingredients that promote externalizing behaviors. These are the ingredients that perpetuate the Type I, bimp cycle, explaining the Schott Foundation *50 State Report on Public Education and Black Males 2010* indicating that the overall 2007/08 graduation rate for African American male students nationwide was an anemic forty-seven percent, and the Charles Lemos "A Nation Incarcerated" paper pointing out that more black 17-year-olds are in prison than in college, one-fifth of black males over 18 are in prison, and about one-ninth of all black males will spend at least one year in jail.

My experiences with adjudicated black youth are most relevant here. In the process of evaluating hundreds of these teens and young-adults, I never failed to ask about their mothers and fathers and about what they planned for their own futures. While they almost always described their mothers with love and affection, the youth typically spoke venomously about their fathers, using epithets such as "ass hole' or "bastard" and citing how their fathers had abandoned them. Lacking in-vivo role models, the same teens and young-adults characteristically aspired to media-hyped, unrealistic careers with street cred, such as rap star or pro athlete.

Ton'Nea Williams, a black woman, also worked with adjudicated black youth. Her story as told by Laura Beil, a free lance writer, provided a first-hand account of the anguish that well-intentioned black women experience when trying be a surrogate mother and father to an in-the-hood, hard-core bimp.

According to Ms. Beil's radio documentary, immediately after graduating college, Ms. Williams accepted a position at a juvenile detention center in the Little Rock area where 12 year old Kenneth Williams was her first "client." (Although Ton'Nea and Kenneth, coincidentally, had the same last name, they were not related in any way.) From the outset, Ton'Nea fell for the polite, needy little boy from a dysfunctional home. Thus began an approximately seven year "mentorship" that long outlived Ms. Williams employment at the facility. She did virtually everything she could to "save" Kenneth from himself, including counseling him, having him eat at her home, and even paying him to babysit her children.

For a short period, Kenneth seemed to be doing well. In fact, there was a time when Ton'Nea thought of him as a "poster child" for her methods. But on December 18, 1998, Ms. Williams' world began to change: that was the day of Kenneth's arrest on one count of capital murder, one count of attempted capital murder, two counts of kidnapping, two counts of aggravated robbery, two counts of theft of property, and one count of arson. Unwilling to accept that her Kenneth had robbed and shot two University of Arkansas students, killing one, Ton'Nea testified as a character witness. Despite her support, however, the jury found Kenneth Williams guilty and sentenced him to life in prison without parole.

Still, Ms. Williams could not believe that Kenneth was guilty. She resigned from her detention center job, started youth basketball camps, and crossed the state, giving speeches about ways to reform youth. Then, Ton'Nea experienced another devastating shock. Kenneth had escaped from prison and, in the process of fleeing, he had shot a man seven times and had killed another in a head-on collision. This time the court not only found Kenneth guilty, but also sentenced him to death.

Tortured by the thought that she had failed to do all necessary to save the 12 year-old boy, Kenneth—her first client—Ton'Nea Williams decided to visit him in prison to determine where she went wrong, and Laura Beil went with her to record the event.

During the two hour session, Kenneth, wearing a large cross around his neck, repeatedly explained that there was nothing that Ms. Williams or anyone could have done to stop him from doing what he wanted to do. He first spoke about the excitement that streamed through him when he first had considered the possibility of killing someone. Then Kenneth claimed that while in prison he had held a photo of the living woman that he had murdered alongside of her autopsy photo. During that segment of the session, he feigned the body language of a repentant man, including covering his eyes with his hands and hunching his shoulders. But both Ms. Williams and Ms. Beil saw through the deception, noting that when he looked up from his charade there was not a single tear in his eyes.

The absence of remorse indicated an especially ruthless psychopath. Kenneth Williams had shot Dominique Herd, a female University of

Arkansas, in the head, execution style. Before he did, Williams interrogated the woman and her male friend asking their states of origin. When the female student said that she lived in Dallas, Kenneth replied, "'I don't like the niggers from Dallas anyway,' and started shooting the couple, emptying the gun." (Lexisone, 2011) Williams also had emptied his gun into the back of his fleeing carjacking victim. Moreover, after being apprehended after the head-on collision that killed an innocent motorist, the state troopers accompanied Kenneth Williams to view the dead victim, thinking that he might be remorseful. Instead, Williams spit on the lifeless body.

At the very start of his reunion with Ms. Williams, Kenneth commented that other prison inmates had been interviewed by a television news team. That thought of being spotlighted apparently lingered in his mind such that in the final minutes of the session, Kenneth Williams advised Ton'Nea and Laura to bring a video camera to document any subsequent visit with him.

According to Laura Beil, the meeting with Kenneth did not resolve Ton'Nea Williams' torment. In fact, after all that she had been through, Ton'Nea never lifted the mantel of responsibility and guilt from her shoulders. For instance, Ms. Williams wondered whether something "like the Little League" could have turned the boy's life around, although Ms. Beil thought that "all the Little League in the world was not going to stop Kenneth." So, here once more, we find a well-intentioned black person inadvertently inclined to reinforce a hard-core bimp in his propensity to deny personal culpability, to project blame, and to maintain an external locus of control for the crimes that he committed.

Ton'Nea Williams, one-shot million man marches, and sanctimonious high definition television specials will not "rescue" African American boys. Multi-millions of black fathers consistently fathering and otherwise supporting their children and their children's mothers is the best prescription for black boys and black girls (as it is for white boys and white girls). Publicizing and celebrating black men and black women who properly parent their children and who want no part of the bimp lifestyle also would be "nice."

I must add, parenthetically, that I was pleasantly surprised and heartened to see a May 2011 Oscar Meyers commercial featuring a black man. The man, apparently returning from work, starts to open the door to his home to find his children oblivious to each other due to preoccupation with each of their own personal electronic devices. He then surreptitiously clicks-off the circuit breaker, disconnecting the electricity and plunging the home into darkness. In the final frame, the entire family is in the back yard, barbecuing, relating, and enjoying each other. This is the Type II social "propaganda" that Type I black males need to be bombarded with. This is the Type II propaganda that also could benefit Type I white males and males of all shades.

The "New" Black Family

Black fathers and mothers living and parenting together was the norm in the not-too-distant past, but not now. The U.S. Census Bureau News noted the following relevant facts:

> African Americans were less likely than non-Hispanic whites to be currently married (35 percent compared with 57 percent).
>
> Nearly one-half (48 percent) of all African American families were married-couple families; for non-Hispanic white families, the corresponding figure was 82 percent.
>
> African Americans have larger families than non-Hispanic whites. For example, 20 percent of African American married-couple families consisted of five or more members, compared with 12 percent of their non-Hispanic white counterparts.

More children and less marriage, however, are only part of the problem. The distribution of marriage, education, and income also are troubling. In her *Psychology Today* 2010, article, "Love in Limbo, The paradoxes of dating and mating," Linda Young fills in the details. She explains that 70% of black women are unmarried at any point in time, as opposed to 24% of white women. Young reports shocking gender-specific achievement disparities between black men and women: The most educated black females—those with master's and doctoral degrees—are said to outnumber the most educated black men at a ratio of 209 to 100. Income, understandable, correlates with education. "Love in Limbo" asserts that while twice as many white men than white women earn $40,000 to $74,999, at that income bracket, black women exceed black men 125/100. At the $100,000 and over level, white men outpace white women 450/100, whereas black women best black men 157/100. Young does point out one place wherein black men make more money than black women. Is this one, small opportunity to provide an extraordinarily "rich" environment for African American women and their offspring? Sadly, it is not. On the contrary, the author informs us that, "The gender disparity switches at the highest income levels [black male salary greater than black female salary] but at those incomes there is a surge in black men (but not women) marrying interracially."

Another black male-female discrepancy is noteworthy here: Barack Obama's approach to assigning responsibility for African American problems. In *The Audacity of Hope* when discussing his ideas for reversing inner-city turmoil, he writes, "We could begin by acknowledging that perhaps the single biggest thing we could do to reduce such poverty is to encourage teenage girls to finish high school and avoid having children out of wedlock." Now, while the advice in and of itself is irreproachable, it blames women and fails to address men. Given all that we have said about black male incarceration, violence, irresponsible fathering, and educational and occupational failure, I find it astounding that Barack Obama could isolate females as the "biggest single" target for overcoming black poverty. Someone also should remind Barack that virtually every pregnant out-of-wedlock teenage black girl has a corresponding out-of-wedlock teenage, or older, black boy hiding somewhere in the hood.

High achieving black women are the women most likely to raise, and not just love, their sons (and daughters), the women most likely to take the lead in "lifting up" the entire African American subculture. But high achieving black women, whose numbers greatly exceed their black male counterparts, present challenges for gender equanimity. "Nightline" addresses the issue on April 9, 2010 with host, Vicki Mabrey, and a panel of 2 black women, Sherri Shepherd, comedienne, actress, and television personality, and Jacque Reid, television and radio personality, plus 3 black men, Jimi Izrael, writer, journalist, and radio personality, Steve Harvey, author comedian, and Hill Harper, film, television and stage actor and author.

Ms. Mabrey began by citing statistics similar to those I mentioned above, specifically saying that the number of college-educated black women surpasses black men by 1.8 million and that twice as many black women than black men attend college. Perhaps that introductory frame primed the rancorous discussion that followed. Izrael took up the challenge immediately, complaining that many black women expect a "perfect" black man, a condition that he called, "the Denzel principle." He patronizingly suggested that black women are not perfect and recommended that each black woman should look for someone who is "the person that she is." Shepherd responded that she only wants a man who is willing to fix her broken "rotisserie," be a father to her 5-year-old son, respect and like women, and be willing to help her with tasks that she considers important, such as, unfurling her cornrows.

Addressing herself to Izrael, moderator Mabrey interjected, "You wrote in the Denzel Principle that too many women try to turn their man into a cross between their girlfriend and a lap dog." The discourse then devolved into a "be real" discussion, that, for a short time, broke the tension sufficiently for Shepard to play the white-scapegoating race card, underscoring her pandering allegiance to black men, commenting, "You will still have a woman in your corner, saying 'baby I know they [white people] put you down but I am here, cornrows or wig'." Almost immediately, Hill Harper tried to redirect everyone to the critical issue, advising that they really needed to talk about the black family and its deterioration. But that was Steve Harvey's cue to take the stage. Harvey jumped in with the absurd claim that, "It is not in a man's DNA" to help with cornrows. Here we see, once again, the paranoid-like sensitivity of some black men to anything that remotely threatens the swagga-suffused hyper-masculine African American mythology. Harvey provided one more reason to believe that bimp defenses ultimately win out; self-serving Type I male form and flash prevails over Type II male substance and family values. The recurrent real-man theme and its associated bimp behaviors are primary reasons for black poverty, black crime, and for the impasse in black-white interracial dialogue and relationships.

CHAPTER 18

Con Vick

Inhumane Individuals

Earlier I mentioned that Black Entertainment Television rewarded two members of the Jena 6 for their hyper-masculine aggression and predation. Consider now the saga of National Football League quarterback, Michael Vick who made out quite a bit better than Jena 2/6. Vick and his ultra-fantastic machismo machine so embodies Type I masculinity that he could write the book on it.

As abstracted from Biography.com, Michael Vick's personal history goes like this:

Vick's teenage parents were unmarried at the time of his birth, raising him in a gang and drug infested area of Newport News, Virginia. Yet, despite his difficult childhood circumstances, through dedication and talent Michael Vick developed into a first-rate football player during his two years at Virginia Tech. He, in fact, was so good that the Atlanta Falcons selected him as their first round choice in the 2001 National Football League draft, awarded a sixty-two million dollar, six-year contract and sweetened the pot with an additional fifteen million dollar bonus. Well on his way to becoming wildly famous and fabulously wealthy, Vick had been granted an opportunity of a lifetime. Would he rise to the occasion?

After mostly watching and waiting during his first year, Michael Vick played often and outstandingly well in seasons two and three. By season four, 2004, however, Vick's star already had begun to lose a little luster. Heretofore positive expectations faded, replaced by concerns that the quarterback was becoming increasingly arrogant, associating with undesirables, and making poor decisions. During the same year, police captured two men who were using Michael Vick's truck to run marijuana. Yet, the quarterback's financial future continued to streak upward and onward. Len Pasquarelli of ESPN.com wrote on Christmas 2004, that Michael Vick had just signed the biggest total pay package in pro football history, a contract extension that, if completed as intended, would have paid Vick approximately $120,000,000.

As his salary increased, so did Vick's crises. In 2005, he avoided a court date only by settling with a woman who claimed that he had infected her with a "sexual disease." In 2007, Michael Vick first denied then admitted to housing, funding, and running a dogfighting ring on his Smithville, Virginia property. By year's end, the former superstar received a sentence of twenty-three months in prison and restitution charges just short of one million dollars. As bad as it was, however, the situation got even worse. In two separate 2009 cases, the Royal Bank of Canada and Wachovia won a combined total of 3.6 million dollar judgments against Michael Vick for loan defaults, and the next year the United States Department of Labor claimed that he unlawfully had used over one million dollars from the pension plan of one of his businesses.

Of all of his troubles, the dogfighting conviction most threatened Michael Vick's short—and long-term future. As details of the abuse emerged, many Americans were incensed by the depth and breadth of its cruelty. An investigative report, published on August 28, 2008 by the United States Department of Agriculture, Office of Inspector General, described the May 23 and June 5, 2007 testimony of "confidential witness, number one" who said that during public dog fights when interested persons paid admission to watch and/or wager, Vick stayed upstairs, fearing someone would recognize him. No wonder Vick was concerned, given the depravity of the enterprise that the witness detailed:

> Vick, Peace, and Phillips thought it was funny to watch the pit
> bull dogs belonging to Bad Newz Kennels injure or kill the other
> dogs . . . In mid-April of 2007, Vicks, Peace, Phillips and Allen
> were rolling [testing fighting prowess] dogs at the property. Vick
> Peace and Phillips killed approximately seven dogs by hanging

and drowning at this time. Allen did not take part in the killing of the dogs. Vick Peace and Phillips hung approximately three dogs by placing a nylon cord over a 2X4 that was nailed to two trees next to the big shed. They also drowned approximately three dogs by putting the dogs' heads in a five gallon bucket of water. XX [name redacted on the transcript] also observed as Vick and Phillips killed a red pit bull dog, by slamming it to the ground several times before the dog died, breaking its neck or back.

In an August 14, 2007 interview, after he had pleaded guilty, Phillips spoke of having met Vick in 7th grade, becoming best friends, and playing middle—and high-school basketball and football together. He said that through an acquaintance named "Taylor," he and Vick became "involved" in dogfighting in 2001. On August 14 and October 9, 2007, Peace validated much of confidential witness, number one's testimony, saying that

> In 2002, he, Vick, Phillips, and Taylor "rolled" (tested) dogs at XX [information redacted in the transcript] to determine if they were good fighters. They would kill the poor fighters by shooting, electrocuting, or drowning them. Almost all the dogs they killed were buried on the XX [information redacted on the transcript] property. On occasion, he would want to give away a dog that would not fight. However, Vick stated "They got to go," meaning that they needed to be killed. Many times Vick, Phillips, and Taylor killed dogs when he was not present. Taylor would tell him about the dogs that did not test well, and would say "They didn't make it," meaning they were killed.

We see, then, that Michael Vick's dogfighting cruelty was a not a momentary, impulsive aberration; in fact, Vick treated animal torture so cavalierly that he produced shirts and head-bands bearing his Bad Newz Kennels logo to advertise his "business." As Vick emerged from prison on May 20, 2009, young men were watching, from sea to shining sea. Just as Pete Rose had disgraced baseball and was forever banned from his sport, Vick never would set foot on a gridiron again. Well, at least not for several weeks.

No. Michael Vick did not forfeit his "right" to play football, to hell with all that gibberish about role models. Within three months after his feet hit the pavement outside Leavenworth Penitentiary, on August 13, 2009, Vick signed a two-year Philadelphia Eagles contract with a potential total payout of 9.8 million dollars. Michael the con, or should I say ex-con, had joined forces with his National Football League franchise to con the American public.

Humane Society?

How did Michael Vick manage to finagle his way back into football? He did it through the most skillfully orchestrated and executed media and public relations scam since the election of Barack Obama. As with Obama, the stakes were high. Vick's success would enable lots of "big" people—inside and outside sports—to augment their power positions, to make lots of big bucks, and to prove themselves eminently virtuous while doing so. They all anticipated a double success—Vick and his handlers/benefactors—enacted via tried and true double standards, double speak, and double bind strategies. You can be sure that every word was parsed, every sentence rehearsed, and every action pre-planned.

As with Obama, and as typical in conspiracies of virtually all types, we know little of the specific back room deals brokered on behalf of Michael Vick. We do glean a hint of the intrigue, however, from the statements and writings of Wayne Pacelle, CEO of the Humane Society. On April 20, 2011, during a public radio feature regarding animal abuse, Marty Moss Coane spoke with Pacelle about the Vick case.

> Coane: . . . . the decision by the Humane Society to reach out to him [Vick]. Was that your idea?
>
> Pacelle: It was . . . actually he reached out to us, toward the end of his his ah prison term at Leavenworth Penitentiary. He, basically, through some of his intermediaries, asked me. My first response was absolutely not, no way, never. Ahm, I considered him radioactive. What he did was despicable . . . The second thing is, knowing as much as we do about dog fighting, we saw that the biggest growth area for dogfighting was in urban centers

like Philadelphia, like Chicago, Los Angeles where young men and boys, often African American, not exclusively by any means, are getting pit bulls for the wrong reason and are squaring them up in fights in abandoned building and back allies, either on the street . . .

Coane: The reaction initially was that Michael Vick was using the Human Society to try to get back into football.

Pacelle: There's no question that he needed to redeem himself. And, and we were a highly credible third party validator for him. But we were also looking to take advantage of his own story, his own experience, to try to leverage this case to do more good for animals . . . If Michael, you know, was playing me and working me, that's not going to embarrass me, that's going to embarrass him . . . I want to use creative strategies to attack the problem and I know we can't just do things the way we used to do them. We've got to reach out to this diverse community of people who are involved in so many forms and you know that this cause has been too Anglo. It hasn't had a conversation with

Coane: Too Anglo, meaning too white?

Pacelle: Too Caucasian, right. Too white. We need to have a conversation with these young kids who are not having a conversation about their responsibility to animals . . . . It's easy for this to get, you know, off-track which is what happened with Vick. He told me that he started dogfighting in Newport News when he was 7 or 8 years old. And all the kids were involved. They were chasing cats with pit bulls and killing cats; then they were fighting the dogs.

This interview begins with Coane naturally presuming that the Humane Society, in the form of their CEO, approached Michael Vick, but, of course, that supposition proved false. Rather, Vick's "intermediaries" did the approaching. This Vick-oriented "when you have a basket of lemons make lemonade" strategy made perfect sense. There was no getting around Michael's record of cruelty, so let's just flip him from sinner to saint. After a minimum of seven years as a dog executioner, overnight he would become an evangelizing disciple of all that is animal humane and animal noble, an itinerant preacher, sauntering from one den of iniquity to another, preaching the gospel of St. Pacelle and saving wayward souls. Vick's motivation? Repentance. Salvation. He entertained nary a thought of the fortune or fame that he could reap in the NFL. No way that he could have imagined making tens or hundreds of millions by playing a little football.

Should we be surprised that race entered into the equation? Though quick to minimize it, Wayne Pacelle does refer to dogfighting as a "growth industry," predominantly in inner-city neighborhoods steeped in the bimp tradition. He admits that his organization had been preaching too long to the "Anglican" choir. Not until Coane calls him on it, does Pacelle straightforwardly acknowledge that his organization traditionally avoided targeting the heart with no soul of the problem. Eventually, he reveals that Michael Vick claimed that "all the kids were involved" in Newport News, presumably meaning all the kids with whom Vick associated, and Vick, himself, disclosed that he began his animal cruelty at "7 or 8" years of age. If this is true, it is a crystal clear indictment of a bimp culture of crime. In any case, the "everybody did it" claim is classic Michael Vick in that he implicitly projects blame for his personal criminality onto the neighborhood in order to get himself off the hook. The projection is fully consistent with material in *The Bond*, Wayne Pacelle's book, wherein he recounts Vick's initial reaction to being questioned about his animal abuse:

> Just two days after the raid, Vick denied any knowledge of dogfighting on the property, claiming that he rarely visited this home and that the people he allowed to stay there had taken advantage of his generosity. "It's unfortunate I have to take the heat," he told reporters in New York City on April 27 [2007], a day before the NFL draft. "Lesson learned for me." It would be several months before Vick would recant that lie and the many others he told following the raid.

Reinforcing Deviance and Forward Passing It

What of the Michael Vick's Humane Society collaboration? How did that go? Did it help?

By cooperating with Vick, The Humane Society had nothing to lose and everything to gain: animal rights publicity, entre into the African American community, sympathy, and funding: perhaps even the marketing core of a book on human-animal bonding. Wayne Pacelle claimed that he and his Society decided to use Vick to do "good," and that is fine. But were there other ways to "use" him? For instance, couldn't the Society have capitalized on the Vick scandal by forming an African American, inner-city, permanent taskforce comprised of veterinarians or other animal-oriented persons living in the targeted communities? By doing so, the Humane Society would have put into place a self-perpetuating, self-reinforcing system that would endure over time and place. Moreover, it would have reinforced the essential notion that everyday black citizens have the power to "rescue" their children and to take back their own neighborhoods. Instead, they got Vick whose sincerity Pacelle, himself, questioned repeatedly in *The Bond*, as when Michael Vick spoke about his profound fondness for animals: "I had pet birds. I love watching the Discovery Channel and nature shows."

Michel Vick's father, Michael Boddie, presented a portrait of young Michael's animal interests at odds with his son's pronouncements. USAToday.com on August 23, 2007 cited an Atlanta Journal-Constitution interview with Boddie in which he said that his son was dogfighting in the family's backyard, at least since 2001. Moreover, the father advised, "I wish people would stop sugarcoating it," that his son "likes" dogfighting, and has the finances to make it happen. In short, "This is Mike's thing. And he knows it."

If the Humane Society had a vested interest in cooperating with Michael Vick, it paled in comparison to the NFL's stake. The National Football League needed a good excuse to keep one of the most hyped, most highly paid, most coveted quarterback in history on the field, and to keep millions of football fans in the stands or in front of their televisions. The Vick handlers-inspired, Humane Society plan could not have been better, providing a perfect excuse to claim that Vick had been rehabilitated. Once the Eagles saw an opening, they jumped at the chance to grab Michael Vick and to dump their aging, first-string quarterback, Donovan McNabb.

Vick's Eagles, of course, are located in Philadelphia, a town with a large inner-city black population. MJD, a sports.yahoo.com author, cites the Associated Press that reported how dogfighting surged after Vick came to town, rocketing from 245 cases in 2008 to 903 cases in 2009. Similarly, Vernon Clark, Peter Mucha, and Robert Moran of the *Philadelphia Inquirer* write on April 11, 2011 about the arrest of 17 people snagged in a police raid on a dog fighting ring. The article explains that police confiscated guns and large quantities of drugs, including heroin, cocaine, and marijuana. A preliminary investigation already had revealed that four suspects either had served time or were being indicted on drug cases and one had an earlier "cruelty to animals" conviction. Here, as often, we found a confluence of animal cruelty, gun violence, and drug abuse.

As if his negative modeling of animal abuse was not enough, Michael Vick even managed to communicate a crime does, in fact, pay message to young men within the City Brotherly Love. Just as two members of the Jena 6 received special recognition from Black Entertainment Television after their hyper-masculine aggression and predation, Vick got his day in the sun, as well, proving once more that no bimp abomination need go unrewarded. On December 23, 2009, the Philadelphia Eagles voted ex-con Vick the Ed Block Courage Award. No, Vick had not rushed into a burning building to rescue a recumbent Rottweiler in respiratory distress. It was because . . . ah . . . because. What was that courageous behavior? Well, what did Mikey say was the reason? "I've overcome a lot, more than probably one single individual can handle or bear," said he. Oh yes, that's right! Another sterling, self-aggrandizing bimp hero destined to inspire America's youth—black and white—with his intrepid magnificence.

Almost exactly one year after Vick had won the Block award, Barack Hussein Obama also jumped on the I-love-Mike bandwagon, calling Philadelphia Eagles owner Jeffrey Lurie. Why? To say he appreciated that Laurie gave Vick "a second chance." One readily can understand Obama's attention to the quarterback and to football: a "real black man" and a real bimp sport. At the time, things must have been slow for Barack, given the then-recent collapse of the American economy, the housing crisis, the employment crisis, the health care crisis, the wars in Iraq and Afghanistan, and the rabid Congressional rancor.

The Obama endorsement of Michael Vick could have been predicted. It is transparently obvious that Barack, the racial-identity conflicted, opportunistic, dark-triad personality, satisfies several of his most fundamental personality needs by advertising his affections for persons such as Michael Vick: he beats back his own not-black-enough racial demons, preempts Uncle Tom criticisms, mollifies black and white raceketeers, and banks more black and ultra-liberal votes for future political campaigns.

So, soon after Vick comes out of jail, he manages a courage award from his team, a self-congratulatory soliloquy, and a presidential endorsement: double speak con jobs of the highest order. One cannot help wonder whether all of this, especially the presidential "citation," would have been conferred if Michael Vick were white.

The Superstar, The President, Dark-Triads, Bimps, and The Doubles

Barack Obama's favorable endorsement of Michael Vick was all but assured, given that Vick is an African American football star who captured nationwide attention. Moreover, despite the fact that Vick, but not Obama, is authentically and completely black and has impeccable street cred, Barack likely fancied some similarities between himself and Vick. For instance, both had Type I fathers. We already have spoken about the absconding Barack senior. Michael Vick's dad, Michael Boddie, too, allegedly was "not there" for his son, and, according to episode 5 of a Black Entertainment Television documentary about Vick, Boddie was "a hard drug user who was in and out of his family's life." There is no denying that the absences of Barack's and Michael's Type I fathers helped to establish the family conditions and childhood experiences that made them who they are today.

Yet, literally millions of American children have Type I fathers; the more fundamental essence of Obama's and Vick's similarities are similarities in the ways that they, themselves, participated in creating their own disingenuous personalities and in the ways they have professionally "marketed" them.

As elaborated repeatedly, Barack Obama has a dark-triad personality involving narcissism, Machiavellianism, and psychopathy. Michael Vick also is dark-triad. Narcissism is apparent in his repeated "I'm so wonderful" pronouncements. Unlike Obama, Vick's psychopathy is of the hard-core, criminal, animal-abusing type. The Machiavellianism of Vick, aided and abetted by his handlers, has become particularly apparent since his incarceration. Through Machiavellian manipulation, Vick has managed to play the public like a rap CD, attempting to convince everyone that he has suffered the passion of Christ, that he, in fact, is the victim in the whole sorry saga, and is a worthy successor to St. Francis of Assisi.

Michael Vick illustrates, too, similarities and differences between a dark-triad personality and a bimp orientation. While he has a dark-triad personality structure, that was neither a necessary nor sufficient condition for making Michael, Michael. Barack Obama, for instance, is a poster child for the dark-triad, but a pitiful excuse for a real bimp. Of course, no one in his right mind would aspire to the presidency and behave in a blatantly bimp manner. Imagine holding one's crotch and spewing four letter expletives while giving a State of the Union speech before Congress. That probably would not "go down" so well. The natural Machiavellianism of most professional dark-triad personalities ensures that they keep their bimp proclivities out of sight. For instance, whenever a dark-triad United States president campaigns against tobacco companies and for the prevention of smoking among teenagers, he is careful that he, himself, only smokes behind closed, locked doors.

Many, but in no way most, athletes, can get away, at least, with soft-core bimp behavior. And Vick proves that hard-core is by no means totally excluded. Michael Vick came out of the hood with authentic bimp credentials that he earned throughout his youth. The more refined, overtly genteel features of his extant dark-triad personality, by contrast, are of recent vintage and, no doubt, attributable to "coaching."

Like Barack Obama, Vick and his handlers have played the doubles as good as it gets. Given the comments of Wayne Pacelle from the Humane Society,

Michael Vick's African American heritage and in-the-hood cred made the CEO convert from viewing Vick as "despicable" to desirable—double standards of the first order. Since Vick's conviction, double speak has run with more abandon than Vick ever demonstrated on the gridiron. In a few short months, the words courage, hero, and inspirational speaker have superseded coward, villain, and disgraced role model in speaking about Michael. And, surely, people who say the things that I have said in this section will be double-binded into submission, maligned as virulent racists, cold, heartless, and unwilling to give a young black man from an impoverished background a second chance.

CHAPTER 19

Forgive?

Forget?

With the exception of "Reverend" Jeremiah Wright and like-minded Afrocentrics, religious leaders preach the moral value of reconciliation. (Desmond Tutu did.) Physicians and psychologists advise that forgiveness literally contributes to health, homeostasis, and longevity. Even world leaders give the nod to alliances with former foes.

Sometimes the bitterest enemies forgive and become staunch allies.

Five decades ago, America was awash with pain, mourning about 292,000 servicemen and servicewomen killed and about 672,000 wounded by the Japanese and Germans. Millions of our citizens had lost fathers, mothers, brothers, sisters, uncles, aunts, and cousins. The hurt was fresh and personal; the perpetrators were obvious. Americans had reasons to be preoccupied with, virtually consumed with, anti-Japanese and anti-German rancor. Today, Japanese and Germans trust and support us, and we them—economically, politically, and, even, militarily.

Consider the following incomplete, alphabetical list of countries against whom America literally has waged war: Afghanistan, Austro-Hungarian Empire, Barbary States of North Africa, Bulgaria, China, England, France, Germany, Grenada, Iraq, Italy, Libya, Mexico, North Korea, Ottoman Empire, Panama, Philippines, Southern USA, and Spain. Should we have maintained those belligerencies in perpetuity? Should we blame those countries for any and all American problems that currently exist, or should we forget the past and promote and maintain cooperation?

The battlegrounds overseas also have a domestic equivalent—gender wars.

In our country, women always have gotten the short end of the political and financial stick, and the long end of the neglect and abuse stick. Women could not vote until 1920, fifty years after African American males did. The National Organization for Women website cites a 2005 statistic suggesting that every day an average of three women are been killed by "an intimate partner."

With all that female suffering, women have just as much right as blacks to complain. Wives could remind their husbands and male acquaintances incessantly about the "legacy of sexism." Psychiatrist Theodore Rubin and other mental health specialists suggest, in fact, that some emotionally compromised people do accumulate a slush fund of angry memories that they manipulate for personal advantage. But most women refrain from routinely using the legacy of sexism as a weapon against the men in their lives so long as those particular men treat them respectfully. The women refrain because they know that doing so facilitates constructive cross-gender relationships that make life better for them, their families, their communities, and their nation.

So why have black and white Americans taken so long to reconcile?

I already have expressed my belief that the natural black-white healing and reconciliation process has been squelched by double standards, double speak, and double binds initiated and sustained by racializers, raceketeers, race cadets, governmental officials, media, marketers, some social scientists and the some non-social science intelligentsia. Now for a scientific explanation.

In the September 2010 *Psychological Bulletin*, Ryan Fehr, Michele J. Gelfand, and Monisah Nag noted that almost 800 forgiveness articles, books, chapters, and dissertations had been written through 2005—testimony to the importance of the topic. But, because they perceived the literature as unwieldy, they initiated a meta-analytic study to evaluate and integrate the mass of data, so that it could be better understood and utilized. Fehr and his associates chose to focus on the victim, organizing their review using a "Tripartite Forgiveness Typology" that involved cognitions (thoughts), affects (feelings), and constraints (obstacles). I must underscore that the literature reviewed aggrieved individuals, not groups, so please "forgive" me for constraints on extrapolations to blacks and whites as group members.

Thoughts

The meta-analysis suggested, as expected, that victim thoughts were important in facilitating forgiveness. The more that the offense was framed as severe, intentional, and directly caused by the blamed person, the less likely that he would be forgiven. The more that the victim obsessed about the injury, the less likely that she would forgive. Apologies by the offender helped encourage reconciliation.

Victim traits also were significant. Those with personalities oriented toward thinking described as "agreeable," "forgiving," and "perspective taking" forgave most readily.

Of the three variables investigated—cognition, affect, and constraint—cognition was most determinative in differentiating forgiving from non-forgiving victims. Moreover, although enduring victim thinking traits were predictive of their willingness to forgive, situation-dependent thinking was more important.

Affects

In their analysis of the role of affects, Fehr and his associates specifically cautioned that the studies they reviewed assessed explicit emotions; that is, reportable and reported feelings, rather than relying on measures of implicit feelings, such as hidden ones revealed by formal psychological testing. This suggested that those being studied could have been either unaware of their "true" emotions about forgiveness or unwilling to be honest in disclosing them. But other studies have supported the overall validity of emotion self-report.

Persons characterized by trait neuroticism (anxiety proneness), trait depression, and trait anger tended not to forgive. Situation-specific negative emotion, generally, and situation-specific anger, specifically, operated against forgiveness while situation-specific empathy facilitated forgiveness.

Constraints

In the constraints domain, two traits and three situation-specific factors emerged as meaningful. Traits associated with a propensity to forgive were orientation toward religion and orientation toward compliance with standards of social desirability. The situation-specific variables positively associated with forgiveness all involved the victim's wish not to impair their relationship with the offending person. Since victims with this situation-specific quality valued the victim-offender relationship, as is logical, the closer the victim's attachment to the offender, the more she experienced relationship satisfaction, and the more she was committed to the relationship, the greater the chance that she would forgive him.

Implications for Black-White Forgiveness

Some white people have read this section shaking their heads, thinking "forgiveness?" "For what?" To which I reply that I have unbridled empathy and fully agree with any white individual refusing to accept responsibility for racial offenses that they never committed. I do not write this section for those people, but for white apologists and black race-mongers, like Jeremiah Wright, who have a compelling need to find a racial scapegoat and to extract a racial pound of flesh.

The meta-analysis does provide some explanation for the absence of racial reconciliation in contemporary America, even if the explanation is "common sense." Fehr and his associates give scientific support to the notion that enduring personality traits of the "victims" are important. Agreeable, forgiving, and perspective taking people are more likely to forgive, as are religious people and those with a strong need to comply with standards of social desirability. On the other hand, persons high in trait neuroticism (anxiety proneness), trait depression, and trait anger are not.

But while enduring personality traits weakly predict willingness to forgive, situational factors have greater explanatory power. How one feels about the offending person at the moment strongly influences forgiveness. We are inclined to forgive those who hurt us if we have strong attachment and commitment to him and if he has pleased us in the past.

The thoughts that cruise through our mind as we contemplate forgiveness are pivotal, too. Obsessing about the injury and framing it as severe and deliberate militate against our willingness to get over it. While experiencing transient negative emotion, particularly anger, we are ill-prepared to forgive.

Does contemporary American culture promote conditions that make racial reconciliation likely? In a word, "no." As we have seen, black and white raceketeers, governmental officials, media, marketers, social scientists, and the non-social science intelligentsia spotlight and magnify any and all black-white differences. Any black entertaining thoughts of forgiveness must withstand a withering barrage of racial negativity. That is, the cognitive, emotional, and constraint-situational factors so essential to facilitating a climate of reconciliation find no support in our society. Quite the contrary. The message is that blacks inclined to forgive and forget are naïve, not black enough, or Uncle Toms. The raceketeer socially sanctioned attitude is that African Americans need to be angry, paranoid, and swagging in their interactions with honkies. Black forgiveness of whites would be traitorism.

Identity slave masters want blacks and whites to live in two different worlds, at least mentally. As you undoubtedly recall, the divisive ones succeeded mightily during the O. J. Simpson fiasco. Terri Conley, Joshua Rabinowitz, and Curtis Hardin documented the discord, showing that reality perception depended on racial affiliation. In the September 2010 *Journal of Personality and Social Psychology*, they reported research examining people involved in cooperative problem-solving dyads (2 person groups). Some dyads were same-race and some were cross-race, black and white. At points during the cooperative activity the participants were reminded of the Simpson trial, causing relationship harmony to be significantly affected. "As predicted, thoughts of Simpson caused decrements in quality of interpersonal perceptions and behaviors for different-ethnicity dyads but increases for same-ethnicity dyads." Moreover, those in accord about

Simpson liked each other more than those at odds about him, regardless of whether the dyads were black, white, or black and white.

America is an estuary inherently capable of nurturing and sustaining its people. But the long, serpentine river that feds the estuary carries not only life-enhancing components but also effluence issuing out of thousands of upstream community tributaries. To survive and thrive, black and white people need to filter out the pollutants and sequester the nutrients. Most of our citizens adapt well to the estuary's conditions. These survivors are black and white professional, skilled and unskilled, unemployed, and retired persons that we encounter every day. But some unlucky blacks and whites, poisoned by hateful propaganda that trickles into the estuary from racializers, raceketeers, and race cadets, devolve into racial criminals, bimps, and addicts. The black and white troubled ones do not differ demonstrably from each other. Every race and every group has its criminals, bimps, and addicts. Only one thing separates the maladapted blacks from the maladapted whites and from people of other races: In addition to having every excuse that persons of other races have to pardon their misbehavior, maladapted blacks have an army of racializers, raceketeers, and race cadets that sanction externalizing excuses for personally and socially damaging, even criminal, behaviors.

Whether they like it or not, and contrary to anti-racial reconciliation propaganda, black and white people do live in the same world. Reality is reality. Citizens of the twenty-first century United States must oppose raceketeers, focus on real here-and-now issues, talk to each other, and forget about Rodney King-like and O.J. Simpson-like incidents.

CHAPTER 20

Rorschach Barack, the Dreamy-Eyed Electorate, and the Future

Barack Obama is the closest thing to a political Rorschach that has ever swaggaed up to a podium. He resembles seven of the ten inkblot cards used to assess personality in that the seven are combinations of black, white, and gray. Like the seven, Barack has been ambiguous. Persons looking at Obama have been able to project onto him their wishful thoughts and feelings, so long as the observer enjoyed the charade. During the presidential campaigns of 2008, the American citizenry rushed headlong to play racial pretend, oblivious to the consequences. Whites wanted Obama to be black from the start. Blacks, at first, knew he was half-white, but subsequently "forgot"—all except Wanda Sykes.

Obama, then, shines as a sterling example for all those who aspire to a bogus, dark-triad racial identity. But, as I have stated previously, he is neither crazy nor criminal in the conventional senses of those words. Unlike a dark-triad, hard-core, Red Bull bimp, he is a soft-core, Bud Light refined kind of dark-triad personality. His narcissism is the narcissism of an insecure, identity-conflicted child. His Machiavellianism is the Machiavellianism of a sanctimonious know-it–all. And his psychopathy is the psychopathy of an emotionally vacuous individual who knows what he should feel, but he just cannot seem to feel it authentically except when his self-esteem or racial identity is on the line.

Barack Obama became President Barack Hussein Obama due to his masterful ability to mobilize dark-triad personality prowess, especially Machiavellian prowess, to manipulate America's longstanding racial problems. His Barry appeals to whites. As Barack, he courts rebellious young people. Hussein provides street cred with Black Muslims and other black extremists. The president turns on his Soetoro face when encountering overseas USA-disparaging people-of-color, and he shouts "Obama" loud and proud whenever anyone questions whether he is African enough.

In politics, context is everything, and context was Barack Obama's best friend: two wars, a flagging economy, and a much maligned Republican president excoriated daily by a biased press for eight long years. Above all, there was race, race, race. How grand to have a pretend black president! Blacks would be happy. Guilt-ridden, self-flagellating whites could exorcize their demons and be on the "right side of history" to boot. And what about the raceketeers—black, white, and all gradations in-between? Raceketeers eagerly anticipated a citizenry primed to be even more racially gullible and malleable than usual—ready, willing, and able to listen to the racializing pontificators and, even, to pay for the privilege of being duped.

The racial identity politics of Barack Obama represents merely one high-profile application of the racial double standards, double speak, and double binds ubiquitous in 21ˢᵗ century America. Blacks and people-of-color embody the preferred color standard when it comes to allocation of governmental and non-governmental resources, everything from federal employment opportunity to private multinational corporations that fund special inner-city projects. Black demagogues get away with double speaking, as when, for example, they scream "code talk" if whites refer to blacks as articulate while using their own code talk in "brotha-ing" each other on a race basis. And double binds are a regular feature of white racial discourse whenever whites raise issues "embarrassing" to blacks, or whenever they advocate for themselves in white-black disputes.

So, a racially disingenuous man became a racially disingenuous president on the backs of a racially disingenuous electorate due to racial doubles. For instance, blacks were praised for 95-96% "vote for the black guy" business-as-usual practices while whites were criticized because "only" about 43% of whites voted for Barack. Double speak definitely figured in the victory. No one could mention that Obama had a Muslim middle name but McCain regularly was disparaged as an angry, boring, dull, old white man. When Caucasians, whether Geraldine Ferraro, or the then-Senator, and now Vice President, Joe Biden, explicitly said what everyone implicitly knew, they not only were shouted down, but also given the loud and clear message that they had no right even to address the issue that they had raised.

The racial identity dysfunctional segment of American society has enabled Barack Obama to market himself as one able to unite people, despite his inability to unite the black and white sides of himself. He says he has been a bipartisan legislator, but his voting record shows the opposite. Obama has integrity, but counts among his closest associates a racist, racializing minister, a murderous bomber, and a convicted slum lord housing developer. He pledges to end "politics as usual," but rams though a pet healthcare bill that he wanted, despite the fact that neither he, nor anyone else, had studied it long enough to know how it would affect healthcare, liberty, or the economy. Barack rationalizes that everyone will like it someday. Obama says that there will be no lobbyists in his administration, then later decides that maybe a few wouldn't be so bad. He calls Wall Street business people "fat cats" on December 14, 2009 (Williamson, 2009) after he has won the presidential election; then on June 21, 2011 when he is beginning his reelection campaign, he summons that same group into the White House for a comingled advisory/campaign fund raising session (Weil, 2011). Obama values independence of the press but launches a "freeze out Fox News" campaign when they say things that hurt his feelings. He is a sterling example to youth, but during his adolescence and early adulthood he rampantly abused alcohol and illicit drugs and smoked cigarettes incessantly; in fact, he smoked throughout virtually all of his adult years and probably still does. He is "brilliant," but will not release his school records. Obama is a proud American but has trouble recalling how many states are in our union and does not know a corpsman from a "corpse, MAN!" He believes fatherhood is a sacred trust, yet he chose a job that frequently causes him physically to leave his young daughters and almost always is no more than half available to them mentally; this when he could have been Vice President under Hillary Clinton while his children were young, and then run for president after they had matured.

Thus far, Rorschach Barack has used his ambiguous persona flawlessly. But, just as happens with repeated exposure to the Rorschach Test, Obama has begun to lose his now-you-know-me-now-you-don't magic. With each passing day, people tire of him and his self-serving façades. Americans are starting to realize that a man who cannot look the reality of his bi-racial identity squarely in the eye cannot make reality-based decisions concerning our people and our nation.

When viewed in the context of contemporary American society, Barack Obama's fantasies and realities—private ones and shared ones—provide invaluable lessons about him and about ourselves. By scrutinizing his situation, we learn that double standards, double speak, and double binds pose virtually insuperable barriers to one's authentic personal identity formation and maintenance, and to others' capacities to routinely, accurately, and matter-of-factly accept the identities of those whom they encounter. The man with five names is a man out of touch with all his five easy pieces. Now, one final example from Obama's life: something that I briefly touched on previously, but that warrants elaboration at this point.

In *Dreams from My Father*, Barack recounts a search-for-identity trek at age 27 that begins in Europe and ends in Africa. In the chapter, he describes all things white either dismissively or contemptuously. Reading a book written by a white Briton makes him angry. Obama resents the "easy familiarity" that a white fellow airplane passenger has with him, and ruminates about whether he should be angry with the man for expressing his honest opinions about Africa. Editorializing about three weeks spent criss-crossing Europe, Barack notes that after only seven days he "realized" that the entire European continent "just wasn't mine. I felt as if I were living out someone else's romance . . . I began to suspect that my European stop was just one more means of delay, one more attempt to avoid coming to terms with the 'Old Man'" [his father].

The excerpt reveals Barack Obama's enslavement: not to the evil white man, but to his own "evil" thoughts and feelings. Even though every somatic cell in his body contains as many white as black chromosomes, Obama cannot accept the simple reality of his physical "integration." Unable to embrace the totality of his being, he literally divides the physical and interpersonal worlds into black versus white. Why isn't Europe his? Why is Africa his? Because Barack Obama tells himself those things; because Barack Obama does not have enough of Eric H. Holder junior's "racial courage" to accept reality and to "tell it like it is."

As shown earlier, Obama, himself, both inadvertently and directly, has informed us that he has had many chances to learn the negative repercussions of raceketeering and strident, excessive pro-black advocacy. For example, his white mother complained that black spokespersons painted all whites as racists. The white wind-chime voice lady that Barack Obama allegedly courted said that she could not tolerate incessant black anger. And Barack's white Illinois Senate colleague told him that black carping about imaginary racisms did not move him to their positions, but only made him more conscious of being Caucasian.

Obama did not learn the lessons of those relationships with white people. Instead, over his lifetime, he has accumulated a slush fund of pseudo-black negativity to justify his private racial-identity anger, dipping into it whenever he disingenuously racialized an event, such occurred regarding black Henry Lewis Gates junior versus white policeman, James Crowley.

Previously I suggested that Barack Obama's race-conflicted personality has been central to the conduct of his election and presidency. Nowhere was that more apparent than in Obama's mangled management of the financial default crisis of July 2011 when he and John Boehner stood in opposition to one another.

Consider the interpersonal background of the protagonists.

As noted earlier, twice in public, broadcasted venues Barack Obama mocked John Boehner in a very personal, emasculating manner. You recall that, in May 2009, the President made fun of the Speaker of the House's "skin tone," implying a girly attention to his complexion. In March 2011, Barack repeated his skin-centered mockery and implied a girly tendency toward tearfulness as well. In July 2011, Obama needed Boehner and vice versa in order to broker a deal on the national budget and an impending default. Many in the media and in politics framed the Obama-Boehner opposition as a battle that would test the mettle of each protagonist—a one-on-one alpha male competition. (Jesse Jackson might have said that it would show which of the two men had the biggest nuts.) In fact, Erica

Werner (2011) literally used the terms "fight" and "test of leadership" to describe the Obama-Boehner negotiations. Boehner lamented that the situation had become a "mano a mano" struggle, meaning hand-to-hand combat—the most macho form of battle. Interestingly, Obama spoke of being "left at the altar now a couple of times."

Left at the altar? What does that odd, apparently out-of-context reference have to do with race and macho? Plenty, since it refers to Barack Obama's identity conflict. As mentioned previously, Barack writes in *Dreams from My Father* about his parents' marriage saying, ". . . how and when the marriage occurred remains a bit murky, a bill of particulars that I've never quite had the courage to explore. There's no record of a real wedding, a cake, a ring, a giving away of the bride. No families were in attendance; it's not even clear that people back in Kansas were fully informed. Just a small civil ceremony, a justice of the peace."

Clearly, there is more to Barack's slip of the tongue than first catches the ear. Given the multiple failed marriages of his mother and father, marriage undoubtedly remains a hot-button personality issue for Barack. "Left at the altar" also connotes a President who originally had been in the "manly" position of waiting for his bride's father to "give" her to him. Finally, "left at the altar now a couple of times" suggests that Obama—a dark-triad person who has lived a life requiring constant pampering and reassurance—feels hurt, abandoned, and disrespected when others do not deliver what he wants. To be disrespected is to be without street cred. No insecurely biracial man who has bought into the racketeer definition of black swagga can tolerate the thought of being "dissed."

To paraphrase a much heralded politician: There is no black Barack Obama. There is no white Barack Obama. There is only a black and white Barack Obama. Mr. President, it is time to get real. Don't allow yourself to be showcased in a photo beside your white mother, grandmother, and grandfather only when it is politically expedient, as after you misspoke in Allentown, Pennsylvania. Be the proactive racial reconciliation leader who would make Martin Luther King junior proud. Have the racial courage to acknowledge being half white when you stand before the Congress of Racial Equality, the NAACP, the Congressional Black Caucus, the Black Entertainment Awards crowd, and the scores of other race-based black advocacy groups to which you pander. Accepting the reality of who you are merely requires you to appreciate and acknowledge the indisputable fact of your dual racial heritage. When that day comes, America can start consistently calling you what you are: the first biracial president. That would be a giant leap forward for you and for all of us.

But we should not be too hard on Barack Obama. As the presidential election of 2008 illustrates, many Americans see race as he sees it. They find nothing wrong with double standards, double speak, and double binds that are enacted with a noble, pro-black purpose. Nothing wrong with looking for and finding white racism, even if they must dream-up the concept of "micro racial transgressions" to rationalize their beliefs. Those Americans fail to see how the doubles have created and sustained the "cold war" racial mentality and chasm that separates us. More disturbing, those Americans do not recognize that the doubles massively contribute to black problems regarding family, education, vocation, and crime. Those Americans do not see that what seems a harmless endorsement of black swagga and hyper-masculinity unwittingly creates a climate that contributes to black violence against blacks, whites, and all shades in-between. Bimp-supportive Americans are like barber-physicians of olden days who intended to help their patients via bloodletting, but only made them sicker.

Slavery ended almost 150 years ago. The unanimous Supreme Court decision, Brown v. Board of Education of Topeka on May 17, 1954 initiated a slow, but inexorable movement toward practical racial integration. I say "practical" because, in today's world, racial similarity is a significant similarity, and people affiliate based on their perception of interpersonal similarity. For the time being at least, there is nothing inherently wrong with black or white people preferring their "own" community gathering places. Those kinds of preferences will persist as long as American Barack Obamas define similarity, first and foremost, as racial sameness. Those kinds of preferences will persist as long as blacks call blacks, but not whites, "brothas" and "sistas." Those kinds of preferences will persist as long as a gullible American citizenry swallows the double standards, double speak, and double binds relentlessly promoted by self-serving racializers, raceketeers, race cadets, governmental officials, media, marketers, some social scientists, and some non-social science intelligentsia. Accordingly, I agree that we continue to live in a non-post-racial America. Nevertheless, there is hope, hope because the numbers of biracial and multiracial people are growing and those people are becoming more visible and more outspoken. Some day they will reach critical mass, and that day will begin a new period wherein we do judge people as individuals and not by the color of their skin. When that day arrives, racial identity slave masters will be out of business.

The Obamafuscation of America is a merely a symptom of the doubles that preceded him by decades. But the emergence of Barry Barack Hussein Soetoro Obama has potentiated identity and race problems—a tsunami of deception and manipulation, inundating our nation with racial identity phonies and racial demagogues. Like Noah, I have taken refuge on an ark, one with at least two of every type citizen—black, white, and all shades in between. We are searching for high ground, hoping to find a site from which to rebuild our nation racially. Sometimes the seas are rough and give us pause, but we remain resolute and hopeful. Periodically, we send out a dove, but so far it always has returned to the ark.

A day will come when the dove does not return: that will be the day when America ceases to be a land of racial identity hypocrisy, double standards, double speak, and doubles binds. There also will be a day when a completely all-black woman or man properly claims to be the first truly one-hundred percent African American president and whom people acknowledge accordingly. Then Barry Barack Hussein Soetoro Obama either will re-experience the anguish attendant to redefining his identity once again, or he will foolishly maintain the disingenuous racial charade that he has promulgated to date. Eric H. Holder junior is watching to determine the extent of Barack's racial courage. The clock is ticking. One day, America will be happy to accept Barack Obama, all 46 chromosomes worth of him—as the first biracial president. And, on that day, many will be prompted to use the reality of his genuine racial identity as a bridge to accepting biracials and multi-racials across the nation.

Holder was correct about one thing: Interracial reconciliation requires forthcoming dialogue. In a previous book, *Conversation: Striving, Surviving, and Thriving*, I suggested that conversations are initiated and sustained because human beings have an inherent need to relentlessly and expectantly search for messages and relationships in order to overcome an, usually unconscious, existential sense of isolation and vulnerability. Through conversation, we continually search for answers to essential questions and for interpersonal contact that we hope will make us feel good, better than we currently feel, or at least homeostatic in the sense that we will have our preexisting and, therefore, relatively "comfortably" expectations confirmed.

For honest interracial dialogue to proceed, then, all American speakers must expect implicitly that their race-oriented conversation will make them feel okay, or better, and interpersonally connected. Whites, especially, must believe that the process and/or outcome of interracial discourse will not be contentious or biased against them; otherwise, they will have no incentive to talk at all. Everyone needs to know that his or her comments and questions will be received respectfully, and that there is some chance of a positive outcome as a result of the verbal exchange. To paraphrase George Orwell, if those conditions are granted, all else follows.

EPILOGUE

Barry Barack Hussein Soetoro Obama, Identity, and Racial Hypocrisy in America: Double Standards, Double Speak, and Double Binds has addressed the derisive challenge laid down by Eric Himpton Holder junior, United States Attorney General who, on February 18, 2009 in a speech at the Department of Justice African American History Month Program, called America a "nation of cowards" regarding race relations. I have chosen to answer Holder by structuring the book around Barack Obama because I regard him as the epitome of racial cowardice and a foremost contemporary perpetrator of racial identity manipulation and the racial doubles.

I contend that America is not a nation of racial cowards. Rather, Americans' difficulty with racial issues, in large measure, is a response to the actions of a powerful cadre of well-connected elitists, such as Barack Hussein Obama junior and Eric Himpton Holder junior who manipulate race for their self-serving purposes. Mostly government, civic, and media leaders, these captains of misery underscore and inflate any and all racial discontent or discord to feed their egos and/or their wallets. Raceketeers have conditioned Americans toward either racial harangues or self-protective avoidance of anything that can be construed as racial forthcoming. Our citizens have been brainwashed such that when black people talk about race, whites are expected to listen, but not the converse. The prevailing cultural ethos teaches that blacks know about racism; their experiences are lessons for whites. African Americans can be blunt, even crude, during their racial lecturing, given that they are "standing up for their people." On the other hand, because of social conditioning, almost no one wants to hear racial honesty from white people, especially from white men. Whites who even mention race are merely exposing their ignorance and perpetuating their virulent white racism.

Barack Obama's presidency continues to provide us a unique opportunity to move race relations forward. White, black, yellow, red, biracial, and mixed Americans of all varieties are infinitely more alike than different. All groups want to be proud of their heritage. And all people resent when another group enjoys extraordinary attention or privilege. People in the here-and-now want to be treated for what they do and who they are, not for what their parents, grandparents, or totally non-related but similarly colored others have done. America cannot move race relations briskly forward by continuously looking backward.

Let *Barry Barack Hussein Soetoro Obama, Identity, and Racial Hypocrisy in America: Double Standards, Double Speak, and Double Binds* serve as an invitation for a one-on-one truly honest, racially courageous, and respectful dialogue between Eric Holder and myself regarding issues in black and white. Our racial dialogue must be one of two people addressing concrete real life situations, enacted without notes, teleprompters, or tutoring by professional debate coaches. That is, the discussion must be extemporaneous and unrehearsed, as would be any authentic racial discussion between any two United States citizens. In contrast to Mr. Holder's African American History Month Program, the venue for our meeting should include an audience representative of the entire American population and not a select, exclusive, racially unbalanced club brought together merely to one-sidedly celebrate one black racial hero.

Eric Holder does not fear frank, constructive, courteous race talk, especially with a common, everyday white person such as I. Our meeting will give him an authentic grassroots forum so that he can elucidate the details of what he believes racial dialogue can and should be. My value to the conversion resides not in my intellect, experience, or education, but in my ordinariness. While I am not everyman, I am a common man who makes a determined effort to speak honestly. After so insistently advocating for respectful discourse on his chosen topic, Holder will not shrink from an opportunity to speak honestly and openly. Attorney General Holder surely is no racial coward.

That brings me to my final and most essential point: an issue infinitely larger than Obama, me, or this book.

Not so long ago, a woman or man, literally, could stand on a soapbox in the town square, be heard, and, in so doing, could influence the citizenry and its leaders. Today, with electronic media at our fingertips, we incorrectly presume that free expression is at an all-time high. But is it?

In writing this book about Barack Obama and race, I have come to realize that institutionalized discourse manipulation has the upper hand. Having written previously about conversation analysis, I originally intended to apply that science extensively to Obama and race.

Conversation analysis, as one would expect, demands verbatim transcripts not only of who said what but how. Paraphrase does not substitute for literal quotes. Seems simple enough. Merely transcribe the to-be-analyzed discourse and make your point.

Not so easy. How does one get the discourse? From print or electronic media giants. And therein lies the challenge: intellectual property. Only by getting the giants' written approval or by risking retaliation can one perform a proper conversation analysis.

Here we have a classic free speech versus intellectual property clash that strikes at the heart of our democracy. Discourse is not just objective facts, easily paraphrased. To paraphrase is to risk losing the essence of a message, whether the essence lies in the original words' denotation (literal meaning), connotation (subjective meaning) or, more likely, both. Subjective elements, in particular—perceived speaker characteristics, specific word nuance, phraseology, general connotation, inflection, context and the like—make all the difference in communication, for instance, permitting African Americans to use the word "nigger" with impunity, but causing all hell to break loose when whites use that despicable word. One cannot perform an adequate conversation analysis, critique, or, even, a significantly meaningful commentary of any sort without showing the literal words that prompted the response. When media giants shelter their literal words from us, they forestall meaningful challenge to their preferred and proffered rendition of information reality.

Now, more than ever, with media conglomerates biased for or against almost everything of personal and national significance, the average citizen must be allowed verbatim quotes to support or oppose the information assailing her or him from every direction. The issue is paramount for democracy

339

in our age of information manipulation and overload. Americans cannot know what is what if they cannot freely and openly discuss the specific details of the information being force-fed. And if you think "blog," think again. Blogs are not significantly different than any other means of written expression. Like all the others, blogs get much of their "data" from information transmitted through media giants. It is time to give all citizens unfettered permission to widely and verbatim quote and evaluate information proffered by the Walt Disney Company and by every similar Mickey Mouse organization in the United States.

If our country is to remain a bastion of liberty, Americans must be grated total freedom to discuss and critique every word and every nuance of the media-propaganda pummeling us every day. There certainly is a need for companies to protect their intellectual property when that property is essential to the conduct of their business and when its protection does not work against the best interests of our nation. But no single person and no media giant has the right to prevent our citizens from reproducing media information presented to us as fact when that reproduction will be used solely to evaluate the validity of the media's "proprietary information" and the impact that it has on our individual, collective, and national well-being.

Many contemporary Americans have sounded the alarm about the power of wealthy communications magnates to subvert free thought and criticism. Apropos of our present discussion, Neil Postman hit the nail on the head with his *Amusing Ourselves to Death: Public Discourse in the Age of Show Business.* The Penguin cover of that 1985 book explained that Postman "alerts us to the real and present dangers of this state of affairs . . . Before we hand over politics, education, religion, and journalism to the show-business demands of the television age, we must recognize the ways in which the media shape our lives and the ways we can, in turn, shape them to achieve our highest goals."

Accordingly, just as a grassroots effort is required to overcome racism, we need such an effort to pass legislation that gives every citizen the right to critique any and all of the literal information propaganda that media giants try to stuff down own throats. If you agree, let's start a movement to campaign against racializing, racekettering, and against the media's stranglehold on our abilities to communicate via critique. To join the campaign, email me: counterdoubles@aol.com.

REFERENCES

ABC Action News. 6:00 P.M. Broadcast. July 5, 2010. A witness to the July 4, 2010 falshmob violence claimed that he observed people, including an Asian man, being punched in the face for no apparent reason.

Abclocal.com. No author listed. Convicted rapist sentenced for Philadelphia attacks. ABClocal.com March 10, 2011. http://abclocal. go.com/wpvi/story?section=news/crime&id=8005854

Abcnewsradio online.com. blog. March 30, 2011 "By Election Day, Westly had joined the elite circle of 'bundlers,' http://abcnewsradioonline.com/ politics-news/did-obama-administration-play-favorites-with-energy-loans.html

African Americans by the Numbers. U.S. Census Bureau. The U.S. Census Bureau News. http://www.infoplease.com/spot/bhmcensus1.html

Aguiluz, Erline. Domenique Wilson Charged with Rape and Armed-Robbery. Philadelphia Daily News November 4, 2010. http:// philadelphiacriminallawnews.com/2010/11/domenique-wilson-charged-with-rape-and-armed-robbery.html#more

Alexander, Michelle. The New Jim Crow: Mass Incarceration in the Age of Colorblindness. New York: the New Press, 2010.

Alinsky, Saul. Rules for Radicals. New York: Vintage Books, Random House, 1971

AllAfrica.com August 12, 2010. President Robert Mugabe launched the fast-track land reform programme in 2000. http://www.newsnet14. com/2010/03/12/land-reform-and-the-lingering-zimbabwe-food-crisis/

Allen, Mike. Clinton aide accuses Obama of plagiarism. February 18, 2008. http://www.politico.com/news/stories/0208/8570.html

Alter, Jonathan. The Promise: President Obama, Year One. New York: Simon & Schuster, 2010.

Alvarez, Alex. Mediaite: Roland Martin Livetweets Dave Chappelle's Strange Comedy Set. July 25, 2011. http://www.rolandsmartin.com/blog/index. php/2011/07/25/cnns-roland-martin-livetweets-dave-chappelles-strange-comedy-set/?utm_source=feedburner&utm_medium=feed&utm_campa ign=Feed%3A+RolandSMartin+%28Roland+S.+Martin+News+Update s%29

Amazon.com product description of: Tatum, Beverly Daniel. Why Are All the Black Kids Sitting Together in the Cafeteria?

Ambinder, Marc. Obama Denounces Wright. April 29, 2008. http:// www.theatlantic.com/politics/archive/2008/04/obama-denounces-wright/52893/

Andersen, Christopher. Barack and Michelle: portrait of an American marriage New York: Harper Collins, 2009.

Anderson, Rob. Maureen Dowd Attacks Michelle Obama. The Editorialist. April, 2007. http://blog.washingtonpost.com/editorialist/2007/04/ todays_columns_maureen_dowd_at.html

Associated Press. Greek Organizations Not Welcomed In Pennsylvania. Newsone.com. July 12, 2010. http://newsone.com/nation/associated-press/ black-greek-organizations-not-welcomed-in-pennsylvania/

Associated Press. 'Green revolution' Nobel winner Norman Borlaug dies. Usatoday.com. September 12, 2009. http://www.usatoday.com/news/ nation/2009-09-13-bolaug-obit_N.htm

Associated Press. NBA gets high marks for diversity in new study. Nba. com. Posted June 10, 2009. http://www.nba.com/2009/news/06/10/ NBA.diversity.ap/index.html

Associated Press. No Author listed. Ludacris' song points to dilemma for Obama. Democrat wants hip-hop world's support, but not art's cultural divisiveness. http://www.msnbc.msn.com/id/25963955/ns/politics-decision_08/t/ludacris-song-points-dilemma-obama/

Associated Press. White House defends invite to rapper Common. Wednesday, May 11, 2011. http://abclocal.go.com/wpvi/story?section=news/entertainment&id=8125276

Atiba Goff, Phillip, Claude M. Steele, Paul G. Davies. The Space Between Us: Stereotype Threat and Distance in Interracial Contexts. Journal of Personality and Social Psychology, January, 2008

Avila, Oscar. Obama's census-form choice: 'Black' The president keeps it simple, but his decision stirs discussion about identity among mixed-race Americans. Los Angeles Times. April 04, 2010|. http://articles.latimes.com/2010/apr/04/nation/la-na-obama-census4-2010apr04

Bacon, Perry. Caucus lines up for white Steve Cohen over black rival. Washington Post. July 20, 2010. http://www.washingtonpost.com/wp-dyn/content/article/2010/07/19/AR2010071905006.html

Ball, Howard. The Bakke Case: Race, Education, and Affirmative Action. Lawrence, Kansas: University of Kansas Press, 2000.

Barbara Fredrickson. University of North Carolina Positive Emotions and Psychophysiology Lab web pagehttp://www.unc.edu/peplab/barb_fredrickson_page.html

Barbash, Fred & Harry Siegel. Van Jones resigns amid controversy. Politico. September 6, 2009. http://www.politico.com/news/stories/0909/26797.html

Barbieri, Rich. CNN poll: Americans don't like health care bill. CNNMoney.com. March 22nd, 2010. http://politicalticker.blogs.cnn.com/2010/03/22/cnn-poll-americans-dont-like-health-care-bill/

Barlas, Thomas. Vineland man killed by fallen tree was an adoptive dad to six children. Press of Atlantic City. Posted: Thursday, July 29, 2010; updated July 30, 2010. http://www.pressofatlanticcity.com/news/top_three/article_6b5f3ad6-9b7a-11df-85dd-001cc4c03286.html

Baumeister, Roy F., Bratslavsky, Ellen, Finkenauer, Catrin, & Vohs, Kathleen D. (2001). Bad is stronger than good. Review of General Psychology, 5, 323-370.

BBC News. No author listed. I was forced to kill my baby. April 2, 2002. http://news.bbc.co.uk/2/hi/uk_news/1899609.stm

Beil, Laura. Lifers. In: Thugs. (radio show) This American Life. July 29, 2011. http://www.thisamericanlife.org/radio-archives/episode/442/thugs

Ben-Yaacov, Shai. Catch and Wreck. (Radio broadcast). Why.org. March 23, 2010.

Biden, Joe. Meet the Press. NBC. September 9, 2007. Joe Biden quote: "If you tell me I've got to take away this protection for these kids in order to win the election, some things aren't worth it."

Bing.com. MSNBC Tucker Carlson. Jena 6 given standing ovation at BET awards October 19, 2007. http://www.bing.com/videos/watch/video/jena-6-applauded-at-bet-awards/6uhyhck

Biography.com. Michael Vick's personal history. http://www.biography.com/articles/Michael-Vick-241100

Black Entertainment Television. Episode 5 summary of a documentary about Michael Vick. Boddie [Vick's father] was " a hard drug user who was in and out of his family's life." http://www1.bet.com/OnTV/BETShows/michaelvick/michaelvick_episodeguide_recap5

Bloomquist, Sara and David Henry. "Unruly crowd" forms after 4th of July celebration. Abclocal.go.com. July 5 2010. http://abclocal.go.com/wpvi/story?section=news/local&id=7537449

Boren, Cindy. President Obama praises Eagles for giving Michael Vick a chance. Washington Post. Posted at December 27, 2010. http://voices. washingtonpost.com/early-lead/2010/12/obama_reportedly_praises_ eagle.html

Bosman, Julie. THE CAUCUS; Pastor Defends Himself. New York Times. April 25, 2008. http://query.nytimes.com/gst/fullpage.html?res=9 802E3DD1638F936A15757C0A96E9C8B63&ref=billmoyers

Brookover, Bob & Jeff McLane. Vick wins Ed Block Courage Award. Philly.com. December 23, 2009. http://www.philly.com/philly/sports/ Vick_wins_Ed_Block_Courage_Award.html

Brown, Jim. Ken Hutcherson Pastor: Obama has no 'black experience' to speak of. OneNewsNow. July 3, 2009. http://www.onenewsnow.com/ Culture/Default.aspx?id=588946

Brownstein, Ronald. Why the white working class is alienated, pessimistic. National Journal, May 31, 2011. http://beta.news.yahoo.com/blogs/ exclusive/why-white-working-class-alienated-pessimistic-141725366. html

Buchanan, Patrick J. The Color of Crime. No Date. http://buchanan.org/ blog/pjb-the-color-of-crime-826

Bureau of Justice Statistics of the United States Department of Justice. On average, blacks murder whites at a rate 277 percent higher than whites murder blacks. http://bjs.ojp.usdoj.gov/index.cfm?ty=kfa

Caleb. Dan Rather: 'Obama couldn't sell watermelons.' Western Journalism. March 9, 2010. http://www.westernjournalism.com/dan- rather-obama-couldnt-sell-watermelons/

Carney, Jay. Press Briefing. April 4, 2011. http://www.whitehouse. gov/the-press-office/2011/04/11/press-briefing-press-secretary-jay- carney-4112011

Carpenter, Amanda. Green jobs czar signed 'truther' statement in 2004. Washington Times. September 3, 2009. http://www.washingtontimes. com/weblogs/back-story/2009/sep/03/green-jobs-czar-signed-truther-statement-in-2004/

Carpenter, Amanda. Special Advisor for Green Jobs, Van Jones. Washington Times. September 4, 2009. http://www.washingtontimes.com/weblogs/ back-story/2009/sep/04/another-apology-may-be-coming-from-van-jones/

CBS Evening News. You'll Never Know Who Helps Whom. December 19, 2008.

Cbs3.com. No author listed. 'Flash Mob' Blamed For South Philly Rampage. Cbs3.com "South Philly rampage" Cbs3.com. June 2, 2009. http://cbs3.com/topstories/Teens.Destrucitve.Rampage.2.1025684.html

Cbsnews.com No author listed. Plea Bargain Wraps Up "Jena 6" Case. No Contest Plea Ends Case Of Black Teens Accused Of Beating White Schoolmate In La. Cbsnews.com. June 26, 2009. http://www.cbsnews. com/stories/2009/06/26/national/main5116800.shtml

Cbsnews.com. No author listed. Caught on Tape: Teens Beat Pregnant Teen on Bus. Cbsnews.com. December 17, 2010. http://www.cbsnews. com/stories/2010/12/17/earlyshow/main7159518.shtml

Celebrity values. No Author listed. George Clooney Takes on Major Issues. http://www.celebrityvalues.com/george_clooney.html

Center for Unconventional Security Affairs. Invisible Children 2008 Human Security Award. University of California, Irvine. 2008. http:// www.cusa.uci.edu/news/invisible_children.html

Charles J. Ogletree, Charles J. Presumption of Guilt: The Arrest of Henry Louis Gates junior and Race, Class and Crime in America. New York: St. Martin's Press, 2010.

Chivvis, Dana. Obama's African Relatives Think His Father Was Murdered. Aolnews.com. October 18, 2010. http://www.aolnews.com/2010/10/18/ obamas-african-relatives-think-his-father-was-murdered/

Chrisite, Ron. Acting White: The Curious History of a Racial Slur. New York: St. Martin's Press, 2010.

Churcher, Sharon. A drunk and a bigot—what the US Presidential hopeful HASN'T said about his father. Daily Mail, updated at 22:51 27. January 2007. htttp://www.dailymail.co.uk/news/article-431908/A-drunk-bigot—US-Presidental-hopeful-HASNT-said-father-. html#ixzz1LnCz3GXx

Cillizza, Chris. The Fix. Harry Reid apologizes for "light skinned" remark about Obama. Washington Post. No date listed. http://voices. washingtonpost.com/thefix/senate/harry-reid-apologizes-for-ligh.html

Clinton, Hillary. January 21, 2008. CNN and the Congressional Black Caucus Institute Democratic Primary debate. Hilary Clinton: Barack was ". . . practicing law and representing your contributor, Rezko, in his slum landlord business in inner-city Chicago."

Clinton, William J. Obama: Biggest fairy tale. New Hampshire campaign stop. January 2008.

CNN and Congressional Black Congress. Presidential Debate January 23, 2008. CNN's Joe Johns asked Barack Obama whether he thought former President Bill Clinton was the nation's 'first black president http:// politicalticker.blogs.cnn.com/2008/01/22/obama-is-bill-clinton-really-a-brother-id-have-to-see-him-dance/

CNN articles. Obama's half brother says father abusive. November 04, 2009. http://articles.cnn.com/2009-11-04/politics/obama. half.brother_1_brother-of-president-obama-half-brother-father?_s=PM:POLITICS

CNN Newsroom March 28, 2009. (Video). T.J. Holmes conducting an interview with Marc H. Morial, president and CEO of the National Urban

League, during which Morial was asserting what he believed the national government and Barack Obama needed to do for black America.

CNN Politics. Joe Wilson says outburst to Obama speech 'spontaneous.' September 10, 2009. http://articles.cnn.com/2009-09-10/politics/obama.heckled.speech_1_illegal-immigrants-illegal-aliens-rep-joe-wilson?_s=PM:POLITICS

Coates, Christopher. Transcript: U.S. Commission on Civil rights. Testimony of Christopher Coates. September 24, 2010. http://pajamasmedia.com/files/2010/09/christopher_coates_testimony_9-24-10.pdf

Cohen, Janet Langhart, Book TV After Words host, discussing with Ron Christie his book, "Acting White." April, 2011. http://www.booktv.org/Program/12072/After+Words+Ron+Christie+Acting+White+hosted+by+Janet+Langhart+Cohen.aspx

Colbert Report. Interview at the Washington office with Eleanor Holmes Norton. July 27, 2006. http://www.colbertnation.com/the-colbert-report-videos/72238/july-27-2006/better-know-a-district—district-of-columbia—eleanor-holmes-norton

Conan, Neal & Junia Yearwood interview. Op-Ed: Advanced Placement Isn't For Every Student. Talk of the Nation. April 25, 2011. http://www.npr.org/2011/04/25/135710864/op-ed-advanced-placement-isnt-for-every-student

Conley, Terri D.; Joshua L. Rabinowitz, & Curtis D. Hardin. O. J. Simpson as shared (and unshared) reality: The impact of consensually shared beliefs on interpersonal perceptions and task performance in different—and same-ethnicity dyads. Journal of Personality and Social Psychology, 99(3), 2010, 452-466.

Corsi, Jerome R. Honolulu Star Bulletin June 20, 1962. Obama articles don't mention wife, son. WorldNetDaily. Posted: November 18, 2010. http://www.wnd.com/?pageId=229417#ixzz1LnRWA4AE

Corsi, Jerome R. The Obama nation : leftist politics and the cult of personality. New York: Simon & Schuster, 2008.

Council for Christian Colleges & Universities (CCCU). Award for Advancing Racial harmony to North Park University. http://www.cccu.org/news/prestigious_awards_presented_at_forum_on_christian_higher_education

Crawford, Jan. Alito Winces as Obama Slams Supreme Court Ruling. Crossroads with Jan Crawford. January 28, 2010. http://www.cbsnews.com/8301-504564_162-6149295-504564.html

Crimes of War Project. http://www.crimesofwar.org/

Cunningham, Hugo, S. "Pravda" as a higher "truth." 2003. http://www.cyberussr.com/rus/pravda-istina-e.html

Dale, Maryclaire. Lawsuits: Whites told they can't teach blacks. The Daily Times, May 18, 2011.

Davis, F. James. Who Is Black? College Park, Pennsylvania: Penn State University Press, 2001.

Dean, Mensah. Savage home invasions earn him lots of prison time. Philly.com. March 11, 2011. http://articles.philly.com/2011-03-11/news/28680424_1_home-invasions-state-prison-spruce-street-apartment

Deroy Murdock. Team Obama turns blind eye to voter intimidation. 'Cracker, you're about to be ruled by a black man.' Washington Times. July 8, 2010. http://www.washingtontimes.com/news/2010/jul/8/team-obama-turns-blind-eye-to-voter-intimidation/

Dickerson, Debra. Colorblind: Barack Obama would be the great black hope in the next presidential race—if he were actually black. Salon. January 22, 2007. http://www.salon.com/news/opinion/feature/2007/01/22/obama

Dickerson, Debra. Memo to Obama: Talk the jobless off the ledge. Washington Monthly, January-February 2011. http://www.washingtonmonthly.com/features/2011/1101.dickerson.html#Byline

Dirner, Cullen. Tim Scott Will Not Join Congressional Black Caucus: 'My Campaign Was Never About Race.' ABC News. December 01, 2010. http://blogs.abcnews.com/thenote/2010/12/tim-scott-will-not-join-congressional-black-caucus-my-campaign-was-never-about-race.html

Dowd, Maureen. Isn't It Ironic? New York Time. June 12, 2010. http://www.nytimes.com/2010/06/13/opinion/13dowd.html

Duncan, Mike. State Pulls Series of License Plates. Mike Duncan. CNN Headline News. Jul 23, 2008. http://www.todaysthv.com/news/story.aspx?storyid=69726

Dunkel, Curtis S. & Jon A. Sefcek. Eriksonian lifespan theory and life history theory: An integration using the example of identity formation. Review of General Psychology, 13(1), 2009, 13-23.

Duval, Thomas Shelley, & Silvia, Paul J. (2002). Self-awareness, probability of improvement, and the self-serving bias. Journal of Personality and Social Psychology, 82, 49-61.

Dyson, Michael Eric. Explained that black people understand "racial politics." Radio Times (audio). May 19, 2009.

Edwards, John. CNN Democrat Presidential Candidate Debate, Myrtle Beach, South Carolina, January 21, 2008. http://archive.redstate.com/stories/elections/2008/unleash_the_democrats

Edwards, Tamela. "Parenting Across the Color Line" 6ABC series. April 2011.

Ehmke, Layton , Justine Jablonska, & John Lund. In Altgeld Gardens, problems run deeper than Fenger violence. Medill Reports Chicago. October 27, 2009. http://news.medill.northwestern.edu/chicago/news.aspx?id=143467

Elder, Larry. Showdown. New York: St. Martin's Press, 2002.

Elder, Larry. Newsweek Whitewashes Al Sharpton. Real Clear Politics. August 5, 2010. http://www.realclearpolitics.com/articles/2010/08/05/newsweek_whitewashes_al_sharpton_106619.html

EspnMLB. No Author Listed. Less than 9 percent of players black. April 21, 2011. http://sports.espn.go.com/mlb/news/story?id=6401971

Erikson, Erik H. Identity: Youth and Crisis (Austen Riggs Monograph) 1968 New York: Norton.

Faber, Judy. CBS Fires Don Imus over Racial Slur. CBS News. April 12, 2007. http://www.cbsnews.com/stories/2007/04/12/national/main2675273.shtml

Farm Journal. No author listed. Borlaug Urges Shift To Gene Revolution. June 25, 2003. AgBioWorld. http://www.agbioworld.org/biotech-info/topics/borlaug/borlaug-articles.html

Fehr, Ryan, Michele J. Gelfand & Monisha Nag. The road to forgiveness: A meta-analytic synthesis of its situational and dispositional correlates. Psychological Bulletin, 136(5), 2010, 894-914.

Ferguson, Niall. "Egypt: How Obama Blew It." Newsweek. February 21, 2011.

Fiedler, Elizabeth. Ditch Cancun. Students ditch Cancun and opt for Camden for spring break. whyy.org March 31, 2009. http://whyy.org/cms/news/education/2009/03/31/students-ditch-cancun-and-opt-for-camden-for-spring-break/5224

Firstbrook, Peter. The Obamas : the untold story of an African family. New York: Crown, 2010.

Fox News Television. Broadcast interview. Herman Cain: a black, 2012 conservative political candidate, asks a black supporter, "But why are you whispering?" February 17, 2011.

Freedland, Jonathan. Obama guilty of naivety, says former Israeli diplomat. Guardian.co.uk, September 17, 2009. http://www.guardian.co.uk/world/2009/sep/17/obama-naivety-israeli-diplomat-attack

Freedland, Jonathan. Obama not walking the walk. Fox News (Television segment), 14:45 hours, May 18, 2011.

Fudge, Marcia. Interviewed by reporters in Washington, D.C, as she and others, mostly Congressional Black caucus members, advocate for eliminating voter identification requirements. July 13, 2011. http://www.youtube.com/watch?v=VEZNnoQVLSM

Gallup Poll conducted at the end of April 2010 revealed that 51% of our citizens who knew about the Arizona Immigration Law favored it and only 39% opposed. http://politicalticker.blogs.cnn.com/2010/04/30/natl-poll-more-favor-than-oppose-arizona-immigration-law/

Gates, Bill. Fond farewell: Norman Borlaug. Time. December 2009.

Gavrilovic, Maria. Barack Obama in Kissimmee, Florida: "You've got my sister; she looks like Selma Hayak. I don't know if you've seen her. She looks Latin." CBS news. May 21, 2008.

Genocide Intervention. No author listed. One Courageous Man, One Daunting Mission: Carl Wilkens http://www.genocideintervention.net/our_programs/carl_wilkens_fellowship/about_carl_wilkens

Gerstein, Josh. Obama on terror trials: KSM will die. November 18, 2009. http://www.politico.com/news/stories/1109/29661.html

Gettleman, Jeffrey. Albinos, Long Shunned, Face Threat in Tanzania New York Times. June 8, 2008. http://www.nytimes.com/2008/06/08/world/africa/08albino.html

Goldberg, Bernard. A Slobbering Love Affair: The True (And Pathetic) Story of the Torrid Romance Between Barack Obama and the Mainstream Media. Washington, D.C: Regnery, 2009

Goldberg, Ross. Obama's Years at Columbia Are a Mystery: He Graduated Without Honors. Special to the New York Sun. September 2, 2008. http://www.nysun.com/new-york/obamas-years-at-columbia-are-a-mystery/85015/

Google search early 2011 of the word "nigger" produced 2,640 titles.

Gorant, Jim. The lost dogs: Michael Vick's dogs and their tale of rescue and redemption. New York: Penguin, 2010.

Gordon, Sarah. Gangland Chicago: Call For Troops On Streets. Sky News Online. April 27, 2010. http://news.sky.com/skynews/Home/World-News/Chicago-Gang-Violence-National-Guard-Needed-On-Streets-Of-Obamas-Adopted-City/Article/201004415620766?lpos=World_News_News_Your_Way_Region_6&lid=NewsYourWay_ARTICLE_15620766_Chicago_Gang_Violence:_National_Guard_Needed_On_Streets_Of_Obamas_Adopted_City

Gottman, John. Gottman Relationship Institute. Homepage, July, 2011. http://www.gottman.com/

Graham, Kristen. Philly Safe Schools Advocate back? March 28, 2011. http://www.philly.com/philly/blogs/school_files/Philly-Safe-Schools-Advocate-back.html

Grier, William & Price Cobbs. Black Rage. New York: Basic Books, 1968.

Grimes, Nikki. Barack Obama: Son of Promise, Child of Hope. New York: Simon & Schuster Books for Young Readers, 2008.

Haley, Alex. Roots: The Saga of an American Family. New York: Doubleday Garden City, 1976.

Halperin, Mark & John Heileman. Game Change: Obama and the Clintons, McCain and Palin, and the Race of a Lifetime. New York: Harper Collins, 2010.

Hamsher, Jane. Obama Mocks Public Option Supporters. Firedoglake.com blog. September 17, 2010. http://fdlaction.firedoglake.com/2010/09/17/obama-mocks-public-option-supporters/

Harnden, Toby. Exclusive: Barack Obama is 'aloof' says British ambassador to US. October 2, 2008. http://www.telegraph.co.uk/news/worldnews/northamerica/usa/barackobama/3125120/Barack-Obama-is-aloof-says-British-ambassador-to-US.html

Harris Interactive. President Obama Heads into Midterms at Lowest Approval Rating of Presidency: Two-thirds of Americans believe country going off on the wrong track. October 25, 2010. http://www.harrisinteractive.com/Hi_assets/TopHitPageNews.html

Hastings, Michael. The Runaway General. Rolling Stone. July 8-22, 2010.

Hilton, Perez. Dave Chappelle BOOED Off Stage At Miami Charity Show! PerezHilton.com. Undated. http://perezhilton.com/tag/alonzo_mournings_summer_groove_charity_event/

Historylink.org comments: ". . . it is something of a mystery whether the pregnancy or true love brought on the marriage." Free Online Encyclopedia of Washington State History. http://www.historylink.org/index.cfm?DisplayPage=output.cfm&file_id=8897

Hoft, Jim. "Kenneth Gladney not black enough" to protect—He's an "Uncle Tom" (Video). Gateway Pundit. Published: July 9, 2010. http://dailycaller.com/2010/07/09/racist-naacp-leader-says-%E2%80%9Ckenneth-gladney-not-black-enough%E2%80%9D-to-protect-%E2%80%93-he%E2%80%99s-an-%E2%80%9Cuncle-tom%E2%80%9D-video/

Holmes, T. J. CNN news broadcast. T.J. Holmes speaking about Obama's "swagga." April 25, 2009.

Hotels.com commercial. Naked black man in a tub with a white and Asian man blowing into the water. http://www.kongregate.com/forums/9/topics/ [and] http://angrywhitedude.com/tag/hotelscom/

http://www.statemaster.com/graph/peo_tot_bla_pop_percap-total-black-population-per-capita

Huffington Post. Beating Death Of Derrion Albert, 16, Caught On Video. First Posted: September 27, 2009. http://www.huffingtonpost.com/2009/09/27/beating-death-of-derrien_n_301319.html

Huffington Post. No author listed. Chris Matthews: "I Felt This Thrill Going Up My Leg" As Obama Spoke. February 13, 2008. http://www.huffingtonpost.com/2008/02/13/chris-matthews-i-felt-thi_n_86449.html

Hutchinson, Bill. Jesse Jackson slams Cavaliers' owner Dan Gilbert for treating LeBron James like a 'runaway slave'. New York Daily News. July 12, 2010. http://articles.nydailynews.com/2010-07-12/news/27069662_1_lebron-james-slave-cavaliers-owner-dan-gilbert

Icasualties. Statistics regarding battlefield deaths in Iraq an Afghanistan. http://icasualties.org/Iraq/index.aspx (Iraq) ; http://icasualties.org/OEF/index.aspx (Afghanistan)

Inskeep, Steve. Wrong Place, Wrong Time. Morning Edition. February 9, 2010.

Jackson, John H. Schott Foundation 50 State Report on Public Education and Black Males. 2010 http://www.blackboysreport.org/files/schott50statereport-execsummary.pdf

Jackson, John L. junior. Racial Paranoia: The Unintended Consequences of Political Correctness, The New Reality of Race in America. New York: Basic Books, 2008.

Javier, Rafael A. & Mario Rendon. The Ethnic Unconscious and Its Role in Transference, Resistance, and Counter transference: An Introduction. Psychoanalytic Psychology, 12, 513-520, 1995.

John. Lights out for Van Jones. Powerline Blog. Posted: September 5, 2009. http://www.powerlineblog.com/archives/2009/09/024444.php

Johnson, Alex. Barack Obama elected 44th president 'Change has come to America,' first African American leader tells country. MSNBC. November 5, 2008. http://www.msnbc.msn.com/id/27531033/

Johnson, Scott. Fleeing From South Africa: Fourteen years after apartheid, why are the best and the brightest leaving Africa's most successful state? Newsweek. February 14, 2009. http://www.newsweek.com/2009/02/13/fleeing-from-south-africa.html

Johnston, Angus. Fake White Student Union Flyers at West Chester University. StudentActivism.net. December 2, 2010. http://studentactivism.net/2010/12/02/fake-white-student-union-flyers-at-west-chester-university/

Jones, Joyce. Sheila Jackson Lee Is Being Sued By a Former Congressional Aide. Black Entertainment Television blog. http://www.bet.com/news/politics/2011/07/14/jackson-lee-is-being-sued-by-a-former-congressional-aide.html

Jones, Paul. Upper Darby chief says flash mobs hard to infiltrate. Philadelphia Inquirer. June 28, 2011. http://www.philly.com/philly/news/pennsylvania/20110628_Upper_Darby_chief_says_flash_mobs_hard_to_infiltrate.html

Jonsson, Patrik. New Black Panther Party voter intimidation case: 'Bombshell' for Obama? Christian Science Monitor. September 24, 2010. http://www.csmonitor.com/USA/Politics/2010/0924/New-Black-Panther-Party-voter-intimidation-case-Bombshell-for-Obama

Kavanagh, Tom. Democrat Frank Caprio Says Obama Can 'Shove It' for Not Endorsing Him. Politics Daily, October 25, 2010. http://www.politicsdaily.com/2010/10/25/obama-can-shove-it-for-not-endorsing-him-frank-caprio-says/

Kelley, Raina. Play the race card. Newsweek, September 28, 2009.

Kelly, Megyn. Non-profit Under Fire For White Male-Only Scholarships. (Video). Fox News. March 2, 2011. "http://video.foxnews.com/v/4564066/college-scholarships-for-white-men-only

Kennedy, Kathleen Townsend, Robert F. Kennedy junior & Kerry Kennedy. Kennedys for Clinton. Los Angeles times. January 29, 2008. http://www.latimes.com/news/printedition/asection/la-oe-kennedy29jan29,0,624676.story

Kennedy, Randall. Nigger. New York: Vintage Books Random House, 2002.

King, Martin Luther junior. Where Do We Go from Here: Chaos or Community? Boston: Beacon Press, 1967.

Kurzban, Robert & Mark R. Leary. Evolutionary origins of stigmatization: The functions of social exclusion. Psychological Bulletin, 127(2), 2001, 187-208.

Kushner, Melissa. In 2010, Melissa received New York University's Robert Wagner School of Public Service Torch Award. Goods for Good website. http://www.linkedin.com/pub/melissa-kushner/6/559/9a0

Landler, Mark & Helene Cooper. Obama Seeks a Course of Pragmatism in the Middle East.

New York Times. March 10, 2011. http://www.nytimes.com/2011/03/11/world/africa/11policy.html

Langer, Ellen, Pirson, Michael, & Delizonna, Laura. (2010). The mindlessness of social comparisons. Psychology of Aesthetics, Creativity, and the Arts, 4, 68-74.

Larkin, Todd. The N Word. (Video Documentary). Trio Films. 2004.

Legault, Lisa, Jennifer Gutsell and Michael Inzlicht. Ironic Effects of Anti-Prejudice Messages: How Motivational Interventions Can Reduce (but also increase) Prejudice. Psychological Science, 2011.

Lemos, Charles. A Nation Incarcerated: The American Gaol Crisis. February 7, 2010. http://mydd.com/2010/2/7/a-nation-incarcerated-the-american-gaol-crisis

Leo, Alex & Nico Pitney. Wanda Sykes Kills At White House Correspondents' Dinner (VIDEO). Huffington Post. First Posted: May 09, 2009. http://www.huffingtonpost.com/2009/05/09/wanda-sykes-video-of-whit_n_201280.html

Lewis, Elliot. Fade: My Journeys in Multi-Racial America. New York: Carroll & Graf, 2006.

Lewis, Matt. Daily Caller Exposes 'Journolist' Attempts to Kill Stories About Rev. Jeremiah Wright. Politicsdaily. July 20, 2010. http://www.politicsdaily.com/2010/07/20/daily-caller-exposes-journolist-attempts-to-kill-stories-about/

Lexisone. No author listed. Kenneth Williams vs. The State of Arkansas. Supreme Court of Arkansas. Opinion delivered February 1, 2001. August 3, 2011. http://www.lexisone.com/lx1/caselaw/freecaselaw?action=OCLGetCaseDetail&format=FULL&sourceID=beehcb&searchTerm=ecDG.UEba.aadj.efae&searchFlag=y&l1loc=FCLOW

Linthicum, Kate. Obama elitist, says Lady Rothschild. Los Angeles Times. September 18, 2008. http://articles.latimes.com/2008/sep/18/nation/na-trailrothschild18

Lowery, Joseph. President Obama's Inauguration benediction. January 20, 2009.

Mabrey, Vicki. Why Can't a Successful Black Woman Find a Man? Television Broadcast. April 9, 2010.

Mac Donald, Heather. The Times' Crime Confusions Persist. Error and distortion at the paper: Heaven help us, of record. City-Journal. January 5, 2009. http://www.city-journal.org/2009/eon0105hm.html

Madblackwoman. You people are just sick. http://www.topix.com/forum/city/wyndmoor-pa/TLUM584VG87VSU9KV

Main, Bruce. President. Urban Promises website. http://urbanpromiseinternational.org/contact/leader-contacts/

Malkin, Michelle. "Maxine Waters: Swamp Queen." April 27, 2011. http://michellemalkin.com/2011/04/27/maxine-waters-swamp-queen/

Malkin, Michelle. Culture of Corruption: Obama and His Team of Tax Cheats, Crooks, and Cronies. Washington, D.C.: Regnery, 2009.

Mandara, Jelani, Fatima Varner, and Scott Richman. Do African American mothers really "love" their sons and "raise" their daughters? Journal of Family Psychology, Vol 24(1), 2010, 41-50.

Marcus, Llyod. "A Black Man, The Progressive's Perfect Trojan Horse." On March 25, 2010. http://www.lloydmarcus.com/?p=1114

Martin, Michel. Biracial Americans Discuss Obama's Identity. Tell Me More. June 11, 2008. http://www.npr.org/templates/story/story.php?storyId=91375775

Martin, Roland. Comment about Dave Chappelle's Meltdown at the 15th Annual Summer Groove show in Hollywood, Florida. CNN News. July 26, 2011.

Massie, Mychal. Jesse Jackson—for blacks or himself? WorldNetDaily.com WorldNetDaily.com Posted: September 16, 2003. http://www.wnd.com/news/article.asp?ARTICLE_ID=34622#ixzz1M5JiJIYx

Mayhill Fowler, Maryhill. Obama Exclusive (Audio): On V.P And Foreign Policy, Courting the Working Class, and Hard-Pressed. San Francisco fundraiser. Posted: April 11, 2008. http://www.huffingtonpost.com/mayhill-fowler/obama-exclusive-audio-on_b_96333.html

McCreary, Joedy. Tom Walter Donates Kidney To Kevin Jordan: Wake Forest Baseball Coach Gives Kidney To Outfielder. Huffington Post. February 02, 2011. http://www.huffingtonpost.com/2011/02/08/tom-walter-kevin-jordan-kidney_n_820233.html

McCusker, Peter J. Conversation: Striving, Surviving, and Thriving, Searching for Messages and Relationships. Bloomington, IN: IUniverse, 2004.

McFeatters, Dale. An entourage more royal than the Queen's. Scripps Howard News Service. March 31, 2009. http://www.scrippsnews.com/node/42183

McPhee, Michele & Sara Just. Obama: Police Acted 'Stupidly' in Gates Case Abcnews.go.com. July 22, 2009. http://abcnews.go.com/US/story?id=8148986&page=1

Media Matters. Chris Wallace: Obama not appearing on Fox News because of "pettiness" and "childishness" Fox & Friends (Video). September 19, 2009.http://mediamatters.org/mmtv/200909190001

Meet the Press. Barack Obama when asked if he would be a 2008 presidential candidate: "You know, I am a believer in knowing what you're doing when you apply for a job." November 8, 2004.

Mendell, David. Obama : from promise to power. New York: Harper Collins, 2007.

Meyer, Bill. Obama: Talking to enemies strengthens U.S. April 19, 2009. http://www.cleveland.com/world/index.ssf/2009/04/obama_says_talking_to_enemies.html

Mezzacappa, Dale. School Days II: Fiasco at South Philly High. Metropolis. January 26, 2010. http://www.phlmetropolis.com/2010/01/school-days-ii-fiasco-at-south-philly-high.php

Mihoces, Gary. Vick's dad cites son's involvement in dogfighting. Usatoday. com. August 23, 2007 Updated August 24, 2007. http://www.usatoday. com/sports/football/nfl/falcons/2007-08-23-vick-thursday_N.htm

Miller III, G.W. Asian Students Under Assault. Seeking refuge from school violence. Philadelphia Weekly. September 1, 2009. http://www. philadelphiaweekly.com/news-and-opinion/Asian-Students-Under-Assault.html

Miller, Jennifer. Chef: Blacks Prey on Hispanics. Daily Local. June 29, 2008.

Mills, David. Sister Souljah's Call to Arms: The rapper says the riots were payback. Are you paying attention? Washington Post. May 13, 1992. http://www.washingtonpost.com/wp-dyn/content/article/2010/03/31/AR2010033101709.html

MJD. Since Vick's arrival, dogfighting reports are up in Philly. Sports. yahoo.com. Posted: April 01 02:21pm EDT [No year listed. Year probably is 2011]. http://sports.yahoo.com/nfl/blog/shutdown_corner/post/Since-Vick-s-arrival-dogfighting-reports-are-up?urn=nfl-231672

Moore, Michael. Stupid White Men. New York: Harper Collins, 2001.

Morning Joe (television broadcast). Niall Ferguson is interrogated about his Newsweek article entitled, "Egypt: How Obama Blew It." MSNBC. March 14, 2011.

Moss-Coane, Marty. (radio broadcast). Rape and War in the Congo. Radio Times. June 8, 2011. http://whyy.org/cms/radiotimes/2011/06/08/rape-in-the-congo/

Newell, Mike & Allison Steele. 32 people shot in 3 days of Philly violence. Philadelphia Inquirer. June 27. 2011. http://articles.philly. com/2011-06-27/news/29708082_1_bouncer-shootings-people-shot

MSNBC. No Author Listed. University of Illinois denies William Ayers emeritus status over book dedication to Bobby Kennedy's killer. Updated:

September 24, 2010. http://www.msnbc.msn.com/id/39340313/ns/ us_news-life/t/u-ill-denies-william-ayers-emeritus-status-over-book-dedication-bobby-kennedys-killer/

Munro, Neil. 'Burn a Bush'? Michelle Obama invites rapper Common to a poetry reading. Daily Caller. May 09, 2011. http://dailycaller. com/2011/05/09/burn-a-bush-michelle-obama-invites-rapper-common-to-a-poetry-reading/

NAACP home page. February 2011. http://www.naacp.org/content/ main/

NAACP. Incarceration Trends in America. http://www.naacp.org/pages/ criminal-justice-fact-sheet.

Nagin, Ray. Chocolate city speech. Martin Luther King junior Day, January 16, 2006.

Nagourney, Adam & Jeff Zeleny. Obama Formally Enters Presidential Race. New York Times, February 11, 2007. http://www.nytimes. com/2007/02/11/us/politics/11obama.html

NBC special. Disaster relief for New Orleans. Kanye West: "George Bush doesn't care about black people!" September 2005.

Neville, Helen A., Brendesha M. Tynes, & Shawn O. Utsey. Handbook of African American Psychology, Thousand Oaks, CA: Sage, 2009.

New York Times. No author listed. Washington D.C.'s Marion Barry. Times Topics. Updated March 2, 2010. http://topics.nytimes.com/topics/ reference/timestopics/people/b/marion_s_jr_barry/index.html

New Yorker (cover) Barack and Michelle in black radical attire, fist bumping. July 2008.

NewsCore. No Author listed. Jordan 'thankful' for coach's kidney. Updated February 09, 2011. http://msn.foxsports.com/other/story/wake-forest-baseball-player-thankful-for-kidney-transplant-from-coach-020911

Newsweek. No author listed. Busted: The Churchill Flap. Newsweek. com February 21, 2009. Last updated at 9:25 AM, September 1, 2010. "Churchill out, Martin Luther King in: First glimpse at President Obama's revamped and thoroughly modern Oval Office." http://www.newsweek. com/2009/02/20/busted-the-churchill-flap.html

Nicholas, Peter. Confessions from the campaign trail: You spend 18 hours a day covering Obama, you wish he'd loosen up. Los Angeles Times. October 28, 2008. http://articles.latimes.com/2008/oct/28/nation/ na-peter28

Nicholas, Peter. Confessions from the campaign trail: You spend 18 hours a day covering Obama, you wish he'd loosen up. Los Angeles Times. October 28, 2008. http://articles.latimes.com/2008/oct/28/nation/ na-peter28

Nobel Prize.org. All Nobel Prizes. http://nobelprize.org/nobel_prizes/ lists/all/

Noguera, Pedro Antonio. The Trouble with Black Boys. Motion Magazine. May 13, 2002. http://www.inmotionmagazine.com/er/pntroub1.html

Norton, Michael I., Frost, Jeana H., & Ariely, Dan. (2007). Less is more: The lure of ambiguity, or why familiarity breeds contempt. Journal of Personality and Social Psychology, 92, 97-105.

Obama, Barack H. The Audacity of Hope: Thoughts on Reclaiming the American Dream. New York: Crown, 2006.

Obama, Barack H. Dreams from my father: A Story of Race and Inheritance. New York: Crown, 1995.

Obama, Barack H. "In the next hundred days, our bipartisan outreach will be so successful that even John Boehner will consider becoming a Democrat. After all, we have a lot in common. He is a person of color, although not a color that appears in the natural world." White House Correspondents' Association. May 9, 2009.

Obama, Barack H. "Now suddenly if you don't have your papers and you took your kid out to get ice cream, you can be harassed; that's something that could potentially happen." MSNBC April 27, 2010. http://www.msnbc.msn.com/id/36800689/ns/politics-white_house/

Obama, Barack H. 2004 Democratic National Convention Keynote Address. Fleet Center in Boston. July 27, 2004.

Obama, Barack H. ABC News airs Barack Obama's ". . . cling to their guns and religion" November 6, 2008.

Obama, Barack H. ABC News airs Barack Obama's self-serving speech: ". . . I can no more disown him [Wright] than I can disown the black community . . ." March 18, 2008.

Obama, Barack H. On My Faith and My Church. Huffington Post. Posted: March 14, 2008. http://www.huffingtonpost.com/barack-obama/on-my-faith-and-my-church_b_91623.html

Obama, Barack H. The Tonight Show. NBC. Obama inadvertently comments that his 129 bowling score is "like the Special Olympics or something." March 19, 2009.

Obama, Barack H. United States Senate. "Mr. President, I rise today, both humbled and honored by the opportunity to express my support for renewal of the expiring provisions of the Voting Rights Act of 1965 . . . We need to make sure that minority voters are not the subject of deplorable intimidation tactics when they do get to the polls." July 20, 2006.

Obama, Barack H. (transcript). April 19, 2011. Town Hall speech at Northern Virginia Community College in Annandale. Barack Obama: that's not who we are". http://www.whitehouse.gov/the-press-office/2011/04/19/remarks-president-town-hall-annandale-virginia

Obama, Barack H. Being the father I never had. People. June 20, 2011.

Obama, Barack H. (transcript). September 6, 2011 at the Milwaukee Area Labor Council's annual LaborFest celebration, Barack Obama:

"They talk about me like a dog." http://projects.washingtonpost.com/ obama-speeches/speech/386/

Obama, Barack H. Remarks by the President to the National Council of La Raza. The White House. Office of the Press Secretary. Marriott Wardman Park Hotel. Washington, D.C. July 25, 2011.

Obama, Michelle. "For the first time in my adult life, I'm really proud of my country." abcnews blog. February 19, 2008. http://blogs.abcnews. com/politicalpunch/2008/02/michelle-obam-1.html

O'Connor, John. The State: South Carolina's Homepage. NAACP nailed a State House statue of Washington into a coffin-like enclosure to hide it. January 18, 2011. joconnor@thestate.com. http://www.thestate. com/2011/01/17/1650881/rally-draws-1200-to-state-house.htm

Odom, Vernon. Philadelphia police chief on flash mobs: We'll lock them up. Abclocal.go.com. March 23, 2010. http://abclocal.go.com/wpvi/ story?section=news/local&id=7345048

Online News Hour. Report on a New York Times series regarding the state of race relations in our country that included questions and comments from Patrick Madden of New York, New York. Pbs.org July 2000. http:// www.pbs.org/newshour/forum/july00/nytrace.html Pbs.org July 2000,

Orwell, George. 1984. New York: Harcourt, 1949.

Pacelle, Wayne & Marty Moss Coane. Humane Society's Wayne Pacelle on 'The Bond' Radio Times (Audio). April 20, 2011.

Pacelle, Wayne. The Bond: Our Kinship with Animals, Our Call to Defend Them New York: Harper Collins 2011.

Paige, Roderick Raynor. Rod Paige: Naked Partisans—The NAACP betrays black Americans. (The Wall Street Journal July 17, 2004.) Cited and Posted by Puzzleman, Freerepublic.com. July 17, 2004. http://www. freerepublic.com/focus/f-news/1173155/posts

Parker, Star. Why corrupt Charlie Rangel was re-elected. November 20, 2010. http://www.wnd.com/index.php?pageId=230457

Pasquarelli, Len. Total package is biggest in NFL history. ESPN. com July 25, 2004. http://sports.espn.go.com/nfl/columns/story?columnist=pasquarelli_len&id=1952387

Paulhus, Delroy L. & Kevin Williams "Shedding Light on the Dark-triad of Personality: Narcissism, Machiavellianism, and Psychopathy." University of British Columbia, Presented at 2001 SPSP Convention in San Antonio Society for Personality and Social Psychology of the University of British Columbia.

PBS Newshour. Democrat vs. Democrat: Liberal Divisions Emerge Over Tax Cuts. (Hamsher, Jane) December 6, 2010. http://www.pbs.org/newshour/bb/politics/july-dec10/taxcuts_12-06.html

Pergram, Chad & The Associated Press. No author listed. Rangel Censured by House for Ethics Violations. FoxNews.com. December 02, 2010. http://www.foxnews.com/politics/2010/12/02/house-votes-censure-rangel-ethics-violations/

Personal experience. Perpetual Prosperity Pumps Foundation bin to send sneakers to Ghana, West Africa.

Phillips, Susan. Teacher says she quit because of racial violence at city school. Whyy.org. December 9th, 2009. http://whyy.org/cms/news/education/2009/12/09/teacher-says-she-quit-because-of-racial-violence-at-city-school/25064

Pinterits, E. Janie; Paul V. Poteat, & Lisa B. Spanierman. The White Privilege Attitudes Scale: Development and initial validation. Journal of Counseling Psychology, 56(3), 2009, 417-42.

Pollowitz, Greg. Chris Wallace zings NRA Director Tom Donilon on waterboarding double standards. Real Clear Politics. http://www.conservativesforamerica.com/sister-toldjah/chris-wallace-zings-nra-director-tom-donilon-on-waterboarding-double-standards

Postman, Neil. Amusing Ourselves to Death: Public Discourse in the Age of Show Business. New York: Penguin, 1985.

Powell, Colin. Meet the Press. Colin Powell endorses Barack Obama. October. 19, 2008.

Powers, Doug. A Sheila Jackson Lee Twofer. Michelle Malkin guest blogger. July 16, 2010. http://michellemalkin.com/2010/07/16/a-sheila-jackson-lee/

Remnick, David. Was President Obama's father murdered? newyorker.com. Posted: October 18, 2010. http://www.newyorker.com/online/blogs/newsdesk/2010/10/barack-obama-sr.html.

Remnick, David. The bridge : the life and rise of Barack Obama . New York: Vintage, 2010.

Report of the United States of America Submitted to the U.N. High Commissioner for Human Rights In Conjunction with the Universal Periodic Review. State Department Report on Human Rights, August 20, 2010. http://www.state.gov/documents/organization/146379.pdf

Reuters.com. No author listed. Brutal Jasper, Texas, Hate Crime Remembered Ten Years Later in San Francisco. Reuters Press Release 2009. From June 22, 2008. http://www.reuters.com/article/2008/06/22/idUS53462+22-Jun-2008+BW20080622

Rhee, Foon. Obama calls for bipartisan cooperation. Boston.com. January 19, 2009. http://www.boston.com/news/politics/politicalintelligence/2009/01/obama_calls_for_2.html

Rich, John A. Wrong Place, Wrong Time. Baltimore, MD: John Hopkins University Press, 2009.

Ripley, Amanda. Should Schools Bribe Kids? A major new study reveals an uncomfortable truth—it can work (if it's done right). Time. April 19, 2010.

Robinson, Eugene. An Inarticulate Kickoff. Washington Post. February 1, 2007. http://www.washingtonpost.com/wp-dyn/content/article/2007/02/01/AR2007020101495.html

Rock, Chris. Bring the Pain: controversial and celebrated skit, Niggas vs. Black People. 1996.

Rose, Charlie. The 2009 Time 100. Time. April 20, 2009. http://www.time.com/time/specials/packages/article/0,28804,1894410_1893836_18 94433,00.html

Rubin, Theodore Isaac. The Angry Book. New York: Touchstone, 1969.

Rumorfix. No author listed. Dave Chappelle Apologizes For Meltdown. July 24, 2011. http://rumorfix.com/2011/07/dave-chappelle-apologizes-for-meltdown/

Runkle, Jim. Domenique Wilson Sentenced to 70-196 Years in State Prison. 'Evil' rapist won't see light at the end of tunnel. Lockhaven.com. June 8, 2010. http://www.lockhaven.com/page/content.detail/id/518670.html

Ryan, Richard M. & Edward L. Deci. Self-determination theory and the facilitation of intrinsic motivation, social development, and well-being. American Psychologist, Vol 55(1), Jan 2000, 68-78.

Sahadi, Jeanne. Debt ceiling FAQs: What you need to know. CNN Money.com. May 18, 2011. http://money.cnn.com/2011/01/03/news/economy/debt_ceiling_faqs/index.htm

Salwen, Kevin & Hannah Salwen. Book Excerpt: The Power of Half. Abcnews.go.com. http://abcnews.go.com/WN/power-half-kevin-hannah-salwen-book-excerpt/story?id=9768341

Savage, Charlie. A Judge's View of Judging Is on the Record. New York Times. May 14, 2009. http://www.nytimes.com/2009/05/15/us/15judge.html

Sawyer, Diane. Children of the Mountains Struggle to Survive. (Television broadcast). ABC 20/20. February 2009.

Schneider, Marc. Whoopi Goldberg Misfires in Attack on Article About Black Oscar Winners. AOL Original Posting. February 14, 2011. http://www.popeater.com/2011/02/14/whoopi-goldberg-new-york-times-black-oscar-winners/

Scott, Janny. A Singular Woman: The Untold Story of Barack Obama's Mother. New York: Riverhead, 2011.

Seelye, Katharine & Julie Bosman. Ferraro's Obama Remarks Become Talk of Campaign. New York Times. March 12, 2008. http://www.nytimes.com/2008/03/12/us/politics/12campaign.html

Seelye, Katharine & Julie Bosman. Ferraro's Obama Remarks Become Talk of Campaign. New York Times. March 12, 2008. http://www.nytimes.com/2008/03/12/us/politics/12campaign.html

Shea, Danny. Elisabeth Hasselbeck Cries After Sparring With Whoopi Over N-Word (VIDEO). Huffington Post. July 17, 2008.

Sherwell, Philip. Bill Clinton holds court in White House after Barack Obama exits stage. The Telegraph. December, 2010. Telegraph.co.uk. http://www.telegraph.co.uk/news/worldnews/us-politics/8195852/Bill-Clinton-holds-court-in-White-House-after-Barack-Obama-exits-stage.html

Silva, Mario. Rihanna, Chris Brown fight ignited by a 'booty call?' Blogs. mercurynews.com. February 11th, 2009. http://blogs.mercurynews.com/aei/2009/02/11/rihanna-chris-brown-fight-ignited-by-a-booty-call/

Sixty Minutes. Bob Simon: America's Gift: Fighting HIV/AIDS in Uganda. April 4, 2010.

Skiba, Katherine. Michelle Obama makes surprise visit to Haiti. Chicago Tribune. April 13, 2010. http://archive.chicagobreakingnews.com/2010/04/michelle-obama-makes-surprise-visit-to-haiti.html

Slamonline. No Author Listed. Study: 2011 NBA Racial and Gender Report Card. June 16, 2011. http://www.slamonline.com/online/nba/2011/06/study-2011-nba-racial-and-gender-report-card/

Smith, Ben. Muslim Women Moved From Obama TV Shot. CBS News. June 18, 2008. http://www.cbsnews.com/stories/2008/06/18/politics/politico/main4191084.shtml

Smith, Ben & Jeffrey Ressner. Exclusive: Obama's lost law review article. News.yahoo.com & Politico. August 22. (No year listed). http://news.yahoo.com/s/politico/20080822/pl_politico/12705

Smith, Stephen. Adrian Peterson: NFL like "modern-day slavery." CBS News. March 15, 2011. http://www.cbsnews.com/8301-31751_162-20043503-10391697.html

Snickers commercial. Mr. T's Banned Snickers Commercial. No author listed. Posted on: August 1, 2008. http://www.spike.com/video-clips/sqkpzi/mr-ts-banned-snickers-commercial

Southall, Ashley. Obama, Barack. Obama Vows to Push Immigration Changes. New York Times. The Caucus Blogs. October 25, 2010. http://thecaucus.blogs.nytimes.com/2010/10/25/in-appeal-to-hispanics-obama-promises-to-push-immigration-reform/

Southwest Airlines commercial. Asian Americans can dance. 2008-2009. http://www.nikkeiview.com/blog/2008/04/13/asian-americans-can-dance/

Spratt, Charlotte. Cognac-swigging Kanye West storms MTV stage and grabs microphone during Taylor Swift's acceptance speech. Daily Mail. Updated at 4:52 PM on 16th September 2009. http://www.dailymail.co.uk/tvshowbiz/article-1213280/Kanye-West-ruins-Taylor-Swifts-big-MTV-acceptance-speech-storms-stage.html

Stein, Sam. Clyburn: Palin 'Intellectually' Incapable Of Understanding Arizona Shootings. Huffington Post. January 12, 2011. http://www.

huffingtonpost.com/2011/01/12/clyburn-palin-arizona-intellectually-inc_n_807871.html

Stephanopolis, George & Cokie Roberts. This Week with George Stephanopolis. ABC. September 21, 2008. Boring white men statement.

Stephens, Bret. Obama Smart? A case study in stupid is as stupid does. Wall Street Journal. August 9, 2011. http://online.wsj.com/article_email/SB10001424053111904140604576495932704234052-lMyQjAxMTAxMDAwOTEwNDkyWj.html?mod=wsj_share_email_bot

Stern, Gary M. Black Issues in Higher Education. January 1997.

Stiehm, Jamie. Oval Office rug gets history wrong. The Washington Post. September 4, 2010. http://www.washingtonpost.com/wp-dyn/content/article/2010/09/03/AR2010090305100.html

Stix, Nicholas. Christopher Newsom The Knoxville Horror: The Crime and the Cover-Up Report Special to American Renaissance News. January 6, 2007. http://www.amren.com/mtnews/archives/2007/05/the_knoxville_h.php

Stix, Nicholas. The Knoxville Horror: The Crime and the Cover-Up. Special to American Renaissance News. May 14, 2007. http://www.amren.com/mtnews/archives/2007/05/the_knoxville_h.php

Strain, Christopher, B. Reload: Rethinking Violence in American Life. Nashville, Tennessee: Vanderbilt University Press, 2010.

Sweet, Lynn. Obama at the 2011 Gridiron Club dinner. Transcript. The scoop from Washington. Chicago Sun Times. March 14, 2011. http://blogs.suntimes.com/sweet/2011/03/obama_at_the_2011_gridiron_clu.html

Taff, Brian. Hoops for Hope in King of Prussia. July 31, 2010. http://abclocal.go.com/wpvi/story?section=news/local&id=7586072

Tantaros, Andrea. Michelle Obama as a "modern-day Marie Antoinette." New York Daily News. August 7, 2010.

Tapper, Jake and Jennifer Parker. Jesse Jackson Apologizes for Open Mic Slight Against Obama. July 10, 2008. http://abcnews.go.com/GMA/Vote2008/story?id=5346657&page=1

Tapper, Jake. Blog. Jake Tapper's January 5, 2011 blog . Senator Obama's Vote Against Raising the Debt Ceiling and the Assassination of Salman Taseer: Abc news blog. January 05, 2011. http://blogs.abcnews.com/politicalpunch/2011/01/senator-obamas-vote-against-raising-the-debt-ceiling-and-the-assassination-of-salman-taseer-todays-q.html

Tapper, Jake. Blog. Gibbs: Senator Obama Only Voted Against Raising Debt Ceiling in 2006 Because He Knew It Would Pass Anyway. Abc news blog. January 05, 2011. http://blogs.abcnews.com/politicalpunch/2011/01/gibbs-senator-obama-only-voted-against-raising-debt-ceiling-in-2006-because-he-knew-it-would-pass-an.html.

Tapper, Jake. Halperin Decries 'Disgusting' Pro-Obama Media Bias in Election Coverage. ABC News First. November 24, 2008. http://blogs.abcnews.com/politicalpunch/2008/11/halperin-decrie.html

Tapper, Jake. Michelle Obama: "For the First Time in My Adult Lifetime, I'm Really Proud of My Country." Blogs.abcnews.com. February 18, 2008. http://blogs.abcnews.com/politicalpunch/2008/02/michelle-obam-1.html

Tatum, Beverly Daniel. Why Are All the Black Kids Sitting Together in the Cafeteria? New York: Basic Books, 1997.

Taylor, Rob. Philly Police Trying to Cover Up Violent Flash Mob Attack at 4th of July Celebration. Red-alerts.com. Posted in Intel by Rob Taylor on July 5, 2010. http://www.red-alerts.com/intel/philly-police-trying-to-cover-up-violent-flash-mob-attack-at-4th-of-july-celebration/

Teo, Thomas. Psychology without Caucasians. Canadian Psychology/Psychologie Canadienne, 50, 2009, 91-97.

Thai, Xuan and Ted Barrett. Biden's description of Obama draws scrutiny. CNN, January 31, 2007. http://articles.cnn.com/2007-01-31/politics/biden.obama_1_braun-and-al-sharpton-African American-presidential-candidates-delaware-democrat?_s=PM:POLITICS

The British Psychological Society. Research Digest. 2009. One nagging thing you still don't understand about yourself. David Buss, specialist in Individual Differences and Evolutionary Psychology at the University of Texas. http://bps-research-digest.blogspot.com/2009/10/

Thomas, Kenneth R. Macrononsense in multiculturalism. American Psychologist, 63, May-Jun 2008, 274-275.

Thompson, Chalmer E. & Dorienna M. Alfred. Black Liberation Psychology and Practice. In: Neville, Helen A., Brendesha M. Tynes, & Shawn O. Utsey. Handbook of African American Psychology, Thousand Oaks, CA: Sage, 2009.

Thompson, Krissah. Cornel West's criticism of Obama sparks debate among African Americans. Washington Post, May 18, 2011. http://www.washingtonpost.com/politics/cornel-wests-criticism-of-obama-sparks-debate-among-African Americans/2011/05/18/AFlGTf6G_story.html

Thompson, Mike. Courage of a Congo survivor. Today Programme BBC. October 14, 2008. http://news.bbc.co.uk/today/hi/today/newsid_7657000/7657461.stm

Time (magazine cover). "Does Temperament Matter?" October 27, 2008.

Tomasky, Michael. Thoughts on the NPR Fiasco. The Guardian. Posted by Realclearpolitics.com. March 10, 2011. http://www.realclearpolitics.com/2011/03/10/thoughts_on_the_npr_fiasco_251802.html

Transparency International Global Coalition Against Corruption.. http://www.transparency.org/policy_research/surveys_indices/cpi/2009/cpi_2009_table

Trice, Dawn Turner. Obama, McCain should lead us beyond whispers of riots. Chicago Tribune. October 27, 2008. http://articles.chicagotribune.com/2008-10-27/news/0810260265_1_police-brutality-riots-suppression-tactics

United States Department of Agriculture, Office of Inspector General. Investigative report, Bad Newz Kennels. Smithfield, Virginia—Animal Fighting. August 28, 2008. http://www.usda.gov/oig/webdocs/BadNewzKennels.pdf

University of California Santa Barbara. Department of Black Studies catalog, 2010

Urban Dictionary. Explains nappy headed hoe. http://www.urbandictionary.com/define.php?term=nappy%20headed%20hoe

Urbandictionary.com defines "ballcuzzi." http://www.urbandictionary.com/define.php?term=ballcuzzi

Urbina, Ian. No Survivors Found After West Virginia Mine Disaster. New York Times, April 09, 2010. http://www.nytimes.com/2010/04/10/us/10westvirginia.html

Van Biema, David. Can Megachurches Bridge the Racial Divide?" Time. January 11, 2010.

Vanden Brook, Tom. Clinton: Obama's words were 'elitist and divisive'. USA TODAY. Updated April 14, 2008. http://www.usatoday.com/news/politics/election2008/2008-04-13-clinton-reax_N.htm

Vernon & Peter Mucha. 17 people arrested in Philadelphia raids on dog-fighting ring. Philadelphia Inquirer. April 11, 2011. Articlesphilly.com. http://articles.philly.com/2011-04-11/news/29406644_1_dog-fighting-ring-pennsylvania-spca-first-raid

Viral email. February 2008. Reaction to Michelle Obama's derisive remarks about not being proud of our country.

Viral email. February 2011. Negative United States economic changes attributed to Barack Obama.

Viral email. Jones, Roger Starner. Jackson, Mississippi. Clarion Ledger. August 23, 2009 "Why Pay for the Care of the Careless?" http://www.snopes.com/politics/soapbox/starner.asp

Viral email. Robert David Hall. http://www.snopes.com/politics/soapbox/imtired.asp

Volpe, Trisha. Mob robbers hit convenience stores in St. Paul. Kare11.com. February 24, 2011. http://www.kare11.com/news/article/909497/396/Mob-robbers-hit-convenience-stores-in-St-Paul

Wallace, Chris. Interview of Secretary of Treasury Timothy Geithner by Chris Wallace. Fox News Sunday. July 24 2011. http://video.foxnews.com/v/1076242494001/secretary-geithner-talks-debt-ceiling-deadline/

Wall Street Journal, Review and Outlook April 14, 2011. No author listed. The Presidential Divider, Obama's toxic speech and even worse plan for deficits and debt. http://online.wsj.com/article/SB10001424052748703730104576260911986870054.html

Walletpop. No author listed. Black-white population and crime statistics. April 7, 2010. http://www.statemaster.com/graph/peo_tot_bla_pop_percap-total-black-population-per-capita

Walletpop. No author listed. Fifteen safest states in which to live, based on 2010 crime rankings. http://www.walletpop.com/blog/2010/04/07/the-15-safest-state-to-live-in-based-on-2010-crime-rankings/

Wallis, Daniel. Somali sea gangs lure investors at pirate lair. Reuteers.com. http://www.reuters.com/article/idUSTRE5B01Z920091201

Watkins, Boyce. Tavis Smiley and Al Sharpton fight about Barack Obama (Audio). Syndication One News-Talk radio Network. February 23, 2010. http://blip.tv/boyce-watkins/tavis-smiley-and-al-sharpton-fight-about-barack-obama-3278610

Watkins, Paul. A Promise of Redemption. Sunday New York Times Sunday Book Review. August 6, 1995. http://www.nytimes.com/1995/08/06/books/review/06obama-dreams.html?ex=1216699200&en=8635963f0d911271&ei=5070

Webster, Stephen. The Wichita Massacre. American Renaissance. July 16, 2002. http://www.freerepublic.com/focus/news/716976/posts

Wehner, Peter. A Disaster for the Gulf Coast, A Disaster for Obama. Politics Daily. June 17, 2010. http://www.politicsdaily.com/2010/06/17/the-oil-spill-disaster-for-the-gulf-disaster-for-obama/

Weil, Dan. Obama Takes Heat for WH Meeting with Wall St. Execs. NewsMax, June 21, 2011. http://www.newsmax.com/Politics/obama-wall-street-executives/2011/06/21/id/400866

Werner, Erica. Obama, Boehner Debt Ceiling Fight Has Become A Test Of Leadership. Huffington Post, July 30, 2011. http://www.huffingtonpost.com/2011/07/30/obama-boehner-debt-ceiling_n_913950.html?icid=maing-grid7|main5|dl1|sec1_lnk3|82273

Wikipedia. Bono and Geldof. http://en.wikipedia.org/wiki/Bono. http://en.wikipedia.org/wiki/Bob_Geldof

Williams, Joseph. Supreme Court rules in favor of Conn. Firefighters. Group accused city of racial discrimination. The Boston Globe, June 30, 2009. http://www.boston.com/news/local/connecticut/articles/2009/06/30/supreme_court_rules_in_favor_of_conn_firefighters/

Williams, Walter E. Up From The Projects: An Autobiography. Stanford, CA: Hoover Institution Press, 2010.

Williamson, Elizabeth. Obama Slams 'Fat Cat' Bankers. Wall Street Journal. December 14, 2009. http://online.wsj.com/article/SB126073152465089651.html

Witt, Howard. Jena 6 defendant charged in Texas assault. Chicago Tribune. February 7, 2008. http://www.chicagotribune.com/news/local/chi-jena_webfeb08,0,233491.story

Womack, Sarah. Black boys 'need role models not rappers'. The Telegraph. August 10, 2007. http://www.telegraph.co.uk/news/uknews/1559904/Black-boys-need-role-models-not-rappers.html

Woods, Tiger. "I'm just who I am, whoever you see in front of you." Oprah Winfrey Show. April 24, 1997.

Worldbank.org. Michael Jones (contact). Press Release No:2009/323/ECA. Global Crisis Pushing Almost 35 Million People Back Into Poverty And Vulnerability In Europe And Central Asia. April 24, 2009. http://web.worldbank.org/WBSITE/EXTERNAL/NEWS/0,,contentMDK:22155627~pagePK:34370~piPK:34424~theSitePK:4607,00.html

Wright, Jeremiah. ABC News airs Jeremiah Wright's "god damn America" rant. March 13, 2008.

Young, Linda. Love in Limbo, The paradoxes of dating and mating. Psychology Today. July 17, 2009. http://www.psychologytoday.com/blog/love-in-limbo/200907/dating-decisions-good-fast-or-cheap

Younge, Gary. Tiger Woods: Black, white, other. The Guardian. Saturday 29 May 2010. http://www.guardian.co.uk/sport/2010/may/29/tiger-woods-racial-politics

Zeleny, Jeff. As Author, Obama Earns Big Money and a New Deal. New York Times, March 19, 2009. ttp://www.nytimes.com/2009/03/20/us/politics/20disclose.html

Zeleny, Jeff. Obama Stands by Daschle. New York Times. February 2, 2009. http://thecaucus.blogs.nytimes.com/2009/02/02/obama-stands-by-daschle/

Ziegler, John. Media Malpractice. (Video) Synergetic Distribution, 2010.

Made in the USA
Lexington, KY
13 November 2012